# INTRODUCTORY
## MICRO AND MACRO
# ECONOMICS

# INTRODUCTORY MICRO AND MACRO ECONOMICS

## CHATTERJEE SIR

**HONS. (ECONOMICS),
M.A. IN ECONOMICS,
M.A. in BUSINESS ECONOMICS,
M.Phil. in ECONOMICS,
B. Ed**

PARTRIDGE

A Penguin Random House Company

**To order additional copies of this book, contact**
Partridge India
000 800 10062 62
www.partridgepublishing.com/india
orders.india@partridgepublishing.com

# Contents

## INTRODUCTORY MICRO ECONOMICS:

# INTRODUCTORY MACRO ECONOMICS:

# Acknowledgement:

Tremendous and overwhelming support of my wife Sonali and my son Kaustav and my friends and my students encouraged me to write this economics book.

I acknowledge with sincere gratitude my indebtedness to my parents for blessing me from heaven to complete this book. I dedicate this economics book to my parents as my token of love and respect for them.

Last but not least, I would like to thank Partridge Publishing Company (A Penguin Random House Company) who extended genuine support for publishing this economics book.

SANJIB CHATTERJEE

# Preface

Ⅰt gives me immense pleasure to place before the students and learned teachers of economics, the first edition of the Economics text book "Introductory Micro and Macro-Economics" for class – XII.

This book has been designed strictly according to new syllabus introduced by Central Board of Secondary Education (CBSE) for the board examination to be held in 2014 along with value based questions and for All India Senior School Certificate. The subject matter of this book has been presented in a lucid manner so as to be intelligible to all students, who have a working knowledge of English. The main objective in this book is to expose the various concepts in a simple and crisp manner and thus help the students of different levels to understand the subject matter very clearly so that they can remember for a long time.

This edition contains a large no. of fully solved analytical questions with special care of necessary graphical presentation so that it becomes easier for the students to clear their concept. The new syllabus concentrates upon Micro and Macro Economics and their related aspects. This edition is a precise analysis of both the parts and I have made a sincere effort to deal with each topic of syllabus diligently.

Appendix contains part wise and chapter wise division of the subject Economics into two Micro and Macro economics and at last there are hundreds of Multiple Choice Questions for the Common Proficiency Test (CPT). Therefore the students will be highly benefitted not only for Board Examination but also to clear the Entrance Test for C.A. Examination. If it is useful to the students then only my sincere effort of last eighteen years teaching experience will be successful.

It is always not possible to make a work hundred percent error free without the co-operation of readers. Therefore any kind of suggestions for further improvement of the book will be thankfully acknowledged.

## SALIENT FEATURES OF THIS ECONOMICS BOOK ARE:

- ❖ Very simple language
- ❖ A comprehensive coverage of the present syllabus of C.B.S.E.
- ❖ Exposition of the text is clear and precise
- ❖ Innovative techniques have been used for presenting each topic in the book
- ❖ The analysis in each chapter has been developed step by step in a systematic manner on the basis of logical reasoning
- ❖ To present the topics simple and convenient, diagrams and schedules have been given, wherever required
- ❖ Chapter wise test questions from previous question papers of C.B.S.E. are given at the end of each chapter
- ❖ Expected important questions along with the marks are also given at the end of each chapter
- ❖ Special attention has been given for the students for Common Proficiency Test (CPT) with Multiple Choice Questions-answer
- ❖ Value based questions and answers also are presented in the book with special care
- ❖ A specially designed time schedule is presented to complete answers of different questions of different marks in C.B.S.E. examination in within stipulated time.

With best wishes,
Sanjib Chatterjee
sanjibchatterjee21@gmail.com

# Various Questions and their Marks and Expected Time to Complete the Answers in the Board Examination of Class-XII:

| WEIGHTAGE OF VARIOUS TYPES OF QUESTIONS | No. OF QUESTIONS | TOTAL MARKS | EXPECTED TIME TO COMPLETE THE ANSWERS (minutes) |
|---|---|---|---|
| 1. LONG ANS. QUESTIONS | 6 QUESTIONS | 6 MARKS EACH, I.E. 36 | 60 |
| 2. S.A. QUESTIONS-I | 6 QUESTIONS | 4 MARKS EACH, 24 | 40 |
| 3. S.A. QUESTIONS-II | 10 QUESTIONS | 3 MARKS EACH, 30 | 50 |
| 4. VERY S.A. QUESTIONS | 10 QUESTIONS | 1 MARK EACH, 10 | 15 |
| | 32 QUESTIONS | 100 | 2 HOUR 45 MINUTES |
| | | | 15 MINUTES REVISION |

NOTE: The Question paper will include Value Based Question/Questions to the extent of 5 Marks.

# Syllabus

# Central Board Of Secondary Education, New Delhi

## SUBJECT: ECONOMICS

**CLASS – XII**           **TIME – 3**          **HOURS MARKS: 100**

### PART – A: Introductory Micro-Economics:

| UNITS | No. OF PERIODS | MARKS | Very Short Answer (1 mark) | Short Answer (3 or 4 marks) | Long Answer (6 marks) |
|---|---|---|---|---|---|
| 1. Introduction | 10 | 04 | 1 (1 Q.) | 3 (1 Q.) | - |
| 2. Consumer's Equilibrium and Demand | 32 | 18 | 1 (2 Qs.) | 3 (2Qs), 4 (1 Q.) | 6 (1 Q.) |
| 3. Producer's behaviour and supply | 32 | 18 | 1 (1 Q.) | 3 (1 Q.), 4 (2 Qs.) | 6 (1 Q.) |
| 4. Forms of Market and Price Determination | 22 | 10 | 1 (1 Q.) | 3 (1 Q.) | 6 (1 Q.) |
| 5. Simple Applications of tools of Demand and Supply | 08 | -- | | | |
| TOTAL | 104 | 50 | | | |

### PART – B: Introductory Macro-Economics:

| UNITS | No. OF PERIODS | MARKS | V.S.A. (1 mark) | S.A. (3 or 4 marks) | Long Ans. (6 marks) |
|---|---|---|---|---|---|
| 6. National Income and related Aggregates | 30 | 15 | - | 3 (3 Qs.) | 6 (1 Q.) |
| 7. Money and Banking | 18 | 08 | 1 (2 Qs) | -- | 6 (1 Q.) |
| 8. Determination of Income and Employment | 25 | 12 | 1 (2 Qs) | 4 (1 Q.) | 6 (1 Q.) |
| 9. Government Budget and the Economy | 17 | 08 | - | 4 (2 Qs) | -- |
| 10. Balance of Payments | 14 | 07 | 1 (1 Q.) | 3 (2 Qs) | -- |
| TOTAL | 104 | 50 | | | |

NOTE: The Question paper will include Value Based Question/Questions to the extent of 5 Marks.

# INTRODUCTORY MICRO ECONOMICS:

# Chapter - 1

## (Introduction To Economics):

### ▪ What is economics?

The word 'Economics' is derived from Greek words "Oikonomia" which means "Management of Households". The word "Oikonomia" is consisted of two words like "Oikos" which means "Household" and "Nomos" which means "laws or management". At first it was being used as Political economy. Even in India Kautilya in his famous book 'Arth-Shastra' explained 'Economics' as economic activities and political activities.

However the word 'Economics' was used to explain how a country's people earn their income and how they spend the income on their necessities and luxuries goods and services.

Different economists have defined Economics in different ways:

A) Adam Smith, the father of modern economics, in his book "An Enquiry into the Nature and Causes of Wealth of Nation" published in 1776, defined Economics as the Science of Wealth.

B) J. B. Says defined Economics as the Science which treats of wealth.

C) Marshall defined Economics as a study of mankind in the ordinary business of life; it examines that part of individual and social action which is most closely connected with the attainment and with the use of the material requisites of well being.

D) Lionel Robbins in his book, "Nature and Significance of Economics Science", defines economics as the science which studies human behaviour as a relationship between ends and scarce means which have alternative uses.

In short Economics can be defined as a social science which is concerned with the efficient uses and proper utilization of limited resources for the achievement of the economic growth.

## ▪ What is an economy?

An economy is defined as a system which provides livelihood to the people. This system helps to produce goods and services and enables the people to earn their incomes.

## ▪ Types of economies:

Economies are classified in the following way:
On the basis of MEANS OF PRODUCTION:

A) **CAPITALIST ECONOMY:** In this economy means of production are privately owned by the individuals and the main aim is profit maximization. There is no interference of the Government.
For example, America, Australia, England.

B) **SOCIALIST ECONOMY:** In this economy means of production are owned by the Government and the main aim is social welfare maximization. Central Planning authority plays most important role for decision making.
For example, China, Cuba, Russia.

C) **MIXED ECONOMY:** In this economy means of production are owned by partly by the Government and partly by the private individuals. The main aim of the Government is social welfare maximization and main aim of private sector is profit maximization.
For example, India, Pakistan, Srilanka.

**On the basis of Economic Development:**

a) **Developed Economy:** It is one in which per capita income is very high and the standard of living of people is also very high. For example, USA, Switzerland, Canada.

b) **Developing Economy:** It is one in which per capita income is not so high like developed countries. For example India, Pakistan, Srilanka.

c) **Underdeveloped Economy:** It is one in which per capita income is very low and standard of living is also low. For example, Nepal, Bhutan, Bangladesh.

## ▪ Distinction between Planned economy and Market economy:

| BASIS | PLANNED ECONOMY | MARKET ECONOMY |
|---|---|---|
| 1. Meaning | This economy is controlled by central planning authority. | This economy is controlled freely by the market forces. |
| 2. Objective | Its main objective is to maximise social welfare. | Its main objective is to maximise profit. |
| 3. Operation | This economy is operated by the Government with the help of central planning authority. | This economy is operated by market demand and supply forces without the direct intervention of Government. |
| 4. Ownership of property | Private ownership of property is under the control of Government. | There is no limit of private ownership of property. |

## ▪ ECONOMIC PROBLEM AND ITS CAUSES:

An economic problem is essentially a problem which arises due to necessity of choice.

The main causes of economic problems are as follows:

i) **UNLIMITED HUMAN WANTS:** Human wants are unlimited. No man can satisfy all his wants fully. As one want is satisfied another crops up. Therefore unlimited wants causes an economic problem.

ii) **LIMITED RESOURCES:** Economic resources are scarce in comparison to its demand. If resources are not limited then there might be no economic problem.

iii) **ALTERNATIVE USES OF RESOURCES:** Economic resources are not only scarce in supply but these also have alternative uses. For example, a piece of land can be used for production of rice or wheat or can be used for construction of a multiplex or can be used for a school or hospital. This problem of choice causes an economic problem.

iv) **URGENCY OF WANTS:** All wants are not equally important. A man always tries to satisfy that want first which is more urgent compared to others.

## ▪ Economizing of resources and its needs:

Economizing of resources means optimum uses of available resources in the economy. It is needed because of the following reasons:

a) Limited resources can be used fully to satisfy maximum wants.
b) Production can be maximum.
c) Wastage should be minimum.

## ▪ Classification of Economics into Micro economics and Macro economics and their differences:

Professor Ragner Frisch in 1933 divided economics into two branches-Micro economics and Macro economics. The major differences between micro and macro economics are as follows:

| Basis | Micro economics | Macro economics |
|---|---|---|
| 1. Meaning | It is that branch of economics which deals with individual economic units. | It is that branch of economics which deals with aggregate economic units. |

| 2. Objective | Its main objective is optimum utilization of limited resources for maximum production. | Its main objective is to determine aggregate output, national income and employment in the economy. |
|---|---|---|
| 3. Determinants | Its main determinants are demand and supply. | Its main determinants are aggregate demand and aggregate supply. |
| 4. Method of study | It deals with partial equilibrium analysis. | It deals with general equilibrium analysis. |
| 5. Example | Individual demand, individual supply, etc. | Aggregate demand, aggregate supply, national income etc. |

## ▪ The problem of allocation of resources:

According to Prof. Samuelson, there are three fundamental and interdependent problems in an economy which are together called problem of allocation of resources. These are as follows:

### (a) What to produce and how much?

This problem deals with which goods will be produced in an economy-whether consumer goods like wheat, cotton, furniture etc., or capital goods like machineries. Since the resources are limited so the economy has to make a choice of production of goods and what quantities of goods. The economy needs to make a choice in the production of goods because the resources are limited. If the resources are not limited then this problem of choice will not occur in any economy.

### (b) How to produce?

This problem deals with the decision of which technology will be used to produce the goods in an economy—Whether labour intensive technology or capital intensive technology. It is a problem of choice of technique which determines input requirement.

21

Labour intensive technology-where labour is used more and capital is used less—For example-handloom industries. A country like India follows labour intensive technology because labour is cheap and abundant.

Capital intensive technology—Where capital is used more and labour is used less—for example power loom industries. A country like America follows capital intensive technology because capital is abundant.

## (c) For whom to produce?

This problem deals with how the produced output will be distributed among the individuals in an economy. It is of two types:

Personal distribution—This refers to how the produced output will be distributed among different individuals. This depends upon the individual's income. The rich person will purchase more and the poor person will purchase less.

Functional distribution—This refers to how the produced output will be distributed among the owners of different factors of production in the form of factor prices like wages, rent, interest and profit.

## ▪ The central problems of an economy:

According to A. J. Brown, an economy is a system by which people get their living.

An economy can also be defined as the sum total of all economic activities like production, consumption, investment, savings, distribution and exchange.

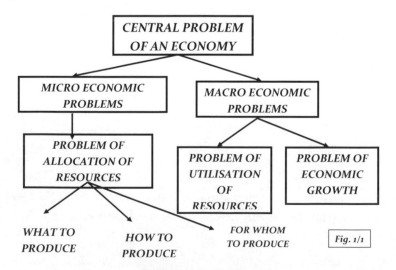

Fig. 1/1

"Central problems" refers to the problems which are fundamental and common to all economies. Every economy faces these problems.

According to Prof. Samuelson, there are three fundamental and interdependent problems in an economy which are together called problem of allocation of resources. These are as follows:

## (a) What to produce and how much?

This problem deals with which goods will be produced in an economy-whether consumer goods like wheat, cotton or capital goods like machineries. Since the resources are limited so the economy can't produce all goods and services. So it has to make a choice of production of goods and what quantities of goods. The economy needs to make a choice in the production of goods because the resources are limited. If the resources are not limited then this problem of choice will not occur in any economy.

## (b) How to produce?

This problem deals with which technology will be used to produce the goods in an economy—Whether labour intensive technology or capital intensive technology.

Labour intensive technology-where labour is used more and capital is used less—For example-handloom industries. A country like India follows labour intensive technology because labour is cheap and abundant.

Capital intensive technology—Where capital is used more and labour is used less—for example power loom industries. A country like America follows capital intensive technology because capital is abundant.

## (c) For whom to produce?

This problem deals with how the produced output will be distributed among the individuals in an economy. It is of two types:

Personal distribution—This refers to how the produced output will be distributed among different individuals. This depends upon the individual's income. The rich person will purchase more and the poor person will purchase less.

Functional distribution—This refers to how the produced output will be distributed among the owners of different factors of production in the form of factor prices like wages, rent, interest and profit.

An eminent economist Lipsey has added two more economic problems in addition to the problem of allocation of resources which are as follows-

### (d) Fuller utilization of resources:

Fuller utilization of resources is an important objective of every economy. This problem deals with how the limited resources can be utilised efficiently without wastage so that production becomes maximum. So this problem states about the full employment of all resources (land, labour, capital) in an economy.

### (e) Economic Growth:

Resources available in the economy determine the capacity to produce in any economy which depends on investment. If the investment in the economy increases then resources will be utilised more efficiently and the production will increase and the growth of economy will take place.

## ▪ Production Possibility Curve (PPC) or Transformation Curve and its Assumptions and properties:

Production Possibility Curve is a curve which shows different possible combination of production of two goods with the help of available resources and technology. This curve is also called transformation curve or production possibility frontier because the combinations of goods on the PPC indicate the transformation of output from one to another.

### Assumptions of production possibility curve:

i)   Economy produces only two goods.
ii)  Resources and technology are given and unchanged.
iii) Resources are fully and efficiently utilised.
iv)  Resources can be shifted from one good to another good.

The fourth assumption reflects that M.O.C (Marginal Opportunity Cost) or marginal rate of transformation increases.

**Properties:**

1. Production Possibility Curve slopes downward: The production possibility curve slopes downward from left to right. This means if the production of one output is increased then the production of other will be decreased.
2. Production possibility curve is concave to the origin: This means slope of PPC increases. It is because of increasing marginal opportunity cost.
3. PPC shows only what a country can potentially produce and not what it actually produces.

## ▪ Explanation of Production Possibility Curve with the help of a hypothetical schedule and diagram:

Production Possibility Curve is a curve which shows different possible combination of production of two goods with the help of available resources and technology. This can be explained with the help of following schedule and diagram.

| Production possibilities | A | B | C | D | E | F |
|---|---|---|---|---|---|---|
| Rice (x) | 0 | 1 | 2 | 3 | 4 | 5 |
| Wheat (y) | 15 | 14 | 12 | 9 | 5 | 0 |
| MRT | - | 1:1 | 2:1 | 3:1 | 4:1 | 5:1 |

Table: 1/1

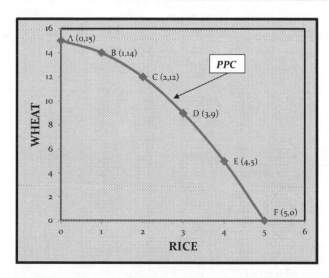

Fig. 1/2

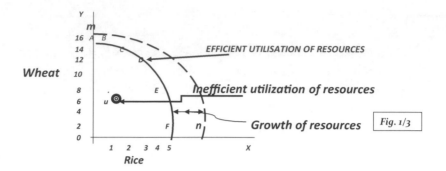

Fig. 1/3

In the above diagram all the points on the PPC like A,B,C,D,E,F, are indicating fuller or efficient utilization of resources and any point under the Production Possibility Curve or to the left of PPC like point 'u' indicates inefficient or under utilization of resources. The shifting of PPC from 'AF' to 'mn' indicates growth of resources.

## ▪ Reasons for Shifting of Production Possibility Curve (PPC) to the right:

Shifting of PPC to the right indicates efficient uses of resources and increases in the employment. This is shown by the following diagram where PPC shifts to right wards from AB to MN.

PPC shift to the right because of the following reasons:

i)   When the resources of an economy increases by the discovery of new resources.
ii)  When there is improvement in technology.
iii) When the productive capacity of the economy increases.

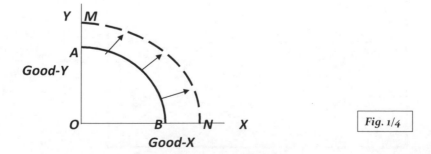

Fig. 1/4

## ▪ Reasons for Shifting of Production Possibility Curve (PPC) to the left:

Shifting of PPC to the left indicate inefficient or under utilization of resources and massive unemployment. This is shown by the following diagram where PPC shifts to leftwards from 'RS' to 'LP'.

PPC shift to the left because of the following reasons:

    i)   When the productive capacity decreases.
    ii)  When the technology becomes obsolete.
    iii) When there is depreciation of machineries.

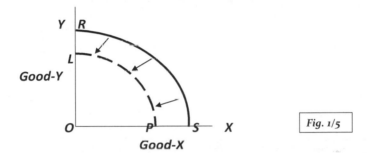

Fig. 1/5

## ▪ The concept of opportunity cost with the help of example.

According to Benham, Opportunity cost of an activity is defined as the next best alternative that could be produced instead by the same factors or by equivalent group of factors, costing the same amount of money.

    According to Professor Knight Opportunity cost is the cost of producing one commodity in terms of another.

    Opportunity cost arises whenever the resources are limited and have alternative uses.

**Assumptions:** opportunity cost is based on the following assumptions:

    i)   There is perfect competition in the market.
    ii)  There is no change in technology.
    iii) There is full employment in the economy.
    iv) There is production of only two goods.

For example, suppose a producer with same cost of cultivation produces rice of Rs. 20, 000 or wheat of Rs. 15,000 in a given piece of land. Now if he decides to produce only rice then he has to sacrifice production of wheat of Rs. 15,000. So the opportunity cost of rice will be Rs. 15, 000 of wheat which is given up.

## ▪ Marginal opportunity cost (MOC) or Marginal Rate of Transformation with the help of a diagram.

The marginal opportunity cost or Marginal Rate of Transformation of a particular good along the PPC is defined as the rate at which quantity of one good is sacrificed for the increase of production of another good.

It can be clear by the following example.

| Rice (X) (gained) | Wheat(Y) (sacrificed) | MOC ($\frac{\Delta Y}{\Delta X}$) or MRT |
|---|---|---|
| 0 | 10 | - |
| 2 | 9 | 10-9/2-0=0.5 |
| 5 | 7 | 9-7/5-2=0.67 |
| 8 | 4 | 7-4/8-5=1 |
| 10 | 0 | 4-0/10-8=2 |

*Table: 1//2 1/2*

$$MRT = \frac{\text{units of one good sacrificed}}{\text{More units of another good produced}} = \frac{\Delta Y}{\Delta X}$$

Here MOC = Sacrifice of wheat/Gain of Rice
= BM /MC
= ΔY/ΔX;

Since, NC/ND > MB/MC, this implies that as one moves from point A to point E on the transformation curve, MOC increases.

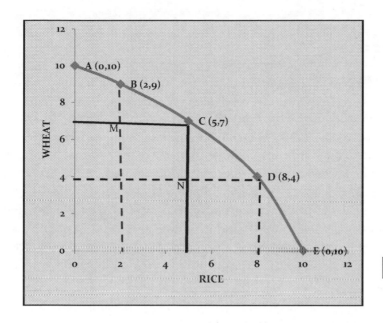

Fig. 1/6

If the slope of marginal opportunity cost (MOC) increases then PPC will be concave; if the slope decreases then PPC will be convex and if the slope is constant then PPC will be a straight line.

## ▪ Distinction between Positive and Normative Economic statements:

| Basis | Positive Science | Normative Science |
|---|---|---|
| 1. Meaning | It refers to that statement which says 'what it is or it was'. | It refers to that statement which says 'what ought to be'. |
| 2. Basis | It is based on real facts. | It is only suggestive. |
| 3. Value judgment | In this value judgments are not given. | In this value judgments are given. |
| 4. Verifications | It can be verified. | It cannot be verified. |
| 5. Examples | Indian economy is a mixed economy. | If production increases price rise can be checked. |

## ▪ Economic problems with the help of PPC:

The central problems of an economy can be explained with the help of PPC in the following way:

(i) **What to produce and how much?**—This problem deals with which goods will be produced in the economy and in what quantities. Since the resources are limited it is not possible to increase the production of one good without decreasing the production of other good. In the following diagram A, B, C, D is different combination of two goods, good-x and good-y. Point B shows that the economy produces OY1 of Good-Y and OX1 of Good-X. If the economy produces more of Good-X i.e.; X1X2 then it has to sacrifice the production of Good-Y i.e.; Y1Y2. This is so because resources are limited.

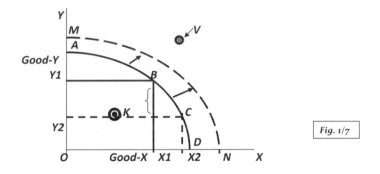

Fig. 1/7

(ii) **How to Produce**—this problem deals with which technology will be used-i.e.; whether labour intensive technology or capital intensive technology. PPC helps to solve this problem. For example if the technology used in the production becomes obsolete then economy will produce at some points inside the PPC like point-K in the above diagram. This will encourage the economy to improve the technology so as production takes place at some point like points A, B, C, and D on the PPC.

(iii) **For whom to produce or choice of technique?**—This problem deals with the distribution of output in the economy. PPC helps to solve this problem. If combination of goods are such that it indicates production in favour of luxury goods which means rich people's taste are more preferred compared to the poor people in the economy. So if necessary, changes can be made in the production of goods.

**(iv) Fuller utilization or efficient utilization of resources**—All the points like A, B, C, D on the PPC indicate resources are fully or efficiently utilized. But any point inside the PPC like point-K indicates under utilization or inefficient utilization of resources.

**(v) How to achieve Economic Growth**—The economy normally cannot produce any combination outside the PPC like point-V in fig-1. If the economy wants to produce such a combination like point V, then it has to mobilize additional resources by new inventions or innovations or by discovery of new sources of materials. Then the PPC will shift to the right which implies economic growth.

The shifting of PPC from AD to MN indicates Growth of Resources.

## ▪ Does production take place only on the PP curve?

Not necessary. If the resources are fully and efficiently utilised in the economy then production takes place on the Production possibility curve as shown by the points A, B, C, D in the above Fig-1. On the other hand if the resources are not fully and efficiently utilized then production takes place below the PPC like point 'K' (which shows problem of unemployment and inefficiency in the economy) as shown in the above fig-1.

## ▪ The subject matter of economics:

Professor Ragner Frisch in 1933, first time classified Economics into Micro and Macro Economics.

Micro Economics deals with

a) Product Pricing-which studies theory of demand and theory of supply.
b) Factor Pricing—which studies theory of wages, rent, interest and profit.
c) Welfare economics.

Macro Economics deals with

d) Theory of income and employment.
e) Theory of General Price Level.
f) Theory of Economic Growth.
g) Theory of Distribution.

## ▪ IS ECONOMICS A SCIENCE OR AN ART?

It is an important objective of study of economics to know whether economics is a science or an art or both. The economists are divided with their own logics while explaining the answer to the above question.

There are some economists like Friedman, Lord Robins, Marshall etc. argued that economics is a science. We should know what is science?

Science is a systematic body of knowledge concerning the relationship between causes and effects of a particular phenomenon.

Economics is regarded as science because facts relating to economics activities are observed and explained and like science the economics laws are verified.

But there are some economists like Pigou, Keynes etc. who argued that economics is an art. Art is defined as the practical application of knowledge in order to attain certain objectives.

Economics is an art because it helps us not only to know the problem but also it suggests solving the problem.

However some economists argued that economics cannot be called as exact science like Physics or Chemistry because economics laws cannot be examined in any laboratory. Therefore it is better to say that economics is social science. So at last to conclude it can be said that economics is both science and as well as an art.

## ▪ SOME IMPORTANT OBJECTIVE QUESTIONS-ANSWERS AT A GLANCE-

**Q.1.** State two characteristics of economic resources

**Ans. 1)** Economic resources are limited.
   **2)** Economic resources can be used alternatively.

**Q.2.** what is meant by scarcity?

**Ans.** Scarcity is a situation in which supply of resources are less than the demand for resources.

**Q.3.** what does a movement from one point to another along the PPC indicate?

**Ans.** It indicates the changes of combination of two goods i.e. more of one is produced at the cost of sacrificing of another.

**Q.4.** why is PPC concave to the origin?

**Ans**. It is because of increasing marginal opportunity cost.

**Q.5.** when can PPC be a straight line?

**Ans.** If the marginal opportunity cost is constant.

**Q.6.** what is economics all about?

**Ans.** Economics is about making choices in the presence of scarcity.

**Q.7.** How can you differentiate between market economy and planned economy?

| BASIS | MARKET ECONOMY | PLANNED ECONOMY |
|---|---|---|
| 1. Definition. | It is a free economy in which the economic problems are solved through price mechanism i.e. by demand and supply forces. | It is an economy in which economic decisions are taken by the Government or Central Planning authority. Demand and supply forces are controlled or regulated. |
| 2. Means of production. | Means of production are owned by private individuals. | Means of production are owned and controlled by the Government. |
| 3. Objective. | Profit maximization | Social welfare maximization |

| 4. Economic growth. | Economic growth depends on market forces. | Economic growth depends on economic planning like five year plans of Government. |
| 5. Role of Government. | Role of Government is very limited. Govt. Does not interfere in the production process. | Government plays an active role in the production process. |

**Although water is very useful to the people compared to the uses of diamond, yet it is cheaper but diamond is costlier? Answer with reason.**

Water is no doubt very essential and useful commodity to the people compared to diamond. Water is cheaper because water is abundantly available whereas diamond is scarce.

The value of any commodity in the economy is inversely related to its availability.

If the commodity is abundantly available then its value becomes less (like water). On the other hand if any commodity is very scarce in the economy then its value is very high (like diamond).

__*__*__*__*__*__*__*__*__*__*__*__*__

# IMPORTANT QUESTIONS:

1. Define economics.
2. What is meant by micro economics?
3. What is scarcity?
4. Write the scarcity definition of economics.
5. Write two examples of micro economics.
6. What is meant by positive economic statement?
7. What is meant by normative economic statement?
8. Why does the problem of choice rise?
9. State two characteristics of economic resources which give rise to economic problem.
10. Define economizing of resources.
11. What is the need of economizing of resources?
12. State three problems of allocation of resources.
13. State the central problem 'what to produce'.
14. State the central problem 'For whom to produce'.
15. State the problem 'how to produce'.
16. Define production possibility frontier.
17. Define opportunity cost.
18. What is meant by marginal rate of transformation or marginal opportunity cost?
19. Why is production possibility curve (PPC) concave?
20. What does leftward shift of PPC indicate?
21. What does rightward shift of PPC indicate?
22. What is meant by efficient utilization of resources?
23. What is meant by inefficient utilization of resources?
24. When can a PPC be straight line?
25. What do you mean by alternative uses of resources?

## 3 OR 4 MARK QUESTIONS:

1.  An economy produces two goods good-X and good-Y according to different combinations. Calculate marginal opportunity costs of good-X from the following table.

| Good-X | 0 | 1 | 2 | 3 | 4 |
|--------|--------|--------|--------|--------|--------|
| Good-Y | 100000 | 90000 | 78000 | 62000 | 42000 |

2.  If Marginal Opportunity Cost remains constant then what will be the shape of PPC?

    Ans. It will be a straight line starting from OY axis to OX axis.

3.  A PPC is drawn for wheat and cloth.

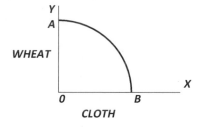

### WHAT WILL BE THE SHAPE OF PPC?

a)  If there is improvement in technology of production of only wheat?
b)  If there is improvement in the technology of production of only cloth?
c)  If the technology improves for the production of both goods?
d)  If the existing technology for the production of both goods becomes obsolete?
e)  If resources are not fully employed?
f)  If efficiency of resources increases?
g)  If all resources are equally efficient in production of all goods?

3.  Distinguish between micro and macro economics.
4.  How can you differentiate between positive and normative economic statement?
5.  Explain the problem of allocation of resources.

6. What is meant by economic problem? Why does it arise?
7. Explain the central problems of an economy.
8. State the characteristics of economic resources which leads to economic problem.
9. What is meant by economizing of resources? What are its needs?
10. What is meant by Production Possibility Curve (PPC)? How can you draw a PPC from production possibility schedule?
11. Explain the central problem what to produce with the help of PPC.
12. Define marginal rate of transformation or marginal opportunity cost with the help of a hypothetical schedule.
13. Why is PPC concave? When can it be a straight line?
14. Write the causes and effects of right ward shift of PPC.
15. Write the causes and effects of left ward shift of PPC.
16. Explain the concept of opportunity cost with the help of an example.
17. How can you explain the fact with the help of PPC when a lot of people died and properties were destroyed due to Tsunamis?
18. Why does the economic problem arise? Explain any one central problem with the help of PPC.
19. Do you think choice of technique is a central problem? Why?
20. How can you explain 'For whom to produce' is a central problem?
21. Do you think an economy always produces only on PPC? Justify your answer with the help of a diagram.
22. Distinguish between a centrally planned economy and a market economy.
23. How can you draw the Production possible frontier when MRT is constant?
24. Identify which of the following are the subject matter of micro or macro economics?

   a) Supply of output by a firm
   b) Cotton and textile industry
   c) Government budget
   d) General Price level
   e) Determination of price of output

# Chapter - 2

## Consumer's Equilibrium:

## ▪ Concept of consumption:

Consumption is defined as the use of utility of goods and services to satisfy human wants.

## ▪ Who is called a consumer?

A consumer is an economic agent who consumes goods and services to satisfy human wants. A consumer may be an individual or a group of individuals or an organization.

## ▪ Utility and its different aspects:

Utility refers to the power of a good or service which satisfies human wants. In other words utility is want satisfying power of a commodity. Utility is anything which can satisfy human wants.

Utility, in cardinal sense, has two aspects—Total Utility and Marginal Utility.

(i) **Total Utility**—According to Leftwich, "Total utility refers to the entire amount of satisfaction obtained from consuming various quantities of a commodity".

In other words, Total Utility is the sum of all the utilities derived from consumption of total number of units of a commodity. TU = ∑MU

**(ii) Marginal Utility**—According to Boulding, "Marginal Utility is the increase in total utility results from a unit increase in consumption".

In other words, Marginal Utility can be defined as the change in the total utility resulting from a one-unit change in the consumption of a commodity per unit of time.

$$\text{Marginal Utility} = \frac{\text{Change in Total Utility}}{\text{Change in quantity consumed}} = \Delta TU/\Delta Q$$

## • The law of diminishing marginal utility:
## • Reasons for its operation and its limitations:

The law of diminishing marginal utility states that as a consumer consumes more units of a commodity the utility derived from each successive units of it goes on diminishing.

According to Professor Samuelson, "As the amount consumed of good increases the marginal utility of the good tends to decrease."

This law is based on the following **assumptions:**

i) Utility can be measured by cardinal numbers.
ii) Marginal utility of money remains constant.
iii) There is a continuous consumption of the commodity.
iv) Size of the consumed unit of commodity must be appropriate.
v) There is no change in the income of consumer.
vi) There is no change in the price of the goods.
vii) There is no change in the taste and habits of the consumer.

This law can be explained by the following table and diagram-

| Units of Commodity | Marginal Utility |
|:---:|:---:|
| 1 | 6 |
| 2 | 4 |
| 3 | 2 |
| 4 | 0 |
| 5 | -2 |

Table: 2/1 1/2

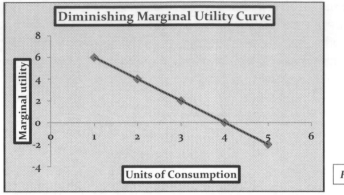

*Fig. 2/1*

From the above table and diagram it is clear that as a consumer consumes more units of a commodity the marginal utility from each successive unit decreases. So the MU curve slopes downwards from left to right.

- **CAUSES OF OPERATION OF THIS LAW:**

  1. This law operates because commodities are not perfectly substitutes.
  2. There is hardly any want which cannot be fully satisfied.

- **Exceptions of this law :**

**The marginal utility instead of decrease it increases for the followings:**

  a) This law is not applicable for collection of rare coins, rare stamps or rare articles of any author or collection of rare paintings of an artist.
  b) It is not applicable for misers who acquire more and more of wealth and marginal utility each time increases with acquiring of wealth.
  c) If the initial units of a commodity are less than the appropriate quantity then instead of decreasing the marginal utility increases as the consumer consumes more units of the same commodity.

## ▪ The relationship between Total Utility and Marginal Utility:

  (i) **Total Utility**—According to Leftwich, "Total utility refers to the entire amount of satisfaction obtained from consuming various quantities of a commodity".

In other words, Total Utility is the sum of all the utilities derived from consumption of total number of units of a commodity. TU =∑MU

**(ii) Marginal Utility**—According to Boulding, "Marginal Utility is the increase in total utility results from a unit increase in consumption".
In other words, Marginal Utility can be defined as the change in the total utility resulting from a one-unit change in the consumption of a commodity per unit of time.

$$\text{Marginal Utility} = \frac{\text{Change in Total Utility}}{\text{Change in quantity consumed}} = \Delta TU/\Delta Q$$

The relationship can be explained by the following table and diagram-

| UNITS CONSUMED (x) | MU | TU |
|---|---|---|
| 1 | 6 | 6 |
| 2 | 4 | 10 |
| 3 | 2 | 12 |
| 4 | 0 | 12 |
| 5 | -2 | 10 |

Table: 2/2

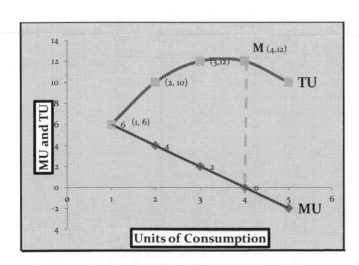

Fig. 2/2

On the basis of above table and diagram the relationship between TU and MU can be explained in the following way:

1. As long as MU decreases and positive, TU increases (up to 3 units).
2. When MU = 0, TU is maximum (as shown by point M) (in case of 4th unit).
3. When MU decreases and negative then TU decreases (in case of 5th unit).

## ▪ Consumer's equilibrium in case of single commodity:

Consumer's equilibrium refers to a situation in which a consumer gets maximum satisfaction out of his given income and price of the good and he has no tendency to change his consumption pattern.

The utility analysis of Consumer's equilibrium can be studied by two approaches.

Firstly by cardinal approach, where utilities of different commodities can be measured by cardinal numbers like 1, 2, 3 and so on. This approach was led by Marshall.

And secondly the consumer's equilibrium can be studied by ordinal approach i.e. indifference curve approach which was led by J. R. Hicks and R.G.D. Allen. This was further developed by Professor Samuelson for Revealed Preference Theory.

## ▪ CONDITION OF CONSUMER'S EQUILIBRIUM for (SINGLE COMMODITY):

$$\frac{MUX}{PX} = MUm$$

Or,    MUx = Px. Mum.

(Here MUx is marginal utility of commodity X, and Px is price of commodity X, and Mum is marginal utility of money.)

**ASSUMPTIONS:**

i)   Utility can be measured by cardinal numbers.
ii)  Marginal utility of money remains constant.
iii) There is a continuous consumption of the commodity.

iv) Size of the consumed unit of commodity must be appropriate.

v) There is no change in the income of consumer.

vi) There is no change in the price of the goods.

vii) There is no change in the taste and habits of the consumer.

The consumer's equilibrium can be explained by the following table and diagram-

Since MU curve diminishes and price of commodity is constant, so MUx/Px also diminishes.

| UNITS OF CONSUMPTION | MUx | Px | MUx/Px | Mum | MUx/Px |
|---|---|---|---|---|---|
| 1 | 12 | 2 | 6 | 4 | Is more than Px |
| 2 | 10 | 2 | 5 | 4 | |
| 3(Equilibrium) | 8 | 2 | 4 | 4 | MUx/Px=MUm |
| 4 | 6 | 2 | 3 | 4 | MUx/Px |
| 5 | 4 | 2 | 2 | 4 | Is less than Px |
| 6 | 2 | 2 | 1 | 4 | |

Table. 2/3

In the above table it is clear that at 3$^{rd}$ unit of consumption of commodity the consumer is equilibrium because here the condition of equilibrium is satisfied i.e. MUx/Px = Mum.

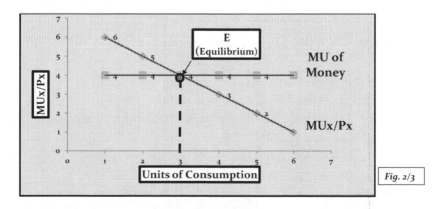

Fig. 2/3

In the above diagram point-E is the equilibrium point in which the condition of consumer's equilibrium i.e., (MUx/Px) = MUm is satisfied and the consumer gets maximum satisfaction. Here the consumer buys 3 units of commodity.

If the consumer consumes less than 3 units, then (MUx/Px) > MUm, so he consumes more. On the other hand at less price his demand increases and he consumes more.

If the consumer consumes more than 3 units, then (MUx/Px) < Mum; So he is not interested to consume more than 3rd unit.

Therefore he maximizes his satisfaction at 3rd units of consumption where the condition of consumer's equilibrium (MUx/Px) = MUm is satisfied.

## Consumer's equilibrium in case of two commodities:

Consumer's equilibrium refers to a situation in which a consumer gets maximum satisfaction out of his given income and prices of the goods and he has no tendency to change his consumption pattern.

### CONDITION OF EQUILIBRIUM (TWO COMMODITIES):

MUx/Px = MUm

And    Muy/Py = Mum.

SO, MUx/PX = Muy/PY = MUm

(Here MUx,MUy are marginal utilities of commodity –x and Commodity-y, Px, Py are prices of commodity-x and commodity-y, and Mum is marginal utility of money.)

### ASSUMPTIONS:

i)    Utility can be measured by cardinal numbers.
ii)    Marginal utility of money remains constant.
iii)    There is a continuous consumption of the commodities.
iv)    Size of the consumed unit of commodities must be appropriate.
v)    There is no change in the income of consumer.
vi)    There is no change in the prices of the goods.
vii)    There is no change in the taste and habits of the consumer.

This law can be explained by the following table and diagram.

| UNITS OF CONSUMPTION | MUx | Px | MUx/ Px | MUy | Py | MUy/ Py |
|---|---|---|---|---|---|---|
| 1 | 24 | 2 | 12 | 30 | 3 | 10 |
| 2 | 20 | 2 | 10 | 24 | 3 | 8 |
| 3 | 16 | 2 | 8 | 18 | 3 | 6 |
| 4 | 12 | 2 | 6 | 12 | 3 | 4 |
| 5 | 8 | 2 | 4 | 6 | 3 | 2 |

*Table. 2/4*

Let Px = Rs. 2 and Py = Rs. 3 and the consumer has Rs. 17 to buy both the goods X and Y.

In order to maximize his satisfaction the consumer does not equate the marginal utilities because the prices of both the goods are different. So, he equates the last rupee spent on two goods i.e., MUx/Px = MUy/Py.

From the above table it is clear that the consumer gets maximum satisfaction out of his spending of Rs. 17, when he consumes 4 units of good X and 3 units of good Y. It is because he gets total utilities of (144 utils); He gets 24+20+16+12 = 72 utils from good X and 30+24+18 = 72 utils from good Y.

No other allocation of money or combination of consumption out of his Rs. 17 can yield him more satisfaction than this.

Here the equilibrium condition of consumer is also satisfied:
i.e., MUx/Px = MUy/Py = Mum = 6.

This can be explained by the following diagram.

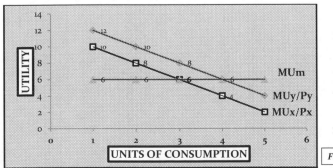

*Fig. 2/4*

This can be explained by the following diagram (diagram without scale)

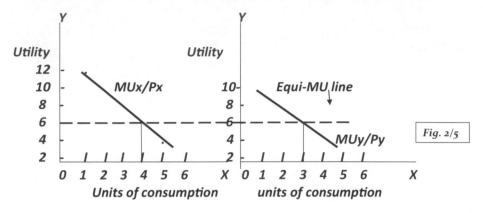

Fig. 2/5

In the above diagram the consumer is equilibrium at that point where he buys 4 units of Good-X and 3 units of Good-Y and the equilibrium condition is satisfied i.e. MUx/Px = Muy/Py. This law is called law of Equi-Marginal Utility.

❖ **Consumer's Equilibrium in case of non-economic or free goods:**

Here the consumer does not pay any price for the consumption of good because the good is non-economic good or free good.

| Output | MU (utility gained) | Price (Utility sacrificed) |
|--------|---------------------|-----------------------------|
| 1 | 6 | Zero |
| 2 | 4 | Zero |
| 3 | 2 | Zero |
| 4 | 0 | Zero |
| 5 | -2 | Zero |

Table. 2/5

The rational consumer will restrict his consumption at 4th unit where marginal utility of the good and the price of the good are equal. This point of satiety denotes consumer's equilibrium as shown by point E in the following diagram.

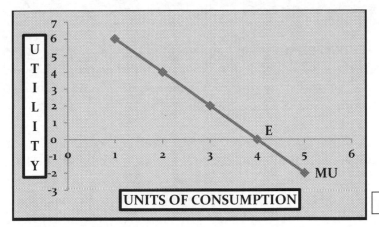

*Fig. 2/6*

## ▪ Indifference Curve and its Properties (Ordinal Approach):

The concept of indifference curve was propounded first by the economist Edgeworth. Later Hicks and Allen used indifference curve as ordinal approach to explain consumer's behaviour.

An indifference curve is a curve which shows different combination of two goods that yield equal level of satisfaction to the consumer.

According to Ferguson, "An indifference curve is a combination of goods, each of which yield the same level of total utility to which the consumer is indifferent."

An indifference map refers to a group of indifference curves where higher indifference curve shows more satisfaction compared to the lower indifference curves.

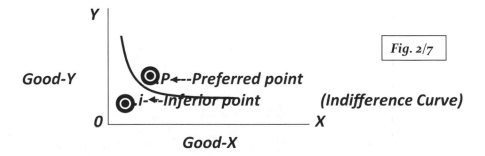

*Fig. 2/7*

## ▪ PROPERTIES OF Indifference curve:

1. **SLOPING DOWNWARDS:** An indifference curve always slopes downwards from left to right. It means if a consumer wants to consume more of a good then he has to consume less of other good in order to maintain the same level of satisfaction.

2. **CONVEX TO THE ORIGIN:** This property is based on law of diminishing marginal rate of substitution. If an indifference curve is not convex i.e. if it is concave or straight line, then law of diminishing marginal rate of substitution is not applicable there. This can be explained by the following diagram.

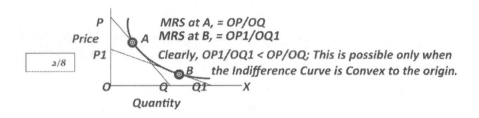

3. **TWO INDIFFERENCE CURVES NEVER INTERSECT EACH OTHER:**
   Each indifference curve shows different level of satisfaction, so they cannot intersect each other.

4. **HIGHER THE INDIFFERENCE CURVE GREATER THE SATISFACTION:**
   Lower indifference curve shows less satisfaction and higher the indifference curve shows more satisfaction.

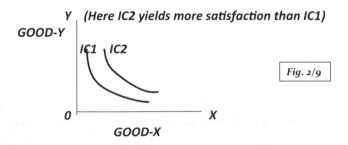

5. **INDIFFERENCE CURVE NEITHER TOUCHES X—AXIS NOR Y—AXIS:**
   No indifference curves touches x-axis or y-axis. It is because if it touches any axis then only one commodity is demanded and the demand for other is zero.

6. **INDIFFERENCE CURVES NEED NOT BE PARALLEL TO EACH OTHER:**
   Indifference curves need not be parallel to each other. They will be parallel only when MRS at different points on two indifference curves diminishes at constant rate otherwise not.

## ▪ Consumer's equilibrium with the help of indifference curve approach or ordinal approach:

Consumer's equilibrium refers to a situation in which a consumer gets maximum satisfaction out of his given income and prices of the goods and he has no tendency to change his consumption pattern.

**The students are advised to clear the concept of Price line or Budget line (discussed later in this chapter) before to present indifference curve approach.**

**ASSUMPTIONS:**

   a) Consumer is rational whose main aim is to maximize satisfaction.
   b) Income of the consumer is given and constant.
   c) Price of the goods is given and constant.
   d) There is perfect competition in the market.
   e) Goods are divisible.

• **CONDITIONS FOR CONSUMER'S EQUILIBRIUM:**

   i) Price line should be tangent to the indifference curve,

   i.e., $MRS_{xy} = P_x/P_y$.

Or, Slope of the Indifference curve = Slope of the Budget line.

   ii) Indifference curve must be convex to the origin.

The consumer's equilibrium can be explained by the following diagram.

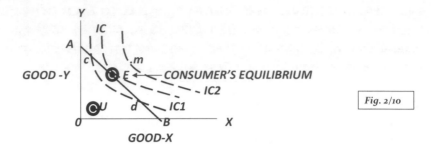

Fig. 2/10

In the above diagram if the consumer prefers any point to the left of indifference curve like point-U then consumer's income is not fully utilised and he does not get maximum satisfaction compared to point E. On the other hand the consumer cannot attain any point like m, because it is beyond his budget line AB. Therefore he gets maximum satisfaction only at point E. **Here both the conditions of consumer's equilibrium are satisfied (indifference curve is convex to the origin and MRSx,y = Px/Py).** So this point E is called consumer's equilibrium point.

The consumer cannot choose points 'c' and'd' although 'c' and 'd' are on the same budget line but they are on lower indifference curve IC1. On the other hand he cannot choose point 'm' because it is out of his budget line. Therefore he prefers point 'E' which is on higher indifference curve IC compared to IC1 and he gets maximum satisfaction. So this point 'E' is called as the consumer's equilibrium point.

## ▪ Distinction between utility approach and indifference approach:

| BASIS | UTILITY APPROACH Developed by Prof. Marshall (cardinal approach) | INDIFFERENCE CURVE APPROACH Introduced by J.R.Hicks (Ordinal approach) |
|---|---|---|
| 1. Approach: | 1. It is based on cardinal concept. | 1. It is based on ordinal concept. |
| 2. Main limitation: | 2. The main limitation of this approach is that it assumes that utility of any commodity depends only on that commodity. Then we cannot study substitute and complementary goods by this approach. | 2. This approach is free from such assumption. |

| 3. MU of Money: | 3. In this approach Marshall assumes constant marginal utility of money. | 3. This approach is free from such assumption. |
|---|---|---|
| 4. Division of Price effect: | 4. This approach fails to divide price effect into income effect and substitution effect. | 4. This approach helps to divide price effect into income and substitution effect. |
| 5. Giffen's paradox: | 5. This approach fails to explain Giffen's paradox. | 5. This approach helps to explain Giffen's paradox. |
| 6. Realistic: | 6. It is not so realistic. | 6. It is more realistic. |

## ▪ Concept of Marginal Rate of Substitution:

The Marginal rate of Substitution shows how much of one commodity is sacrificed by a consumer to gain how much of another commodity. In other words MRS is defined as a rate at which a consumer is willing to sacrifice one commodity for gaining another commodity.

The concept of diminishing MRS is an important tool for indifference curve analysis. It is slope of an indifference curve.

MRSxy may be defined as the amount of Y commodity that the consumer is willing to give up in order to get an additional unit of X commodity.

MRSxy is also equal to the ratio of marginal utilities of commodity Y and X. Symbolically,

$$MRS_{xy} = = \frac{E/P_x}{E/P_y} = \frac{P_x}{P_y} ; \text{ Here 'E' refers to the expenditure.}$$

$$MRS_{xy} = \frac{MU_x}{MU_y} = \frac{P_x}{P_y} = (-)\frac{\Delta y}{\Delta x} \text{ (Slope of Indifference Curve)}$$

This is shown by the following table:

| COMBINATIONS | GOOD-Y | GOOD-X | MRS OF X FOR Y |
|---|---|---|---|
| A | 15 | 1 | – |
| B | 11 | 2 | 4:1 |
| C | 8 | 3 | 3:1 |
| D | 6 | 4 | 2:1 |
| E | 5 | 5 | 1:1 |

*Table. 2/6*

It is clear from the above table that as a consumer consumes more, he sacrifices Good-Y to gain one unit of Good-X. So MRS diminishes.

This MRS can be explained by the following diagram.

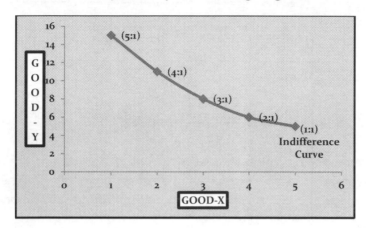

Fig. 2/11

If MRS of x for y commodity diminishes then the indifference curve is convex (as shown in the above diagram)
If MRS increases then the indifference curve is concave;
If MRS is constant then the indifference curve is a straight line.

In the above diagram MRS of Good-X for Good-Y can be written as-
Slope of Indifference Curve, MRSxy = $\dfrac{-\Delta Y}{\Delta X}$ .

**TWO IMPORTANT POINTS:**

(a) If $MRS_{xy} > \dfrac{P_x}{P_y}$, then the consumer sacrifices more of Good-y in order to get additional unit of Good-x and this process continues till both the ratios are equal.

(b) If $MRS_{xy} < \dfrac{P_x}{P_y}$, then the consumer sacrifices less of Good-y in order to get additional unit of Good-x and this process continues till both the ratios are equal.

❖ MRS decreases because a consumer can sacrifice more of a good if the good is abundant to him (up to 'C' combination in the table) and if the good is very scarce then he sacrifices less (combination 'D' and 'E' in the above table).

## ▪ Budget Line and Budget Equation:

A budget line is a graphical presentation of different combination of goods at different prices that a consumer can buy with his given income.

A budget line is the upper boundary of the feasible set of bundles that a consumer can buy with his given income and the prices of two goods.

This is also called price line or budget constraint line.

According to Ferguson, "The price line shows the combinations of goods that can be purchased if the entire money income is spent."

**BUDGET LINE EQUATION**: A budget line equation can be presented in the following way-

$Px.Qx + Py.Qy = M$ : Here Px, Py are prices of two goods and Qx, Qy are quantities of two goods respectively and M refers to Money Income of the consumer.

If Qx is zero, then Qy = M/Py,
If Qy is zero, then Qx = M/Px

> If $Px.Qx + Py.Qy < M$ then it is called as Budget constraint and the whole income is not fully utilised.

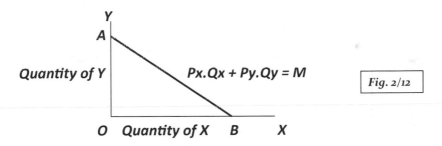

Fig. 2/12

The area AOB is called budget set. Any point in this area AOB is called attainable point whereas any point to the right of budget line or out of the area AOB is called unattainable point.

SLOPE OF the budget line = Px/Py ratio.

## ▪ Shifting of Budget line:

A budget line can be shifted either to the right or to the left depending on the two following factors:

a) If the price of good-x or price of the good-y changes or price of both changes.

b) If the money income of the consumer changes.

## ▪ CHANGES OF BUDGET LINE—

1. **Change in price of only good-x:**

   a) If price of good-x falls then budget line will shift to the right as shown in the following figure.

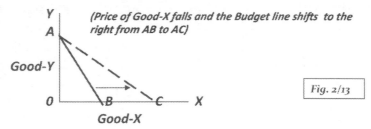

*(Price of Good-X falls and the Budget line shifts to the right from AB to AC)*

Fig. 2/13

   b) If price of Good-X rises then budget line will shift to the left as shown in the following figure.

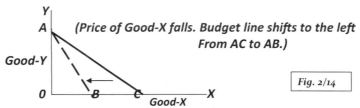

*(Price of Good-X falls. Budget line shifts to the left From AC to AB.)*

Fig. 2/14

2. **Changes in the price of only Good-y.**

   a) If price of Good-y falls then budget line will shift to upwards as shown in the following figure.

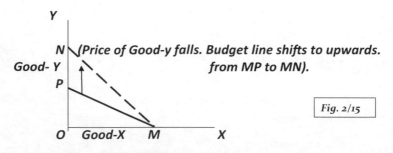

*(Price of Good-y falls. Budget line shifts to upwards. from MP to MN).*

Fig. 2/15

b) If price of Good-y rises then budget line will shift to downwards as shown in the following figure.

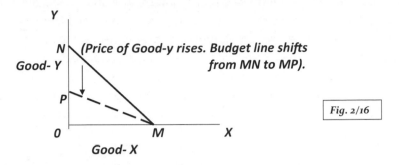

Fig. 2/16

## 3. Changes in the income of consumer:

If the income of the consumer increases then he will buy both the goods more. So his budget line will shift to right.

If his income decreases then his budget line will shift to left.

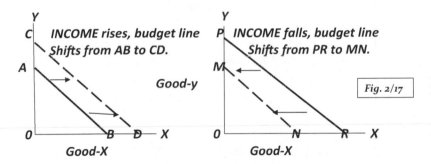

Fig. 2/17

## ▪ What is meant by Monotonic Preferences?

A consumer's preferences is called monotonic only when the consumer prefers a bundle which has more of at least one good and not less of other good out of given two goods compared to other bundles.

Q. A consumer is monotonic in his preferences. Then what will be his selection nature out of the following bundles — (5, 5), (5, 4), (4, 4).

Ans. He will always prefer the bundle (5, 5) compared to the other bundles because he gets more satisfaction from this bundle.

## ▪ BUDGET SET AND CONSUMER'S PREFERENCE:

It refers to the set of bundles of commodities available to a consumer at prevailing prices which the consumer can buy with his given income.

Out of the budget set of commodities a consumer can choose his consumption bundle on the basis of his taste and preferences. While comparing any two bundles the consumer either prefers one to the other or he is indifferent between the two bundles. Even the consumer can rank the bundles in order of his preferences over them. This can be explained by the following example.

Example: 1: A consumer has Rs. 30 which he uses to consume two goods x and y at price Rs. 2 and Rs. 3 respectively.

Here the number of bundles available to the consumer (while full amount is utilised) is as follows: (15, 0), (12, 2), (9, 4), (6, 6), (3, 8), (0, 10).

a) The consumer's most preferred bundle is (6, 6)

Example: 2: A consumer has Rs. 20 which he uses to consume two goods x and y at price Rs. 5 per unit of each good.

Here, the number of bundles available to the consumer (while full amount is utilised) is as follows: (0, 4), (4, 0), (2, 2), (3, 1), (1, 3).

a) The consumer's most preferred bundle is (2, 2)
b) He is indifferent between (1, 3) and (3, 1).
c) If he ranks the bundles then the ranking will be as follows:

| RANKING | BUNDLE |
|---------|--------|
| FIRST | (2, 2) |
| SECOND | (1, 3) AND (3, 1) |
| THIRD | (0, 4) AND (4, 0) |

*Table. 2/7*

## ▪ DERIVATION OF THE SLOPE OF THE BUDGET LINE:

The slope of the budget line can be measured by the following diagram. Let the budget line is P1.Q1 + P2.Q2 = M. Where P1, P2 are the prices of two goods and Q1 and Q2 are quantities consumed respectively and M is the money income of the consumer which is given and constant.

We have taken two points (Q1, Q2), and (Q1+ΔQ1, Q2+ΔQ2) on the budget line.

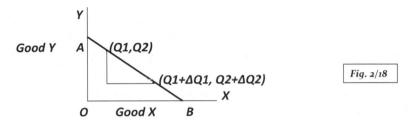

Fig. 2/18

We have P1.Q1 + P2.Q2 = M .... (1)

And P1 (Q1+ΔQ1), + P2 (Q2+ΔQ2) = M .... (2)

By subtracting (2) from (1), we have P1.ΔQ1 + P2.ΔQ2 = 0

Or, $\dfrac{\Delta Q1}{\Delta Q2} = (-) \dfrac{P2}{P1}$ = SLOPE OF BUDGET LINE

The price ratio is the slope of the budget line.

Q. A consumer consumes two goods, good-x and good-y. The prices are Rs.5 and Rs.6 respectively. If consumer's income is Rs.30

Then i)  write the equation of the budget line.
    ii)   How much good-x can be consumed if he spends his income only on good-x?
    iii)  How much of good-y can be consumed if he spends his income only on good-y?
    iv)  What will be the slope of the budget line?

Ans. (i)  Here, if the quantities of two goods are Qx and Qy respectively then the Budget Equation is, 5.Qx + 6.Qy = 30
    (ii)  Qx = 30/5 = 6 units.
    (iii) Qy = 30/6 = 5 units.
    (iv) Slope of the Budget Line = Px/Py = 5/6 = 0.83

3.   If the utility function is U = x2y2 and budget equation is 4x+8y=96

Then find out the number of units of commodities x and y at which the consumer gets maximum satisfaction.

Solution: U = x2y2
Therefore, MUx = 2xy2 and MUy = 2x2y
      4x + 8y = 96
So, Px = 4 and Py = 8
Now according to consumer's equilibrium for two commodities,

We have $\dfrac{\textbf{MUx}}{\textbf{Px}} = \dfrac{\textbf{MUy}}{\textbf{Py}}$

Or, $\dfrac{\textbf{2xy2}}{4} = \dfrac{\textbf{2x2y}}{8}$

Or, x = 2y

Now putting the above value of x in 4x + 8y = 96
We get 4.2y + 8y = 96
Or, y = 96/16 = 6

$$\text{So, } x = 2y = 2.6 = 12$$

So, the required number units of commodities are $x = 12$ and $y = 6$ at which the consumer gets maximum satisfaction.

4. Is there any relation between MU and the supply of any good?

Ans. Yes; MU changes with the change in the supply of a good. If the supply of good is unlimited (free good) then its MU = 0. On the other hand if there is shortage of supply of a good the MU is positive. So, there is inverse relationship between MU and supply of a good.

5. A consumer is given two goods X and Y. If the ratio between marginal utilities and prices of both goods are not equal because of the change in the price of good X, then explain the reaction of the consumer.

Ans. Equilibrium condition of the consumer is $MU_x/P_x = MU_y/Py = Mum$ If the ratios of MU and Prices are not equal:

(a) If Px falls, then, $MU_x/P_x > MU_y/Py$ ; then the consumer will consume more of good X in place of good Y. As a result MUx will decrease and MUy will increase and this situation of substitution will continue until the equilibrium is achieved i.e.

$$MU_x/P_x = MU_y/Py = MUm;$$

(b) If Px rises, then $MU_x/P_x < MU_y/Py$ ; then the consumer will consume more of good Y in place of good X. As a result MUy will decrease and MUx will increase and this situation of substitution will continue until the equilibrium is achieved i.e.

$$MU_x/P_x = MU_y/Py = MUm;$$

—__*__*__*__*__*__*__*__*__*__*__*__*__

# IMPORTANT QUESTIONS:

1. Define marginal utility.
2. Define total utility.
3. How do we get TU from MU?
4. How do we get MU from TU?
5. Define indifference curve.
6. What is Marginal rate of substitution?
7. What happens to TU when MU is positive but decreasing?
8. What happens to TU when MU is negative and decreasing?
9. What happens to TU when MU = 0?
10. What is meant by indifference map?
11. Why indifference curve is convex to the origin?
12. What are the conditions for consumer's equilibrium under cardinal approach?
13. Write the formula for calculating the slope of budget line.
14. Write the formula for calculating the slope of indifference curve.
15. If a consumer is indifferent between combination two bundles of commodities X and Y then what does it signify?

## 3 or 4 MARK QUESTIONS:

1. How can you explain the relationship between TU and MU with the help of hypothetical schedule and diagram?
2. Explain the law of diminishing marginal utility and state its causes.
3. Explain the conditions of consumer's equilibrium for two commodities.
4. What is budget line? Explain the shift of budget line when price of only one commodity changes.

5. Explain the shift of budget line when the income of the consumer changes.
6. If a consumer is given the following utility schedule and price of commodity is given as Rs. 8 per unit then find out at what level of consumption of output he will get maximum Total Utility?

| Units consumed | 1 | 2 | 3 | 4 |
|---|---|---|---|---|
| MU | 12 | 10 | 8 | 6 |

7. State three properties of indifference curve.
8. Explain Marginal rate of substitution with the help of a schedule and diagram.
9. What happens to budget set if both the prices and income of the consumer is double? Answer with reasons.
10. Why is the indifference curve convex to the origin?
11. Why does a budget line slope downwards?

## 6 MARK QUESTIONS:

1. Explain the consumer's equilibrium in case of a single commodity.
2. Explain the consumer's equilibrium in case of two commodities.

Or

Explain the cardinal approach for consumer's equilibrium when a consumer consumes two commodities.

3. Explain the ordinal approach for consumer's equilibrium

Or

Explain the consumer's equilibrium with the help of indifference curve approach.

4. Explain with the help of diagrams different conditions under which the budget line shifts.
5. A consumer is given Rs. 100 which he wants to spend on two goods coke and pastry. The price of each coke is Rs. 10 and the price of each pastry

is Rs. 5. The marginal utility schedules of both goods are given as follows. Find out at what level of consumption of output the consumer gets maximum satisfaction.

| Units | 1 | 2 | 3 | 4 | 5 | 6 | 7 | 8 |
|---|---|---|---|---|---|---|---|---|
| MU of coke | 80 | 70 | 60 | 50 | 40 | 30 | 20 | 10 |
| MU of pastry | 50 | 45 | 40 | 35 | 30 | 25 | 20 | 15 |

(Hints: at 6th units of coke and 8th units of pastry because equilibrium condition is satisfied and total expenditure is also Rs.100)

___*___*___*___*___*___*___*___*___*___*___*___*___*___

# Chapter - 3

## Theory of Demand:

## ▪ Demand and its main Characteristics:

Demand refers to the quantity of a commodity that a consumer is ready to purchase and able to purchase at a particular price during a given time period.

According to Ferguson, "Demand refers to the quantities of a commodity that the consumers are able and willing to buy at each possible price during a given period of time, other things being equal."

'Demand' in Economics is different from desire and want. Desire means only wishes and it is not related to ability to pay e.g. John desires to have a good car. It may be his desire.

If we take another example like, a beggar is shivering in cold and he needs a blanket. This example indicates the beggar's wants. Both the examples are not called 'Demand'.

The main characteristics of demand are as follows:

a)  Willingness to buy a commodity.
b)  Ability to buy a commodity.
c)  To buy a commodity at particular price.
d)  To buy a commodity at particular time period.

## ▪ Distinction between Demand and Quantity demanded of a commodity.

Demand refers to the various quantities of a commodity that a consumer is ready to purchase and willing to purchase at different possible prices, other things remaining constant.

Whereas quantity demanded refers to the particular quantity of a commodity that a consumer is ready to purchase and able to purchase at a given price during a time period, other factors remaining constant.

Demand refers to always price of commodity but quantity demanded refers to specific quantity of a commodity to be purchased at specific price.

Example: A consumer demands 2 oranges at Rs.4 per unit and he demands 4 oranges at Rs.3 per unit. This is an example of demand.

His quantity demanded is that he buys 2 oranges at Rs.4 per unit.

## ▪ Demand schedule:

Demand schedule refers to tabular presentation of inverse relation between different quantities demanded of a commodity and its different prices.

According to Professor Samuelson, "The table relating to price and quantity demanded is called the demand schedule."

Demand schedule is of two types:

(a) **INDIVIDUAL DEMAND SCHEDULE**—It is a table which shows different quantities of a commodity that an individual consumer buys at all possible prices at a given time period.

Table: Individual demand schedule—

| PRICE OF ORANGE(Rs.) | QUANTITY Demanded(units) |
|---|---|
| 1 | 5 |
| 2 | 4 |
| 3 | 3 |
| 4 | 2 |
| 5 | 1 |

*Table. 3/1*

(b) **MARKET DEMAND SCHEDULE**—It is defined as the quantities of a commodity which all consumers buy at all possible prices at a given time period.

Table: Market demand schedule—

| PRICE OF ORANGE(Rs.) | A'S DEMAND | B'S DEMAND | C'S DEMAND | MARKT DEMAND (A+B+C) |
|:---:|:---:|:---:|:---:|:---:|
| 1 | 4 | 5 | 3 | 12 |
| 2 | 3 | 4 | 2 | 9 |
| 3 | 2 | 3 | 1 | 6 |
| 4 | 1 | 2 | 0 | 3 |

*Table. 3/2*

In the above table only 3 consumers are assumed of different nature in the market.

## ▪ Demand curve and construction of individual demand curve from individual demand schedule:

Demand curve refers to graphical presentation of demand schedule reflecting the relationship between different quantities demanded at different possible prices.

According to Lipsey, "The curve which shows the relation between the price of a commodity and the amount of the commodity that the consumer wishes to purchase."

Demand curve is of two types: (a) individual demand curve and (ii) market demand curve.

(a) **INDIVIDUAL DEMAND CURVE:** It is a curve which shows different quantities of a commodity demanded at different prices by an individual consumer. It can be drawn from individual demand schedule.

Table: Individual demand schedule—

| PRICE OF ORANGE(Rs.) | QUANTITY Demanded(units) |
|:---:|:---:|
| 1 | 5 |
| 2 | 4 |
| 3 | 3 |
| 4 | 2 |
| 5 | 1 |

*Table. 3/3*

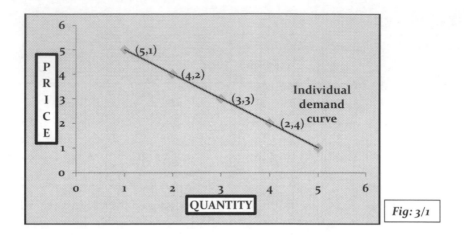

Fig: 3/1

The individual demand curve is drawn from the individual demand schedule which depicts the inverse relationship between the price of a good and its demand.

## ▪ Market demand curve and construction of market demand curve from market demand schedule:

It is a curve which shows total demand of all the consumers in the market of a commodity at different prices. This can be drawn from the market demand schedule in the following way.

Table: Market demand schedule—

| PRICE OF ORANGE(Rs.) | A'S DEMAND | B'S DEMAND | MARKT DEMAND (A+B) |
|---|---|---|---|
| 1 | 4 | 5 | 9 |
| 2 | 3 | 4 | 7 |
| 3 | 2 | 3 | 5 |
| 4 | 1 | 2 | 3 |

Table. 3/4

In the above table only 2 consumers are assumed of different nature in the market.

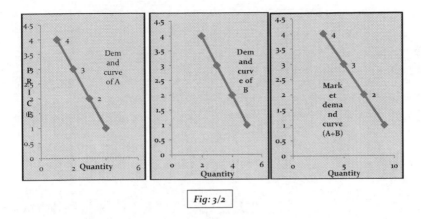

Fig: 3/2

# Law of Demand with the help of hypothetical Schedule:

Law of Demand states, that other factors being constant the demand for a commodity extends with a fall in price and contracts with the rise in price.

According to Professor Samuelson, "Law of demand states that people will buy more at lower prices and buy less at higher prices, ceteris paribus."

Law of demand is based on the following assumptions—

## ASSUMPTIONS:

(i) The income of the consumer remains unchanged.

(ii) The price of related goods remains constant.

(iii) There should be no change in the taste and preference of the consumer.

(iv) There is no change in the expected price of the commodity by the consumer.

(v) There will be no change in the distribution of income and wealth.

(vi) The commodities should be normal.

The Law of Demand can be presented by the following table and diagram.

| PRICE OF ORANGE(Rs.) | QUANTITY Demanded(units) |
|:---:|:---:|
| 1 | 5 |
| 2 | 4 |
| 3 | 3 |
| 4 | 2 |
| 5 | 1 |

Table. 3/5

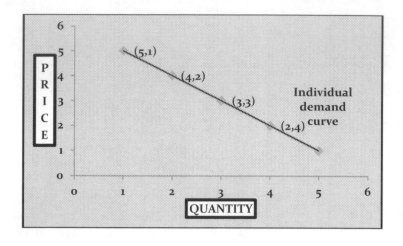

Fig: 3/3

In the above table and diagram it is clear that a consumer demands more at less price and he demands less at high price.

## ▪ Why does demand curve slope downwards?
## ▪ Or why there is an inverse relation between price of a commodity and its demand?

Demand curve is the graphical presentation of inverse relation between the price of a commodity and its price.

It is downward sloping from left to right because of the following reasons.

(i) **LAW OF DIMINISHING MARGINAL UTILITY:** Law of demand is based on the law of diminishing marginal utility. Law of diminishing marginal utility states that phenomenon in which the marginal utility of any commodity diminishes as more and more units of that commodity is purchased. Therefore a consumer will buy an extra unit of a commodity only if he has to pay less price compared to earlier. This means he will buy more if the price falls.

(ii) **INCOME EFFECT:** Income effect means that when the price of a commodity falls then the real income of the consumer rises. Thus, when the price of a commodity falls the purchasing power of the consumer increases and his demand for commodity also increases and vice-versa.

(iii) **SUBSTITUTION EFFECT:** When the price of a commodity falls and the consumer feels it is cheaper than its substitute good, then he buys more of the commodity. Thus, due to favourable substitution effect the demand for a commodity increases and due to unfavourable substitution effect the demand decreases.

(iv) **DIFFERENT USES:** There are many commodities which have alternative uses like milk, land, electricity etc. Milk can be used for drinking or for preparing sweets, cheese, curd etc. With the rise of price, milk is used for few purposes, so the demand for milk falls. On the other hand with the fall in price of milk its demand rises and it is used for many purposes.

(v) **SIZE OF CONSUMER GROUP:** With the fall in price of a commodity the consumers who were not able to buy earlier, they also start to buy, so its demand increases. On the other hand if the price rises then its demand decreases because some consumers are not able to buy who were buying earlier.

(vi) **CONSUMER'S EQUILIBRIUM:** The equilibrium condition for the consumer's equilibrium is $MU_1 = \lambda P_1$; Here $\lambda$ is marginal utility for money. Now if $P_1$ decreases and other factors remain constant, then right hand side will be lower than left hand side (MU1). Since $\lambda$ is assumed to be constant then a new equilibrium will be reached if L.H.S. i.e. $MU_1$ decreases.

It is possible (decrease in $MU_1$) if the consumer consumes more of $Q_1$ commodities. Thus, as $P_1$ decreases, the demand for $Q_1$ increases.

So, there is inverse relation between price of the goods and demand for the goods and the demand curve slopes downwards from left to right.

## • The main determinants of Demand: Or the factors which affect demand for a commodity. Or the Demand functions:

The main factors which affect the demand for a commodity are called determinants of demand. There are some factors which affect individual demand for a commodity which are called individual demand function. This can be written as: Dg = f (Pg, Pr, Yc, T);

Dg—Demand for goods, Pg—Price of goods, Yc—income of the consumer, T—taste and preferences.

## (1) PRICE OF COMMODITY—

With the rise in the price of a normal good its demand contracts and with the fall in the price of it, its demand extends. So there is inverse relation between the price of a commodity and its demand.

## (2) PRICE OF RELATED GOODS—

Related goods are classified into two categories—substitute goods and complementary goods.

    **(a) SUBSTITUTE GOODS**—Substitute goods are those goods which can be used for each other e.g. tea and coffee, Pepsi and coke etc.
If the price of Pepsi rises then the demand for its substitute good i.e. Coke increases. On the other hand if the price of Pepsi falls then demand for its substitute good i.e. coke decreases.

    **(b) COMPLEMENTARY GOODS**—Complementary goods are those goods which jointly satisfy the want for one commodity like car and petrol together satisfies the demand for a car. In this case if the price of car rises then its demand decreases and the demand for petrol also decrease. On the other hand if the price of car falls then its demand increases and the demand for petrol also increase.

**(3) INCOME OF THE CONSUMER**—If the income of the consumer increases then the demand for normal goods rises and the demand for inferior goods falls and vice-versa.

**(4) TASTE AND PREFERENCES**—Other factors remaining constant with the development of taste and preferences the demand for a commodity increases. On the other hand if the taste and preferences under develops then the demand for a commodity decreases.
There are some other factors in addition to the above factors which affect the market demand for a commodity. These factors are like Future expectation (Fe), Number of consumers (N), Distribution of income (D), Government Policy (G) etc.
So the Demand Function becomes $Dg = f (Pg, Pr, Yc, T, Fe, N, D, G)$
The above factors can be explained in the following way:

(5) **FUTURE EXPECTATION**—If a consumer expects that price of a commodity will rise in future then its demand increases at present. On the other hand if the consumer expects that price of a commodity will fall in future then its demand will be less at present and the consumer will wait for future.

(6) **NUMBER OF CONSUMERS**—when the number of consumers for a commodity increases then the demand for the commodity increases. On the other hand if the number of consumers decreases then the demand for the commodity decreases.

(7) **DISTIBUTION OF INCOME**—If in a country income and wealth is distributed in favour of the poor people then the demand for luxury goods in the country decreases and the demand for necessary goods will increase. On the other hand if the income or wealth is distributed in favour of rich people then the demand for luxuries goods in the country will increase and demand for inferior goods will decrease.

(8) **GOVERNMENT POLICY**—Government policy of taxation and subsidy also influences demand for a commodity. If the Government reduces sale tax on commodity like liquor then its price decreases and its demand increases.

## ▪ The movement along the demand curve.

Movement along the demand curve refers to changes in the quantity demanded of a commodity due to change in the price of the commodity other factors remaining constant.

It is of two types: extension of demand and contraction of demand.

(a) **EXTENSION OF DEMAND**—It refers to rise in the demand for a commodity due to fall in its price and other factors remaining constant. This is shown by the following table and diagram.

| PRICE OF COMMODITY (Rs. Per unit) | QUANTITY DEMANDED (UNITS) |
|---|---|
| 3 | 1 |
| 1 | 3 |

Table. 3/6

In the above table it is clear that as the price falls from Rs.3 to Rs.1 its demand rises from 1 unit to 3 units.

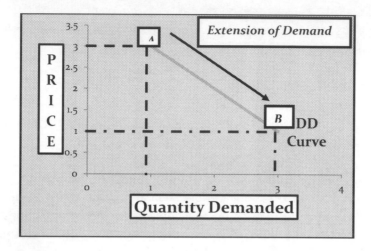

Fig: 3/4

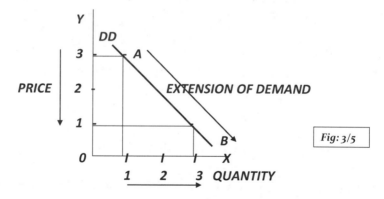

Fig: 3/5

In the above diagram the movement from point A to B is called extension of demand which is due to fall in price of the commodity.

**(b) CONTRACTION OF DEMAND**—It refers to fall in the demand for a commodity due to rise in its price and other factors remaining constant. This is shown by the following table and diagram.

| PRICE OF COMMODITY (Rs. Per unit) | QUANTITY DEMANDED (UNITS) |
|---|---|
| 1 | 3 |
| 3 | 1 |

Table. 3/7

In the above table it is clear that as the price rises from Rs.1 to Rs.3 its demand falls from 3 units to 1 unit.

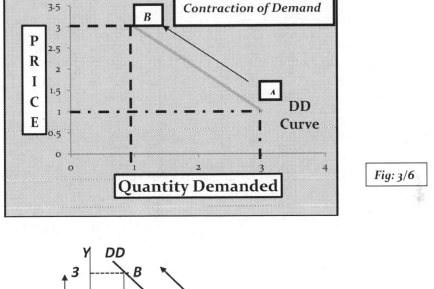

Fig: 3/6

Fig: 3/8

In the above diagram the movement from point A to B is called contraction of demand which is due to rise in price of the commodity.

## ▪ Shift of the demand curve:

Shift of the demand curve refers to the changes in the demand for a commodity not due to price of the commodity but due to the factors like income of the consumer, changes in the number of consumers or due to change in the price of other related goods or change in the taste of the consumers.

It is of two types: Increase in demand and decrease in demand.

73

(i) **INCREASE IN DEMAND**—It refers to increase in the demand for a commodity not due to its price but due to the following factors.

(a) If the income of the consumer increases.
(b) If the number of consumer increases.
(c) If the price of substitute goods increase.
(d) If tax rebates are given.
(e) If the price of complementary goods falls.
(f) If the taste and preferences for the goods develops.

Increase in demand can be explained by the following table and diagram.

| PRICE OF GOODS (Rs. per unit) | INCOME OF CONSUMER (Rs.) | DEMAND FOR GOODS(units) |
|---|---|---|
| 3 | 10,000 | 10 |
| 3 | 15,000 | 15 |

Table. 3/8

From the above table it is clear that demand for goods increases not due to any change in price but due to increase in the income of the consumer.

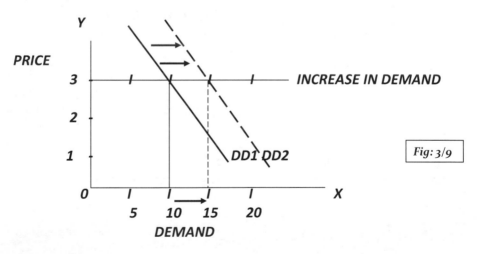

Fig: 3/9

In the above diagram it is clear as the income of the consumer increases the demand for the commodity increases and the demand curve shifts from DD1 to DD2 to the right.

**(ii) DECREASE IN DEMAND**—It refers to decrease in the demand for a commodity not due to price but due to the following factors.

(a) If the income of the consumer decreases.
(b) If the number of consumer decreases.
(c) If the price of substitute goods decreases.
(d) If existing tax rate increases or new tax is imposed.
(e) If the price of complementary goods rises.
(f) If the taste and preferences for the goods under develops.

Decrease in demand can be explained by the following table and diagram.

| PRICE OF GOODS (Rs. per unit) | INCOME OF CONSUMER (Rs.) | DEMAND FOR GOODS(units) | |
|---|---|---|---|
| 3 | 15,000 | 15 | |
| 3 | 10,000 | 10 | Table. 3/9 |

From the above table it is clear that demand for goods decreases not due to any change in price but due to decrease in the income of the consumer.

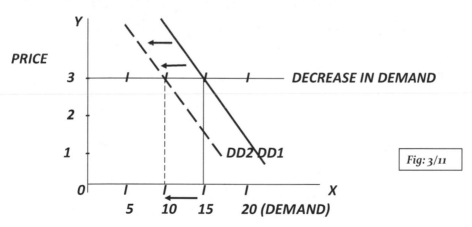

Fig: 3/11

In the above diagram it is clear as the income of the consumer decreases the demand for the commodity decreases and the demand curve shifts from DD1 to DD2 to the left.

# ▪ Distinction between changes in quantity demanded and change in demand:

| Basis | CHANGE IN QUANTITY DEMANDED | CHANGE IN DEMAND |
|---|---|---|
| 1. Definition: | It refers to change in quantity demanded for a commodity due to change in its price only. | 1. It refers to change in quantity demanded due to change in other factors other than price. |
| 2. Expression: | It is expressed in term of movement along the demand curve. | 2. It is expressed in term of shift of the demand curve. |
| 3. Classification: | It is classified into Extension of demand and Contraction of demand. | 3. It is classified into Increase and Decrease of demand. |
| 4. Presentation: | It is presented by downward movement (extension of demand) and upward movement (contraction of demand) of demand curve. | 4. It is presented by rightward shift (increase in demand i.e., DD1to DD2) and leftward shift (decrease in demand i.e., DD1 to DD3) of demand curve. |
| 6. Diagram: |  Fig: Movement along demand curve |  Fig: Shift of demand curve |

- **Distinction between extension of demand and increase in demand:        Or**
- **Distinction between change in quantity demanded and change in demand (increase).**

| Basis | EXTENSION OF DEMAND | INCREASE IN DEMAND |
|---|---|---|
| 1. Meaning: | It refers to rise in demand due to fall in price of the commodity and other factors remain constant. | 1. It refers to increase in demand due to change in other factors other than price of commodity. |
| 2. Expression: | It is expressed by the downward movement of the demand curve. | 2. It is expressed by the rightward shift of the demand curve. |
| 3. Cause: | It is due to fall in price of commodity only. | 3. Its causes are:<br>(i) If the consumer's income increases.<br>(ii) If price of substitute goods increases.<br>(iii) If price of complementary goods falls.<br>(iv) If number of consumers increases. |
| 4. Numerical Example | <table><tr><td>Price of Goods (Rs.)</td><td>Demand For Goods</td></tr><tr><td>3</td><td>1</td></tr><tr><td>1</td><td>3</td></tr></table> | <table><tr><td>Price of Goods (Rs.)</td><td>Demand For Goods</td></tr><tr><td>2</td><td>2</td></tr><tr><td>2</td><td>4</td></tr></table> |
| 5. DIAGRAMATIC PRESENTATION: | | |
| 6. Component: | 6. Component: It is a part of change in quantity demanded. | 6. It is a part of change in demand. |

- **Distinction between contraction of demand and decrease in demand:        Or**
- **Distinction between change in quantity demanded and change in demand (decrease).**

| Basis | CONTRACTION OF DEMAND | DECREASE IN DEMAND |
|---|---|---|
| 1. Meaning: | It refers to fall in demand due to rise in price of the commodity and other factors remain constant. | 1. It refers to decrease in demand due to change in other factors other than price of commodity. |
| 2. Expression: | It is expressed by the upward movement of the demand curve. | 2. It is expressed by the leftward shift of the demand curve. |
| 3. Cause: | It is due to rise in price of commodity only. | 3. Its causes are:<br>(i) If the consumer's income decreases.<br>(ii) If price of substitute goods decreases.<br>(iii) If price of complementary goods rises.<br>(iv) If number of consumers decreases. |
| 4. Numerical Example: | Price of Goods (Rs.) / Demand For Goods<br>1 / 3<br>3 / 1 | Price of Goods (Rs.) / Demand For Goods<br>2 / 4<br>2 / 2 |
| 5. DIAGRAMATIC PRESENTATION: | | |
| 6. Component: | It is a part of change in quantity demanded. | It is a part of change in demand. |

> - **Under what conditions the demand curve of a commodity will shift to the rightwards?**
> - **Or what are the causes of increase in demand?**
> - **Or Why does demand increase?**

The causes for increase in demand or rightwards shift of the demand curve are as follows:

(a) If the income of the consumer increases.

(b) If the number of consumer increases.

(c) If the price of substitute goods increase.

(d) If tax rebates are given.

(e) If the price of complementary goods falls.

(f) If the taste and preferences for the goods develops.

(g) If the consumer expects that price will increase in future.

Increase in demand can be explained by the following table and diagram.

| PRICE OF GOODS (Rs. per unit) | INCOME OF CONSUMER (Rs.) | DEMAND FOR GOODS(units) | |
|---|---|---|---|
| 3 | 10,000 | 10 | |
| 3 | 15,000 | 15 | Table. 3/10 |

From the above table it is clear that demand for goods increases not due to any change in price but due to increase in the income of the consumer.

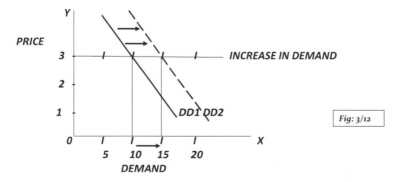

Fig: 3/12

In the above diagram it is clear as the income of the consumer increases the demand for the commodity increases and the demand curve shifts from DD1 to DD2 to the right.

- **Under what conditions the demand curve of a commodity will shift to the leftwards?**
- **Or what are the causes of decrease in demand?**
- **Or Why does demand decrease?**

The causes for decrease in demand or leftwards shift of the demand curve are as follows:

(a) If the income of the consumer decreases.
(b) If the number of consumer decreases.
(c) If the price of substitute goods decreases.
(d) If tax rate increases or new tax is imposed.
(e) If the price of complementary goods rises.
(f) If the taste and preferences for the goods under develops.
(g) If the consumer expects that price will decrease in future.

Decrease in demand can be explained by the following table and diagram.

| PRICE OF GOODS (Rs. per unit) | INCOME OF CONSUMER (Rs.) | DEMAND FOR GOODS (units) | |
|---|---|---|---|
| 3 | 15,000 | 15 | |
| 3 | 10,000 | 10 | Table. 3/11 |

From the above table it is clear that demand for goods decreases not due to any change in price but due to decrease in the income of the consumer.

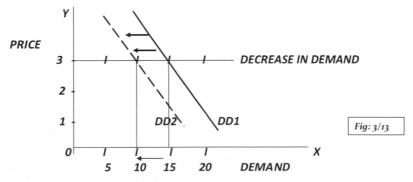

Fig: 3/13

In the above diagram it is clear as the income of the consumer decreases the demand for the commodity decreases and the demand curve shifts from DD1 to DD2 to the left.

- **The exceptions of law of demand:**
- **Or the limitations of law of demand:**
- **Or under what conditions the law of demand is not valid?**

There are some exceptions where the law of demand is not valid i.e. the demand curve slopes upwards from left to right as shown in the diagram—

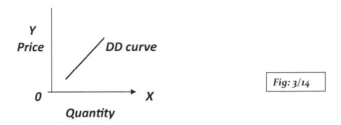

Fig: 3/14

**The Exceptional cases are as follows:**

## (1) CONSPICUOUS CONSUMPTION GOODS OR VEBLEN GOODS:

There are some luxury goods like jewellery, gems, costly carpets, diamond etc. are more demanded by the rich and wealthy persons of the society because the prices of these goods are high. This is against the law of demand. By the name of economist Veblen these goods are called Veblen goods.

## (2) IGNORANCE OF CONSUMER:

Sometimes due to ignorance of consumers, the consumers demand more for those goods if the prices are high and they demand less if the price is low. At this time the consumers are guided by the assumption that the high-priced good is better in quality compared to the lower price goods.

## (3) GIFFEN GOODS:

Giffen goods are those inferior goods whose demand falls even when their price falls. So the law of demand does not hold good for them. Giffen goods are inferior goods with negative income elasticity of demand and positive price elasticity of demand. It is named after Sir Robert Giffen.

## (4) EMERGENCIES:

The law of demand does not hold well during the time of emergencies like war, famine, depression, etc., because in such a time the consumers behave not in normal way as they use to. In such situations consumers due to fear of shortage, demand for necessary goods more at higher price.

## (5) SHARE MARKET:

The law of demand does not hold good for the share market, particularly for those shares whose price falls continuously. This is because it has been seen if the price of any share falls continuously then its demand instead of increase it decreases to the investors.

## (6) EXPECTATION OF PRICE RISE IN FUTURE:

If the consumers expect that the price will rise in future then they demand more at present even if the price at present is high.

## ▪ Distinction between Normal goods and Inferior goods:

| Basis | NORMAL GOODS | INFERIOR GOODS |
|---|---|---|
| 1. Price Effect: | 1. Price effect is negative. It means there is inverse relation between price of goods and demand for goods. | 1. Normally price effect is negative but for the Giffen goods it is positive. |
| 2. Income Effect: | 2. Income effect is positive. It means with the increase in income, the demand for normal goods increases and with the decrease in income, the demand decreases. | 2. Income effect is negative. It means with the increase in income the demand for inferior goods decreases and with the decrease in income the demand increases. |

| 3. Example: | 3. For example: Car, carpet, rice etc. | 3. For example: candle, matchbox, coarse rice etc. |
|---|---|---|

## ▪ The effect of changes in income on the demand for goods:

This question can be answered under the following heads.

### (i)  NORMAL GOODS:

Normal goods are those goods whose demand increases with the increase in the income of the consumer and demand decreases with the decrease in the income of the consumer. So there is positive relation between price of goods and demand for normal goods.

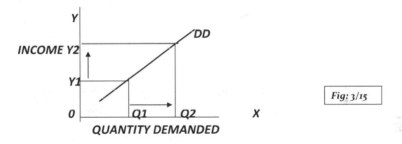

Fig; 3/15

### (ii) INFERIOR GOODS:

Inferior goods are those goods whose income effect is negative. This means with the increase in the income of the consumer the demand for inferior goods decreases and with the decrease in the income of the consumer the demand for inferior goods increases. Here as the income increases from OY1 to OY2 the demand decreases from oq1 to oq2.

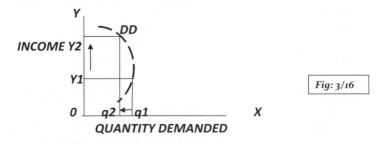

Fig: 3/16

## (iii) NECESSARIES OF LIFE GOODS:

In case of such goods like salt, match box etc. the demand remains constant irrespective of changes in the income of the consumer except a slight increase at initial stage. This is shown in the following diagram.

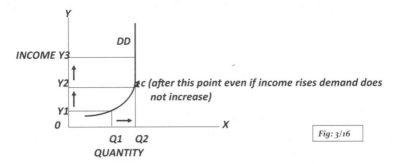

Fig: 3/16

In the above diagram at the initial stage up to OQ2 the demand increases with the increase in income, after that the demand remains constant even the income increases.

- **Q. If there are 50 identical consumers in the market with demand function Q = 30-2P then find out the market demand for the commodity at price of Rs.10 per unit.**

Ans. The market demand = 50 Q = 50 (30-2P)
  = 1500-100P.
  = 1500-100 (10)
  = 1500-1000
  = 500 units.

- **Q. How is the price of related goods affect the demand for a commodity?**

Ans. Related goods are classified into two categories—substitute goods and complementary goods.

(a) **SUBSTITUTE GOODS**—Substitute goods are those goods which can be used for each other e.g. tea and coffee, Pepsi and coke etc.

If the price of Pepsi rises then the demand for its substitute goods i.e. Coke increases. On the other hand if the price of Pepsi falls then demand for its substitute good i.e. coke decreases.

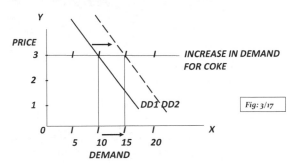

In the above diagram demand curve for coke shifts to the right i.e. demand increases due to increase in the price of Pepsi.

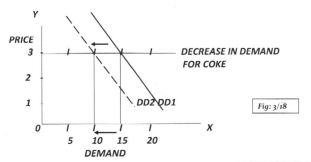

In the above diagram demand curve for coke shifts to the left (i.e. demand decreases) due to decrease in the price of Pepsi.

**(b) COMPLEMENTARY GOODS**—Complementary goods are those goods which jointly satisfy the want for one commodity like car and petrol jointly satisfy the demand for car. In this case if the price of car rises then its demand decreases and the demand for petrol also decrease. On the other hand if the price of car falls then its demand increases and the demand for petrol also increase.

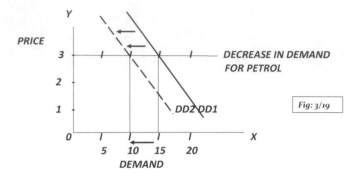

Fig: 3/19

In the above diagram demand curve for Petrol shifts to the left (i.e. demand decreases) due to rise in the price of complementary good car.

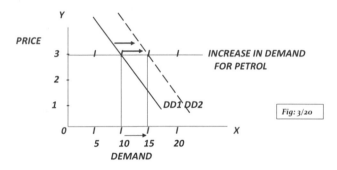

Fig: 3/20

The above diagram shows that the demand curve for Petrol shifts to the right (i.e. demand increases) because of fall in the price of its complementary good i.e. car.

## ▪ Cross price effect.

Cross Price Effect refers to change in the demand for a commodity due to the change in the price of its related goods i.e. substitutes goods or complementary goods.

## ▪ DIAGRAMATIC PRESENTATION OF NORMAL GOODS AND INFERIOR GOODS:

This answer can be explained by using the concept of indifference curve and equilibrium in the following way:

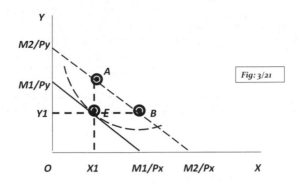

Fig: 3/21

In the above diagram point E is the equilibrium point where the budget line is the tangent to the indifference curve.

(i)   If new equilibrium point after increasing the income of consumer lies between A and B points then it is a normal good.

(ii)  If new equilibrium point is to the left of point A, then good-X is an inferior good.

(iii) If new equilibrium point is to the right of point B, then good-Y is an inferior good.

87

# IMPORTANT QUESTIONS:

1. What is demand?
2. What is meant by law of demand?
3. Define demand schedule?
4. What is meant by normal goods?
5. Define inferior goods.
6. What is meant by market demand?
7. What is meant by extension of demand?
8. Define contraction demand.
9. What is meant by increase in demand?
10. What is meant by decrease in demand?

1. Explain the factors which affect individual demand for a commodity.

   Or

   State the determinants of individual demand for a commodity.

2. Explain the main determinants of market demand for a commodity.

   Or

   Explain the factors which affect market demand for a commodity.

3. How does the change in income of a consumer affect the demand for a commodity?

4. Explain the effect of change in the price of other related goods on the demand for the original good.

5. Why does the demand curve slope downwards from left to right?

   Or

   Why does a consumer consume less at high price of a commodity?

6. Distinguish between extension of demand and contraction demand.

7. Explain the movement along the demand curve or

   Explain the changes in quantity demanded.

8. Distinguish between increase in demand and decrease in demand.

9. Explain the shift of demand curve or

   Explain the change in demand.

10. Distinguish between movement along the demand curve and the shift of the demand curve.

11. Distinguish between changes in quantity demanded and changes in demand (increase).

    Or

    Distinguish between extension of demand and increase in demand.

12. Distinguish between changes in quantity demanded and changes in demand (decrease).

Or

Distinguish between contraction of demand and decrease in demand.

13. Why does demand curve shift to right wards?

Or

Why does demand for a commodity increase at given price?

14. Why does demand curve shift to left wards?

Or

Why does demand for a commodity decrease at given price?

15. Explain the cross price effect of demand.

## 6 MARK QUESTIONS:

1. How can you draw market demand curve from market demand schedule?
2. Explain the market demand function.
3. Explain with the help of a diagram the changes in demand when the income of the consumer changes.
4. Explain with the help of a diagram the changes in demand when the price of related goods changes.
5. Explain the determinants of market demand.
6. What are the limitations of law of demand?
7. Why does demand curve slope downwards from left to right?
8. Distinguish between movement along the demand curve and the shift of the demand curve.

# Chapter - 4

## Price Elasticity Of Demand:

## ▪ Concept of Elasticity of Demand:

Elasticity of Demand is a measure of the degree of responsiveness of quantity demanded of a good to change in its three quantifiable determinants like (1) Price of commodity, (2) Income of the consumer and (3) Price of related commodities.

Accordingly there are three types of Elasticity of Demand:

(1) PRICE ELASTICITY OF DEMAND—
(2) INCOME ELASTICITY OF DEMAND—
(3) CROSS ELASTICITY OF DEMAND—

This concept of elasticity of demand was developed by economists like J.S.MILL and COURNOT but its credit for scientific presentation goes to Dr. MARSHALL.

## ▪ Price elasticity of demand:

According to Professor Boulding, "Price elasticity of demand measures the responsiveness of the quantity demanded to the change in price."

It is measured by the following formula

Elasticity of Demand = (-) $\dfrac{\text{\% change in quantity demanded}}{\text{\% change in Price}}$

$$= (-)\ \frac{\left(\frac{\Delta Q}{Q}\right) \cdot 100}{\left(\frac{\Delta P}{P}\right) \cdot 100} = (-) \left(\frac{\Delta Q}{Q}\right) / \left(\frac{\Delta P}{P}\right)$$

## ▪ Different degrees or types of Price Elasticity of Demand:

In Economics Price Elasticity of Demand is classified into five degrees which are as follows:

### (1) PERFECTLY ELASTIC DEMAND (Ed = ∞):

When the demand for a commodity changes to any extent at the given price then it is called Perfectly Elastic Demand.

In other words, a slight fall in price causes an infinite increase in demand and a slight rise in price will reduce demand to zero. It exists under perfect competition market which is an imaginary situation. Perfectly Elastic demand curve is a horizontal line parallel to X-axis as shown in the following diagram.

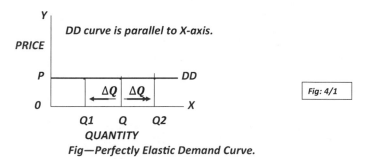

Fig: 4/1

Fig—Perfectly Elastic Demand Curve.

### (2) PERFECTLY INELASTIC DEMAND (Ed = 0):

When the demand for a commodity does not change due to any change in its price then it is called perfectly inelastic demand.

The elasticity of demand in this case is zero. The demand curve will be parallel to Y-axis as shown in the following diagram.

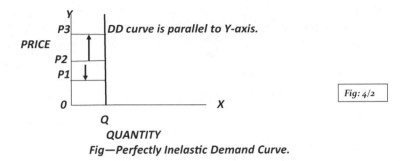

Fig: 4/2

Fig—Perfectly Inelastic Demand Curve.

From the above diagram it is clear that even if the price changes the demand does not change. It exists in case of essential life saving drugs.

## (3) UNITARY ELASTIC DEMAND (Ed = 1):

When percentage change in demand is equal to the percentage change in price of the commodity then the demand is called unitary elastic demand.

The shape of such demand curve is rectangular hyperbola. The areas of all rectangles under this curve are always equal. It exists in case of normal goods. This curve is shown in the following diagram.

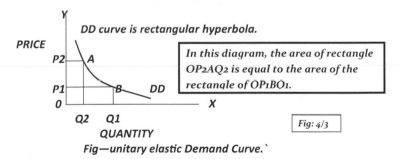

In this diagram, the area of rectangle $OP_2AQ_2$ is equal to the area of the rectangle of $OP_1BQ_1$.

Fig: 4/3

Fig—unitary elastic Demand Curve.`

## (4) MORE ELASTIC DEMAND OR GREATER THAN UNITARY ELASTIC DEMAND (Ed > 1):

When percentage change in demand is more than percentage change in price of goods then it is called more elastic demand or greater than unitary elastic demand.

It exists in case of luxuries goods. This is shown in the following diagram.

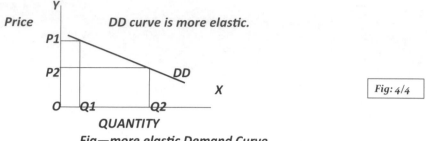

Fig—more elastic Demand Curve.

Fig: 4/4

## (5) LESS ELASTIC OR INELASTIC OR LESS THAN UNITARY ELASTIC DEMAND (Ed < 1):

When percentage change in demand is less than percentage change in price of goods then it is called less elastic demand or less than unitary elastic demand.

It exists in case of necessities like food, fuel etc. This is shown in the following diagram.

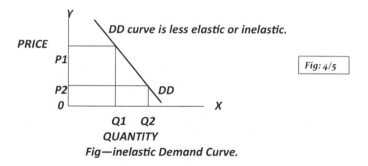

Fig—inelastic Demand Curve.

Fig: 4/5

## ▪ The factors which affect the price elasticity of demand: Or the determinants of price elasticity of demand:

The main determinants of price elasticity of demand for a commodity are as follows:

### (1) HABITS OF CONSUMER:

If the people are accustomed to a particular habit of consuming a particular commodity then they do not bother for price change of that commodity over a particular time period. Therefore the demand for such commodities like cigarette, liquor etc. will be inelastic.

## (2) AVAILABILITY OF SUBSTITUTES:

When a commodity has a large number of substitutes then its demand will be more elastic. For example close up tooth paste has many substitutes like Colgate tooth paste, pepsodent tooth paste, Neem tooth paste etc. Now if the price of Close up tooth paste rises then in the market it has many cheaper substitutes so the demand for tooth paste will be more elastic. On the other hand if a product has fewer substitutes then its demand is less elastic or inelastic.

## (3) TIME PERIOD:

Longer the time period, more elastic is the demand for the commodity. On the other hand, shorter the time period, demand is less elastic or inelastic. This is because in long run the consumer is able to adjust his consumption pattern and he can increase or decrease his demand accordingly.

## (4) PRICE LEVEL:

In case of very high priced goods like diamond, jewellery etc. the demand is less elastic or inelastic. The demand is also inelastic in case of very low price goods like matchbox, salt etc.

On the other hand the demand is more elastic for those goods whose price is in the middle range i.e. neither too expensive nor too cheap.

## (5) INCOME LEVEL:

Generally the demand for those people whose income is either very high or very low is less elastic or inelastic. It is so because rise or fall in the prices has very little effect on their demand. On the other hand the demand for the middle income group people is more elastic because change in price has more effect on their demand.

## (6) NATURE OF GOODS:

In economics all goods are classified into three categories.
They are (a) Necessaries, (b) Comforts and (c) Luxuries.

(a) **NECESSARIES:** Demand for necessaries like salt, electricity, school uniform, food grains, life saving drugs etc. It is less elastic because a consumer has to buy a particular quantity of such commodities, irrespective of their prices.

(b) **COMFORTS:** Demand for comforts like milk, fans, cooler, transistors, cycles etc. changes in almost the same proportion as their price changes. So the demand for such goods is unitary elastic.

(c) **LUXURIES:** Demand for luxuries like car, television, air-conditioner, costly cosmetics, costly garments etc. is more elastic or elastic. It is so because a little change in price has a large effect on the demand for these goods.

### (7) POPORTION OF INCOME SPENT:

When the money spent on a commodity by a consumer is very small proportion of his income, then the demand for such commodities like newspaper, salt etc is less elastic or inelastic. On the other hand if the money spent on a commodity is large proportion of his income then its demand is more elastic.

### (8) DIFFERENT USES OF A COMMODITY:

When a commodity is used for different purposes then its demand will be more elastic. If the price of such commodities falls then it can be used for various purposes like electricity, coal etc. On the other hand goods which can be used for fewer purposes have less elastic demand.

### (9) POSTPONMENT OF USE:

Goods whose demand can be postponed for future have more elastic demand like construction of house. On the other hand goods whose demand cannot be postponed for future, have less elastic demand or inelastic demand like demand for drinking water or demand for food.

## ▪ Different methods to measure Price Elasticity of demand:

There are five methods to measure price elasticity of demand which are as follows—

(i)   TOTAL EXPENDITURE METHOD.

(ii)  PROPORTIONATE OR PERCENTAGE OR FLUX METHOD.

(iii) POINT METHOD OR GEOMETRICAL METHOD.

(iv)  ARC ELASTICITY METHOD.

(v)   REVENUE METHOD.

According to the syllabus of class-XII the first three methods are discussed in question-answer form.

Explain the total expenditure method to measure price elasticity of demand.

Or

How can you measure price elasticity of demand when the price falls and expenditure changes? Or show the effect of an increase in price on total expenditure depends on the value of price elasticity of demand.

The expenditure method was developed by Dr. Marshall. According to this method we can measure whether elasticity of demand is more elastic or less elastic or unitary elastic. This method can be explained by the following table.

| Price (Rs.) | Demand (units) | Total Expenditure | Effect on Total Expenditure | Elasticity of Demand |
|---|---|---|---|---|
| 1 | 6 | 6 | Price rises, | Ed<1 |
| 2 | 5 | 10 | T.E. rises. | |
| 3 | 4 | 12 | Price rises, | Ed = 1 |
| 4 | 3 | 12 | T.E. constant | |
| 5 | 2 | 10 | Price rises, | Ed>1 |
| 6 | 1 | 6 | T.E. falls. | |

Table. 4/1

From the above table we summarize the following facts.

(I)   when price rises and total expenditure increases, or price falls and total expenditure also falls i.e. there is positive relation between price of commodity and total expenditure, then demand is less elastic (Ed<1).

(II) When price rises or falls but total expenditure does not change then demand is unitary elastic (Ed = 1).

(III) When price rises and total expenditure decreases, or price falls and total expenditure increases i.e. there is inverse relation between the price of commodity and total expenditure, then the demand is more elastic (Ed>1).

Total Expenditure can also be explained by the following diagram.

**(Diagram without scale)**

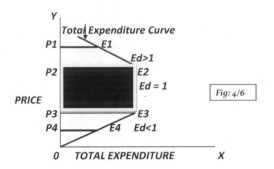

Fig: 4/6

**(Diagram with scale)**

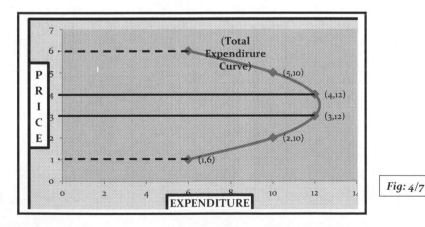

Fig: 4/7

From the above diagram the following facts are very clear.

(a) When price rises from OP4 (Re 1) to OP3 (Rs. 3), total expenditure increases from P4E4 (Rs. 6) to P3E3 (Rs. 12), or when price falls from

OP3 (Rs. 3) to OP4 (Re. 1) then total expenditure falls from P3E3 (Rs. 12) to P4E4 (Rs. 6). So there is positive relation between price and total expenditure and the demand is less elastic (Ed < 1).

(b)  When price rises from OP3 (Rs. 3) to OP2 (Rs. 4) or price falls from OP2 (Rs. 4) to Op3 (Rs. 3) then total expenditure remains unchanged i.e. P2E2 = P3E3=Rs. 12. So the demand is unitary elastic (Ed = 1).

(c)  When price rises from OP2 (Rs. 4) to OP1 (Rs. 6) and expenditure falls from P2E2 (Rs. 12) to P1E1 (Rs. 6), or when price falls from OP1 (Rs. 6) to OP2 (Rs. 4) and expenditure rises from P1E1 (Rs. 6) to P2E2 (Rs. 12). So there is inverse relation between price and total expenditure and the demand is more elastic (Ed > 1).

Explain the Point method or Geometric method to measure price elasticity of demand.

Or

How can you measure price elasticity of demand at different points on a linear demand curve that touches both the axes?

Point elasticity of demand refers to measure price elasticity of demand at different points on a demand curve.

According to this method, the elasticity of demand at any point is measured by the following formula:

$$\text{Elasticity of demand} = \frac{\text{Lower segment of demand curve}}{\text{Upper segment of demand curve}}$$

This method can be explained by the following diagram.

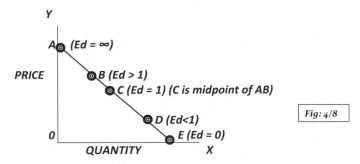

Fig: 4/8

In the above diagram AE is a straight line demand curve that touches both the axes at points A and E. So, A B, C, D, E are different points on this demand curve. Point C is the midpoint of this demand curve. Now elasticity of demand at different points can be calculated by the following way:

(1) At point A, Ed = AE/0 = ∞,
(2) At point B, Ed = BE/BA > 1, (since BE>BA)
(3) At point C, Ed = CE/CA = CE/CE = 1, (since C is midpoint of AE)
(4) At point D, Ed = DE/DA < 1, (since DE<DA)
(5) At point E, Ed = 0/EA = 0.

## ▪ Explain the Flux method or proportionate method or percentage method.

This method is associated with author Flux. According to this method, elasticity of demand is measured by the ratio of percentage change in quantity demanded to a percentage change in price.

$$\text{Elasticity of demand} = \frac{\text{Percentage change in quantity demanded}}{\text{Percentage change in Price}}$$

Let initial price is P and final price is P1. Then change in price = P1-P = $\Delta P$
And % change in Price = (P1-P)/P x 100 = $\left(\frac{\Delta P}{P}\right) \cdot 100$
Similarly, if the initial quantity is Q and final quantity is Q1, then
% change in Quantity = (Q1-Q)/Q x 100 = $\left(\frac{\Delta Q}{Q}\right) \cdot 100$

Therefore,

$$Ed = (-) \frac{\% \text{ change in quantity demanded}}{\% \text{ change in price}}$$

$$= (-) \frac{\left(\frac{\Delta Q}{Q}\right) \cdot 100}{\left(\frac{\Delta P}{P}\right) \cdot 100}$$

$$= (-) \frac{\left(\frac{\Delta Q}{Q}\right)}{\left(\frac{\Delta P}{P}\right)} = (-) \frac{\Delta Q}{\Delta P} \cdot (P/Q)$$

## ▪ If a demand curve is non-linear then how do we measure price elasticity of demand?

In this case we need to draw a tangent to the non-linear demand curve and then we follow the 'Geometric method' to measure price elasticity of demand. This is shown by the following figure.

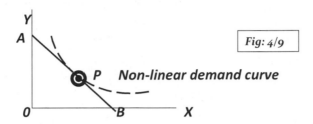

Fig: 4/9

Non-linear demand curve

In the above diagram at point P, price elasticity of demand of the non-linear curve is = PB/PA < 1 (because PB is less than PA).

## ▪ The Importance of price elasticity of demand:

Price elasticity of demand has the following importance:

### (1) PRICE DETERMINATION UNDER MONOPOLY MARKET—

Under monopoly market a monopolist fixes lower price if the price elasticity of demand for the product is elastic. On the other hand if demand is inelastic he fixes high price per unit.

### (2) HELPFUL TO FINANCE MINISTER—

In case of imposition of taxes, a finance minister imposes less tax on those goods which have elastic demand. On the other hand goods having inelastic demand are taxed at a higher rate.

### (3) DISTRIBUTION OF TAX BURDEN—

Elasticity of demand also helps to distribute the tax burden between the producers and consumers. If the demand for goods is inelastic, the burden of indirect tax will be more on consumers. On the other hand, if the demand is elastic the burden of indirect tax will comparatively be more on the producers.

### (4) PRICE DISCRIMINATION—

A monopolist practices price discrimination when price elasticity of demand for different goods for different uses for different consumers for different markets is different. In case of inelastic demand he charges higher price for the product and on the other hand if the demand is elastic then he charges lower price for the product.

### (5) POLICY OF NATIONALISATION—

Government nationalizes those industries and enterprises, the demand for whose products is inelastic e.g. railways, electricity, water supply etc. If these services are allowed to run by the private enterprises then they can exploit the consumers by charging higher prices.

### If two demand curves intersect each other then state which one will be more elastic and why?

The answer can be explained by the following diagram.

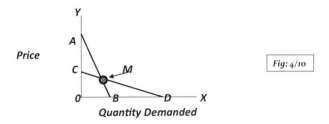

Fig: 4/10

*Quantity Demanded*

In the above diagram the demand curve CD is more elastic compared to the demand curve AB, because CD is more flat than the demand curve AB.

This can be proved by the following way—
In case of AB demand curve at point M, Ed = MB/MA,
I.e. Ed < 1. (Since MB <MA)
In case of CD demand curve at point M, Ed = MD/MC,
I.e. Ed > 1. (Since MD > MC).

**How can you explain that two demand curves have different slopes but with same elasticity of demand?**

This question can be answered by the following diagram:

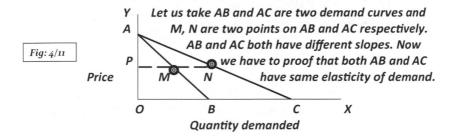

*Fig: 4/11*

*Let us take AB and AC are two demand curves and M, N are two points on AB and AC respectively. AB and AC both have different slopes. Now we have to proof that both AB and AC have same elasticity of demand.*

Proof: At point M, Ed = MB/MA = OP/PA;

At point N, Ed = NC/NA = OP/PA;

So, both AB and AC have same elasticity of demand.

## ▪ NUMERICAL OF PRICE ELASTICITY OF DEMAND—

**1. Price of a commodity falls from Rs.5 to Rs. 3. As a result its demand rises from 80 units to 100 units. Calculate price elasticity of demand.**

| PRICE (Rs.) | QUANTITY DEMANDED |
|---|---|
| 5 | 80 |
| 3 | 100 |
| $\Delta P = -2$ | $\Delta Q = 20$ |

$Ed = (-) (\Delta Q/Q)/(\Delta P/P)$

$\quad = (-) (20/80)/ (-2/5)$

$\quad = (20/80)/ (2/5)$

$\quad = (20. 5/80. 2)$

$\quad = 100/160$

$\quad = 0.625$; Since Ed is 0.625 so it is less elastic demand.

**2. Price of a commodity falls from Rs.5 to Rs. 3. As a result its demand rises from 80 units to 100 units. Calculate price elasticity of demand by total outlay method or expenditure method.**

| PRICE (Rs.) | QUANTITY | TOTAL EXPENDITURE (Rs.) |
|---|---|---|
| 5 | 80 | 5.80 = 400 |
| 3 | 100 | 3.100 = 300 |

From the above table it is clear as the price falls total expenditure also falls so there is positive relation between price and expenditure. Therefore the demand is inelastic i.e. Ed < 1.

**3. A consumer buys 100 units of a commodity at Rs.4 per unit. When the price falls he buys 150 units. If price elasticity of demand is (-) 1, then find out the new price.**

Ans. Given Ed = (-) 1,

| PRICE (Rs.) | QUANTITY |
|---|---|
| 4 | 100 |
| X | 150 |
| $\Delta P = X - 4$ | $\Delta Q = 50$ |

$$Ed = (-) (\Delta Q/Q)/(\Delta P/P)$$
Or,     $1 = (-) 50/100 \div (X-4)/4$
Or,     $1 = (-) 50 \times 4 /100(X-4)$
Or,     $1 = (-) 2/(X-4)$
Or,    $X-4 = -2$
Or,     $X = 2$; So the new price is Re.2.

**Q. 4. Price of a commodity falls from R. 20 per unit to Rs. 15 per unit. As a result the consumer buys from 15 units to 20 units. Calculate the price elasticity of demand by total expenditure method.**

Ans.

| PRICE (Rs.) | QUANTITY | TOTAL EXPENDITURE (Rs.) |
|---|---|---|
| 20 | 15 | 20x15 = 300 |
| 15 | 20 | 15x20 = 300 |

The above table shows due to change in price the total expenditure remains unchanged. Therefore price elasticity of demand is unitary i.e. Ed = 1.

**5. As a result of 20% fall in price of a good, its demand rises from 80 units to 120 units. Calculate price elasticity of demand.**

Ans. % change in demand = $\dfrac{(120-80)}{80} \times 100$

$$= (40/80) \times 100$$

$$= 50\%$$

Price Elasticity of demand = $\dfrac{\% \text{ change in demand}}{\% \text{ change in price}}$

$$= 50\,\%/20\%$$
$$= 50/20$$
$$= 2.5$$

Therefore the demand is greater than unitary (Ed >1).

**6. A 10% fall in price of a good leads to 10% rise in its demand. A consumer buys 60 units of the good at a price of Rs.5 per unit. How many units will he buy if the price falls by 20%?**

Ans. From the above question we have

$$Ed = \frac{\text{\% change in quantity demanded}}{\text{\% change in the price}}$$

$$= 10\%/10\% = 1 \text{ (Unitary elastic demand)}$$

Now we also have,

| PRICE (Rs.) | DEMAND |
|:---:|:---:|
| 5 | 60 |
| 4 | X |
| -1 | X-60 |

20% fall in price of Rs.5 means Rs.1
So the new price is Rs.5-Re.1 = Rs.4
Let the final quantity is X
Then by using the formula we get the following-

$$Ed = (-) ( \Delta Q/Q) \div (\Delta P/P)$$
$$1 = (-) (X-60)/60 \div (-1)/5$$
$$\text{Or, } 1 = (X-60)/60 \times 5/1$$
$$\text{Or, } 12 = X-60$$
$$\text{Or, } X = 12 + 60$$
$$\text{Or, } X = 72$$

So the required quantity is 72.

**7. Suppose there are two consumers in the market for a good and their demand functions are as follows:**

d1 (p) = 20-2p for any price less than or equal to 10 and d1 (p) = 0 at any price more than 10.

d1 (p) = 30-2p for any price less than or equal to 15 and d2(p) = 0 at any price more than 15.

Find out the market demand function.

Ans. Market demand can be calculated by adding the two demand functions i.e. d1 = 20-2p

And d2 = 30-2p

-----------------------------------------

Market Demand (d1 + d2) = 50-4P

## 8. If the demand function is Qx = 720/Px then find out the following:

(a) Total expenditure on good-x when Px rises from Re. 1 to Rs. 6.

(b) What is the value of price elasticity of demand?

(c) What is the shape of the demand curve?

Ans. (a)

| Px (Rs.) | Qx = 720/Px | T.E. = Px.Qx |
|----------|-------------|--------------|
| 1 | 720/1 = 720 | 720 |
| 2 | 720/2 = 360 | 720 |
| 3 | 720/3 = 240 | 720 |
| 4 | 720/4 = 180 | 720 |
| 5 | 720/5 = 144 | 720 |
| 6 | 720/6 = 120 | 720 |

(b) From the above table it is clear that the total expenditure remains constant even if the price rises from Re.1 to Re.6. So the price elasticity of demand will be equal to one. i.e. Ed = 1.

(c) The demand curve will be rectangular hyperbola as shown by the following diagram—

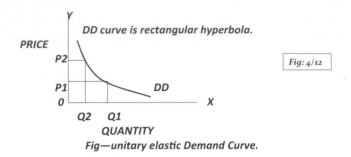

Fig: 4/12

Fig—unitary elastic Demand Curve.

## Q.9. Due to 10% increase in price the demand for a good falls by 10 units. If Ed = 2, then find out the initial Q?

Let the initial demand was Y and the price was x. Then we have the following:

| PRICE (Rs.) | DEMAND |
|---|---|
| X | Y |
| 11X/10 | Y-10 |
| X/10 | -10 |

Now, Ed = (-) $\frac{-10}{Y} \div \frac{X/10}{X}$

$2 = 10/Y \times 10/1$

OR, $2Y = 100$

OR, $Y = 50$

## Q.10. Ed for a good is (-1). At price Rs. 10 a consumer was buying 60 units. If price rises by Rs. 5 then how much will the consumer buy? Calculate by total expenditure method.

Ans. The problem can be presented by the following way:

| PRICE (Rs.) | DEMAND | EXPENDITURE |
|---|---|---|
| 10 | 60 | 600 |
| 10+5=15 | X | 15X |

If Ed = 1, then total expenditure remains constant.

Therefore, 15X= 600
   Or, X = 600/15
   Or, X = 40

So the required quantity is 40 units.

**Q.11. Calculate price elasticity of demand of the following demand function q = 20 – 4p at p = 4.**

Ans. when p=4, then q = 20 – 4x4 = 4

$$e_p = \frac{\delta q}{\delta p} \cdot \frac{p}{q} = \frac{\delta(20-4p)}{\delta p} \cdot \frac{p}{q} = (-4) \times \frac{4}{4} = -4$$

Since, price elasticity of demand is modulus, so price elasticity of demand = 4 i.e. more elastic demand.

**Q.12. Calculate price elasticity of demand of the following demand function q = 240 – 3p at p = 5.**

Ans. When p=5, then q = 240 – 3x5 = 225

$$e_p = (-)\frac{\delta q}{\delta p} \cdot \frac{p}{q} = (-)\frac{\delta(240-3p)}{\delta p} \cdot \frac{p}{q}$$
$$= (-)(-3) \times \frac{5}{225} = 1/15 = 0.66$$

**3. If a demand function is as DD = 19 – 3p – p2 and supply function is SS = 5p – 1 then find out the equilibrium price and equilibrium quantity of output.**

Ans. At equilibrium, DD = SS

Or, 19 – 3p – p2 = 5p – 1

Or, p2 + 8p – 20 = 0

Or, (p + 10)(p - 2)= 0

Therefore, p = - 10 or 2. But price cannot be negative. So price = 2.

When p =2, then DD = 19 – 6 – 4 = 9

And SS = 5.2 – 1 = 9

So, equilibrium price = Rs.2 and equilibrium quantity of output = 9.

**4. A demand function is given as q = 20 – 5p – p2, calculate the elasticity of demand at price Rs.2.**

Ans.  $Ed = (-) \dfrac{\Delta Q}{\Delta P} \cdot \dfrac{P}{Q}$

$= (-) \dfrac{dq}{dp} \cdot \dfrac{p}{q}$

$= (-) \dfrac{p}{q} \cdot \dfrac{d(20-5p-p2)}{dp}$

$= (-) \dfrac{p}{q} \cdot (- 5 - 2p)$

When p = 2, then Ed  $= (-) \dfrac{p}{20-5p-p2} \cdot (- 5p - 2p)$

$= (-) \dfrac{2}{20-10-4} \cdot (- 5 - 4)$

$= (-) \dfrac{2}{6} \cdot (-9)$

$= 3$

**5. If p = 1 – q then calculate TR, MR, AR and Ed**

Or, TR = p.q = q – q2

AR = TR/q = 1 – q

$MR = \dfrac{d(TR)}{dq} = 1 - 2q.$

$Ed = \dfrac{dq}{dp} \cdot \dfrac{P}{q} = 1. (1 - q)/q$

**6. The price elasticity of demand for a commodity-X is ½ of price elasticity of demand for commodity-Y. A consumer demands 120 units of commodity-X at price Rs. 20 per unit. If the price increases by Rs. 10, he buys 90 units of commodity-X. If the price of commodity-Y changes by 15% then what will be the impact on the consumption of commodity-Y by the same consumer?**

Ans. $E_X = \frac{1}{2} . E_Y$

| Price (Rs.) | Quantity |
|---|---|
| 20 | 120 |
| 20+10=30 | 90 |
| ΔP + 10 | ΔQ + -30 |

$E_X = ( ) \frac{\Delta Q/Q}{\Delta P/P} = (-)\frac{-30/120}{10/20} = \frac{1/4}{1/2} = 0.5$

According to the question, $E_Y = E_X.2 = 0.5 \times 2 = 1$

Let the consumption of commodity will be changed by x.

By the formula, $E_Y = \frac{\% \text{ change in quantity demanded}}{\% \text{ change in price}} = \frac{x}{15\%}$

$$\text{Or, } 1 = \frac{x}{15\%}$$
$$\text{Or, } x = 15\%$$

Therefore the consumption of the consumer will also change in equal proportion i.e. by 15%.

**7. If the demand function is q = 20 – 5p – p2 then find out the elasticity of demand at price Rs. 2 per unit.**

Solution: q = 20 – 5p – p2

$$\frac{dq}{dp} = -5 - 2p$$

So,| Ed $= \frac{dq}{dp} . \frac{p}{q}$

$= (-5 - 2p).\frac{2}{20-10-4}$

$= \frac{-18}{6} = -3$

## 8. If Ed = 2.25 and MR = 10 then find out AR or Price.

Solution: We know that

MR = AR (1 – 1/e)
10 = AR (1 – 1/2.25)
10 = AR. (1.25/2.25)
Or, AR = $\frac{2.25 \times 10}{1.25}$ = 18

## 9. If the utility function is U = x2y2 and budget equation is 4x+8y=96 Then find out the number of units of commodities x and y at which the consumer gets maximum satisfaction.

Solution: U = x2y2
Therefore, MUx = 2xy2 and MUy = 2x2y
4x + 8y = 96

So, Px = 4 and Py = 8

Now according to consumer's equilibrium for two commodities,

We have $\frac{MUx}{Px} = \frac{MUy}{Py}$

Or, $\frac{2xy2}{4} = \frac{2x2y}{8}$

Or, x = 2y

Now putting the above value of x in 4x + 8y = 96
We get 4.2y + 8y = 96
Or, y = 96/16 = 6
So, x = 2y = 2.6 = 12

So, the required number units of commodities are x = 12 and y = 6 at which the consumer gets maximum satisfaction.

___*__*__*__*__*__*__*__*__*__*__*__*___

# IMPORTANT QUESTIONS:

## 1 MARK QUESTIONS:

1. What is meant by price elasticity of demand?
2. When is demand inelastic?
3. Define unity elastic demand.
4. If due to 10 % changes in price the demand for a good changes by 10% then what will be price elasticity of demand?
5. What is meant by imperfectly elastic demand?

## 3 or 4 MARK QUESTIONS:

1. What is price elasticity of demand? State three factors those can affect the price elasticity of demand.
2. Distinguish between elastic demand and inelastic demand.
3. Distinguish between perfectly elastic demand and imperfectly elastic demand.
4. How can you measure price elasticity of demand at different points on a linear demand curve?

Or

   Explain the geometric method to measure price elasticity of demand.
5. Explain the expenditure method to measure price elasticity of demand.
6. How can you measure price elasticity of demand by percentage method?
7. Explain the effect of an increase in price on total expenditure depending on the value of price elasticity of demand.
8. Explain the effect of a decrease in price on total expenditure depending on the value of price elasticity of demand.

9. What will be the price elasticity of demand for the following products and why?
   (a) School uniform (b) Lipstick of Lakme company (c) life saving medicine (d) Salt (e) cell phones (f) luxury car.
10. How does the nature of a commodity affect the price elasticity of demand?
11. Numerical:
12. If two demand curves intersect each other then which one will be more elastic and why?

## 6 MARK QUESTIONS:

1. Explain different types of price elasticity of demand

   Or

   Explain different degrees of price elasticity of demand.
2. What is meant by price elasticity of demand? Explain the factors those can affect the price elasticity of demand.
3. How can you measure the price elasticity of demand at different points on a straight line demand curve touching both the axes?
4. Explain the relationship between change in total outlay on a commodity and price elasticity of demand with the help of a schedule and diagram. Numerical:
5. At price Rs. 10 a consumer was consuming 120 units of a commodity. When price falls by Rs. 2 per unit then he consumes 150 units. Calculate price elasticity of demand. (ans. 1.25)
6. At price Rs. 10 a consumer was consuming 120 units of a commodity. When price falls by Rs. 2 per unit then how much will he consume if price elasticity of demand is 1.25? (150 units)
7. At price Rs. 10 a consumer was consuming certain units of a commodity. When price falls by Rs. 2 per unit then he buys 150 units. If price elasticity of demand is 1.25 then how much was he consuming earlier? (120 units)
8. At a certain price a consumer was consuming 120 units of a commodity. When price falls by Rs. 2 per unit then he consumes 150 units. If price elasticity of demand is 1.25 then find out original price? (Rs. 10)

9. At price Rs. 10 a consumer was consuming 120 units of a commodity. When price falls by Rs. 2 per unit then he consumes 150 units. Calculate price elasticity of demand by expenditure method. (Unitary elastic)
10. Due to 20% change in price of a commodity its demand increases from 120 units to 150 units. Calculate elasticity of demand. (Ep = 1.25)
11. Calculate price elasticity of demand of the following demand function Q = 200 – 5P at price Rs. 10. (ans. 0.33)
12. Calculate price elasticity of demand from the following table when price falls from Rs.25 to Rs.15.

| Price (Rs.) | 35 | 25 | 18 | 15 |
|---|---|---|---|---|
| Quantity (units) | 120 | 100 | 90 | 80 |

__*__*__*__*__*__*__*__*__*__*__*__*__

# Chapter - 5

## Production Function And Returns To A Factor:

## ▪ What is meant by Production?

Production is defined as the transformation of inputs into output.

## ▪ Concept of Production function:

Production function is defined as the functional relationship between physical inputs and physical output of a firm over a particular time period.

Algebraically, it can be expressed by the following way:

$X = f$ (a, b, c, d . . .); Where X is output and a, b, c, d are the productive resources and f is the function.

If labour is denoted by L, capital is by K then the production function can be written as

$$Q = f (L, K)$$

In economics theory there are three types of production function:

1. Production function of one variable; Example: Law of variable proportion or law of diminishing marginal return.
2. Production function with two variables; Example: Iso-quant curve.
3. Production function with all variables; Example: Return to scale.

Production function can be studied in the context of short-run and long-run.

## • Short-run and Long-run production function:

**SHORT-RUN PRODUCTION FUNCTION**: It refers to production in short-run or that time period in which some factor inputs are fixed and other factors are variable. Time is so short that additional supply of fixed factor inputs cannot be adjusted. For example, land, plant, machinery, building, top management etc.

**LONG-RUN PRODUCTION FUNCTION**: It refers to production in long-run or that time period in which all factor inputs are variable or no factor is fixed. Time is so long that additional supply of variable factors can be adjusted.

## • Different concepts of Product or Output:

Product or output is defined as the volume of goods produced by a firm during a given period of time.

It has three aspects like total product, average product and marginal product.

### (1) TOTAL PRODUCT or TOTAL PHYSICAL PRODUCT:

It refers to the total quantity of goods and services produced by a firm with given inputs over a specific time period. It can be increased by increasing the supply of variable factors in short-run and all the factors in the long-run.

Symbolically, $T.P = \sum M.P = A.P \times L$ (where L is labour, the variable factor).

**SHAPE OF TP:** TP curve starts from the origin, first increases at increasing rate, then increases at decreasing rate, reaches a maximum and after that it starts decreasing. This is shown by the following diagram—

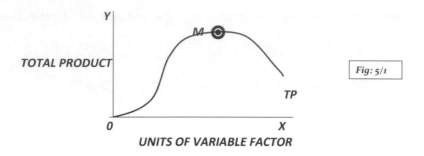

Fig: 5/1

## (2) MARGINAL PRODUCT OR MARGINAL PHYSICAL PRODUCT:

It refers to the change in the Total Product resulting from the employment of one more or less unit of variable factor. It is also defined as the rate at which TP increases due to change in the variable factor.

Symbolically, MP = TPn – TPn-1
   Or, MP = $\Delta TP/\Delta Ql$
Here $\Delta TP$ denotes change in the Total Product.
And $\Delta Ql$ denotes change in the variable factor, labour.

**SHAPE OF MP CURVE:** The MP curve rises first and reaches maximum and then it starts decreasing. When TP is maximum then MP is zero and when TP is decreasing then MP is negative.

MP can be calculated by the following way—

| UNITS OF VARIABLE FACTOR (LABOUR) | TP | MP |
|---|---|---|
| 1 | 2 | 2 |
| 2 | 6 | 4 |
| 3 | 12 | 6 |
| 4 | 16 | 4 |
| 5 | 18 | 2 |
| 6 | 18 | 0 |
| 7 | 16 | -2 |

Table. 5/1

From the above table it is clear that MP curve first rises, reaches maximum and then it starts to decrease and finally it becomes negative.

118

DIAGRAM OF MP CURVE:

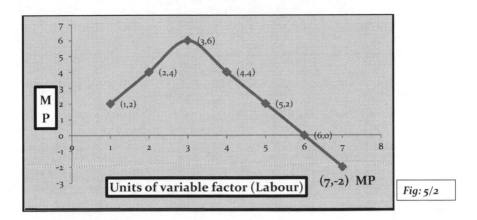

Fig: 5/2

**(3) AVERAGE PRODUCT:** It is defined as the per unit production of a variable factor.

Symbolically, AP = TP/L (TP means total product and L means variable factor, Labour)

**SHAPE OF AVERAGE PRODUCT**: AP curve starts from the origin. At first AP increases at a decreasing rate, reaches at maximum and then it starts falling. AP is inverted-U shaped curve as shown in the following figure.

DIAGRAM OF AP CURVE:

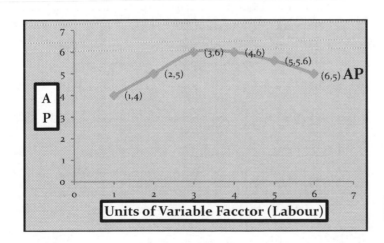

Fig: 5/3

AP can be calculated in the following way—

| Units of labour (L) | TP | AP |
|---|---|---|
| 1 | 4 | 4 |
| 2 | 10 | 5 |
| 3 | 18 | 6 |
| 4 | 24 | 6 |
| 5 | 28 | 5.6 |
| 6 | 30 | 5 |

*Table. 5/2*

From the above table it is clear that AP first increases, then reaches maximum and then it decreases.

## ▪ Different types of production function.

Production function refers to the technical relation between factor inputs and output of a firm over a specific time period.

It is of two types: (1) Variable proportion type production function and (2) Constant proportion type production function.

### (1) VARIABLE PROPORTION TYPE PRODUCTION FUNCTION:

It refers to that production function in which some factors are fixed and other factor inputs are variable. Here the factor input ratio changes at different level of output. This relation is explained by the Law of Variable Proportion. This is shown by the following diagram.

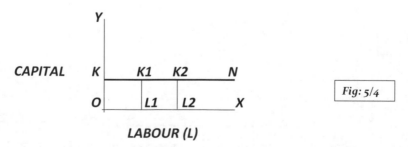

*Fig: 5/4*

In the above diagram the line KN shows that the units of Capital (OK) is fixed and to increase the output the variable factor input Labour is increased from OL1 TO OL2.

Thus, K1L1/OL1 ≠ K2L2/OL2

## (2) CONSTANT PROPORTION TYPE PRODUCTION FUNCTION:

It refers to that production function in which all factor inputs are variable. Here all factor inputs are used in the same proportion whatever may be the output level. In other wards the factor input—output ratio remains constant. This relationship is explained by the returns to scale.

This is shown by the following diagram.

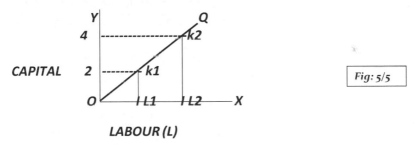

Fig: 5/5

LABOUR (L)

In the above diagram the straight line OQ starts from the origin which shows that the ratio of labour and capital remains constant at different level of output.

Thus, K1L1/OL1 = k2L2/OL2

## ▪ Distinction between variable proportion type production function and constant proportion type production function:

| BASIS | VARIABLE PROPORTION TYPE PRODUCTION | CONSTANT PROPORTION TYPE PRODUCTION |
|---|---|---|
| 1. Time Period | 1. It is studied for the short period only. | 1. It is studied with reference to long period only. |
| 2. factor-Input Ratio | 2. The factor-input ratio changes with the change in the level of output. | 2. The factor-input ratio remains constant at all level of output. |

| 3. Scale of Output | 3. The scale of output does not change. | 3. The scale of output changes. |
| 4. Nature of Factors | 4. Some factors are variable and others remain fixed. | 4. All factors are variable and no factor is fixed. |

## ▪ The relationship between Total Product, Average Product and Marginal Product with the help of a table:

Total Product refers to the total quantity of goods and services produced by a firm with given inputs over a specific time period.

Average Product is defined as the per unit production of a variable factor. Symbolically, AP = TP/L (TP means total product and L means variable factor, Labour).

Marginal Product refers to the change in the Total Product resulting from the employment of one more or less unit of variable factor.

The relationship between TP, AP and MP can be explained with the help of following table—

| UNITS OF VARIABLE FACTOR (LABOUR) | TP | MP | AP |
|---|---|---|---|
| 1 | 2 | 2 | 2 |
| 2 | 6 | 4 | 3 |
| 3 | 12 | 6 | 4 |
| 4 | 16 | 4 | 4 |
| 5 | 18 | 2 | 3.6 |
| 6 | 18 | 0 | 3 |
| 7 | 16 | -2 | 2.2 |

*Table. 5/3*

**Table of TP, AP and MP**

The relationship between TP, AP and MP is as follows:

1) AP curve is the slope of the straight line from the origin to each point on the TP curve. Whereas MP curve is the slope of the TP curve at each point.
2) When MP = AP then AP is maximum in case of 4th unit of labour.
3) When MP = 0 then TP is maximum as shown in the above table in case of 6th unit of labour.
4) TP falls when MP is negative in case of 7th unit of labour.

## ▪ The relationship between TP and MP:

Total Product refers to the total quantity of goods and services produced by a firm with given inputs over a specific time period.

Marginal Product refers to the change in the Total Product resulting from the employment of one more or less unit of variable factor.

The relationship between TP and MP is as follows

DIAGRAM OF TP and MP CURVE:

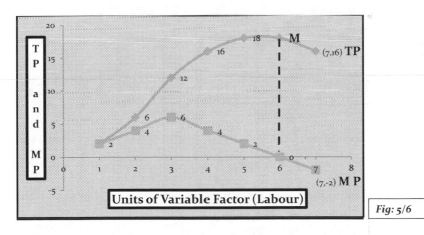

Fig: 5/6

From the above diagram and the table given in answer no.7 we get the following results:

1. As long as TP increases at increasing rate, MP rises.
2. When TP increases at diminishing rate then MP starts diminishing.
3. When MP = 0 then TP is maximum.

123

4.  When MP is negative then TP starts falling.
5.  MP is the slope of TP curve at any point on the TP curve whereas TP is the sum total of MP i.e. TP = $\sum$ MP

## ▪ The relationship between MP and AP:

Average Product is defined as the per unit production of a variable factor. Symbolically, AP = TP/L (TP means total product and L means variable factor, Labour).

Marginal Product refers to the change in the Total Product resulting from the employment of one more or less unit of variable factor.

The relationship between AP and MP can be explained by the following way with the help of above table of TP, AP and MP.

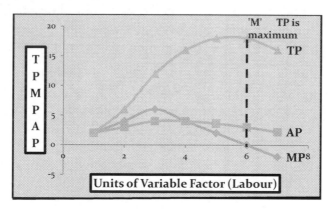

Fig: 5/7

From the above table (given in the answer of Q.NO.7) and diagram we get the following relationship:

1.  Both AP and MP are calculated from TP.

AP = TP/Q and MP = MP = $TP_n - TP_{n-1}$

Or, MP = $\Delta TP/\Delta QL$

2.  As long as MP>AP, AP increases.
3.  When MP = AP then AP is maximum.
4.  When MP<AP, then AP decreases.

## ▪ The term "Law of Return" in Economics:

Law of return refers to changes in the Total product due to change in the factor inputs.

It is of two types: Return to a variable factor and Return to scale.

Return to a variable factor is concerned with short-run production function whereas Return to scale is concerned with long-run production function.

## ▪ The return to a variable factor:

It refers to the change in the Total Product due to change in only one factor of production and all other factor inputs remain fixed. This is concerned with short-run production function.

Total Product in such a situation, will increase at different rates which are as follows:

a) Law of increasing returns.
b) Law of constant returns.
c) Law of diminishing returns.

## ▪ The law of increasing returns or increasing return to a variable factor:

Law of increasing return states that when we employ more and more of variable factor with some fixed factors then total product increases at increasing rate or marginal product increases.

According to Benham, "As the proportion of one factor in a combination of other factors is increased up to a point the marginal productivity of the factor will increase".

This can be explained by the following table and diagram.

| Units of variable factor(labour) | capital | TP | MP |
|---|---|---|---|
| 1 | 2 | 2 | 2 |
| 2 | 2 | 5 | 3 |
| 3 | 2 | 9 | 4 |
| 4 | 2 | 14 | 5 |

Table. 5/4

From the above table it is clear as the units of variable factor increases the Total Product increases at increasing rate and the Marginal Product increases.

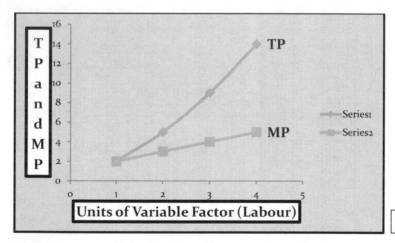

Fig: 5/8

In the above diagram it is clear that TP increases at increasing rate and the MP increases i.e. 2,3,4,5 in this way.

• **REASONS FOR THE APPLICATION OF THIS LAW:**

    **I.** **Better coordination of factors**—As more and more units of variable factors are used with the fixed factors the coordination between fixed and variable factors becomes better and Total Product increases at increasing rate and MP increases.

    **II.** **Specialization**—As more and more of variable factors are used with the fixed factors the efficiency of variable factors increases TP and the MP increases. For example due to process based division of labour the efficiency of variable factor i.e. labours increases and MP increases.

**III. Indivisibility of factors**—initially the fixed factors are not fully utilized. Due to indivisibility of fixed factors when we use more units of the variable factors then it will raise the productivity of the variable factor.

However, this situation of increasing return is not sustainable in an economy because of the following reasons:

a) In short-run some factors remain fixed which cannot be increased in proportion with variable factors.
b) Factors of production are not perfectly substitutable to each other.

## ▪ The law of diminishing returns:

The law of diminishing return states that as the quantity of a variable factor of production is increased along with fixed factors then the marginal product of the additional variable factor will go on diminishing.

According to Professor Benham, "As the proportion of one factor in a combination of other factors is increased, after a point the marginal and average product of that factor will diminish".

### ASSUMPTIONS:

This law is based on the following assumptions—

(1) It is assumed that the production takes place in the short-run.
(2) There is no change in the technique of production.
(3) All units of variable factor are homogeneous.
(4) There is one variable factor and the other factors are fixed.

Now this law can be explained by the following table and diagram:

In this table labour is assumed the variable factor and land is assumed as the fixed factor.

| Units of land (hectare) | Units of labour | TP | MP |
|---|---|---|---|
| 4 | 1 | 5 | 5 |
| 4 | 2 | 8 | 3 |
| 4 | 3 | 10 | 2 |
| 4 | 4 | 11 | 1 |

*Table. 5/5*

From the above table it is clear that as more and more of variable factor is employed TP increases but at diminishing rate and MP diminishes. This law is also called as the law of increasing cost.

The law of diminishing return can also be explained by the following diagram—

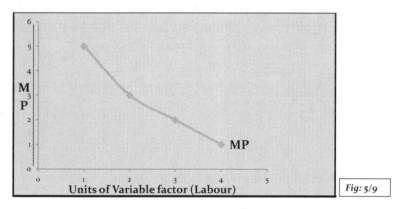

*Fig: 5/9*

In the above diagram it is clear that as more and more of variable factor is used with fixed factor (land) the Marginal Product of variable factor i.e., labour decreases.

• **REASONS FOR OPERATION OF LAW OF DIMINISHING RETURN-**

1. **Fixed factors of production**—It is an important cause for the operation of this law. When the fixed factor is used with the variable factor then its ratio compared to variable factor decreases. Therefore when an extra unit of a variable factor has to produce with the

help of a fixed factor then the marginal return of the variable factor diminishes.

2. **Optimum Production**—after achieving the optimum combination of fixed and variable factor of production, if the production increases by using only variable factor then due to diminishing efficiency of variable factor, the marginal return decreases.

3. **Imperfect Substitutes**—According to MRS. JOAN ROBINSON the imperfect substitution of factors mainly causes the law of diminishing return. Up to a certain limit factors of production can be substituted one for another but after that these factors cannot be substituted for a long time and the marginal return falls.

4. **Scarcity of factors of production**—it is also another important reason for the law of diminishing return.

## ▪ Explain the Law of variable proportion.

The law of variable proportion is explained by different economists in various ways.

The law states as one factor is increased with other fixed factors to increase the production, then at first TP increases at increasing rate and then TP increases at diminishing rate and finally TP falls.

According to Left witch, "The law of variable proportion states that if the input of one resources is increased by equal increments per unit of time while the inputs of other resources are held constant, total output will increase, but beyond some point the resulting output will become smaller and smaller".

According to Professor Samuelson, "The law states an increase in some inputs relative to other fixed inputs, will, in a given state of technology, causes output to increase, but after a point the extra inputs will become less and less".

Actually this law states the relationship between TP, AP and MP and this law is a restatement of the law of diminishing return.

This law is based on certain assumptions:

## ASSUMPTIONS:

(1) State of technology remains constant.
(2) Only one factor is variable and all other factors are fixed.

(3) All units of variable factor are homogeneous and this law depends on the possibility of changes in the ratio between two inputs.

(4) It is assumed that the whole operation is for short-run.

This law can be explained by the following table and diagram:

| Units of land (hectare) | Units of variable factor(labour) | TP | AP | MP | Stages |
|---|---|---|---|---|---|
| 4 | 1 | 2 | 2 | 2 | increasing return |
| 4 | 2 | 5 | 2.5 | 3 | |
| 4 | 3 | 9 | 3 | 4 | |
| 4 | 4 | 12 | 3 | 3 | diminishing return |
| 4 | 5 | 14 | 2.8 | 2 | |
| 4 | 6 | 15 | 2.5 | 1 | |
| 4 | 7 | 15 | 2.14 | 0 | |
| 4 | 8 | 14 | 1.75 | -1 | Negative return |

*Table. 5/6*

From the above table it is clear that as we increase labour one by one unit TP first increases at increasing rate, then at diminishing rate and finally TP falls. This can be explained by the following diagram:

**Law of variable proportion:**

The law of variable proportion determines the shape of Total Product curve. It is also called as the law of diminishing return to factors. It states that if we employ more of one factor of production and other factors remaining constant then its Marginal Product after sometime will diminish. This law can be explained by the following diagram which also presents the relationship between TP, AP and MP. This first diagram is based on the above table.

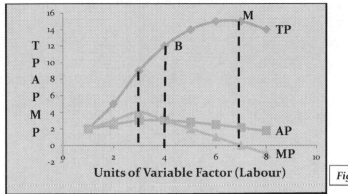

Fig: 5/10

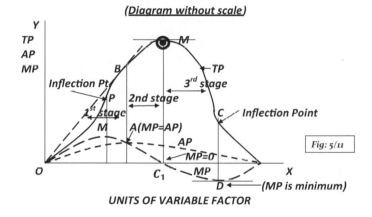

Fig: 5/11

In the above figure, TP is presented by OBC curve;
MP is presented by OMD curve;
AP is presented by OA curve;

In the above diagram, at zero level of output TP = AP = MP. So three curves TP, AP and MP start from the origin. As long as TP is convex MP rises. At point of inflection 'p', MP is maximum. Then after, TP is concave and MP falls.

To the right of maximum point 'M', TP falls and MP is negative, AP decreases. At point 'c' on TP curve again there is an inflection point. Corresponding to point 'c' at point 'D' MP is minimum. So MP has two extreme points. AP remains positive and asymptotic to OX axis.

An eminent economist Cassel has explained the above relationship between TP, AP and MP in the production process by three stages in the following way.

**Stage –1: This stage continues up to point B (4ᵗʰ units of labour) on TP curve i.e. till MP=AP.**

In this stage 1)  AP increases

2)  MP > AP and MP may be increasing (up to corresponding point of inflection) or decreasing (after corresponding point of inflection).

3)  TP first convex from below and then concave but increases.

CAUSES:

(a)  Underutilisation of fixed factor.

(b)  Indivisibility of factors

(c)  Specialisation of variable factor (labour).

**Stage –2: This stage (decreasing return) is shown by the portion between 'B' and 'M' (between 3ʳᵈ and 7ᵗʰ units of labour) on TP curve.**

In this stage 1)  TP increases at diminishing rate.

2)  MP decreases but positive

3)  AP decreases.

At the end of this stage when MP=0 (at 7ᵗʰ unit of labour) then TP is maximum.

CAUSES:

(a)  Optimal use of fixed factor

(b)  Lack of perfect substitutes between factors.

**Stage –3: This stage (negative return) starts (beyond 7ᵗʰ unit of labour) to the right point of M on TP curve.**

(1)  TP decreases and there is again a point of inflection at point C on TP curve.

(2)  MP decreases, negative and this continues up to **point D (where MP is minimum)** corresponding to inflection point C of TP Curve.

(3)  AP decreases but positive and actually AP becomes asymptotic to OX axis.

CAUSES:

(a) Over utilization of fixed factor.

## ▪ Which of the above three stages is more preferred by a producer to produce output and why?

It is an important question whether the producer will produce in the first stage or in the second stage or in the third stage.

A rational producer will not stop its production in the first stage because his main aim is to maximize profit. So he wants to produce more of total product and here MP of fixed factor (land) is negative. In stage-1, AP increases and he does not make best use of fixed factor.

The producer does not prefer to produce in the third stage because in this stage the marginal product of variable factor (labour) is negative. This stage is called as uneconomic region of production function.

Therefore the rational producer always prefers to produce in the second stage because in this stage he maximizes total production by using variable factor in such a manner that its elasticity is less than or equal to one.

In this stage though AP and MP decrease but they are positive. Here both the MP of fixed and variable factor is positive. So it is the best stage for any firm to produce output.

➢ **Explain the Law of variable proportion with the help of a table.**

The increasing return to a variable factor, diminishing return to a variable factor and negative return can be explained by the following table.

| Capital (K) | Labour (L) | TP | MP | AP | STAGES |
|:-----------:|:----------:|:--:|:--:|:--:|:------:|
| 4 | 1 | 2 | 2 | 2 | Increasing |
| 4 | 2 | 5 | 3 | 2.5 | Return |
| 4 | 3 | 9 | 4 | 3 | To a |
| 4 | 4 | 12 | 3 | 3 | Variable factor |

| Capital (K) | Labour (L) | TP | MP | AP | STAGES |
|:---:|:---:|:---:|:---:|:---:|:---:|
| 4 | 5 | 14 | 2 | 2.8 | Diminishing Return to a Variable factor |
| 4 | 6 | 15 | 1 | 2.5 | Diminishing Return to a Variable factor |
| 4 | 7 | 15 | 0 | 2.1 | Diminishing Return to a Variable factor |
| 4 | 8 | 14 | -1 | 1.75 | Negative return |

*Table. 5/7*

> **Concept of constant return to a variable factor:**

It refers to a situation when the TP increases at constant rate i.e. MP is also constant.

This can be explained by the following table and diagram:

| Units of land (hectare) | Units of labour | TP | MP |
|:---:|:---:|:---:|:---:|
| 4 | 1 | 5 | 5 |
| 4 | 2 | 10 | 5 |
| 4 | 3 | 15 | 5 |
| 4 | 4 | 20 | 5 |

*Table. 5/7*

From the above table it is clear that as the variable factor increases with fixed factor land then TP increases at the constant rate i.e. MP is equal to 5 units (constant).

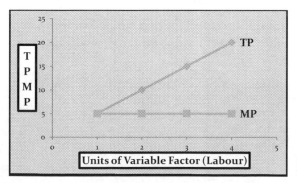

*Fig: 5/12*

From the above table it is clear that TP increases at constant rate and MP is also constant at each unit of variable factor.

134

## • Why is the shape of MP curve inverse of 'U'?

MP at first starts and rises due to increasing return to a factor and then due to constant return MP stabilizes and finally due to diminishing return to a factor MP falls. SO the shape of MP curve becomes inverse of 'U'.

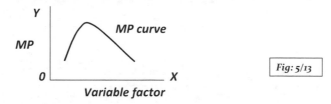

Fig: 5/13

## • Is it possible to avoid the law of variable proportion?

No, it is not possible to avoid this law of variable proportion.

Only we can postpone this law with the help of invention of new substitute product or by innovation of new technique.

# IMPORTANT QUESTIONS:

## 1 MARK QUESTIONS:

1. What is meant by production?
2. Define production function.
3. How do we calculate Total Product from Marginal Products?
4. How do we calculate Marginal Product from Total Product?
5. What happens to TP (or TPP) when MP (or MPP) is equal to zero?
6. Define law of variable proportion.

## 3 or 4 MARK QUESTIONS:

1. Explain the increasing return to a variable factor and state its causes.
2. Explain the diminishing return to a variable factor and state its causes.
3. Explain the constant return to a variable factor and state its causes.
4. Explain the law of variable proportion.
5. Explain the relationship between TP, MP and AP.

## 6 MARK QUESTIONS:

1. Explain the law of variable proportions with the help of a schedule and diagram.
2. What is meant by return to a variable factor? Explain three stages of return to a variable factor.
3. Explain the law of diminishing return to a variable factor and state its causes.

___*___*___*___*___*___*___*___*___*___*___*___*___

# Chapter - 6

## Supply And Elasticity Of Supply:

### Concept of Supply and its main characteristics:

Supply refers to the quantity of a commodity that a seller is ready to sell at a particular price during a given time period.

According to Anatol Murad, "Supply refers to the quantities of a commodity offered for sale at a given price, in a given market at a given period of time, other things being equal."

The main characteristics of supply are as follows:

a) Willingness to sell a commodity.
b) To sale a commodity at particular price.
c) To sale a commodity at particular time period.

### Distinction between Supply and Quantity Supplied of a commodity:

Supply refers to the various quantities of a commodity that a seller is ready to sale in a market at different possible prices, other things remaining constant.

Whereas quantity supplied refers to the particular quantity of a commodity that a seller is ready to sell at a given price during a time period, other factors remaining constant.

Supply refers to always price of commodity but quantity supplied refers to specific quantity of a commodity to be sold at specific price.

Example: A seller sells 2 oranges at Rs.4 per unit and he sells 4 oranges at Rs.6 per unit. This is an example of supply.

His quantity supplied is that he sells 2 oranges at Rs.4 per unit.

## ▪ Concept of supply schedule:

Supply schedule refers to tabular presentation of positive relation between different quantities supplied of a commodity and its different prices.

According to Professor Samuelson, "The table relating to price and quantity supplied is called the supply schedule."

Supply schedule is of two types:

**(a) INDIVIDUAL SUPPLY SCHEDULE**—It is a table which shows different quantities of a commodity that an individual firm sells at all given price, in a given market and at a given time period.

Table: Individual supply schedule—

| PRICE OF ORANGE(Rs.) | QUANTITY Demanded(units) |
|---|---|
| 1 | 1 |
| 2 | 2 |
| 3 | 3 |
| 4 | 4 |
| 5 | 5 |

Table. 6/1

**(b) MARKET SUPPLY SCHEDULE**—It is defined as the quantities of a commodity which all firms sale at a given price, in a given market and at a given time period.

Table: Market supply schedule—

| PRICE OF ORANGE(Rs.) | A'S SUPPLY | B'S SUPPLY | C'S SUPPLY | MARKT SUPPLY (A+B+C) |
|:---:|:---:|:---:|:---:|:---:|
| 1 | 1 | 2 | 0 | 3 |
| 2 | 2 | 3 | 1 | 6 |
| 3 | 3 | 4 | 2 | 9 |
| 4 | 4 | 5 | 3 | 12 |

*Table. 6/2*

In the above table only 3 FIRMS are assumed of different nature in the market.

## ▪ Supply curve and construction of individual supply curve from individual supply schedule:

Supply curve refers to graphical presentation of supply schedule reflecting the positive relationship between different quantities supplied at different possible prices.

According to Lipsey, "The curve which shows the relation between the price of a commodity and the amount of the commodity that the firm wishes to sale is called supply curve."

Supply curve is of two types: (a) individual supply curve and (ii) market supply curve.

(a) **INDIVIDUAL SUPPLY CURVE:** It is a curve which shows different quantities of a commodity supplied at different prices by an individual firm. It can be drawn from individual supply schedule.

Table: Individual supply schedule—

| PRICE OF ORANGE(Rs.) | QUANTITY Supplied(units) |
|:---:|:---:|
| 1 | 1 |
| 2 | 2 |
| 3 | 3 |
| 4 | 4 |
| 5 | 5 |

*Table. 6/3*

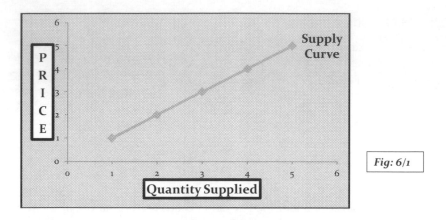

Fig: 6/1

In the above diagram the supply curve is drawn from the supply schedule which shows positive relationship between price of a commodity and its supply.

## ■ Market supply curve and drawing of market supply curve from market supply schedule.

It is a curve which shows total quantities of a commodity offered for sale at various prices by all the firms in the market. This can be drawn from the market supply schedule in the following way.

Table: Market supply schedule—

| PRICE OF ORANGE (Rs.) | A'S SUPPLY | B'S SUPPLY | MARKT SUPPLY (A+B+C) |
|---|---|---|---|
| 1 | 1 | 2 | 3 |
| 2 | 2 | 3 | 5 |
| 3 | 3 | 4 | 7 |
| 4 | 4 | 5 | 9 |

Table. 6/4

In the above table only 2 FIRMS are assumed of different nature in the market.

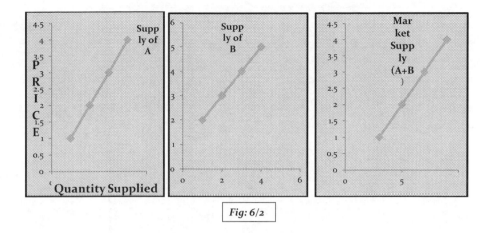

Fig: 6/2

## • The Law of Supply with the help of hypothetical schedule and its assumptions:

The law of supply states, that other factors being constant, the supply of a commodity extends with a rise in price and contracts with the fall in price.

According to Professor Dooley, "Law of supply states that other things remaining the same, higher the price, greater is the quantity supplied and lower the price, the smaller is the quantity supplied."

Law of supply is based on the following assumptions—

### ASSUMPTIONS:

The law of Supply can be explained by the following table and diagram.

(i)   The number of firms remains unchanged.
(ii)  The price of factors of production remains constant.
(iii) There should be no change in the state of technology. (iv) There is no change in the expected price of the commodity by the seller.
(v)   Goal of the firms remains constant. The Law of Supply can be presented by the following table and diagram.

| PRICE OF ORANGE (Rs.) | QUANTITY Demanded (units) |
|---|---|
| 1 | 1 |

141

| | |
|---|---|
| 2 | 2 |
| 3 | 3 |
| 4 | 4 |
| 5 | 5 |

Table. 6/5

In the above table it is clear that a firm sells more at higher price and sells less At lower price.

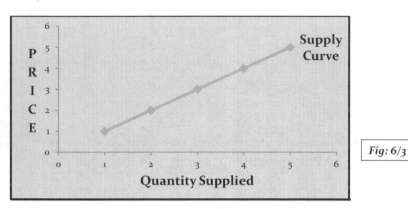

Fig: 6/3

> **Why does supply curve slope upwards? Or why there is a positive relation between price of a commodity and its supply?**

Supply curve is the graphical presentation of positive relation between the price of a commodity and its price.

It is upward sloping from left to right because of the following reasons.

**(1) PROFIT AND LOSSES:** If the price is high then the firms supply more because they expect more profit. On the other hand if the price is less then they supply less because of the possibility of losses.

**(2) ENTRY AND EXIT OF FIRM:** If the price is high then many firms enter into the market because of the high profit, so the supply increases. On the other hand at low price some firms exit from the market so the supply decreases.

**(3) CHANGE IN STOCK:** At higher price the firms bring their existing stock for sale in the market. So the supply increases.

## • The main determinants of Supply
## • Or the factors which affect supply of a commodity:
## • Or the Supply functions:

The main factors which affect the supply of a commodity are called determinants of supply. There are some factors which affect individual supply of a commodity which are called individual supply function. This can be written as Sg = f (Pg, Pr, Pf, G, St);

Where Sg—Supply of goods, Pg—Price of goods, Pr—Price of related goods, Pf—Price of factors of production, G—Goal of the firm, St—state of technology).

### (1) PRICE OF COMMODITY—

With the rise in the price of a good its supply rises and with the fall in the price of it, its supply falls. So there is direct relation between the price of a commodity and its supply.

### (2) PRICE OF RELATED GOODS—

Supply of a commodity also depends on the price of related goods, especially substitute goods. If the price of a commodity remains constant (e.g. Pepsi) and the price of its substitute good (Coke) rises then the producers will prefer to produce substitute goods. Therefore supply of original goods decreases and the supply of substitute goods will increase.

### (3) PRICE OF FACTORS OF PRODUCTION:

When the price of factors of production i.e., price of land, labour, capital increases then the cost of production of output also increases. As a result firm's profit falls. So the supply decreases and vice-versa.

### (4) GOAL OF THE FIRM:

If the goal of the firm is profit maximization then the firms supply more goods at higher price. On the other hand if the goal of the firm is sales maximization the firm supplies more goods at lower price.

## (5) STATE OF TECHNOLOGY:

If the producers use advanced technology then the cost of production of output decreases and profit increases. So the supply increases.

On the other hand if the producers use traditional technology then cost of production increases and profit falls. So the supply decreases.

There are some other factors in addition to the above factors which affect the market supply of a commodity. These factors are like Future expectation (Fe), Number of firms (N), and Government Policy (Gp) etc.

So the Supply Function becomes SS = f (Pg, Pr, Pf, G, S, Fe, N, Gp);

The above factors can be explained in the following way:

(6) **FUTURE EXPECTATION**—If a seller expects that price of a commodity will rise in future then its supply decreases at present. On the other hand if the seller expects that price of a commodity will fall in future then its supply will increase at present.

(7) **NUMBER OF FIRMS**—when the number of Firms for a commodity increases in the market, then the supply of the commodity increases. On the other hand if the number of firms decreases, then the supply of the commodity decreases.

(8) **GOVERNMENT POLICY**—Government policy of taxation and subsidy also influences supply a commodity.

If the Government reduces tax on the inputs then the cost of production of output will decrease and profit will increase and supply increases. On the other hand if the producers are given more subsidies on production then the producers are encouraged to increase supply of goods.

## ▪ The movement along the supply curve:

The movement along the supply curve refers to changes in the quantity supplied due to change in the price of commodity other factors remaining constant.

It is of two types: extension of supply and contraction of supply.

(a) **EXTENSION OF SUPPLY**—It refers to rise in the supply of a commodity due to rise in its price and other factors remaining constant. This is shown by the following table and diagram.

| PRICE OF COMMODITY (Rs. Per unit) | QUANTITY SUPPLIED (UNITS) |
|:---:|:---:|
| 1 | 1 |
| 3 | 3 |

In the above table it is clear that as the price rises from Rs.1 to Rs.3 its supply rises from 1 unit to 3 units.

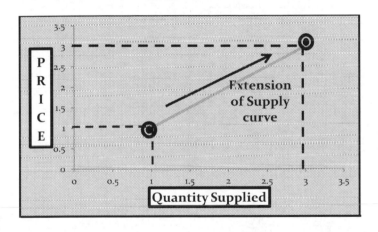

Fig: 6/4

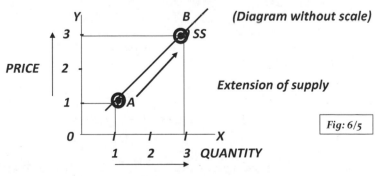

(Diagram without scale)

Extension of supply

Fig: 6/5

In the above diagram the movement from point A to B is called extension of supply which is due to rise in price of the commodity.

**(b) CONTRACTION OF SUPPLY**—It refers to fall in the supply of a commodity due to fall in its price and other factors remaining constant. This is shown by the following table and diagram.

| PRICE OF COMMODITY (Rs. Per unit) | QUANTITY SUPPLY (UNITS) |
|---|---|
| 3 | 3 |
| 1 | 1 |

In the above table it is clear that as the price falls from Rs.3 to Rs.1 its supply falls from 3 units to 1 unit.

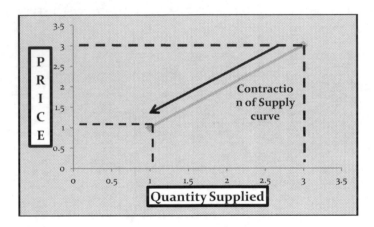

Fig: 6/6

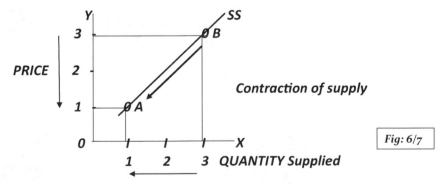

Fig: 6/7

In the above diagram the movement from point B to A is called contraction of supply which is due to fall in price of the commodity.

146

## ▪ Concept of the shift of supply curve:

Shift of the supply curve refers to the changes in the supply of a commodity not due to price of the commodity but due to the other factors like price of factors of production, changes in the number of firms or due to change in the price of other related goods or change in the state of technology.

It is of two types: Increase in supply and decrease in supply.

(i) **INCREASE IN SUPPLY**—It refers to increase in the supply of a commodity not due to price but due to the following factors.

   (a) If the number of firms increases.
   (b) If the price of factors of production decreases.
   (c) If the cost of production decreases.
   (d) If producers are given subsidy to produce output.
   (e) If the advanced technology is used.
   (f) If the firms expect that price will fall in future.

Increase in supply can be explained by the following table and diagram.

| PRICE OF GOODS (Rs. per unit) | NUMBER OF FIRMS | SUPPLY OF GOODS (units) |
|---|---|---|
| 3 | 10,000 | 10 |
| 3 | 15,000 | 15 |

From the above table it is clear that supply of goods increases not due to any change in price but due to increase in the number of the firms.

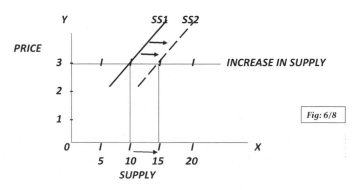

147

In the above diagram it is clear as the number of firms increases the supply of the commodity increases and the supply curve shifts from SS1 to SS2 to the right.

**(ii) DECREASE IN supply**—It refers to decrease in the supply of a commodity not due to price but due to the following factors.

(a) If the number of firms decreases.

(b) If the price of factors of production increases.

(c) If the cost of production increases.

(d) If import duty increases or subsidy is withdrawn.

(e) If the obsolete technology is used.

(f) If the firms expect that price will rise in future.

Decrease in supply can be explained by the following table and diagram.

| PRICE OF GOODS (Rs. per unit) | NUMBER OF FIRMS | SUPPLY OF GOODS (units) |
|---|---|---|
| 3 | 15,000 | 15 |
| 3 | 10,000 | 10 |

From the above table it is clear that supply for goods decreases not due to any change in price but due to decrease in the number of the firms.

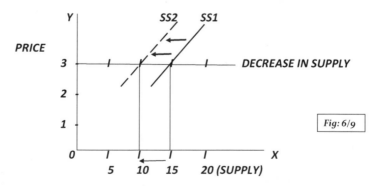

Fig: 6/9

In the above diagram it is clear as the number of firms decreases the supply of the commodity decreases and the supply curve shifts from SS1 to SS2 to the left.

# ▪ Distinction between changes in quantity supplied and change in supply.

| CHANGE IN QUANTITY SUPPLIED | CHANGE IN SUPPLY |
|---|---|
| 1. It refers to change in quantity supplied for a commodity due to change in its price only. | 1. It refers to change in quantity supplied due to change in other factors other than price like change in cost of production, change in technology, change in the price of factors of production etc. |
| 2. It is expressed in term of movement along the supply curve. | 2. It is expressed in term of shift of the supply curve. |
| 3. It is classified into Extension of supply and Contraction of supply. | 3. It is classified into Increase and Decrease of supply. |
| 4. It is presented by upward movement (extension of supply) and downward movement (contraction of supply) of supply curve. | 4. It is presented by rightward shift (increase in supply) and leftward shift (decrease in supply) of supply curve. |
| 5. Fig: Fig: Movement along the supply curve. | 5. Fig: Shift of supply curve. |

- **Distinction between extension of supply and increase in supply:** **Or**
- **Distinction between change in quantity supplied and change in supply (increase).**

| EXTENSION OF SUPPLY | INCREASE IN SUPPLY |
|---|---|
| 1. It refers to increase in supply due to rise in price of the commodity. | 1. It refers to increase in supply due to change in other factors other than price of commodity. |
| 2. It is expressed by the upward movement of the supply curve. | 2. It is expressed by the rightward shift of the supply curve. |
| 3. It is due to rise in price of commodity only. | 3. Its causes are:<br><br>(i)  If the number of firms increases.<br>(ii) If price of factors of production decreases.<br>(iii) If cost of production decreases.<br>(iv) If advanced technology is used. |
| 4. NUMERICAL EXAMPLE: | 4. NUMERICAL EXAMPLE: |

| PRICE OF GOODS (Rs.) | SUPPLY OF GOODS |
|---|---|
| 1 | 1 |
| 3 | 3 |

| PRICE OF GOODS (Rs.) | SUPPLY FOR GOODS |
|---|---|
| 3 | 10 |
| 3 | 15 |

| 5. DIAGRAMATIC PRESENTATION: | 5. DIAGRAMATIC PRESENTATION. |
|---|---|
| 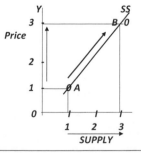 |  |
| 6. It is a part of change in quantity supplied. | 6. It is a part of change in supply. |

- **Distinction between contraction of supply and decrease in supply: Or distinction between change in quantity supplied and change in supply (decrease).**

| CONTRACTION OF SUPPLY | DECREASE IN SUPPLY |
|---|---|
| 1. It refers to decrease in supply due to fall in price of the commodity. | 1. It refers to decrease in supply due to change in other factors other than price of commodity. |
| 2. It is expressed by the downward movement of the supply curve. | 2. It is expressed by the leftward shift of the supply curve. |
| 3. It is due to fall in price of commodity only. | 3. Its causes are:<br>i)  If the number of firms decreases.<br>(ii) If price of factors of production increases.<br>(iii) If cost of production increases.<br>(iv) If obsolete technology is used. |
| 4. NUMERICAL EXAMPLE: | 4. NUMERICAL EXAMPLE: |

| PRICE OF GOODS (Rs.) | SUPPLY FOR GOODS |
|---|---|
| 3 | 3 |
| 1 | 1 |

| PRICE OF GOODS (Rs.) | SUPPLY FOR GOODS |
|---|---|
| 2 | 4 |
| 2 | 2 |

| 5. DIAGRAMATIC PRESENTATION: | 5. DIAGRAMATIC PRESENTATION. |
|---|---|
| Contraction of supply | Decrease in supply |
| 6. It is a part of change in quantity supplied. | 6. It is a part of change in supply. |

Contraction of supply

Decrease in supply

- **Under what conditions the supply curve of a commodity will shift to the rightwards?**
  **Or what are the causes of increase in supply?**
  **Or Why does supply increase?**

(i) **INCREASE IN SUPPLY**—It refers to increase in the supply of a commodity not due to price but due to the following factors.

  (a)  If the number of firms increases.
  (b)  If the price of factors of production decreases.
  (c)  If the cost of production decreases.
  (d)  If producers are given subsidy to produce output.
  (e)  If the advanced technology is used.
  (f)  If the firms expect that price will fall in future.

Increase in supply can be explained by the following table and diagram.

| PRICE OF GOODS (Rs. per unit) | NUMBER OF FIRMS | SUPPLY OF GOODS (units) |
|---|---|---|
| 3 | 10,000 | 10 |
| 3 | 15,000 | 15 |

From the above table it is clear that supply of goods increases not due to any change in price but due to increase in the number of the firms.

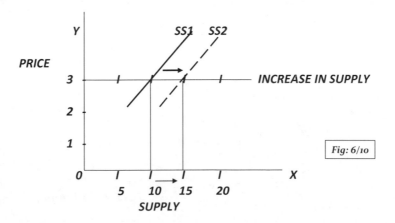

In the above diagram it is clear as the number of firms increases the supply of the commodity increases and the supply curve shifts from SS1 to SS2 to the right.

152

- **Under what conditions the supply curve of a commodity will shift to the leftwards?**
  **Or what are the causes of decrease in supply?**
  **Or Why does supply decrease?**

The causes for decrease in supply or leftwards shift of the supply curve are as follows:

**DECREASE IN supply**—It refers to decrease in the supply of a commodity not due to price but due to the following factors.

(a) If the number of firms decreases.
(b) If the price of factors of production increases.
(c) If the cost of production increases.
(d) If import duty increases or subsidy is withdrawn.
(e) If the obsolete technology is used.
(f) If the firms expect that price will rise in future.

Decrease in supply can be explained by the following table and diagram.

| PRICE OF GOODS (Rs. per unit) | NUMBER OF FIRMS | SUPPLY OF GOODS (units) |
|---|---|---|
| 3 | 15,000 | 15 |
| 3 | 10,000 | 10 |

From the above table it is clear that supply for goods decreases not due to any change in price but due to decrease in the number of the firms.

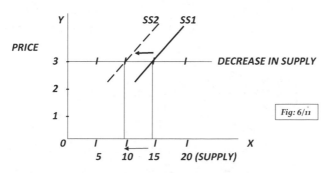

Fig: 6/11

In the above diagram it is clear as the number of firms decreases the supply of the commodity decreases and the supply curve shifts from right to left i.e. from SS1 to SS2.

## ▪ The exceptions of law of supply:
## Or the limitations of law of supply:
## Or under what conditions the law of supply is not valid?

There are some exceptions where the law of supply is not valid i.e. the supply curve does not slope upwards from left to right. The exceptional cases are as follows:

(1) AGRICULTURAL PRODUCTS—If due to natural calamities agricultural production decreases then its supply will not increase even at the high price.
(2) PERISHABLE GOODS—In case of perishable products for example vegetables the producers supply more even at lower price.
(3) SOCIAL DISTINCTION GOODS—In case of social distinction goods like diamond, gold jewelleries the supply will remain limited even if the price tends to rise.
(4) AUCTION OF GOODS—In case of auction of any commodity the supply does not increase even if the price of the commodity increases.

Explain the effect of changes in technology and price of factor inputs and excise tax on the supply of a commodity.

This question can be answered under the following heads.

## (i) CHANGE IN TECHNOLOGY:

If the producers use advanced technology then the cost of production decreases and profit increases. So the supply increases and the supply curve shifts right wards. On the other hand if the producers use traditional technology then cost of production increases and profit falls. So the supply decreases and the supply curve shifts to the left wards as shown in the following figure.

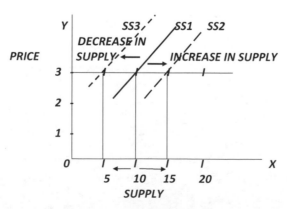

## (ii) PRICE OF FACTOR INPUTS:

If the prices of factor inputs like land, labour, capital increases, then the cost of production of output increases and the profit decreases. So the supply decreases and the supply curve shifts to the left wards. On the other hand if the price of factor inputs falls then the cost of production falls and the profit increases. So the supply increases and the supply curve shifts to the right wards as shown in the following figure.

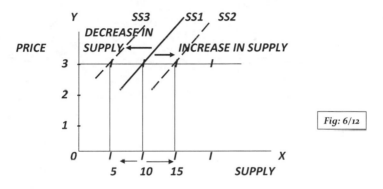

Fig: 6/12

## (iii) EXCISE TAX:

Excise tax is a tax imposed by the Government on the production of goods and services. Generally it is imposed on per unit of production of output by a firm. Therefore it raises average cost and marginal cost of output. If excise tax is levied then the firms will sell less output at present price. Therefore supply of output decreases and the supply curve will shift to the leftwards. If excise tax is withdrawn then the supply will increase and the supply curve will shift to rightwards as shown in the following diagram.

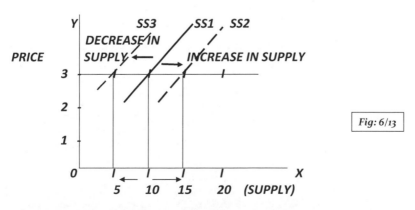

Fig: 6/13

Q. If there are 50 identical firms in the market with supply function Q =10+2P then find out the market supply for the commodity at price of Rs.10 per unit.

Ans. The market supply is, 50 Q

$$= 50 (10+2P)$$
$$= 500+100P.$$
$$= 500+100 (10)$$
$$= 500+1000$$
$$= 1500 \text{ units.}$$

—*—*—*—*—*—*—*—*—*—*—*—*—*—

# Chapter -

## Price Elasticity Of Supply:

According to Professor Samuelson, "Price elasticity of supply measures is the degree of responsiveness of supply of a commodity to a change in its price."
It is measured by the following formula

Elasticity of Supply = $\dfrac{\% \text{ change in quantity supplied}}{\% \text{ change in Price}}$

■ **Different degrees or types of Price Elasticity of Supply:**

In Economics Price Elasticity of Supply is classified into five degrees which are as follows:

**(1) PERFECTLY ELASTIC SUPPLY (Es = ∞):**

When the supply of a commodity changes to any extent at the given price then it is called Perfectly Elastic Supply.

In other words, a slight rise in price causes an infinite increase in supply and a slight fall in price will reduce supply to zero.

Perfectly Elastic supply curve is a horizontal line parallel to x-axis as shown in the following diagram.

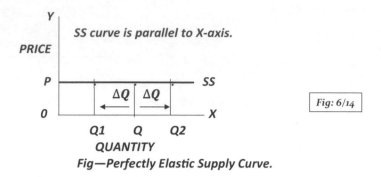

Fig: 6/14

Fig—Perfectly Elastic Supply Curve.

## (2) PERFECTLY INELASTIC SUPPLY (Es = 0):

When the supply of a commodity does not change due to any change in its price then it is called perfectly inelastic supply. The elasticity of supply in this case is zero. The supply curve will be parallel to Y-axis as shown in the following diagram.

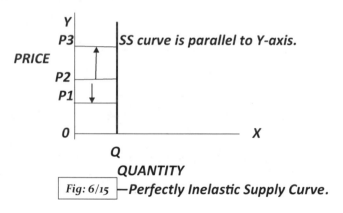

Fig: 6/15 —Perfectly Inelastic Supply Curve.

From the above diagram it is clear that even if the price changes the supply does not change.

## (3) UNITARY ELASTIC SUPPLY (Es = 1):

When percentage change in quantity supplied of a commodity is equal to the percentage change in its price then the supply is called unitary elastic supply. The shape of such supply curve is a straight line with positive slope and starting from the origin. This curve is shown in the following diagram.

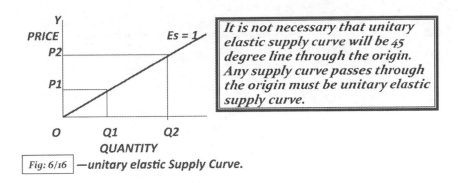

Es = 1

It is not necessary that unitary elastic supply curve will be 45 degree line through the origin. Any supply curve passes through the origin must be unitary elastic supply curve.

Fig: 6/16 —unitary elastic Supply Curve.

## (4) MORE ELASTIC SUPLY OR GREATER THAN UNITARY ELASTIC SUPPLY (ES > 1):

When percentage change in quantity supplied of a commodity is more than percentage change in the price of commodity then it is called more elastic supply or greater than unitary elastic supply.

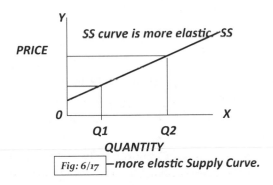

Fig: 6/17 —more elastic Supply Curve.

## (5) LESS ELASTIC OR INELASTIC OR LESS THAN UNITARY ELASTIC SUPPLY (Es < 1):

When percentage change in quantity supplied of a commodity is less than percentage change in the price of commodity then it is called less elastic supply or less than unitary elastic supply. This is shown in the following diagram.

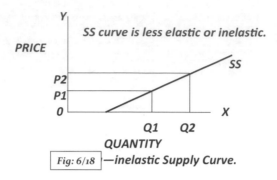

Fig: 6/18 —inelastic Supply Curve.

## ▪ The factors which affect the price elasticity of supply: Or
## The determinants of price elasticity of supply.

The main determinants of price elasticity of supply for a commodity are as follows:

(1) **NATURE OF COMMODITY:** In case of perishable goods like milk, vegetables etc. the supply will be inelastic in short-period because their supply neither can be increased nor can be decreased. On the other hand in case of durable goods like furniture, cell phone supply will be elastic.

(2) **TIME FACTOR:** During short period supply cannot be adjusted with its demand. So supply is inelastic. On the other hand in long-run supply can be easily adjusted with its demand. So supply will be elastic.

(3) **TECHNIQUE OF PRODUCTION:** The goods which are produced by using simple technique they have elastic supply. On the other hand the goods which are produced by using complex technology will have inelastic supply.

(4) **RISK FACTOR:** If a producer bears more risk, then the supply of his product will be more elastic. On the other hand if the producer is unable to bear risk, then the supply of his product will be less elastic.

(5) **STAGES OF LAW OF RETURN:** If the production is subject to law of diminishing return then the supply of goods will be inelastic. On the other hand if the production is subject to law of increasing return then the supply of goods will be elastic.

**(6) FUTURE PRICE EXPECTATION:** If the producer expects price of product will rise in future then its supply will be less at present. On the other hand if the producer expects price of the product will fall in future then its supply will be more at present.

## ▪ Different methods to measure Price Elasticity of supply

We measure price elasticity of supply by the following methods:

(i)  GEOMETRIC METHOD.
(ii) PROPORTIONATE OR PERCENTAGE OR FLUX METHOD.

## ▪ The Point method or Geometric method to measure price elasticity of supply: Or
## ▪ How can you measure price elasticity of supply at different points on a linear supply curve?

This method measures price elasticity of supply at different points on a supply curve. This method is known as geometric method or graphic method. This method can be explained by the following diagram.

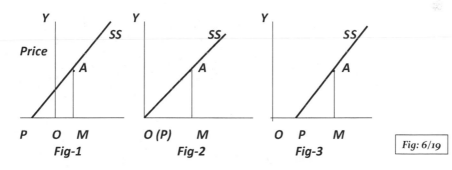

Fig-1          Fig-2          Fig-3          Fig: 6/19

In the above three diagrams SS is the supply curve and a point A is taken on each supply curve to measure price elasticity of supply. From point A the perpendicular AM is drawn in each diagram. Now elasticity of supply can be measured by the following way.

(a)  In fig-1, at point A, Es = PM/OM

Es > 1 (since PM > OM);

(b)  In fig-2, at point A, Es = PM/OM

Es = 1 (since PM = OM);

(c)  In fig-3, at point A, Es = PM/OM

Es < 1 (since PM < OM);

Therefore any supply curve starts from vertical axis has more elastic supply. Any supply curve starts from the origin has unitary elastic supply and any supply curve starts from the horizontal axis has less elastic supply.

## ▪ The Flux method or proportionate method or percentage method:

This method is associated with author Flux. According to this method, elasticity of supply is measured by the ratio of percentage change in quantity supplied to a percentage change in price.

$$\text{Elasticity of Supply} = \frac{\text{Percentage change in quantity supplied}}{\text{Percentage change in Price}}$$

Let initial price is P and final price is P1. Then change in price = P1-P = $\Delta$P
And % change in Price = (P1-P)/P x 100 = $\left(\frac{\Delta P}{P}\right) \cdot 100$
Similarly, if the initial quantity is Q and final quantity is Q1, then
% change in Quantity = (Q1-Q)/Q x 100 = $\left(\frac{\Delta Q}{Q}\right) \cdot 100$

Therefore,

$$Es = \frac{\text{\% change in quantity supplied}}{\text{\% change in price}}$$

$$= \frac{\left(\frac{\Delta Q}{Q}\right) \cdot 100}{\left(\frac{\Delta P}{P}\right) \cdot 100}$$

$$= \frac{\left(\frac{\Delta Q}{Q}\right)}{\left(\frac{\Delta P}{P}\right)} = \frac{\Delta Q}{\Delta P} \cdot (P/Q)$$

## ▪ The Importance of Price Elasticity of Supply:

Price elasticity of supply has the following importance:

### (1) PRICE DETERMINATION:

Elasticity of Supply helps to determine the price of a product especially in the long-run when supply of a product is perfectly elastic. But in short-run when supply is less elastic then it s role is not so important.

### (2) RENT DETERMINATION:

If supply of a factor of production is perfectly elastic then it has no rent. On the other hand if supply of a factor is perfectly inelastic then the entire earning of the factor will be rent. Thus supply of a factor determines rent of the factor.

## ▪ If two supply curves intersect each other then state which one will be more elastic and why?

The answer can be explained by the following diagram.

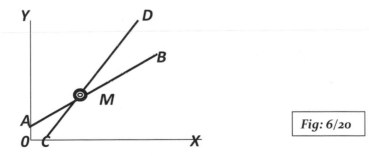

Fig: 6/20

In the above diagram the supply curve AB is more elastic compared to the supply curve CD, because AB is more flat than the supply curve CD.

■ **How can you proof that any supply curve passes through the origin and slopes upward is unitary elastic.**

This can be proved by the following diagram.

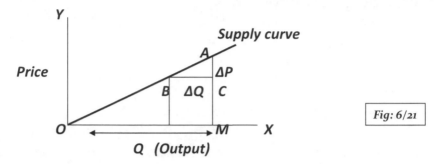

Fig: 6/21

Elasticity of supply at any point A of supply curve is measured by the following formula. Es = $\frac{\Delta Q}{\Delta P} \cdot \frac{P}{Q}$

Δ ABC and Δ AOM are similar triangles. So, the ratios of their sides are equal.

Therefore, AC/BC = AM/OM

Or, $\frac{\Delta P}{\Delta Q}$ = P/Q . . . . . . . . . . .(1)

Putting this value in the formula of Elasticity of Supply, we have

$$Es = \frac{\Delta Q}{\Delta P} \cdot \frac{P}{Q}$$

$$= Q/P \cdot P/Q$$

$$= 1$$

## ▪ NUMERICAL OF PRICE ELASTICITY OF SUPPLY—

1. Price of a commodity rises from Rs.5 to Rs. 8. As a result its supply rises from 80 units to 100 units. Calculate price elasticity of supply by proportionate method.

Ans.

| PRICE (Rs.) | QUANTITY SUPPLIED |
|---|---|
| 5 | 80 |
| 8 | 100 |
| $\Delta P=3$ | $\Delta Q=20$ |

Es = $(\Delta Q/Q)/(\Delta P/P)$
= (20/80)/ (3/5)
= (20/80)/ (3/5)
= (20.5/80.3)
= 100/240
= 0.416

Since Es is 0.416 so it is less elastic supply.

2. Price of a commodity doubles. As a result its supply increases by 20%. If previously a firm was supplying 80 units at Rs.5 per unit then calculate price elasticity of supply by proportionate method.

Ans.

| PRICE (Rs.) | QUANTITY |
|---|---|
| 5 | 80 |
| 10 | 96 |
| $\Delta P=5$ | $\Delta Q=16$ |

Price becomes double. So new price is Re.5x2 = Re.10 and quantity increases by 20%. So new quantity is 80 + 16 = 96

Es = $(\Delta Q/Q)/(\Delta P/P)$
= (16/80)/ (5/5)
= (1/5)/ (1)
= 0.2

So supply is less elastic.

3. A seller sells 100 units of a commodity at Rs.4 per unit. When the price rises he sells 150 units. If price elasticity of supply is unity, then find out the new price.

Ans. Given Es = 1,

And the other information as shown in the table:

| PRICE (Rs.) | QUANTITY |
|---|---|
| 4 | 100 |
| X | 150 |
| $\Delta P = X - 4$ | $\Delta Q = 50$ |

$Ed = (\Delta Q/Q)/(\Delta P/P)$

Or,   $1 = 50/100 \div (X-4)/4$

Or,   $1 = 50 \times 4 /100(X-4)$

Or,   $1 = 2/(X-4)$

Or,   $X-4 = 2$

Or,   $X = 6$

So the new price is Re. 6.

Q.4. Price of a commodity falls from Rs. 20 per unit to Rs. 15 per unit. As a result producer's supply decreases from 150 units to 120 units. Calculate the price elasticity of supply by percentage method.

Ans.

| PRICE (Rs.) | QUANTITY |
|---|---|
| 20 | 150 |
| 15 | 120 |
| 5 | 30 |

Here, % change in Price = (5/20) x100 = 25%

And % change in Quantity supplied = (30/150) x100 = 20%

$$\text{Price Elasticity of Supply} = \frac{\% \text{ change in supply}}{\% \text{ change in price}}$$

= 20% / 25%

= 0.8

So price elasticity of supply is 0.8 i.e. less elastic supply.

5.  As a result of 20% rise in price of a good, its supply rises from 80 units to 120 units. Calculate price elasticity of supply.

Ans. % change in supply = $\underline{(120\text{-}80) \times 100}$
$$\phantom{\% change in supply = } 80$$
$$= (40/80) \times 100 = 50\%$$

Price Elasticity of supply = $\dfrac{\% \text{ change in supply}}{\% \text{ change in price}}$

$$= 50\%/20\%$$
$$= 50/20$$
$$= 2.5$$

Therefore the supply is greater than unitary (Es >1).

6.  A 10% rise in price of a commodity leads to 10% rise in its supply. A producer sells 60 units of the commodity at a price of Rs.5 per unit. How many units will he sell if the price rises by 20%?

Ans. From the above question we have

$$Es = \dfrac{\% \text{ change in quantity supplied}}{\% \text{ change in the price}}$$
$$= 10\%/10\%$$
$$= 1$$

Now we also have,

| PRICE (Rs.) | SUPPLY |
|-------------|--------|
| 5 | 60 |
| 5+1 = 6 | X |
| 1 | X-60 |

20% rise in price of Re.5 means Re.1
So the new price is Re.5 + Re.1 = Re.6
Let the final quantity is X

Then by using the formula we get the following-

$$Es = (\Delta Q/Q)/(\Delta P/P)$$
$$1 = (X-60)/60 \div (1/5)$$
$$Or, 1 = (X-60)/60 \times 5/1$$
$$Or, 12 = X-60$$
$$Or, X = 12 + 60$$
$$Or, X = 72$$

So the required quantity is 72.

7. The price elasticity of supply of a commodity is 2. When its price falls from Rs.10 to Rs. 8 per unit, its quantity supplied falls by 500 units. Calculate the quantity supplied at the reduced price. (C.B.S.E. 2006, Delhi)

Ans.

| PRICE (Rs.) | SUPPLY |
|:---:|:---:|
| 10 | X |
| 8 | X-500 |
| 2 | 500 |

Let previous quantity was X.
Given Es = 2, Now by using the formula
We have, Price Es = $(\Delta Q/Q)/(\Delta P/P)$

$$Es = (500/X) / (2/10)$$
$$2 = (500/X) \times (5/1)$$
$$Or, 2 = 2500/X$$
$$Or, X = 2500/2$$
$$Or, X = 1250$$

So the new quantity at reduced price is 1250-500 = 750 Units.

8. A 15% rise in price of a commodity results in a rise in its supply from 600 to 735 units. Calculate elasticity of supply. (A.I.C.B.S.E.2008 Comptt.)

Ans. Here % change in quantity supplied = (735-600)/600 x 100

= (135/600) x 100

= 22.5 %

And, % change in price = 15%

So, Price Elasticity of Supply = 22.5% / 15%

= 1.5 i.e. more elastic supply.

9.  The price elasticity of supply of commodity X is twice of price elasticity of commodity Y. Now due to 10% change in price of commodity X its supply increases by 15%. A seller was supplying 200 units of commodity Y at price of Rs. 50 per unit, then how much would he supply if the price increases by Rs. 25 per unit?

Ans. $E_X = 2. E_Y$ (Given)

$$E_X = \frac{15\%}{10\%} = 1.5$$

Therefore, $E_Y = 1.5/2 = 0.75$

Let the seller would supply y units when price increases by Rs. 50

$0.75 = \frac{\Delta q/q}{\Delta p/p}$

| Price (Rs.) | Quantity |
|---|---|
| 50 | 200 |
| 50+25=75 | Y |
| Δp=25 | Δq=y-200 |

$$0.75 = \frac{\frac{y-200}{200}}{\frac{25}{50}} = \frac{y-200}{200} \times \frac{50}{25}$$

Or, 0.75 x100 = y – 200

Or, 75 = y – 200

Or, y = 275

So, the required quantity of supply will be 275 units.

___*___*___*___*___*___*___*___*___*___*___*___*__

# Important Questions For Law Of Supply:

1. What is supply?
2. What is meant by law of supply?
3. Define supply schedule?
4. What is meant by stock?
5. Define individual supply schedule.
6. What is meant by market supply?
7. What is meant by extension of supply?
8. Define contraction of supply.
9. What is meant by increase in supply?
10. What is meant by decrease in supply?
11. How are the following two goods X and Y are related?

   a) With the rise in the supply of good-X, the supply of good-Y also rises.
   b) With the rise in the supply of good-X, the supply of good-Y falls.

1. Explain the factors which affect individual supply of a commodity.

   Or

State the determinants of individual supply of a commodity.

2. Explain the main determinants of market supply for a commodity.

   Or

   Explain the factors which affect market supply of a commodity.

3. How does the change in state of technology affect the supply of a commodity?

4. Explain the effect of change in the price of other related goods on the supply for the original good.

5. Why does the supply curve slope upwards from left to right?

6. Distinguish between extension of supply and contraction of supply.

7. Explain the movement along the supply curve or

   Explain the changes in quantity supplied.

8. Distinguish between increase in supply and decrease in supply.

9. Explain the shift of supply curve or

   Explain the change in supply.

10. Distinguish between movement along the supply curve and the shift of the supply curve.

11. Distinguish between changes in quantity supplied and changes in supplied (increase).

    Or

    Distinguish between extension of supply and increase in supply.

12. Distinguish between changes in quantity supplied and changes in supply (decrease).

    Or

Distinguish between contraction of supply and decrease in supply.

13. Why does supply curve shift to right wards?

    Or

Why does supply of a commodity increase at given price?

14. Why does supply curve shift to left wards?

    Or

Why does supply of a commodity decrease at given price?

## 6 MARK QUESTIONS:

1. How can you draw market supply curve from market supply schedule?
2. Explain the market supply function.
3. Explain with the help of a diagram the changes in supply of a commodity when the price of its input changes.
4. Explain with the help of a diagram the changes in supply when There is change in the state of technology.

5. Explain the determinants of market supply.
6. What are the limitations of law of supply?
7. What is meant by a supply curve? Why does supply curve slope upwards from left to right?
8. Distinguish between movement along the supply curve and the shift of the supply curve.

# Important Questions For Elasticity Of Supply:

1. What is meant by price elasticity of supply?
2. When is supply called inelastic?
3. Define unity elastic supply.
4. If due to 10 % changes in price the supply of a good changes by 10% then what will be price elasticity of supply?
5. What is meant by imperfectly elastic supply?

## 3 or 4 MARK QUESTIONS:

1. What is price elasticity of supply? State three factors those can affect the price elasticity of supply.
2. Distinguish between elastic supply and inelastic supply.
3. Distinguish between perfectly elastic supply and imperfectly elastic supply.
4. How can you measure price elasticity of supply at different points on a linear supply curve?

   Or

Explain the geometric method to measure price elasticity of supply.

5. How can you measure price elasticity of supply by percentage method?
6. How does the nature of a commodity affect the price elasticity of supply?
7. How does the Government policy affect the price elasticity of supply?
8. Numerical:

9. If two supply curves intersect each other then which one will be more elastic and why?
10. State the relation between the slope of the supply curve and the elasticity of supply.
11. What will be the price elasticity of supply of the following goods? Answer with reasons.

    a) School uniform; b) Petrol; c) Economics text book; d) medicines; e) Cell phone of branded company; f) Salt; g) lipstick of branded company;

## 6 MARK QUESTIONS:

1. Explain different types of price elasticity of supply

    Or

    Explain different degrees of price elasticity of supply.

2. What is meant by price elasticity of supply? Explain the factors those can affect the price elasticity of supply.
3. How can you measure the price elasticity of supply at different points on a straight line supply curve?

—*—*—*—*—*—*—*—*—*—*—*—*—*—

# Chapter - 7

## Concepts Of Cost Of Production:

Cost of production refers to the expenditure incurred for the factors of production like land, labour, capital etc. and non-factor inputs like raw materials etc. for the production of output.

**Concept of Cost function.**

According to Watson, cost function refers to the functional relationship between the output and cost.

Symbolically, C = f (Q)

Where C is cost of production, Q is output, and f is functional relationship.

According to Koutsoyiannis, cost functions are derived function from the production functions.

**Concept of different types of cost of production:**

Concept of cost of production can be clear by the following way:

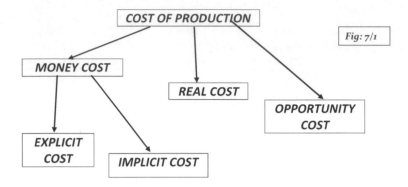

Fig: 7/1

**(1) MONEY COST:** Generally, the term cost of production refers to the money cost which is also known as nominal cost. It refers to all monetary expenditure incurred by a firm to produce and sell its product. It includes the following expenses:

a. cost of raw materials and machinery,
b. wages and salaries,
c. expenses on electricity, fuel,
d. interest on capital,
e. depreciation,
f. insurance charges,
g. transport costs,
h. publicity,
i. Normal profit etc.

According to Hansen, 'The money cost of producing a certain output of a commodity is the sum of all payments to the factors of production engaged in the production of that commodity'.

Money cost includes two types of cost which are as follows:

**(i) EXPLICIT COST:** It refers to those expenses which are actually paid by the firm to purchase or hire the goods and services of other firms. For example, payments for raw material, fuel, power, transport, rent etc.
   According to Leftwich," Explicit costs are those cash payments which firms make to outsiders for their goods and services".

**(ii) IMPLICIT COST:** Implicit costs are costs of those factors of production which are owned and employed by the firm itself. It includes interest on owner's own capital, cost of the self employed services etc.

According to Leftwich, "Implicit costs are costs of self-owned and self-employed resources".

Therefore Total Money Cost is the sum total of explicit costs and implicit costs.

**(2) REAL COST:** This cost was introduced by the classical economists for the first time. Real cost refers to the all payments made to the factors of production to compensate their mental and physical exertions for producing output.

Thus, REAL COST = Efforts, pains, exertions, sacrifices of Factors of productions like labour, capital and abstinence of Entrepreneurs.

**(3) OPPORTUNITY COST:** Opportunity cost is defined as the cost of producing one output in term of another output foregone. In modern times the concept of opportunity cost occupies an important place in economic theory.

According to Professor Benham, "The opportunity cost of anything is the next best alternative that could be produced instead by the same factors or by an equivalent group of factors, costing the same amount of money".

The opportunity cost can be defined by the following diagram:

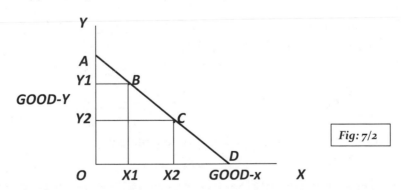

Fig: 7/2

In the above diagram AD line represents different combinations of two goods X and Y those can be produced by the limited resources. Point-B indicates the firm is producing OY1 of good-Y and OX1 of good-X in the economy. Now if the firm wants to produce more of good-X by X1X2 then it has to reduce the production of good-Y by Y1Y2 i.e. it has to sacrifice good-Y by Y1Y2. So opportunity cost of gaining X1X2 is the cost of Y1Y2 which is sacrificed. Thus opportunity cost is defined as the cost of foregone alternatives.

## ▪ Distinction between Explicit cost and implicit cost:

| BASIS | EXPLICIT COST | IMPLICIT COST |
|---|---|---|
| 1. Meaning | It refers to the payments made to the outsiders for their goods and services. | It refers to the cost of self-employed services and self-employed resources. |
| 2. Alternative name | It is known as paid-out costs. | It is known as non-expenditure costs. |
| 3. Entry | It is entered in the books of accounts. | It is not entered in the books of accounts. |
| 4. Examples: | Cost of raw materials, machinery, transportation costs, wages to labour etc. | Rent of owner's own land, interest on owner's own capital etc. |

## ▪ The role of Time element over Cost determination:

Time is very important factor to determine cost of production. The time period is classified into short run and long run. Accordingly there are two types of cost of production like short-run cost and long-run cost of production.

(1) **SHORT-RUN COSTS:** It refers to those costs over a time period in which there are some factors like plant, machinery, land remains fixed. It is sum total of fixed cost and variable cost incurred by a firm to produce output.

(2) **LONG-RUN COSTS:** It refers to those costs over a time period in which all factors are variable and no factor remains fixed. Firm can adjust its supply according to required demand.

## ▪ SHAPE OF TOTAL COST:

The shape of Total Cost Curve depends upon the cost functions. There are three types of cost functions like linear cost function, quadratic and cubic cost function. Out of these three the first two i.e., linear and quadratic cost functions are most commonly used to depict the cost curve.

## 1. LINEAR COST CURVE:

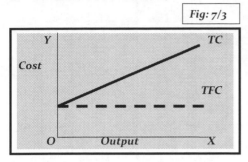

Fig: 7/3

If a firm has fixed cost 'a' which does not depend upon output level, And uses variable factors like labour, raw material of cost of 'b', then in order to produce x units of output, Total Cost (TC) = a + b x; AC = a/x + b; AFC = a/x; AVC = b; And MC = $\frac{d(TC)}{dx}$ = b

## 2. QUADRATIC COST CURVE:

This curve represents (a) diminishing return or increasing cost and (b) increasing return or diminishing cost:

(a) Diminishing return or increasing cost: In this case Total Cost,

(C) = a + b x + c x²; where 'a' is fixed cost, b x variable cost of labour, raw material at first, and c x² is also variable cost when demand for variable factors increases due to increase in the level of output. Here TC increases at increasing rate.

(b) Increasing return or decreasing cost: In this case Total Cost,

(C) = a + b x - c x²; where 'a' is fixed cost, b x variable cost of labour, raw material at first, and c x² is also variable cost. Here TC increases at decreasing rate.

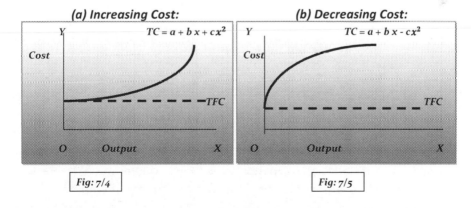

Fig: 7/4    Fig: 7/5

3. **CUBIC COST CURVE:** In this case Total Cost (C) = a + b x - c X²+ d X³; This curve has two bends. This curve at first shows increasing return (or decreasing cost) and after the first bend it shows decreasing return (increasing cost).

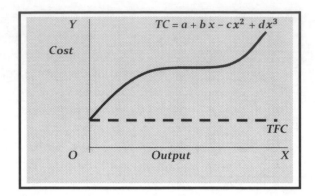

$$TC = a + bx - cx^2 + dx^3$$

Fig: 7/6

## ■ Different variants of Total Cost or Money Cost in short-run:

There are three different variants of Total cost which are as follows:
TOTAL COST, AVERAGE COST AND MARGINAL COST.

**(1) TOTAL COST:** It refers to the total amount of money spent on the production of different levels of output.

According to Dooley, "Total cost of production is the sum of all expenditure incurred in producing a given volume of output".

In short-run Total cost has two parts: Total Fixed Cost and Total Variable Cost. Thus, TC = TFC + TVC; where TC is total cost, TFC is total fixed cost and TVC is total variable cost.

**(i) TOTAL FIXED COST:** It refers to the expenditure incurred by a firm to purchase or hire the services of fixed factors of production.

According to Anatol Murad, "Fixed costs are costs which do not change with change in the quantity of output".

Fixed costs includes the expenditure on rent, depreciation, interest on fixed capital, license fees, normal profit, wages to permanent employees, etc.

These costs are also known as supplementary costs or overhead costs or indirect costs. Fixed cost is shown by the following table and diagram:

| OUTPUT | 0 | 1 | 2 | 3 | 4 | 5 | 6 |
|---|---|---|---|---|---|---|---|
| TFC (Rs.) | 10 | 10 | 10 | 10 | 10 | 10 | 10 |

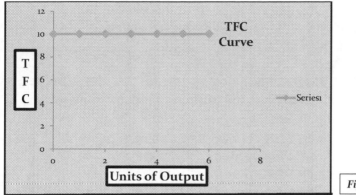

Fig: 7/7

From the above table and diagram it is clear that even if the production of output increases total fixed cost remains fixed. It does not change.

### (ii) TOTAL VARIABLE COST:

Variable costs are those costs which vary with the change in the level of production of output.

According to Dooley, "Variable cost is one which varies as the level of output varies". At zero level of output variable cost is zero. These costs are also called prime costs or direct costs. It includes expenses on raw materials, wages of labour, electricity charges, wear and tear expenses etc. Variable cost can be shown by the following table and diagram.

| OUTPUT | 0 | 1 | 2 | 3 | 4 | 5 | 6 | 7 |
|--------|---|---|---|---|---|---|---|---|
| TVC (Rs.) | 0 | 10 | 18 | 24 | 28 | 32 | 38 | 46 |

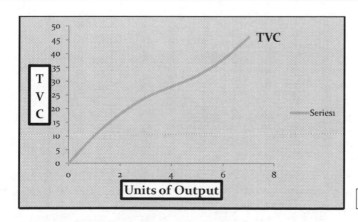

Fig: 7/8

181

From the above table and diagram it is clear that as the production of output increases the variable cost increases. Variable cost becomes zero at zero level of output.

(2) **AVERAGE COST:** Average cost is defined as the cost per unit of production of output. It is the total cost divided by the number of units produced. AC = TC/Q

There are three types of average costs namely

Average total cost, average fixed cost and average variable cost.

(a) **AVERAGE FIXED COST:** It is defined as the fixed cost per unit of production of output. It is calculated by dividing the total fixed cost by the number of units of output.

Symbolically, AFC = TFC/Q

AFC can be shown by the following table and diagram:

| OUTPUT | 0 | 1 | 2 | 3 | 4 | 5 | 6 |
|---|---|---|---|---|---|---|---|
| TFC (Rs.) | 60 | 60 | 60 | 60 | 60 | 60 | 60 |
| AFC (Rs.) | ∞ | 60 | 30 | 20 | 15 | 12 | 10 |

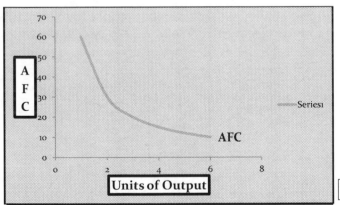

Fig: 7/9

From the above table and diagram it is clear that as the fixed cost is constant at 60, therefore AFC continuously decreases as the production of output increases. But it never becomes zero because TFC never becomes zero. AFC starts from the infinity because at zero level of output TFC is not zero and AFC = TFC/Q, so AFC becomes infinity. Ultimately AFC is rectangular hyperbola which means the area of all rectangles under the AFC becomes equal. AFC is asymptotic to both the axes.

(b) **AVERAGE VARIABLE COST:** It is obtained by dividing total variable cost by the number of units of output.

Symbolically, AVC = TVC/Q;

The AVC curve falls at first up to a certain point and then it starts to rise. Ultimately it takes the shape of English letter 'U' as shown in the following table and diagram.

| OUTPUT | 1 | 2 | 3 | 4 | 5 | 6 | 7 |
|---|---|---|---|---|---|---|---|
| TVC (Rs.) | 20 | 36 | 45 | 56 | 70 | 90 | 140 |
| AVC (Rs.) | 20 | 18 | 15 | 14 | 14 | 15 | 20 |

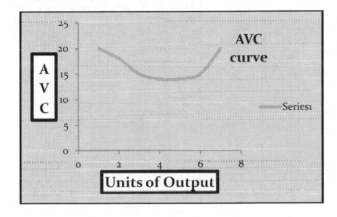

*Fig: 7/10*

From the above table and diagram it is clear that at first AVC decreases, reaches to a minimum then it increases and finally it takes "U" shape.

(c) **AVERAGE TOTAL COST OR AVERAGE COST**: It is defined as the overall cost per unit of output. It is calculated by dividing total cost by the number of units output.

Symbolically, AC = TC/Q;

It is also written as AC = AFC + AVC;

At first AC falls with increase in output up to a certain point, then after reaching its minimum point it starts to increase with the increase in output. AC curve finally takes the shape of English letter "U" but wider than AVC curve. This can be shown by the following table and diagram.

| Output | 1 | 2 | 3 | 4 | 5 | 6 | 7 | 8 |
|---|---|---|---|---|---|---|---|---|
| AC | 18 | 14 | 10 | 11 | 13 | 17 | 20 | 24 |
| AFC | 8 | 5 | 3.3 | 2.5 | 2 | 1.7 | 1.4 | 1.2 |
| AVC | 10 | 9 | 6.7 | 8.5 | 11 | 15.3 | 18.6 | 22.8 |

Table. 7/1

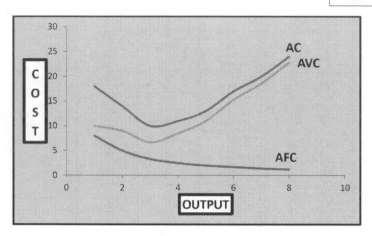

From the above table and diagram it is clear that AC at first diminishes, reaches to its minimum and then it increases with the increase in output.

(3) **MARGINAL COST:** Marginal cost is defined as the addition to total cost caused by producing one more unit of output.

According to Ferguson, "Marginal cost is the addition to the total cost due to the addition of one unit of output.

Symbolically, MC = TCn – TCn-1

Or, MC = $\frac{\Delta TC}{\Delta Q}$; or, MC = = $\frac{\Delta TVC}{\Delta Q}$

This can be explained by the following table and diagram:

| OUTPUT | 0 | 1 | 2 | 3 | 4 | 5 | 6 |
|---|---|---|---|---|---|---|---|
| TC (Rs.) | 40 | 120 | 170 | 180 | 210 | 260 | 340 |
| MC (Rs.) | _ | 80 | 50 | 10 | 30 | 50 | 80 |

Table. 7/2

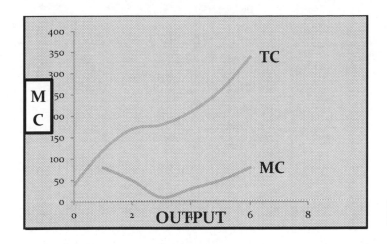

Fig: 7/12

From the above table and diagram it is clear that MC first decreases up to a certain point, then it starts to increase with the increase in output. It is caused by the change in the variable cost.

## ▪ Distinction between Total Fixed Cost and Total Variable Cost:

| BASIS | TOTAL FIXED COST | TOTAL VARIABLE COST |
|---|---|---|
| 1. Meaning | 1. These are the cost of fixed factors. | 1. These are the cost of variable factors. |
| 2. Relation with level of output | 2. These costs are not dependent on the level of output and they remain fixed. | 2. These are dependent on the level of output and they change with the change in level of output. |
| 3. Time period | 3. These are related to short-period. | 3. These are related to long-period. |
| 4. At zero level of output | 4. These costs remain constant even at zero level of output. | 4. These costs are zero at zero level of output. |
| 5. Examples | 5. Examples: salaries of permanent staff, license fees, insurance, cost of plants, machines etc. | 5. Examples: cost of raw materials, electricity, transport charges etc. |

| 6. Diagram | 6. 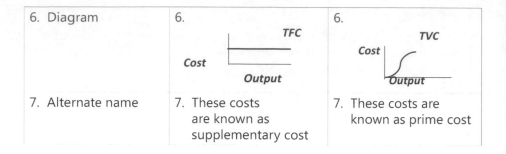 | 6. |
|---|---|---|
| 7. Alternate name | 7. These costs are known as supplementary cost | 7. These costs are known as prime cost |

## ▪ Why short-run average cost curve is "U" shaped?

In short-run average cost curve is "U" shaped. This means at first it decreases up to a certain level then reaching its minimum point, it starts to increase.

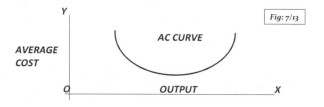

Fig: 7/13

**The reasons for the "U" shape are as follows:**

(i) **BASIS OF AFC AND AVC:** In short-run AC is the summation of AFC and AVC. Therefore the shape of AC depends on the shape of AFC and AVC curves. AFC curve continuously decreases as the production of output increases. On the other hand the AVC at first decreases up to a certain level of output then after that it starts increasing. Therefore the combined shape and behaviour give the shape of AC curve "U"(wider than the AVC curve) shape in short-run.

(ii) **BASIS OF LAW OF VARIABLE PROPORTION:** AC curve is also "U" shaped in short-run because of law of variable proportion. According to this law at first average cost decreases with the increase in output because of law of increasing returns and AC curve reaches to its minimum. After reaching minimum point average cost increases due to law of diminishing returns.

### (iii) AC IS RECIPROCAL IMAGE OF AVERAGE PRODUCTIVITY CURVE:

AC of Labour = TC/Q
Now, ACL = (PL x QL)/Q [Here only labour is assumed variable Factor]
Or, ACL = PL ÷ (Q/QL)
Or, ACL = PL ÷ APL [APL is average productivity of labour, = Q/QL]
Or, ACL = PL/APL; [ACL is average cost of labour]

Since PL is constant, therefore the shape of AC is the reciprocal image of AP (Average Productivity) curve. As production increases AP curve first rises reaches to its maximum and then it falls. Conversely AC curve at first falls, reaches to its minimum then it starts to increase and finally AC curve becomes "U" shaped.

### (IV) INDIVISIBILITIES OF THE FACTOR:

The indivisibilities of factors of production is also another cause for the short-run "U" shaped AC curve. In short-run when the firm raises its production then due to indivisibilities of some fixed factors of production the firm enjoys some internal economies like managerial economies, technical economies, marketing economies etc. As a result AC decreases and reaches to its minimum point. After that due to some diseconomies of scale the AC curve starts to increase and finally AC curve becomes "U" shaped.

## ▪ The relation between MC, AC, and AVC:

The relationship between AC, AVC, and MC can be explained by the following way.

AC = TC/Q; AVC = TVC/Q; MC = TCn—TCn-1
    Or, MC = TVCn—TVCn-1

The relation becomes clear by the following diagram.

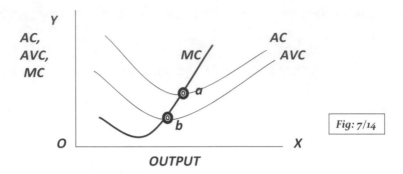

Fig: 7/14

From the above diagram we get the following relationship:

**(A)    AC and MC:**

(1)  As long as MC is less than AC, AC decreases.
(2)  When AC = MC then AC is minimum as shown by the point a.
(3)  When MC is more than AC, then AC increases (beyond point a).

**(B) AVC and MC:**

(4)  AS long as MC is less than AVC, AVC decreases.
(5)  When AVC = MC then AVC is minimum as shown by the point b.
(6)  When MC is more than AVC, then AVC increases (beyond point b).

## ▪ THE RELATION BETWEEN AC AND MC CURVE CAN ALSO BE EXPLAINED BY USING SIMPLE CALCULAS:

Let, C (total cost) = zQ and z = AC and AC = f(X)

Now, $MC = \dfrac{\delta C}{\delta X} = \dfrac{\delta(zQ)}{\delta X}$

By using rule of product differentiation, we have

$$MC = z.\dfrac{\delta Q}{\delta X} + Q.\dfrac{\delta z}{\delta X}$$

Or, MC = AC + Q. (slope of AC);  [Here $\dfrac{\delta Q}{\delta X} = 1$]

If AC > 0 and Q > 0 then we have the following relationship:

- If slope of AC > 0, then MC > AC.
- If slope of AC < 0, then MC < AC.
- If slope of AC = 0, them MC = AC.

NOTE: slope of AC = 0, at the minimum point of AC curve.

## ▪ The relationship between Marginal Cost and Average Cost concept can also be explained in the following way (without calculus):

1. **When AC falls:** Then AC in (n+1) time period is less than AC in nth time period.

   Then, $AC_{n+1} < AC_n$;

   This means, $\dfrac{TC_{n+1}}{n+1} < \dfrac{TC_n}{n}$

   Multiplying both sides by (n+1) we get,

   $TC_{n+1} < \dfrac{TC_n}{n} \times (n+1)$

   Or, $TC_{n+1} < TC_n \times \left(\dfrac{n+1}{n}\right)$

   Or, $TC_{n+1} < TC_n \times \left(\dfrac{n}{n} + \dfrac{1}{n}\right)$

   Or, $TC_{n+1} < TC_n \times \left(1 + \dfrac{1}{n}\right)$

   Or, $TC_{n+1} < TC_n + \dfrac{TC_n}{n}$

   Or, $TC_{n+1} - TC_n < \dfrac{TC_n}{n}$;   Therefore, $MC_n < AC_n$

2. **When AC rises,** Then AC in (n+1) time period is more than AC in nth time period.

Then, $AC_{n+1} > AC_n$

This means, $\frac{TC_{n+1}}{n+1} > \frac{TC_n}{n}$

Multiplying both sides by (n+1) we get,

$TC_{n+1} > \frac{TC_n}{n} \times (n+1)$

Or, $TC_{n+1} > TC_n \times (\frac{n+1}{n})$

Or, $TC_{n+1} > TC_n \times (\frac{n}{n} + \frac{1}{n})$

Or, $TC_{n+1} > TC_n \times (1 + \frac{1}{n})$

Or, $TC_{n+1} > TC_n + \frac{TC_n}{n}$

Or, $TC_{n+1} - TC_n > \frac{TC_n}{n}$;   Therefore, $MC_n > AC_n$ ;

3. **When AC is constant,** Then AC in (n+1) time period is equal to AC in nth time period.

Then, $AC_{n+1} = AC_n$

This means, $\frac{TC_{n+1}}{n+1} = \frac{TC_n}{n}$

Multiplying both sides by (n+1) we get,

$TC_{n+1} = \frac{TC_n}{n} \times (n+1)$

Or, $TC_{n+1} = TC_n \times (\frac{n+1}{n})$

Or, $TC_{n+1} = TC_n \times (\frac{n}{n} + \frac{1}{n})$

Or, $TC_{n+1} = TC_n \times (1 + \frac{1}{n})$

Or, $TC_{n+1} = TC_n + \frac{TC_n}{n}$

Or, $TC_{n+1} - TC_n = \frac{TC_n}{n}$;   Therefore, $MC_n = AC_n$ ;

## ▪ The relation between TVC and MC curves:

$$MC_n = TVC_n - TVC_{n-1}$$

The relationship between MC and TVC will be clear by the following diagram:

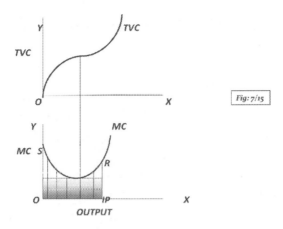

Fig: 7/15

From the above diagram we get the following relationship:

(i) MC is the slope of the TVC at each point of TVC curve whereas TVC is the sum total of MC.

(ii) TVC is an inverse of S-shape but MC is U-shaped.

(iii) When TVC rises at a diminishing rate, then MC decreases.

(iv) When TVC rises at an increasing rate, then MC increases.

(v) Graphically TVC is equal to the area covered under the MC curve. At OP level of output, TVC is equal to the area of OPRS as shown in the above diagram.

## ▪ The relation between TC and MC curves:

MC is the calculated by the difference between TC of two successive units of output.

$$MC_n = TC_n - TC_{n-1}$$

The other relations are as follows:

(i) When TC increases at diminishing rate, then MC decreases.
(ii) When the rate of increase in TC stops diminishing, then MC becomes minimum.
(iii) When TC increases at increasing rate, then MC increases.

## ■ The relation between TC, TVC and TFC:

Total Cost refers to the total monetary expenditure incurred by a firm to produce output. It is the sum of Total Fixed Cost and Total Variable Cost i.e. TC = TFC + TVC.

Total Fixed Cost remains fixed at all level of output, whether the production increases or decreases or becomes zero.

Total Variable Cost increases with the increase in output and decreases with decrease in output and it becomes zero at zero level of output. The relation can be explained by the following table and diagram.

| OUTPUT | TFC | TVC | TC |
|--------|-----|-----|-----|
| 0 | 10 | 0 | 10 |
| 1 | 10 | 10 | 20 |
| 2 | 10 | 18 | 28 |
| 3 | 10 | 24 | 34 |
| 4 | 10 | 30 | 40 |

Table. 7/3

From the above table it is clear that TFC remains fixed at 10 whether production increases, decreases or becomes zero.

Whereas TVC increases as production increases and TVC becomes zero at zero level of output. TC is the sum of TFC and TVC at each level of output.

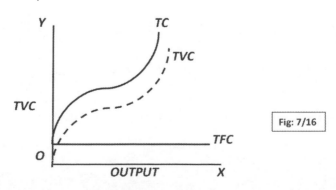

Fig: 7/16

192

From the above diagram it is clear that TVC curve starts from the origin i.e. zero and TFC starts from the vertical axis and parallel to horizontal axis. TC curve starts from the origin of TFC curve i.e. from the vertical axis because at zero level of output, TC = TFC. The gap between TC and TVC indicates the magnitude of TFC.

## ▪ Why is MC curve 'U' shaped?

Marginal cost refers to the changes in the total cost or total variable cost due to one more unit of production of output.

$$\text{Symbolically, } MC_n = TC_n - TC_{n-1}$$
$$\text{Or, } MC_n = TVC_n - TVC_{n-1}$$

MC curve at first decreases because at first TC and TVC increase at diminishing rate and the firm enjoy certain economies.

MC reaches to its minimum point when the rate of increase in TC and TVC becomes minimum.

After reaching to its minimum point, MC curve starts to increase because TC and TVC increase at increasing rate and the firm faces certain diseconomies. Ultimately the shape of the MC curve becomes 'U' shaped as shown in the following diagram.

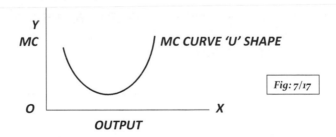

## ▪ The long run cost curves.

In long run all factors are variable and there is no fixed factor. In long run each firm decides its output level with an aim either to maximize profit or to minimize losses by selecting the size of short-run plant. Long run total cost is always either less than or equal to the short-run total cost. We can write as, LTC ≤ STC.

According to Leibhafasky, "The long-run total cost of production (LTC) is the least possible cost of producing any given level of output when all inputs are variable".

The long-run total cost curve starts from the point of origin because all factors are variable. It is shown in the following diagram:

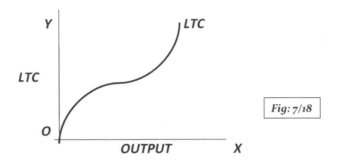

Fig: 7/18

From the above diagram it is clear that LTC curve starts from the origin and increases as the output level increases.

There are two important costs in long-run namely which are as follows:

(i)  LONG-RUN AVERAGE COST (LAC).
(ii)  LONG-RUN MARGINAL COST (LMC).

## ▪ Explain the LAC and LMC and state the relation between LAC and LMC with the help of a diagram.

➤  **LONG-RUN AVRAGE COST:**

LAC refers to the minimum possible cost per unit of producing each level of output in the long period.

According to J. S. Bain, "The long-run average cost curve shows for each possible output, the lowest cost of producing that output in the long-run".

The LAC curve is also known as the 'Envelope' curve because it envelopes all short-run average cost curves. It is also 'U' shaped as shown in the following diagram.

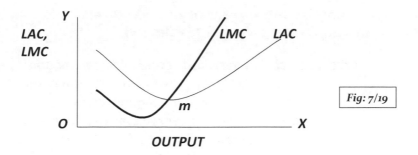

From the above diagram it is clear that LAC is 'U' shaped but wider than SAC curve.

## ➤ LONG-RUN MARGINAL COST (LMC):

Long-run marginal cost is defined as the change in Total Cost due to one more unit of production of output.

According to Robert Awh, "Long-run marginal cost curve is that which shows the extra cost incurred in producing one more unit of output when all inputs can be changed".

It is clear from the above diagram that LMC is also 'U' shaped. LAC and LMC are "U" shaped because at first due to economies of scale the LAC and LMC decreases and reaches to their minimum points. LMC reaches earlier to LAC. After reaching their minimum points LAC and LMC increase due to diseconomies of scale.

## ➤ RELATIONSHIP BETWEEN LAC AND LMC:

From the above diagram the relationship can be written as follows:

(a)  When LMC is less than LAC, then LAC decreases.
(b)  When LAC = LMC, then LAC is minimum.
(c)  When LMC is more than LAC, then LAC rises.

## ▪ But according to modern theory of economics the Long-run Average Cost is 'L' shaped.

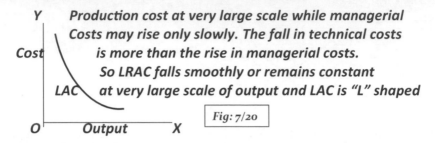

*Production cost at very large scale while managerial Costs may rise only slowly. The fall in technical costs is more than the rise in managerial costs. So LRAC falls smoothly or remains constant at very large scale of output and LAC is "L" shaped*

Fig: 7/20

## ▪ Do you think that Fixed cost has any impact on Marginal cost?

No, Fixed cost has no impact on MC because MC is the addition to Total Variable Cost due to one more unit of production of output whereas the FC remains fixed at each level of output. This is shown by the following:

$MC = TC_n - TC_{n-1}$
$= (TFC_n + TVC_n) - (TFC_{n-1} + TVC_{n-1})$
$= TFC_n - TFC_{n-1} + TVC_n - TVC_{n-1}$
$= TVC_n - TVC_{n-1}$ (since $TFC_n = TFC_{n-1}$)
So TFC has no impact on MC.

## ▪ GRAPHICAL DERIVATION OF AFC FROM TFC:

TFC curve remains fixed at each level of output in short-run. AFC = TFC/Q. The graphical derivation of AFC curve from TFC curve can be explained by the following diagram.

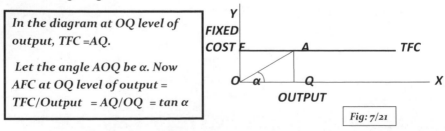

*In the diagram at OQ level of output, TFC = AQ.*

*Let the angle AOQ be α. Now AFC at OQ level of output = TFC/Output = AQ/OQ = tan α*

Fig: 7/21

# GRAPHICAL DERIVATION OF AVC FROM TVC:

TVC increases with the increase of output in short-run. AVC = TVC/Q. The graphical derivation of AVC curve from TVC curve can be explained by the following diagram.

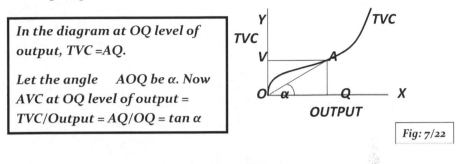

In the diagram at OQ level of output, TVC = AQ.

Let the angle AOQ be α. Now AVC at OQ level of output = TVC/Output = AQ/OQ = tan α

Fig: 7/22

# SHORT-RUN SUPPLY CURVE OF A PERFECTLY COMPETITIVE FIRM:

According to shut-down point, a firm will continue its production as long as P ≥ AVC

If the MC increases then the price of output will increase because the equilibrium price is determined at higher level and it will encourage the firm to sell more. If price is below OP1 then the seller will not sell output. This can be explained by the following diagram.

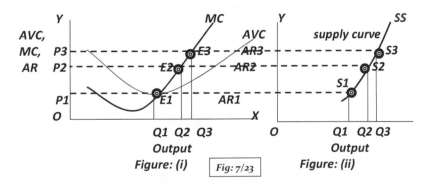

Figure: (i)    Fig: 7/23    Figure: (ii)

In figure (i) at equilibrium point E1, equilibrium price is OP1 and equilibrium output is OQ1. When price rises from OP1 to OP2, and finally to OP3, then the equilibrium output also increases from OQ1 to OQ2 and finally to OQ3.

If we join the price-output combinations like S1, S2 and S3 as shown in figure (ii) then we get the supply curve which shows positive relation between price and output.

Short-run supply curve of a perfectly competitive industry can be drawn by the horizontal summation of supply curves of individual firms.

## ▪ Technological progress and firm's supply curve:

A cost saving technology shows that the firm requires lesser quantity of output to produce the same level of output. As a result MC falls and the MC curve shifts to the right from MC1 to MC2 as shown in the following figure.

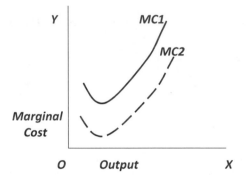

## ▪ Imposition of a unit Tax and supply curve:

A unit tax means that a firm has to pay the amount of tax on each unit of an output that he produces. As a result, the per unit cost of output increases and the MC curve shifts to the left from MC1 to MC2 as shown in the following figure.

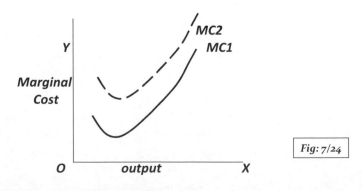

Fig: 7/24

## Why does MC curve intersect AC curve at its minimum point?

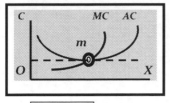

Fig: 7/25

The minimum point of AC curve means at this point AC is constant. This is possible only when MC = AC as shown by point m in the figure.

At point m, if we draw a tangent which shows AC is parallel to the OX axis. It is possible only when AC = MC.

MC will be equal to AC when they intersect each other.

Therefore, MC intersects AC curve only at its minimum point i.e., point 'm'. At point 'm' slope of the tangent to the AC curve is zero i.e. $\frac{d(AC)}{dx} = 0$ (1st order is equal to zero) and at 'm' $\frac{d^2(AC)}{dx^2} > 0$ (2nd order derivative is greater than zero). So only at 'm' AC is minimum. Either to the left or to the right of 'm' AC is not equal to MC.

❖ Why long-run cost curves are flatter than short-run cost curves?

It is because in long-run a firm can adjust its production of output by any number of plants in which cost will be minimized or it can shift its production from one scale to another scale, which is not possible in short-run.

## NUMERICAL:

### Q.1. Calculate (a) TFC, (b) TVC, (c) MC, (d) AC, (e) AFC and (f) AVC from the following cost function.

| OUTPUT | 0 | 1 | 2 | 3 | 4 | 5 | 6 |
|--------|-----|-----|-----|-----|-----|-----|-----|
| TC (Rs.) | 60 | 90 | 100 | 105 | 115 | 135 | 160 |

| OUTPUT | TC | TFC | TVC | MC | AC | AFC | AVC |
|--------|-----|-----|-----|-----|-------|-----|-------|
| 0 | 60 | 60 | 0 | - | ∞ | ∞ | - |
| 1 | 90 | 60 | 30 | 30 | 90 | 60 | 30 |
| 2 | 100 | 60 | 40 | 10 | 50 | 30 | 20 |
| 3 | 105 | 60 | 45 | 5 | 35 | 20 | 15 |
| 4 | 115 | 60 | 55 | 10 | 28.75 | 15 | 13.75 |
| 5 | 135 | 60 | 75 | 20 | 27 | 12 | 15 |
| 6 | 160 | 60 | 100 | 25 | 26.66 | 10 | 16.66 |

Some steps to remember:

I.    At zero level of output, TFC = TC; So TFC = 60 and it remains fixed for all levels of output i.e. at all levels TFC = 60.

II.   TVC is calculated by the difference of TC and TFC, i.e. TVC = TC − TFC.

III.  MC is calculated by the formula, MC = TVCn − TVCn-1.

IV.  AC = TC/Q, AFC = TFC/Q and AVC = TVC/Q.

## Q.2. Calculate MC from the following table.

| OUTPUT | 1 | 2 | 3 | 4 | 5 | 6 |
|---|---|---|---|---|---|---|
| AVC (Rs.) | 30 | 22 | 18 | 15 | 17 | 20 |

| OUTPUT | AVC | TVC = AVC x Q | MC = TVCn − TVCN-1 |
|---|---|---|---|
| 1 | 30 | 30 | 30 |
| 2 | 22 | 44 | 14 |
| 3 | 18 | 54 | 10 |
| 4 | 15 | 60 | 6 |
| 5 | 17 | 85 | 25 |
| 6 | 20 | 120 | 35 |

## Q.3. The following table shows the MC at different level of output by a firm. Calculate AC and AVC when Average Fixed Cost at 2nd level of output is given as Rs. 60.

| OUTPUT | 1 | 2 | 3 |
|---|---|---|---|
| MC (Rs.) | 30 | 15 | 10 |

Ans. Here AFC at 2nd level of output is given as 60

So, TFC = 2 x 60 = 120 and we know that TFC never changes.

| OUTPUT | MC | TFC | TVC | TC | AC | AVC |
|---|---|---|---|---|---|---|
| 0 | - | 60 | 0 | 60 | ∞ | - |
| 1 | 30 | 60 | 30 | 90 | 90 | 30 |
| 2 | 15 | 60 | 45 | 105 | 52.5 | 22.5 |
| 3 | 10 | 60 | 55 | 115 | 38.3 | 18.3 |

**Q.4. Total fixed cost of a firm is given as Rs. 100. Its MC at different level of output is given in the following table. Calculate AVC and TC at each level of output.**

| OUTPUT | 1 | 2 | 3 | 4 |
|---|---|---|---|---|
| MC | 40 | 30 | 35 | 39 |

Ans.

| OUTPUT | MC | TFC | TVC | TC | AVC |
|---|---|---|---|---|---|
| 0 | - | 100 | 0 | 100 | - |
| 1 | 40 | 100 | 40 | 140 | 40 |
| 2 | 30 | 100 | 70 | 170 | 35 |
| 3 | 35 | 100 | 105 | 205 | 35 |
| 4 | 39 | 100 | 111 | 211 | 36 |

**Q.5. Calculate TC and AVC from the following table of cost of production at each given level of output.**

| OUTPUT | 1 | 2 | 3 | 4 | 5 |
|---|---|---|---|---|---|
| AFC | 60 | 30 | 20 | 15 | 12 |
| MC | 32 | 30 | 28 | 30 | 35 |

| OUTPUT | AFC | MC | TFC | TVC | TC | AVC |
|---|---|---|---|---|---|---|
| 0 | ∞ | - | 60 | 0 | 60 | - |
| 1 | 60 | 32 | 60 | 32 | 92 | 32 |
| 2 | 30 | 30 | 60 | 62 | 122 | 31 |
| 3 | 20 | 28 | 60 | 90 | 150 | 30 |
| 4 | 15 | 30 | 60 | 120 | 180 | 30 |
| 5 | 12 | 35 | 60 | 155 | 215 | 31 |

—*—*—*—*—*—*—*—*—*—*—*—*—

# IMPORTANT QUESTIONS:

## 1 MARK QUESTIONS:

1. What is meant by cost of production?
2. Define opportunity cost.
3. Define explicit cost.
4. Define implicit cost.
5. What is meant by fixed cost?
6. Define variable cost.
7. What happens to AC when MC > AC?
8. What happens to AVC when MC > AVC?
9. What is the shape of AFC?
10. What do AC, AVC and MC curves look like in short-run?

## 3 or 4 MARK QUSTIONS:

1. Distinguish between explicit cost and implicit cost.
2. Distinguish between variable cost (prime cost) and fixed cost (supplementary cost).
3. Why is AFC curve rectangular hyperbola?
4. Why is AC curve 'U' shaped in short-run?
5. Why is MC curve 'U' shaped in short-run?
6. Explain the relationship between MC and AC with the help of a schedule and diagram.
7. Explain the relationship between MC and AVC with the help of a schedule and diagram.
8. Can MC rise when AC falls?
9. Classify the following into fixed cost and variable cost:

a) Sales tax; b) Excise duty; c) Salary to permanent workers; d) Transport cost; e) Minimum telephone bill; f) Payment of telephone bill beyond minimum telephone bill; g) License fee

10. Can AC be less than the MC when AC is rising? Answer with reason.

## 6 MARK QUESTIONS:

1. Explain the shape of MC, AC and AVC curves in short run with their causes.
2. Explain the relationship between ATC, AVC and MC with the help of a schedule and diagram.
3. Numerical:

___*___*___*___*___*___*___*___*___*___*___*___*___*___*___

# Chapter - 8

## Concepts Of Revenue:

### • Concept of Revenue and its different types:

Revenue is defined as money receipts from the sale of output by a firm.

According to Dooley, "The revenue of a firm is its sales receipts or money receipts from the sale of a product".

There are three different concepts of Revenue like Total Revenue, Average Revenue and Marginal Revenue.

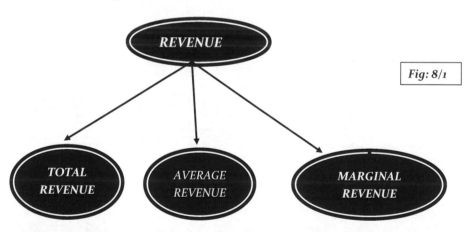

Fig: 8/1

(1) **TOTAL REVENUE:** Total revenue refers to the total amount of money or payments received by a firm from the sale of its products.

According to Dooley, "Total revenue is the sum of all sales, receipts or income of a firm". This means TR = P x Q

Or, TR = $\sum$ MR

**(2) AVERAGE REVENUE:** Average revenue refers to the revenue per unit of sale of a product obtained by a firm.

According to Holland, "Average revenue is the ratio of the total revenue to the quantity sold of the product".

Thus, AR = TR/Q = (P x Q)/Q = P.

**(3) MARGINAL REVENUE:** Marginal revenue refers to the change in the total revenue of a firm resulting from the sale of an extra unit of output.

According to Ferguson, "Marginal revenue is the change in the total revenue which results from the sale of one more or less unit of output".

$$MR = TR_n - TR_{n-1}$$

Or, $MR = \dfrac{\Delta TR}{\Delta Q}$;

## ▪ The relationship between TR, AR and MR under the Perfect competition market:

Under Perfect competition market all the firms are price takers and they are compelled to sell their product fixed by the industry. In this market price remains constant whatever quantities of output the firms sell in the market. Therefore Total Revenue increases at constant rate and AR becomes equal to MR. This can be explained by the following table and diagram:

| OUTPUT | AR = PRICE (Rs.) | TR (Rs.) | MR (Rs.) |
|--------|------------------|----------|----------|
| 1 | 10 | 10 | 10 |
| 2 | 10 | 20 | 10 |
| 3 | 10 | 30 | 10 |
| 4 | 10 | 40 | 10 |
| 5 | 10 | 50 | 10 |

Table. 8/1

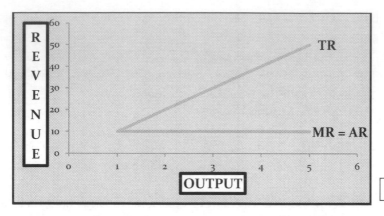

Fig: 8/2

From the above table and diagram we get the following relationship:

(i) AR and MR both remain constant in this perfect competition market. So Price = AR = MR and the curve is parallel to horizontal axis.

(ii) As the production of output increases TR increases at the constant rate.

(iii) TR starts from the origin (at zero level of output) and slopes positively from left to right upward.

## ▪ The relationship between TR, AR and MR under imperfect competition market:

Under imperfect competition market i.e. monopoly or monopolistic competition market goods are sold at different prices. In the imperfect competition market the firms can sell more output by reducing price. Therefore AR and MR will decrease as the sale of output increases. The relationship can be explained by the following table and diagram:

| OUTPUT | PRICE (Rs.) | TR (Rs.) | MR (Rs.) | AR (Rs.) |
|---|---|---|---|---|
| 1 | 6 | 6 | 6 | 6 |
| 2 | 5 | 10 | 4 | 5 |
| 3 | 4 | 12 | 2 | 4 |
| 4 | 3 | 12 | 0 | 3 |
| 5 | 2 | 10 | -2 | 2 |
| 6 | 1 | 6 | -4 | 1 |

Table. 8/2

From the above table it is clear that more output is sold by the firm by reducing price.

From the above table we get the following relationship:

(i) When AR and MR both decrease, then TR increases at increasing rate.

(ii) When MR = 0, then TR is maximum.

(iii) When MR is negative, then TR starts decreasing.

(iv) MR can be positive, can be zero or negative but AR always remain positive.

(v) When MR and AR decreases then MR < AR.

This relationship can also be explained by the following diagram:

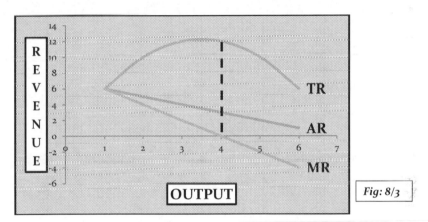

Fig: 8/3

From the above diagram we get the following relationship:

(i) When AR and MR both decrease, then TR increases at increasing rate.

(ii) When MR = 0, then TR is maximum at 4th unit of output.

(iii) When MR is negative, then TR starts decreasing beyond 4th level of output.

(iv) MR can be positive, can be zero or negative but AR always remain positive.

(v) When both MR and AR decreases then MR < AR.

## ▪ The relationship between Marginal revenue and Average revenue concept can also be explained in the following way:

1. **When AR decreases:**

   Then AR in (n+1) time period is less than AR in nth time period.

   Then, $AR_{n+1} < AR_n$;

   This means, $\dfrac{TR_{n+1}}{n+1} < \dfrac{TR_n}{n}$

   Multiplying both sides by (n+1) we get,

   $TR_{n+1} < \dfrac{TR_n}{n} \times (n+1)$

   Or, $TR_{n+1} < TR_n \times \left(\dfrac{n+1}{n}\right)$

   Or, $TR_{n+1} < TR_n \times \left(\dfrac{n}{n} + \dfrac{1}{n}\right)$

   Or, $TR_{n+1} < TR_n \times \left(1 + \dfrac{1}{n}\right)$

   Or, $TR_{n+1} < TR_n + \dfrac{TR_n}{n}$

   Or, $TR_{n+1} - TR_n < \dfrac{TR_n}{n}$;

   Therefore, $MR_n < AR_n$

2. **When AR increases:**

   Then AR in (n+1) time period is more than AR in nth time period.

   Then, $AR_{n+1} > AR_n$;

   This means, $\dfrac{TR_{n+1}}{n+1} > \dfrac{TR_n}{n}$

   Multiplying both sides by (n+1) we get,

   $TR_{n+1} > \dfrac{TR_n}{n} \times (n+1)$

   Or, $TR_{n+1} > TR_n \times \left(\dfrac{n+1}{n}\right)$

   Or, $TR_{n+1} > TR_n \times \left(\dfrac{n}{n} + \dfrac{1}{n}\right)$

   Or, $TR_{n+1} > TR_n \times \left(1 + \dfrac{1}{n}\right)$

   Or, $TR_{n+1} > TR_n + \dfrac{TR_n}{n}$

   Or, $TR_{n+1} - TR_n > \dfrac{TR_n}{n}$;

   Therefore, $MR_n > AR_n$

### 3. When AR is constant,

Then AR in (n+1) time period is equal to AR in nth time period.

Then, $AR_{n+1} = AR_n$;

This means, $\dfrac{TR_{n+1}}{n+1} = \dfrac{TR_n}{n}$

Multiplying both sides by (n+1) we get,

$TR_{n+1} = \dfrac{TR_n}{n} \times (n+1)$

Or, $TR_{n+1} = TR_n \times (\dfrac{n+1}{n})$

Or, $TR_{n+1} = TR_n \times (\dfrac{n}{n} + \dfrac{1}{n})$

Or, $TR_{n+1} = TR_n \times (1 + \dfrac{1}{n})$

Or, $TR_{n+1} = TR_n + \dfrac{TR_n}{n}$

Or, $TR_{n+1} - TR_n = \dfrac{TR_n}{n}$ ;

Therefore, $MR_n = AR_n$

**The shape of AR and MR curves under different market conditions:**

## (A) SHAPE OF AR and MR CURVES UNDER PERFECT COMPETITION MARKET:

Perfect competition is a market situation in which there are large number of sellers and buyers and the product is homogeneous.

In this market the firms are price taker and the industry is price maker. The firms can not influence the price of product. Therefore in this market AR = MR = Price and the revenue curves are perfectly elastic i.e. parallel to horizontal axis.

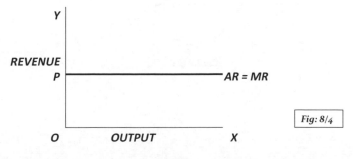

Fig: 8/4

## (B) SHAPE OF AR and MR CURVES UNDER MONOPOLY MARKET:

Monopoly market is a situation in which there is only one seller and product has no close substitute.

In this market the single firm or the industry is price maker. The firm can sell more by reducing price. The firm can either control the price or the quantity of output but not both at the same time. The AR and MR curves are less elastic and MR < AR, as shown in the following diagram:

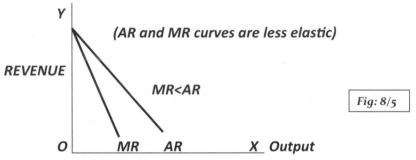

Fig: 8/5

## (C) SHAPE OF AR and MR CURVES UNDER MONOPOLISTIC COMPETITION MARKET:

This market refers to a market situation in which there is large number of sellers (but less than perfect competition) and product is differentiated.

In this market the firms can sell more by reducing price. The firms have not full control over the price of product. In this market the revenue curves are more elastic and MR < AR as shown in the following figure:

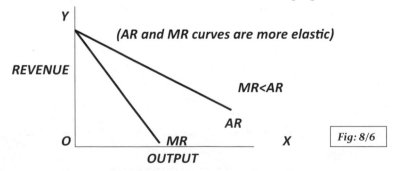

Fig: 8/6

## The relationship between TR and MR:

### (1) TOTAL REVENUE:

Total revenue refers to the total amount of money or payments received by a firm from the sale of its products.

This means TR = P x Q

Or, TR = $\sum$ MR

### (2) MARGINAL REVENUE:

Marginal revenue refers to the change in the total revenue of a firm resulting from the sale of an extra unit of output.

MR = TRn – TRn-1

Or, MR = $\dfrac{\Delta TR}{\Delta Q}$ ;

The relationship between TR and MR can be explained by the following diagram.

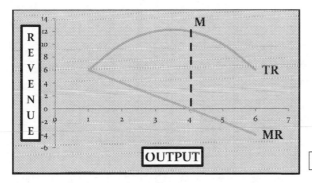

Fig: 8/7

From the above diagram and from the Table No. 8/2, we get the following relationship.

(i) When MR is positive and decreases (up to 3$^{rd}$ level of output), TR increases at a diminishing rate.

(ii) When MR = 0 at 4$^{th}$ level of output, then TR is maximum (point M in the above diagram).

(iii) When MR is negative (5$^{th}$ level of output onwards), then TR starts decreasing.

(iv) When TR increases at constant rate then MR is constant.

## ▪ The relationship between AR and MR when a firm is able to sell more quantity of output

    (i)  At the same price.

    (ii)  Only by lowering price.

### (i) At the same price:

At the same price means the price is constant. The price does not change. Since price is constant the Average Revenue (AR) is also constant. This implies the Marginal Revenue (MR) is equal to Average Revenue. This can be explained by the following table and diagram.

| PRICE (Rs.) | OUTPUT | TR=P.Q | $MR = \frac{\Delta R}{\Delta Q}$ | AR = PRICE |
|:---:|:---:|:---:|:---:|:---:|
| 5 | 1 | 5 | 5 | 5 |
| 5 | 2 | 10 | 5 | 5 |
| 5 | 3 | 15 | 5 | 5 |

*Table. 8/3*

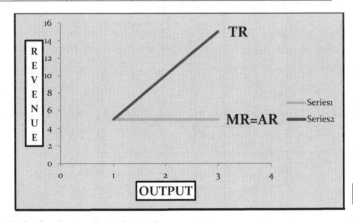

*Fig: 8/8*

### (ii) Only by lowering the price:

    If by lowering the price of a product more products can be sold then the Average Revenue (AR) will decrease. AR decreases only when the Marginal Revenue (MR) is less than Average Revenue (AR). Thus, when a firm increases sales by reducing the price of the product then AR will decrease and MR < AR. This is shown by the following table and diagram.

| PRICE (Rs.) | OUTPUT | TR=P.Q | $MR=\frac{\Delta R}{\Delta Q}$ | AR = PRICE | MR<AR |
|:---:|:---:|:---:|:---:|:---:|:---:|
| 6 | 1 | 6 | 6 | 6 | |
| 5 | 2 | 10 | 4 | 5 | MR < AR |
| 4 | 3 | 12 | 2 | 4 | MR < AR |
| 3 | 4 | 12 | 0 | 3 | MR < AR |
| 2 | 5 | 10 | -2 | 2 | MR < AR |
| 1 | 6 | 6 | -4 | 1 | MR < AR |

Table. 8/4

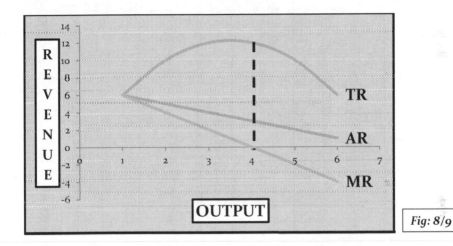

Fig: 8/9

NOTE: To draw downward sloping AR and MR curve in the same diagram, students must remember when MR touches OX axis (i.e. MR = 0), then the line drawn from that point (MR = 0) to the AR (point k) must indicate price elasticity of demand = 1.

The upper part of AR curve shows Price elasticity of demand is more than one and the lower part of AR curve shows price elasticity of demand is less than one.

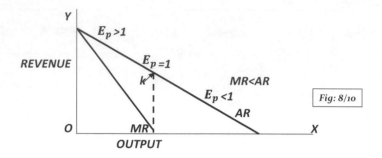

Fig: 8/10

The above relationship is obtained from the following relationship.

$$e_p = \frac{AR}{AR - MR}$$ ; where $e_p$ price elasticity of demand and AR is average revenue and MR is marginal revenue.

(a) If $e_p = 1$, MR = 0
(b) If $e_p > 1$, MR is positive
(c) If $e_p < 1$, MR is negative.

NOTE: To draw downward sloping AR and MR curve in the same diagram, students must remember that MR curve lies half-way from the AR curve and vertical axis.

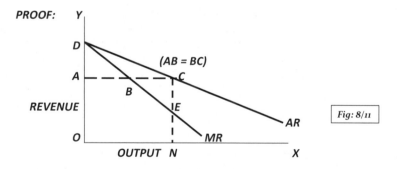

Fig: 8/11

In the above diagram, from Δ ABD and Δ BCE,

We have, < ECB = < BAD (both are right angles)
< CBE = < ABD (vertically opposite)
And < ADB = < CEB (alternate angles)

Therefore, Δ ABD and Δ BCE are similar triangles.

So, AB = BC

It means MR curve lies half way from the AR curve and the vertical axis i.e., AB = BC.

## NUMERICAL EXAMPLES:

### 1. Calculate TR, MR and AR from the following table:

| PRICE (Rs.) | 7 | 6 | 5 | 4 | 3 | 2 | 1 |
|---|---|---|---|---|---|---|---|
| OUTPUT | 1 | 2 | 3 | 4 | 5 | 6 | 7 |

Ans.

| PRICE (Rs.) | OUTPUT | TR=P.Q | MR=$\frac{\Delta R}{\Delta Q}$ | AR = PRICE |
|---|---|---|---|---|
| 7 | 1 | 7 | 7 | 7 |
| 6 | 2 | 12 | 5 | 6 |
| 5 | 3 | 15 | 3 | 5 |
| 4 | 4 | 16 | 1 | 4 |
| 3 | 5 | 15 | -1 | 3 |
| 2 | 6 | 12 | -3 | 2 |
| 1 | 7 | 7 | -5 | 1 |

Table. 8/5

### 2. Calculate TR, MR and AR from the following table when each unit of a good is sold at Rs. 6.

| PRICE | 7 | 6 | 5 | 4 | 3 | 2 | 1 |
|---|---|---|---|---|---|---|---|
| OUTPUT | 1 | 2 | 3 | 4 | 5 | 6 | 7 |

Since each unit is sold at Rs. 6, then this means price is constant. This is possible only in perfect competition market.

| PRICE (Rs.) | OUTPUT | TR=P.Q | MR=$\frac{\Delta R}{\Delta Q}$ | AR = PRICE |
|---|---|---|---|---|
| 6 | 1 | 6 | 6 | 6 |
| 6 | 2 | 12 | 6 | 6 |
| 6 | 3 | 18 | 6 | 6 |
| 6 | 4 | 24 | 6 | 6 |
| 6 | 5 | 30 | 6 | 6 |
| 6 | 6 | 36 | 6 | 6 |
| 6 | 7 | 42 | 6 | 6 |

Table. 8/6

## Q.3. Calculate TR and MR from the following table.

| Units of Output | TR (Rs.) | MR (Rs.) | AR (Rs.) |
|:---:|:---:|:---:|:---:|
| 1 | — | — | 10 |
| 2 | — | — | 10 |
| 3 | — | — | 10 |
| 4 | — | — | 10 |

## Q.5. Complete the following table:

| Units of output | TR (Rs.) | AR (Rs.) | MR (Rs.) |
|:---:|:---:|:---:|:---:|
| 1 | 10 | — | — |
| 2 | — | 9 | 8 |
| 3 | 24 | — | — |
| 4 | — | 7 | 4 |
| 5 | 30 | 6 | — |
| 6 | — | — | 0 |
| 7 | — | 4 | — |

Table. 8/7

—*—*—*—*—*—*—*—*—*—*—*—*—

# IMPORTANT QUESTIONS:

1. What is meant by revenue?
2. Define total revenue.
3. Define marginal revenue.
4. What is meant by average revenue?
5. How do we get TR from MR?
6. How do we get MR from TR?
7. What happens to TR when MR is equal to zero?
8. What is the shape of MR and AR curve under perfect competition market?
8. What happens to MR when TR increases at increasing rate?
9. What happens to MR when TR increases at diminishing rate?

1. Explain the relationship between TR and MR with the help of a schedule and diagram.
2. How can you show the relationship between MR and AR?
3. Explain the shape of revenue curves under perfect competition market?
4. Why is the TR curve under perfectly competitive market a straight line passing through the origin?
5. Explain the MR and AR curves under monopoly market.
6. How can you compare the AR and MR curves under monopoly and monopolistic competition market?

## 6 MARK QUESTIONS:

1. How can you explain the relationship between TR, AR and MR with the help of a hypothetical schedule and diagram?
2. Calculate TR, AR and MR from the following revenue schedule

| Price (Rs.) | 8 | 7 | 6 | 5 | 4 | 3 | 2 | 1 |
|---|---|---|---|---|---|---|---|---|
| Quantity demanded | 1 | 2 | 3 | 4 | 5 | 6 | 7 | 8 |

3. From the above table explain the relationship between TR and MR by using diagram.

__*__*__*__*__*__*__*__*__*__*__*__*__*__

# Chapter - 9

## Producer's Equilibrium:

### Who is called a Producer?

A producer is an economic agent whose main aim is to maximize profit. Generally it refers to a firm which produces goods and services with an aim to maximize profit. Profit is the difference between total revenue earned by a firm and total cost incurred by a firm. i.e. Profit = Total Revenue – Total Cost.

### What is meant by producer's equilibrium?

A producer is said to be in equilibrium when it produces that level of output at which profit is maximized and it has no tendency to change its level of output.

### Different approaches of Producer's Equilibrium:

There are two approaches of producer's equilibrium namely:

(a) Total Revenue-Total Cost approach and
(b) Marginal Revenue-Marginal Cost approach.

## • TR-TC approach of Producer's Equilibrium when price is decreasing: Or TR-TC approach under imperfect competition market.

A rational producer will expand output if he thinks he can increase his profits by doing so or he can contract output if he thinks he can avoid losses. He will be in equilibrium position at that level of output at which his money profits are maximum and he has no tendency to change the level of output.

➤ **Conditions of equilibrium under TR-TC approach:**

    (i)   The vertical distance between Total Revenue and Total Cost is maximum.
    (ii)  TR and TC have the same slope.

Producer's equilibrium with TR-TC approach can be explained by the following diagram:

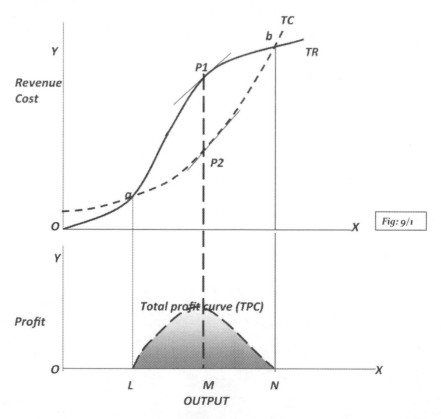

Fig: 9/1

In the above diagram the points a and b present the break even points because at these points Total Revenue and Total Cost both are equal and the firm enjoys only normal profit.

The profit area is presented by the area aP1bP2 covered by the TR and TC curves. The maximum profit is obtained at OM level of output where the vertical distance between TR and TC is greatest. Any level of output less than OM level but more than OL level yield the firm less profit than at OM level. Similarly any level of output more than OM level but less than ON level of output will yield the firm less profit than at OM level. So the firm maximizes profit only at OM level of output (shown by the Total Profit curve-TPC in the second diagram), where both the TR and TC curves have same slope. So at this OM level of output the firm is in equilibrium and OM is called equilibrium output.

**LIMITATION:** It is very difficult to find out the vertical distance between TR and TC because we have to draw many tangents before to reach the equilibrium point.

## • TR-TC approach of producer's equilibrium under Perfect competition market:

A rational producer will expand output if he thinks he can increase his profits by doing so or he can contract output if he thinks he can avoid losses. He will be in equilibrium position at that level of output at which his money profits are maximum and he has no tendency to change the level of output.

➢ **Conditions of equilibrium under TR-TC approach:**

(i)   The vertical distance between Total Revenue and Total Cost is maximum.
(ii)  TR and TC have the same slope.

Producer's equilibrium in the prefect competition market, with TR-TC approach can be explained by the following diagram:

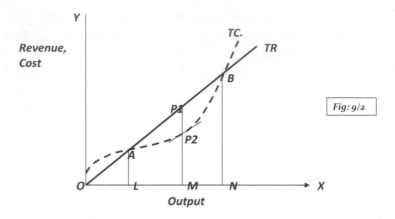

Fig: 9/2

In the above diagram the points A and B present the break even points because at these points Total Revenue and Total Cost both are equal and the firm enjoys only normal profit.

In this market since the price is given and constant and the firms have no role to influence the price, so Price = AR = MR. Therefore TR starts from the origin slopes positively upwards and increases at constant rate.

The profit area is presented by the area AP1BP2 covered by the TR and TC curves. The maximum profit is obtained at OM level of output where the vertical distance between TR and TC is greatest. Any level of output less than OM level but more than OL level yield the firm less profit than at OM level. Similarly any level of output more than OM level but less than ON level of output will yield the firm less profit than at OM level.

So the firm maximizes profit only at OM level of output where both the TR and TC curves have same slope. So at this OM level of output the firm is in equilibrium and OM is called equilibrium output.

## ▪ MR-MC approach of producer's equilibrium:

A producer is said to be in equilibrium when it produces that level of output at which profit is maximized and it has no tendency to change its level of output.

The producer's equilibrium can be explained separately under perfect competition market and imperfect competition market in the following way.

# ▪ UNDER PERFECT COPETITION MARKET:

According to this approach under perfect competition market

Where P = AR = MR, the producer will be in equilibrium when the following conditions are satisfied.

(i) MR = MC and
(ii) MC cuts MR from below.

This can be explained by the following diagram.

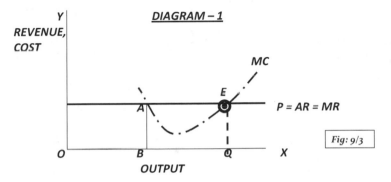

From the above diagram – 1, it is clear that at point A and at point E, MR = MC i.e. first condition is satisfied only. But at point E both the conditions are satisfied. So point E is called the equilibrium point where MR = MC and MC cuts MR from below and OQ is called equilibrium level of output.

# ▪ SHORT-RUN AND CONCEPT OF PROFIT UNDER PERFECT COMPETITION MARKET:

Short-run is that time period in which the firms can change their level of output by changing some variable factors like labour, raw materials etc, whereas other factors remain fixed.

➤ **In short-run the firms face three following situations:**

**(a) Normal Profit:** It is that amount of minimum profit which is required for the firms to remain in the business. In this case the firm's Price = AR =

AC. This is shown by the above diagram 1. Here point E is the equilibrium point where MR = MC and MC cuts MR from below and Price or AR = AC = EQ. So the firm earns only normal profit.

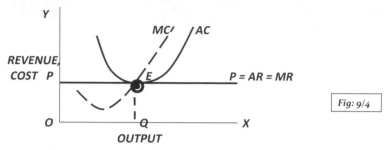

Fig: 9/4

(b) **Supernormal Profit:** It arises when firm's Price or AR > AC. This is shown by the following diagram.

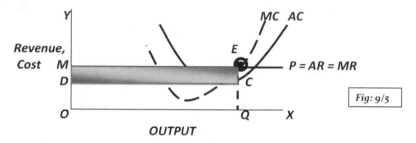

Fig: 9/5

Here point E is the equilibrium point.

And Price = AR = EQ and AC = CQ. Since Price > AC, so the firm earns supernormal profit. Per unit super-normal profit = EQ − CQ = EC. Total super-normal profit area = ECDM area.

(c) **Minimum Losses:** It arises when firm's Price or AR < AC. This is shown in the following diagram.

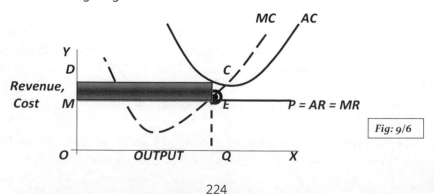

Fig: 9/6

Here point E is the equilibrium point.

And Price = AR = EQ and AC = CQ. Since Price < AC, so the firm suffers losses. Per unit loss = CQ – EQ = CE.

Total minimum losses area = ECDM area.

## ▪ (B) UNDER IMPERFECT COMPETITION MARKET:

According to MR-MC approach under imperfect competition market, where MR is less than AR and downward sloping (more output is sold by reducing price), the producer will be in equilibrium when the following two conditions are satisfied.

(i)   MR = MC and
(ii)  MC cuts MR from below.

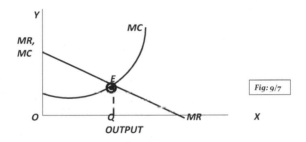

Fig: 9/7

From the above diagram (9/7) it is clear that at point E, MR = MC and MC cuts MR from below. So both the conditions of producer's equilibrium are satisfied. Therefore point E is called producer's equilibrium point and OQ is called equilibrium output. If the firm produces any output more than the OQ level or less output than the OQ level then the firm's profit will not be maximum.

## ▪ Break-even point and shut-down point with the help of diagram:

### ➢ BREAK-EVEN POINT:

In micro economics break-even point is said to occur when either TR = TC or AR = AC.

This can be explained by the following diagrams.

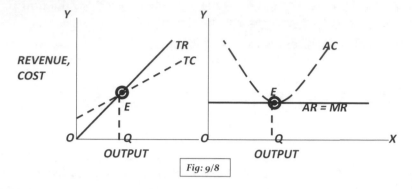

Fig: 9/8

From the above two diagrams it is clear that break-even point occurs at point E where TR =TC or AR = AC and break-even point output is at OQ level of output. At this break-even point the firm earns only normal profit.

## ▪ SHUT-DOWN POINT:

**In short-run,**

Shut-down point occurs when the price is so critically low that a firm is just able to cover its variable cost only, incurring the loss of fixed cost of production. The price line passes through the minimum point of the AVC curve.

In other wards it is a situation when TR = TVC or AR = AVC.

This can be explained by the following diagram.

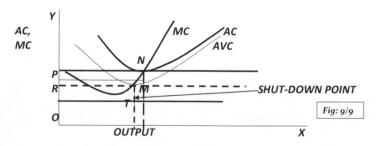

Fig: 9/9

From the above diagram it is clear that the firm is equilibrium at point N, where equilibrium price is OP and this equilibrium Price = AC. If the price falls to OR then the firm's losses becomes RPNM which is equal to Total Fixed

Cost. Although at both the points N and m the firm is at equilibrium. At this point R, Price = AVC.

But if the price falls below OR i.e. less than AVC then the firm discontinues its production for the time being because it fails even to cover the variable cost. Therefore point T is called Shut-down point as shown in the above diagram.

So we can conclude that a firm in short-run can shut-down if the Price falls below the Average Variable Cost i.e. P < AVC or in other words a firm will continue its production if at equilibrium, price is equal or greater than AVC i.e. P ≥ AVC.

In long-run, the shut-down point is the minimum of LRAC curve.

## ▪ Equilibrium of a competitive firm when it is earning only normal profit:

A firm earns normal profit only when AR = AC =MR = MC. At this point the firm sells its output at a price which is equal to minimum Average Cost as shown in the following diagram.

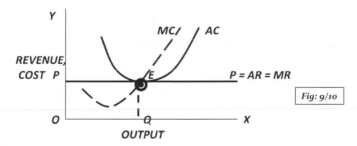

From the above diagram it is clear that the firm is equilibrium at point E, where MR = MC and MC cuts MR from below. So the equilibrium price is OP and equilibrium output is OQ. At this price OP the Average Revenue and Average Cost are equal. So the firm earns only normal profit.

## ▪ What happens to AR when MR is (i) greater than AR, (ii) Equal to AR and (iii) less than AR?

   (i)  when MR is greater than AR, then AR increases.

   (ii)  When MR is equal to AR, then AR is maximum.

   (iii)  When MR is less than AR, then AR decreases.

## Q. State the relation between MR and AR when a firm is

   (i)   Selling more quantity of output at the same price, and
   (ii)  Selling more quantity of output by reducing price.

Ans. (i)  when a firm sells more quantity of output at the same price then the market is perfect competition market. So Price = AR = MR.
   (ii)  When a firm sells more quantity of output by reducing price then the market is imperfect competition market. So MR < AR.

### PROFIT MAXIMISATION CONDITIONS:

For a firm to maximize profit at positive level of output must satisfy following three conditions.

1.  The price of the product is equal to the marginal cost (P = MC).
2.  The marginal cost is non-decreasing.
3.  In short-run, P $\geq$AVC and in Long-run, P $\geq$AC.

## Short-run equilibrium conditions for a firm:

1.  MC must be equal to MR
2.  MC cuts MR from below or MC will be greater than MR after the equilibrium point.
3.  In short-run, P $\geq$AVC

## Why will profits be maximum when MR = MC?

The profit maximizing equilibrium condition can be explained by the following diagram.

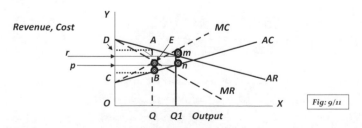

Fig: 9/11

228

In the above diagram point 'E' is the equilibrium point in which MR = MC and MC cuts MR from below. OQ is equilibrium level of output. At this OQ output, Profit per unit = AR – AC =AQ – BQ = AB

And Total Profit area = ABCD. Now the question is whether this profit is maximum or not at the equilibrium level of output?

(a) If the firm produces more output like OQ1, then AR = mQ1 and AC = nQ1. So profit per unit = mQ1 – nQ1= mn
And Total Profit area = mnpr;
Since, from the diagram it is clearly visible, ABCD > mnpr;
Therefore profit is maximum at equilibrium level of output.

(b) On the other hand if the firm produces les than OQ level of output, then MR < MC and profit is less.

Therefore profit is maximum when MR = MC and MC cuts MR from below.

## ▪ Why profit will be maximum when MR = MC?

Mathematically it can be shown by the following:
Profit = TR – TC
By first order derivative with respect to Q (output) and setting equal to zero,
We have $\pi$ = TR – TC

Or, $\dfrac{d\pi}{dQ} = \dfrac{d(TR)}{dQ} - \dfrac{d(TC)}{dQ} = 0$

Or, $\dfrac{d(TR)}{dQ} = \dfrac{d(TC)}{dQ}$

Or, MR = MC.

## NUMERICAL

**Q.1. From the following schedule find out the level of output at which the producer is in equilibrium, using MC and MR approach. Give reasons for your answer.**

| PRICE PER UNIT (Rs.) | OUTPUT (UNITS) | TC (Rs.) |
|:---:|:---:|:---:|
| 8 | 1 | 6 |
| 7 | 2 | 11 |
| 6 | 3 | 15 |
| 5 | 4 | 18 |
| 4 | 5 | 23 |

Ans.

| Price (Rs.) | Output | TC | TR | MR | MC | Profit =TR-TC |
|:---:|:---:|:---:|:---:|:---:|:---:|:---:|
| 8 | 1 | 6 | 8 | — | — | 2 |
| 7 | 2 | 11 | 14 | 6 | 5 | 3 |
| 6 | 3 | 15 | 18 | 4 | 4 | 3 |
| 5 | 4 | 18 | 20 | 2 | 3 | 2 |
| 4 | 5 | 23 | 20 | 0 | 5 | -3 |

*Table. 9/1*

From the above table it is clear that the producer is equilibrium at 6 units of output because at this level of output the profit is maximum and MR = MC.

If the firm produces more output than 6 units then profit decreases. On the other hand if the firm produces less than 6 units of output then profit even remains equal (here at 2 units of output) but it does not satisfy the equilibrium condition i.e. at this point MR is not equal to MC.

**Q.2. From the following schedule find out the level of output at which the producer is in equilibrium, using MC and MR approach. Give reasons for your answer.**

| Output (units) | Price (Rs.) | TC (Rs.) |
|---|---|---|
| 1 | 7 | 7 |
| 2 | 7 | 15 |
| 3 | 7 | 22 |
| 4 | 7 | 28 |
| 5 | 7 | 33 |
| 6 | 7 | 40 |
| 7 | 7 | 48 |

Ans.

| Output (units) | Price (Rs.) | TC (Rs.) | TR | MR | MC | Profit |
|---|---|---|---|---|---|---|
| 1 | 7 | 7 | 7 | 7 | — | 0 |
| 2 | 7 | 15 | 14 | 7 | 8 | -1 |
| 3 | 7 | 22 | 21 | 7 | 7 | -1 |
| 4 | 7 | 28 | 28 | 7 | 6 | 0 |
| 5 | 7 | 33 | 35 | 7 | 5 | 0 |
| 6 | 7 | 40 | 42 | 7 | 7 | 2 |
| 7 | 7 | 48 | 49 | 7 | 8 | 1 |

Table. 9/2

From the above table it is clear that the producer is equilibrium at 6 units of output because at this level of output the profit is maximum and MR = MC.

If the firm produces more output than 6 units then profit decreases. On the other hand if the firm produces less than 6 units of output then also profit decreases.

## Q.3. Complete the following table:

| OUTPUT (Units) | PRICE (Rs.) | TR (Rs.) | MR (Rs.) |
|---|---|---|---|
| 4 | 9 | 36 | — |
| 5 | — | — | 4 |
| 6 | — | 42 | — |
| 7 | 6 | — | — |
| 8 | — | 40 | — |

Ans.

| Output(Units) | Price | TR (Rs.) | MR (Rs.) |
|---|---|---|---|
| 4 | 9 | 36 | — |
| 5 | 8 | 40 | 4 |
| 6 | 7 | 42 | 2 |
| 7 | 6 | 42 | 0 |
| 8 | 5 | 40 | -2 |

*Table. 9/3*

—*—*—*—*—*—*—*—*—*—*—*—*—

# IMPORTANT QUESTIONS:

1. What is meant by producer's equilibrium?
2. State the general profit maximising condition of a producing firm.
3. State the conditions of producer's equilibrium of a firm under perfect competition market.
4. Define normal profit.
5. Define shut-down point.
6. What are the conditions for profit maximisation of a firm in short-run?
7. What are the conditions for profit maximisation of a firm in long-run?

## 3 or 4 MARK QUESTIONS:

1. How can you explain producer's equilibrium with the help of TR and TC approach?
2. Define producer's equilibrium and state its conditions.
3. Explain producer's equilibrium with the help of MR and MC approach under perfect competition market.
4. Explain producer's equilibrium with the help of MR and MC approach under imperfect competition market.
5. Numerical:

## 6 MARK QUESTIONS:

From the above schedule find out the level of output at which the producer is in equilibrium, using MC and MR approach. Give reasons for your answer.

| Output | 1 | 2 | 3 | 4 | 5 | 6 | 7 |
|---|---|---|---|---|---|---|---|
| Price (Rs.) | 6 | 6 | 6 | 6 | 6 | 6 | 6 |
| TC (Rs.) | 7 | 15 | 22 | 28 | 33 | 40 | 48 |

# Chapter - 10

## Forms Of Market:

## Concept of a Market:

In economics, market does not necessarily mean a particular place. It refers to a mechanism that helps to interact between the buyers and sellers to purchase and sell their goods and services.

According to Prof. Edwards, "A market is that mechanism by which buyers and sellers are brought together. It is not necessarily a fixed place".

## The basis of classification of markets:

Markets may be classified as:

**(A) On the basis of area,**
as (i) Local market, (ii) National market and (iii) World market.
**(B) On the basis of time, as market price on a particular day,**
(i) Short-period Price, (ii) Long-period Price and or Secular price.
**(C) On the basis of nature of competition,**
(i) Perfect competition, (ii) Imperfect competition that includes Monopoly, Monopolistic competition and Oligopoly

## The main features of Perfect Competition market.

Perfect competition market is a situation in which there are large number of buyers and sellers and the product is homogeneous.

According to Mrs. Joan Robinson, "Perfect competition prevails when the demand for the output of each producer is perfectly elastic".

Its main features are as follows:

1) **LARGE NUMBER OF BUYERS AND SELLERS**: The number of sellers and number of buyers are very large in this market. Each seller sells so little and each buyer buys so little that no one can influence the price of the product. Each firm is called as price taker or quantity adjuster. The firm's action is controlled from outside by the industry. No buyer can influence the total demand and no firm can influence the total supply in this market.

2) **HOMOGENEOUS PRODUCT**: All the firms in this market produce identical product or homogeneous product. This means the product of each firm is perfectly substitute for any other firm's product. The above two conditions make clear that in this market AR curve of each firm will be horizontal i.e. the firms will be price takers.

3) **FREE ENTRY AND FREE EXIT OF FIRMS:** It means if there is any super normal profit in short-run then in long-run new firm can enter into the market. On the other hand if the existing firms are making losses in the short-run, then in long-run some of them can exit from the market. As a result of 'free entry' the long-run price will cover only long-run average cost and each firm earns only normal profit.

4) **PERFECT KNOWLEDGE:** In this market all buyers, sellers and resources owners have perfect knowledge. No seller can charge higher price and no buyer can buy at lower price the product. Even the resources owners know the respective prices of their factors of production in the market. So there is no exploitation in this market.

5) **PERFECT MOBILITY OF FACTORS OF PRODUCTION:** In this market the factors of production are perfectly mobile. Factors of production are free to seek their employment in any industry wherever they like. Sellers must be able to sell their goods and services wherever the price is highest. And resources must be able to secure employment at their highest prices.

6) **ABSENCE OF TRANSPORT COSTS:** There is no transport cost in this market to prevail the same price. Otherwise if transport cost is incurred then the price cannot remain same through the whole market.

7) **ABSENCE OF SELLING COSTS:** In this market the sellers do not spend any money on advertisement or publicity because the price is uniform and the product is homogeneous.

8) **UNIFORM PRICE:** In this market the price is uniform. No individual firm or buyer can influence the price of the product. Price is determined by the industry and the firms are price takers only. So in this market P = AR =MR and revenue curves are perfectly elastic as shown in the following diagram.

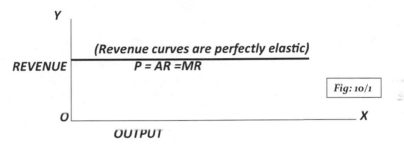

## ▪ Distinction between Perfect competition and Pure competition:

Economists sometimes distinguish between 'Pure' and 'Perfect competition". The distinction is only of degree.

The concept of pure competition is mainly propounded by Prof. Chamberlin. According to him a market which satisfies only the following characteristics is called pure competition.

(a) There are large number of buyers and sellers.
(b) The product is homogeneous.
(c) There is free entry and free exit of firms.

Thus it is clear that 'Pure competition" is a part and parcel of "Perfect competition" and pure competition is more realistic. In addition to the above three conditions "Perfect competition market" satisfies some other characteristics which are as follows:

(i) Perfect knowledge of buyers and sellers regarding the market conditions.
(ii) Perfect mobility of factors of production.

(iii) There is absence of transport cost.

(iv) There is absence of selling costs.

## • Under Perfect competition market the firms are price takers and industry is price maker:

Perfect competition market is a market situation in which there are large number of buyers and sellers and the product is homogeneous.

The number of sellers and number of buyers are very large in this market. Each seller sells so little and each buyer buys so little that no one can influence the price of the product. Each firm is called as price taker or quantity adjuster. The firm's action is controlled from outside by the industry. No buyer can influence the total demand and no firm can influence the total supply in this market.

The price of the product is determined jointly by the market demand and market supply forces. This is shown in the following diagram.

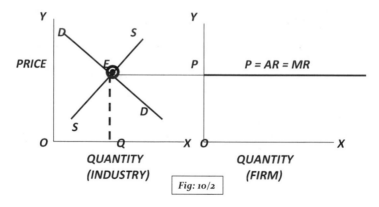

Fig: 10/2

In the above diagram the price of the product is determined by the interaction of market demand and market supply curves and each firm is compelled to sell their product at this price. Since no firm can influence the price of the product and price is fixed, so the price = AR = MR in this market. This price is called equilibrium price.

In this market the firms have no independent pricing policy because there are large numbers of firms and the product is homogeneous and there is no restriction on the entry and exit of the firms in this market.

## ▪ Monopoly market and its important features:

Monopoly market is a market situation in which there is only one seller and the product has no close substitute.

According to Koutsoyiannis, "Monopoly is a market situation in which there is a single seller, there are no close substitutes for commodity it produces, and there are barriers to entry".

Main Features of MONOPOLY market:

1) **SINGLE SELLER AND LARGE NUMBER OF BUYRS:** In this market there is only one seller of the product and he has full control over the supply of the product. In this market there is no difference between a firm and an industry. There is large number of buyers but less than the Perfect competition market.

2) **NO CLOSE SUBSTITUTES:** Pure monopoly has no substitute but simple monopoly market has no close substitute of his products. In this market the product is unique and its cross elasticity of demand is zero.

3) **RESTRICTIONS OF NEW FIRMS:** In this market there are some restrictions for the entry of new firms which are due to following reasons:

   (i) Legal rights for the production of the output exclusively by the monopolist.
   (ii) Natural barrier over the supply of raw materials.
   (iii) Economies of large scale of production.

4) **PRICE MAKER:** In this market since the monopolist is the only seller therefore it has full control over the price of the product. The monopolist is price maker. The monopolist can either control the price or the quantity of product at a time but he cannot control both the price and quantity at a time.

5) **PRICE DISCRIMINATION:** Since the monopolist is a single seller therefore he can charge different price from different consumers for the same product which is known as price discrimination. Price discrimination depends on elasticity of demand. If elasticity of demand is high then he

charges low price and if the elasticity of demand is less then he charges higher price of the product.

Price discrimination is of different types like

(a) Personal price discrimination,
(b) Use wise price discrimination,
(c) Geographical price discrimination.

6) **DOWNWARD SLOPING DEMAND CURVE:** The demand curve in the monopoly market is downward sloping. It means he can sell more of a product by reducing price. If his aim is profit maximization then he can sell less quantity of product at higher price. In this market MR is less than AR and they are less elastic as shown in the following figure.

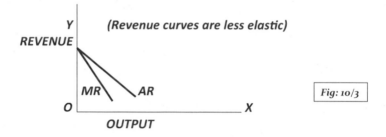

Fig: 10/3

## ▪ Reasons for arising Monopoly market:

Monopoly market structure may arise due to any of the following reasons:

1) **PATENT RIGHT:** When a firm introduces new product or new technology then it applies to the Government to obtain patent certificate by which it gets exclusive right over the new product and/or new technology. No firm can produce the same product or can use that technology for which they have no patent right. So in this way firm can enjoy monopoly right.

2) **LICENSING BY THE GOVERNMENT:** A monopoly market emerges when Government gives a firm license, i.e., exclusive legal right to produce a product or service in a particular area for particular time period. For example Railway services in India.

3) **FORMING A CARTEL:** Sometimes some firms unite and form a group and control their pricing and output decisions in such a way as to get the benefits of monopoly. Such a group formation is called 'Cartel'.

4) **NATURAL MONOPOLY RIGHT:** Sometimes a firm enjoys monopoly right as a natural phenomenon. For example, if a firm has the ownership of spring of water in an island. Then he has full control over the price of spring water i.e. he enjoys monopoly market.

## • Monopolistic competition market and its important features:

Monopolistic competition market is a market situation in which there is large number of sellers and buyers and the product is differentiated.

According to J. S. Bain, "Monopolistic competition is found in the industry where there are a large number of small sellers, selling differentiated but close substitute products".

Actually perfect competition market and monopoly market are extreme market situations. In reality the market which is easily available that is monopolistic competition. For example, firms producing Lux, Liril, Dove, soaps or firms producing Tata tea, Lipton tea or Brook Bond tea or firms producing Colgate, Close up or Pepsodent tooth paste are examples of monopolistic competition market.

Main Features of MONOPOLISTIC COMPETITION market are as follows:

1) **LARGE NUMBER OF BUYERS AND SELLERS:** Like perfect competition market, in this market also there are large numbers of sellers and buyers (less than perfect competition). But the size of each seller is very small so it has limited control over the price of product.

2) **PRODUCT DIFFERENTIATION:** It is the most important feature that the product of each firm is different from others due to its size, colour, quality, shape, outlook etc. Product of one firm is close substitute to the product of other firms. For example tooth pastes of Colgate, Close-up, and Pepsodent etc. are the examples of product differentiation in monopolistic competition market.

3) **FREEDOM OF ENTRY AND EXIT OF FIRMS:** Like perfect competition market, there is not absolutely freedom for the firms to enter into this market because of legal patent right. Any new firm if attracted by the supernormal profit in this market can enter into the market but it is not allowed to produce the same product which is already patented.

4) **SELLING COST:** Each firm spends a lot of money on the advertisement and publicity of its product in newspaper, cinemas, radio, television etc., in order to promote the sales of its product. All these expenses are termed as selling cost.

5) **INDEPENDENT PRICE POLICY:** In this market each firm has its own independent price policy in order to maximize profit. If a firm wants to sell more, then it has to reduce its own price. So AR and MR curves downward slope from left to right.

6) **LIMITED MOBILITY**: In this market the factors of production and goods and services are less than perfectly mobile because the producer charges transport costs and marginal productivity of each factor is not equal.

7) **IMPERFECT KNOWLEDGE**: Buyers and sellers in this market have imperfect knowledge because they fail to compare the price of one product with another due to product differentiation. Similarly the owners of factors of production are ignorant about the price of their services paid by other firms.

8) **NATURE OF DEMAND CURVE:** In this market a slight fall in the price of the product attracts more consumers because the product has close substitute. So the demand curve is more elastic and downward sloping and MR < AR.

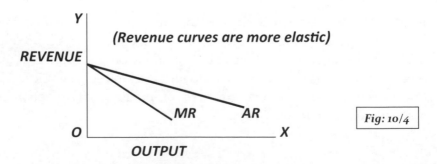

Fig: 10/4

9) **NON-PRICE COMPETITION:** In this market each firm competes with each other not through the price of the product but due to some sales promotion activities like free gift with the main product. Such activities are known as non-price competition. Its main aim is to increase the sales of the product and to maximize profit.

❖ Price and equilibrium determination under monopoly market:

Price and equilibrium output can be determined with respect to time period into the (a) Short Period and (b) Long Period:

Short-period: It is that time period in which some factors like machineries, plant remain fixed and other factors are variable.

Long Period: It is that time period in which all factors are variable and no factors remain fixed.

A monopolist in short-run faces three situations like

(i) Super-normal profit, (ii) Normal profit and (iii) Minimum losses.

(i) **Super-normal Profit**: A monopolist earns super-normal profit when price at equilibrium is more than Average Cost (P > AC).

In the following diagram, E is equilibrium point, OQ is equilibrium level of output, AR = AQ and AC = BQ; Since, AR > AC, the firm earns Super-normal profit of AB per unit. And Total Supernormal profit area = ABCD

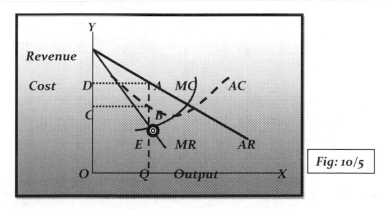

Fig: 10/5

(ii) **Normal Profit:** A monopolist earns normal profit when P = AC. This is shown by the following diagram.

In the diagram, E is equilibrium point (MR = MC), OQ is equilibrium level of output, AR = AQ and AC = AQ. Since, AR = AC, the firm earns only normal profit.

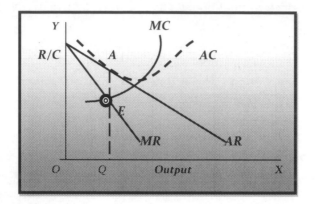

Fig: 10/6

**(iii) Minimum losses:** A monopolist suffers losses when P < AC. This is shown by the following diagram.

In the diagram, E is equilibrium point (MR = MC), OQ is equilibrium level of output, AR = BQ and AC = AQ. Since, AR < AC, the firm suffers losses AB per unit. And Total losses area = ABCD

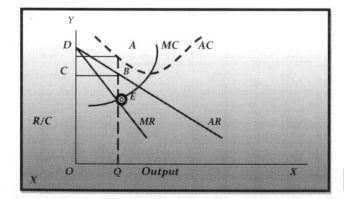

Fig: 10/7

## ▪ Oligopoly market and its main features:

Oligopoly market is a market situation in which there are a few big firms produce goods which are either homogeneous (like steel and fertilizers) or differentiated (like cars, scooters etc.).

Oligopoly markets range from a minimum of two firms (Duopoly market) to a few firms.

Oligopoly markets are generally of two types:

  (i)   Non-collusive Oligopoly market and
  (ii)  Collusive Oligopoly markets.

**(i)  Non-collusive Oligopoly market:** Non-collusive Oligopoly market refers to that market in which each firm competes with other and they do not come to any agreement regarding their product and pricing and distribution of product policy.

**(ii) Collusive Oligopoly market:** Collusive Oligopoly market refers to that market in which rival firms agree to create a centralized agency to fix the price, output and area of distribution and marketing on the basis of mutual agreement. This is called as cartel.
OPEC is a good example of cartel.

Main Features of Oligopoly Market are as follows:

**1)  A FEW FIRMS:** There is a few firms, but large in size and they dominate the market with substantial share of output.

**2)  NATURE OF PRODUCT:** The nature of product is either homogeneous or differentiated.

**3)  MUTUAL INTERDEPENDENCE:** This is an important feature of this market. Since the market is dominated by a few firms, therefore price and output decisions of one firm will affect the other firms and any decision can only be taken after deep consideration of the possible reaction of the rival firms in the market. Since decision making is closely connected with price-output policies, therefore any firm in Oligopoly market cannot act independently.

**4)  INDETERMINATE DEMAND CURVE:** In this market demand curve cannot be determined due to high degree of interdependency among different firms. Therefore it is not possible to predict change in price. When a firm reduces price to earn extra profit then the other firms also reduce the price of their product, as a result the first firm does not obtain the expected profit. So there is no clear existence of a single demand curve.

5) **PRICE RIGIDITY:** In Oligopoly market each firm reacts unexpectedly and immediately to the change in the price made by other firm. Therefore no firm takes the initiative to change the price of its product. So the price remains rigid and it is not flexible.

6) **SELLING COST:** In Oligopoly market selling cost plays a very important role to increase the sales of a particular firm's product. In this market advertising can become a life-and-death matter where a firm which fails to keep up with advertising budget of its rival firm, may find that the customers are switching over the rival firm's product. Therefore all firms in this market spend a large amount of money for advertisement of product.

7) **CONCEPT OF CARTEL:** With a view to avoid competition in oligopoly market, firms may form a cartel. It means some firms may form a group and jointly decide the price, production and marketing of their products so that joint profit becomes maximum compared to individual profit. It is a situation of collusive oligopoly market. Its example is that firms producing oil jointly form a group called OPEC (Organization of Petroleum Exporting Countries).

## Why is the demand curve in Oligopoly market not determined?

Since the Oligopoly market is dominated by a few and big firms, therefore price and output decisions of one firm will highly affect the other firms and any decision can only be taken after deep consideration of the possible reaction of the rival firms in the market. Since decision making is closely connected with price-output policies, therefore any firm in Oligopoly market cannot act independently.

In this market demand curve cannot be determined due to high degree of interdependency among different firms. Therefore it is not possible to predict change in price. When a firm reduces price to earn extra profit then the other firms also reduce the price of their product, as a result the first firm does not obtain the expected profit. So there is no clear existence of a single demand curve.

**Why there are only a few firms in Oligopoly market?**

Oligopoly market is a market situation in which there is a few firms, but large in size and they dominate the market with substantial share of output.

Example: automobile industry in India.

However, the number of firms in this market is very limited because of the following reasons:

a) **Large Investment**: In oligopoly market the production of output and its advertisement requires a large amount of investment. Therefore the firms which are not able to afford such huge investment cannot enter in to the market.

b) **Patent right**: In this market the firms are well established by their patent rights of their product which raise the bar for the new firms to enter the market.

c) **Cartel**: In this market the firms enjoy monopoly rights by forming cartel which keeps the new firms out of the market.

## ▪ Distinction between Perfect Competition and Imperfect competition market:

| BASIS | PERFECT COMPETITION | IMPERFECT COMPETITION |
|---|---|---|
| 1. Meaning: | It refers to a market in which there are a large number of sellers and buyers. | It refers to a market in which there are large number of sellers and buyers but less than the perfect competition. |
| 2. Nature of product: | Product is homogeneous. | Product may be homogeneous or may be differentiated. |
| 3. AR and MR curves. | AR = MR at each level of output. | MR < AR and both slope downwards. |

| | PERFECT COMPETITION | IMPERFECT COMPETITION |
|---|---|---|
| | | |

| 4. Utilization Capacity: | Factors of production are fully utilised to their full capacity. | Factors of production are not fully utilised to their full capacity. |
|---|---|---|
| 5. Selling cost. | Selling cost is not required. | Selling cost helps to increase the sales of product. |

## ■ Comparison of four markets i.e. perfect competition, monopoly, monopolistic competition and oligopoly market.

| BASIS | PERFECT COMPETITION | MONOPOLY MARKET | MONOPOLISTIC MARKET | OLIGOPOLY MARKET |
|---|---|---|---|---|
| 1. No. of sellers and buyers. | Large number of sellers and buyers. | One seller but large number of buyers, less than perfect competition | Large number of sellers and buyers but less than perfect competition. | Few but giant sellers and large number of buyers. |
| 2. Nature of product. | Homogeneous | Homogeneous or differentiated | Differentiated | Homogeneous or differentiated |
| 3. Price | Uniform | Not uniform because of price discrimination. | Not uniform because of product differentiation. | Undetermined. |
| 4. selling cost | Not required | Not significant | Very important | Very important |
| 5. Demand curve | Perfectly elastic | Less elastic | More elastic | Indeterminate. |
| 6. Revenue curves | $P = AR = MR$ | $MR < AR$ | $MR < AR$ | Indeterminate. |
| 7. Control over Price | Firm has no control over price of product. | Monopolist has full control over price of product. | Firm has partial control over price of product. | Depends upon particular model. |
| 8. Entry and exit of firms | Free entry and exit of the firms. | Very restricted of entry and exit. | Not absolutely free. | Restricted of entry and exit. |
| 9. Nature of Profit | Normal profit because $AR = AC$ | Super normal profit because $AR > AC$ | Normal profit because $AR = AC$ | Super normal profit because $AR > AC$. |

## ■ How can you explain that a firm under Perfect competition market in long run always earns normal profit?

Perfect competition market is a situation in which there are large number of buyers and sellers and the product is homogeneous.

According to Mrs. Joan Robinson, "Perfect competition prevails when the demand for the output of each producer is perfectly elastic".

In short-run a firm in perfect competition market can earn either normal profit or super normal profit or face minimum losses. This market has some important features like free entry and exit, homogeneous product, uniform price and the buyers and sellers both have perfect knowledge regarding the market.

Therefore if there is any super normal profit in short-run, then new firms can be attracted by this and they will enter into the market. As a result supply of product will increase and the price will decrease until Price = AC. If Price = AC, then the firm will earn only normal profit.

On the other hand if there is a loss in short-run, then some firms can exit the market. As a result supply of product will decrease until Price = AC. If Price = AC, then the firm will earn only normal profit.

SO in the long-run finally a firm under Perfect competition market always earns only normal profit.

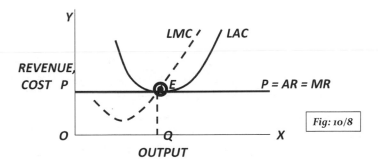

Fig: 10/8

In the above diagram at equilibrium, AR=AC=EQ or OP which indicates that firms in long-run earn only normal profit.

# ▪ IMPLICATIONS OF CERTAIN FEATURES OF PERFECT COMPETITION MARKET:

## 1. Large number of buyers and sellers:

(i) In this market 'large number of sellers' does not specify any number. It refers to number of sellers is too large that a single seller's share in the total market supply of the goods is trivial.

(ii) Trivial or immaterial share means that if any one firm increases or decreases its supply of goods then the existing market price remains unaffected.

(iii) The market price in this market is determined by the interaction of market demand and market supply forces. No individual firm can influence the price.

(iv) Each individual seller has to accept this price determined by the industry. For this reason each firm is called as price taker and industry is price maker.

(v) Similarly 'large number of buyers' has the same implication. Any single buyer's share in total market demand is so trivial that he cannot influence the market price of his own by changing his demand. In other words the buyer is also called as price taker.

## 2. Homogeneous product:

(i) The 'homogeneous product' refers to the products which the buyers buy are identical in this market. The buyers are not able to distinguish the product of one firm from others.

(ii) The implication of this 'homogeneous product' is that since the buyers treat the products as identical so they are not ready to pay different price for the product of any firm. Each buyer pays the same price for the products of all firms in this market.

(iii) On the other hand if any firm wants to sell its product at different prices will not be successful because each buyer in this market has perfect knowledge.

(iv) Finally the price of the product remains uniform.

### 3. Free entry and free exit of firms in this market:

(i) 'Freedom of entry into the market' refers to that there is no natural or artificial barrier (legal restriction or patent right etc.) for a new firm to enter the market. Firms enter the market when they think the entry will be profitable.

(ii) 'Freedom of exit' refers to that there is no barrier for a firm to exit from the market. They can leave anytime whenever they wish.

(iii) The important implication of this feature is that no firm in this market in long-run can earn super normal profit. Each firm in long-run earns only normal profit (AR = AC) which is necessary to remain in the business.

(iv) If there is more than normal profit in this market then new firms enter the market and supply increases and the price comes down. Finally normal profit prevails i.e. AR = AC.

(v) If there are any losses in this market, then some firms who wish to exit the market, they exit. As a result supply of output decreases and price goes up. Finally normal profit prevails i.e. AR = AC.

### 4. Firms and buyers have perfect knowledge:

(i) In this market of perfect competition the buyers and sellers have the perfect knowledge.

(ii) The implication of 'perfect knowledge of sellers' refers to that no firm can charge higher price than the existing uniform price in this market. The buyers will not pay higher price because they have perfect knowledge about the market.

(iii) The buyers do not pay higher price due to ignorance. On the other hand the firms do not accept lower price due to ignorance. So there is no ignorance factor.

(iv) In this market all firms have uniform cost structure and they have no cost advantage. Since all the firms have uniform cost and the price is also uniform, therefore all the firms earn only uniform profits.

__*___*___*___*___*___*___*___*___*___*___*___*___*__

# IMPORTANT QUESTIONS:

1. What is meant by market?
2. Define perfect competition.
3. Define monopoly market.
4. Define monopolistic competition market.
5. What is meant by pure competition?
6. Define oligopoly market.
7. In which market always MR = AR?
8. Draw AR and MR curves in a perfectly competitive market.
9. Draw AR and MR curves in a monopolistic competition market.
7. What is meant by price discrimination?
8. Define product differentiation.
9. Draw AR and MR curves in a monopoly market.
10. What is meant by non-price competition?
11. In which market the firm is price maker?
12. n which market the product of each firm is different from others?

1. Explain any three features of perfect competition market.
2. Explain any three features of pure perfect competition market.
3. Explain any three features of monopoly competition market.
4. Explain any three features of monopolistic competition market.
5. Explain any three features of oligopoly market.
6. How can you explain that under perfect competition market the firms are price taker and industry is price maker?
7. Distinguish between perfect competition and monopoly market.
8. Distinguish between monopoly and monopolistic competition market.

9. State the implication of product differentiation.
10. State the implication of price discrimination.
11. Distinguish between collusive and non-collusive oligopoly market.
12. Will a monopolist firm continue its production in short-run even if it incurred a loss?
13. Why does the situation of monopoly arise?
14. Explain the reasons for downward sloping demand curve under monopolistic competition market.
15. Explain why the demand curve facing a firm under monopolistic competition is more elastic than that of monopoly firm.

## 6 MARK QUESTIONS:

1. Explain the main features of monopolistic competition market.
2. State the main characteristics of oligopoly market.
3. Write the main features of perfect competition market.
4. How can you differentiate the monopoly market and monopolistic competition market?
5. Distinguish between perfect competition and monopoly market.

__*__*__*__*__*__*__*__*__*__*__*__*__

# Chapter - 11

## Price Determination Under Perfect Competition:

### • Concept of Equilibrium; Equilibrium Price; and Equilibrium Quantity of Output in a market:

Perfect competition market refers to a market situation in which there are large number of buyers and sellers and the product is homogeneous.

Equilibrium, in general sense refers to a balance or a state of rest when two equal forces operate oppositely.

In economics, equilibrium refers to a situation in which two forces like demand made by the consumers and supply made by the producers, balance each other equally corresponding to a particular price.

Equilibrium Price refers to that price at which market demand forces is equal to market supply forces. In other wards Equilibrium Price is that price at which quantity demanded is equal to quantity supplied. This equilibrium price is also known as 'Market Price' or "Price under Perfect competition market". At this price there is neither excess demand nor excess supply. So this price remains stable.

Equilibrium quantity of output refers to that quantity at which quantity demanded is equal to quantity supplied.

### • Determination of Equilibrium Price under Perfect competition market:

Perfect competition market is a situation in which there are large number of buyers and sellers and the product is homogeneous.

Under Perfect competition market, the equilibrium price is determined by the market demand and market supply forces in the following way.

**(a) Market Demand:** Market demand refers to total demand made by all the consumers for a particular product to satisfy their wants.

The market demand curve can be drawn from the following market demand schedule which shows as the price rises the quantity demanded decreases.

**(b) Market Supply:** Market Supply refers to total supply made by all the firms for a particular product. The market supply curve can be drawn from the following market supply schedule which shows as the price rises more quantity is supplied.

| PRICE (Rs.) | MARKET DEMAND (UNITS) | MARKET SUPPLY (UNITS) | REMARKS |
|---|---|---|---|
| 10 | 50 | 10 | EXCESS DEMAND |
| 20 | 40 | 20 | EXCESS DEMAND |
| 30 | 30 | 30 | **EQUILIBRIUM** |
| 40 | 20 | 40 | EXCESS SUPPLY |
| 50 | 10 | 50 | EXCESS SUPPLY |

*Table. 9/3*

From the above schedule it is clear that both the demand and supply are the functions of price. At price Rs.10 and Rs.20, the demand is 50 and 40 units respectively but at the same time supply is 10 and 20 units respectively. So there is excess demand in the market.

On the other hand at price Rs.40 and Rs.50, the demand is 20 and 10 units respectively but at the same time supply is 40 and 50 units respectively. So there is excess supply.

Ultimately at price Rs. 30, the quantity demanded is equal to quantity supplied.

So the price Rs.30 is called equilibrium price because at this price quantity demanded is equal to quantity supplied. The determination of equilibrium price can be explained by the following diagram.

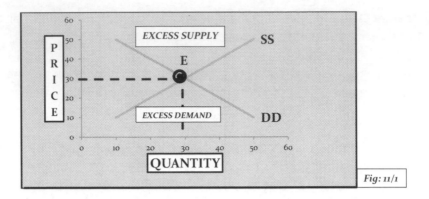

Fig: 11/1

From the above diagram it is clear that the market is in equilibrium at point E, where quantity demanded (30 units) is equal to quantity supplied (30 units) and equilibrium price is determined at OP (here Rs. 30) and equilibrium quantity is at OQ (30 units).

At price more than Re.30, Supply > Demand, implies Excess Supply.
At price less than Re.30, Demand > Supply, implies Excess Demand.

At last it is concluded that the equilibrium price is that price at which market demand is equal to market supply and this price has a tendency to persist. If at a price market demand is not equal to market supply, then there will be either excess demand or excess supply and the price will have tendency to change until once again market demand is equal to market supply.

Equilibrium price can change when demand or supply or both changes.

## ▪ How can the equilibrium price be changed in an Economy?

The equilibrium price can be changed by the following way.

    (i)   When only demand changes.
    (ii)  When only supply changes.
    (iii) When both the demand and supply change.

The detail descriptions of the above cases are explained in the following way with the help of different diagrams.

# ▪ What happens to the equilibrium price when only demand changes?

In this question changes in demand means both the increase in demand and decrease in demand.

(a) When demand increases only i.e. supply is constant.
This can be explained by the following diagram.

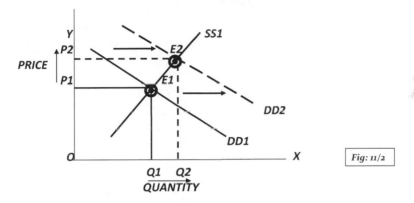

Fig: 11/2

In the above diagram E1 is the equilibrium point where OP1 is equilibrium price and OQ1 is equilibrium quantity.

When demand increases new equilibrium point becomes E2, where OP2 is new equilibrium price and OQ2 is new equilibrium quantity of output.

So equilibrium price increases from OP1 to OP2.

(b) When demand decreases only i.e. supply constant.
This5 can be explained by the following diagram.

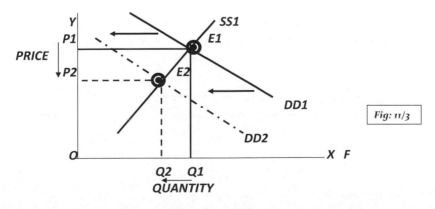

Fig: 11/3

257

In the above Fig-1(b), E1 is the equilibrium point where OP1 is equilibrium price and OQ1 is equilibrium quantity.

When demand decreases new equilibrium point becomes E2, where OP2 is new equilibrium price and OQ2 is new equilibrium quantity.

So equilibrium price decreases from OP1 to OP2.

## ▪ What happens to equilibrium price when only supply changes?

In this question changes in supply means both the increase in supply and decrease in supply.

(a) When supply increases only i.e. demand is constant.
This can be explained by the following diagram.

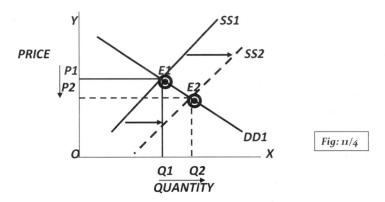

Fig: 11/4

In the above diagram E1 is the equilibrium point where OP1 is equilibrium price and OQ1 is equilibrium quantity.

When Supply increases new equilibrium point becomes E2, where OP2 is new equilibrium price and OQ2 is new equilibrium quantity of output.

So equilibrium price decreases from OP1 to OP2.

(b) When supply decreases only i.e. demand is constant.
This can be explained by the following diagram.

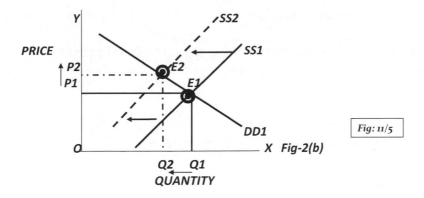

Fig: 11/5

In the above diagram E1 is the equilibrium point where OP1 is equilibrium price and OQ1 is equilibrium quantity.

When Supply decreases new equilibrium point becomes E2, where OP2 is new equilibrium price and OQ2 is new equilibrium quantity of output.

So equilibrium price increases from OP1 to OP2.

## ▪ What happens to equilibrium price when demand increases and supply decreases?

This can be explained by the following diagram.

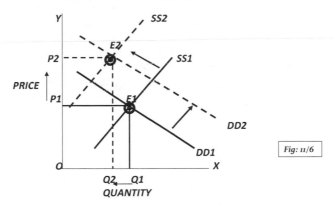

Fig: 11/6

In the above diagram E1 is equilibrium point, where demands curve DD1 and supply curve SS1 intersect each other and they are equal.

Here equilibrium price is OP1 and equilibrium quantity is OQ1.

When demand increases i.e. demand curve shifts to right wards, and supply decreases i.e. supply curve shifts to left wards then new equilibrium point is E2. Here new equilibrium price is OP2 and new equilibrium quantity is OQ2.

So equilibrium price increases from OP1 to OP2 and equilibrium quantity of output decreases from OQ1 to OQ2.

## ▪ What happens to the equilibrium price when demand decreases and supply increases?

This can be explained by the following diagram.

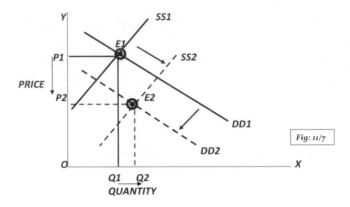

Fig: 11/7

In the above diagram E1 is equilibrium point, where demand curve DD1 and supply curve SS1 intersect each other and they are equal.

Here equilibrium price is OP1 and equilibrium quantity is OQ1.

When demand decreases i.e. demand curve shifts to left wards, and supply increases i.e. supply curve shifts to right wards then new equilibrium point is E2. Here new equilibrium price is OP2 and new equilibrium quantity of output is OQ2.

So equilibrium price decreases from OP1 to OP2 and equilibrium quantity of output increases from OQ1 to OQ2.

# ▪ What happens to the equilibrium price when demand is perfectly elastic and supply changes?

This answer can be written by the following way.

   (a) When demand is perfectly elastic and supply increases as shown in the diagram.
   (b) When demand is perfectly elastic and supply decreases as shown in the diagram.

(a) When demand is perfectly elastic and supply increases.

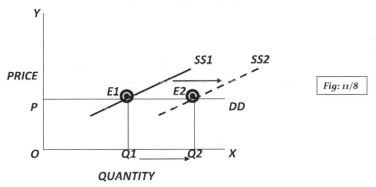

Fig: 11/8

In the above diagram E1 is the equilibrium point, where perfectly elastic demands curve DD and the supply curve SS1 intersects each other and they are equal. Here OP is equilibrium price and OQ1 is equilibrium quantity of output.

   When supply increases then supply curve shifts to right wards and new equilibrium point is E2. Now new equilibrium price remains same as OP, and only the equilibrium quantity of output increases from OQ1 to OQ2.

(b) When demand is perfectly elastic and supply decreases.

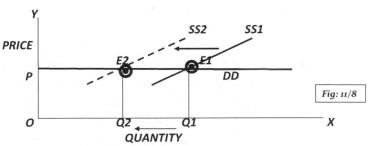

Fig: 11/8

In the above diagram E1 is the equilibrium point, where perfectly elastic demand curve DD and the supply curve SS1 intersect each other and they are equal. Here OP is equilibrium price and OQ1 is equilibrium quantity of output.

When supply decreases then supply curve shifts to left wards and new equilibrium point is E2. Now new equilibrium price remains same as OP, and only the equilibrium quantity decreases from OQ1 to OQ2.

## ▪ What happens to the equilibrium price when supply is perfectly elastic and demand changes?

This answer can be written as follows.

    (a) When supply is perfectly elastic and demand increases and
    (b) When supply is perfectly elastic and demand decreases.

(a) When supply is perfectly elastic and demand increases:
This is explained by the following diagram.

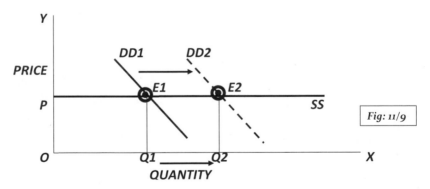

Fig: 11/9

In the above diagram E1 is the equilibrium point, where perfectly elastic Supply curve SS and the demand curve DD1 intersect each other and they are equal. Here OP is equilibrium price and OQ1 is equilibrium quantity of output.

When demand increases then demand curve shifts to right wards and new equilibrium point is E2. Now new equilibrium price remains same as OP, and only the equilibrium quantity of output increases from OQ1 to OQ2.

(b) When supply is perfectly elastic and demand decreases.
This is explained by the following diagram.

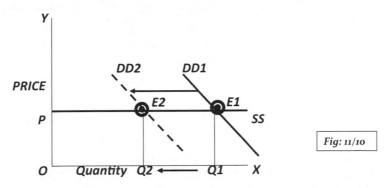

Fig: 11/10

In the above diagram E1 is the equilibrium point, where perfectly elastic Supply curve SS and the demand curve DD1 intersect each other and they are equal. Here OP is equilibrium price and OQ1 is equilibrium quantity of output.

When demand decreases then demand curve shifts to left wards and new equilibrium point is E2. Now new equilibrium price remains same as OP, and only the equilibrium quantity of output decreases from OQ1 to OQ2.

- ## What happens to the equilibrium price when demand is perfectly inelastic and supply changes?

This answer can be explained by the following diagram.

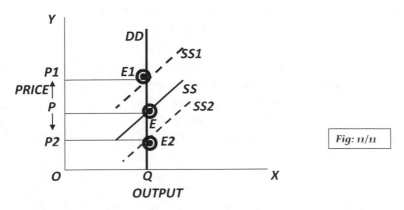

Fig: 11/11

The above diagram shows that E is the equilibrium point where equilibrium price is OP and equilibrium quantity is OQ.

When supply decreases i.e. supply curve shifts upward, then new equilibrium point is E1 and new equilibrium price is OP1 i.e. equilibrium price increases from OP to OP1 but equilibrium quantity remains same as OQ.

On the other hand when supply increases i.e. supply curve shifts down wards, then new equilibrium point is E2 and new equilibrium price is OP2 i.e. equilibrium price decreases from OP to OP2 but equilibrium quantity remains same as OQ.

## ▪ What happens to the equilibrium price when supply is perfectly inelastic and demand changes?

This answer can be explained by the following diagram.

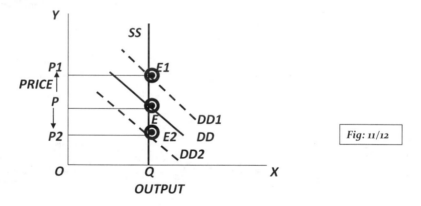

Fig: 11/12

The above diagram shows that E is the equilibrium point where equilibrium price is OP and equilibrium quantity is OQ.

When demand increases i.e. demand curve shifts upward, then new equilibrium point is E1 and new equilibrium price is OP1 i.e. equilibrium price increases from OP to OP1 but equilibrium quantity remains same as OQ.

On the other hand when demand decreases i.e. demand curve shifts down wards, then new equilibrium point is E2 and new equilibrium price is OP2 i.e. equilibrium price decreases from OP to OP2 but equilibrium quantity remains same as OQ.

**▪ Explain the effects of simultaneous shift of demand and supply curves on equilibrium price and quantity. Or Explain with the help of a diagram a situation when both demand and supply curves shift to the right but equilibrium price remains unchanged.**

Simultaneous change in demand and supply has many possibilities but here we will discuss two main possibilities i.e.

(i) Effect of simultaneous increase in demand and supply and

(ii) Effect of simultaneous decrease in demand and supply.

## (i) EFFECT OF SIMULTANEOUS INCREASE IN DEMAND AND SUPPLY:

It has following three possibilities:

### (a) WHEN INCREASE IN DEMAND IS MORE THAN INCREASE IN SUPPLY:

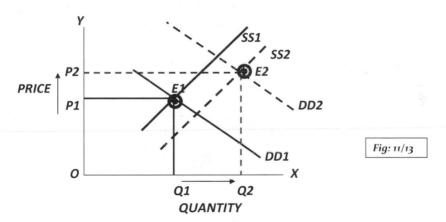

Fig: 11/13

In the above diagram E1 is the equilibrium point where equilibrium price is OP1 and equilibrium quantity is OQ1.

When demand increases more than increase in supply then both the demand and supply curves shift right wards and new equilibrium point is E2. New equilibrium price is OP2 and new equilibrium quantity is OQ2.

So equilibrium price increases from OP1 to OP2 and equilibrium quantity of output increases from OQ1 to OQ2.

### (b) WHEN INCREASE IN DEMAND IS EQUAL TO INCREASE IN SUPPLY:

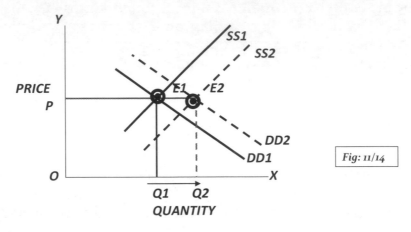

Fig: 11/14

In the above diagram E1 is the equilibrium point where equilibrium price is OP and equilibrium quantity is OQ1.

When demand increases equal to increase in supply then both the demand and supply curves shift right wards and new equilibrium point is E2.

New equilibrium price remains same as OP and new equilibrium quantity of output is OQ2.

So equilibrium price remains unchanged and only the equilibrium quantity increases from OQ1 to OQ2.

### (c) WHEN INCREASE IN DEMAND IS LESS THAN INCREASE IN SUPPLY:

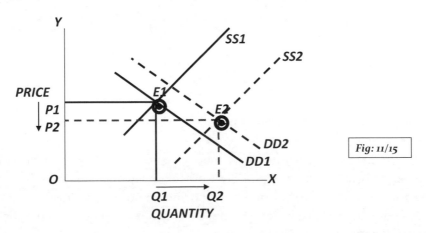

Fig: 11/15

In the above diagram E1 is the equilibrium point where equilibrium price is OP1 and equilibrium quantity is OQ1.

When demand increases less than increase in supply then both the demand and supply curves shift right wards and new equilibrium point is E2.

New equilibrium price is OP2 and new equilibrium quantity of output is OQ2.

So equilibrium price decreases from OP1 to OP2 and the equilibrium quantity of output increases from OQ1 to OQ2.

## ▪ Effect of simultaneous decrease in demand and supply:

It has three following possibilities which are explained along with diagrams.

### (a) WHEN DECREASE IN DEMAND IS MORE THAN DECREASE IN SUPPLY:

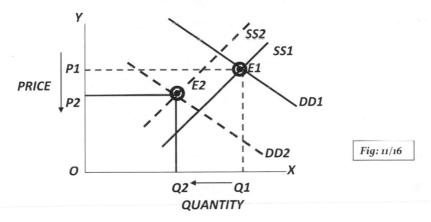

Fig: 11/16

In the above diagram E1 is the equilibrium point where equilibrium price is OP1 and equilibrium quantity is OQ1.

When demand decreases more than decrease in supply then both the demand and supply curves shift to left wards and new equilibrium point is E2. New equilibrium price is OP2 and new equilibrium quantity is OQ2.

So equilibrium price decreases from OP1 to OP2 and equilibrium quantity decreases from OQ1 to OQ2.

## (b) WHEN DECREASE IN DEMAND IS EQUAL TO DECREASE IN SUPPLY:

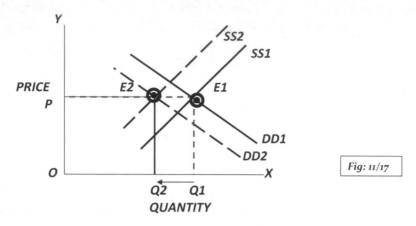

Fig: 11/17

In the above diagram E1 is the equilibrium point where equilibrium price is OP and equilibrium quantity is OQ1.

When demand decreases equal to decrease in supply then both the demand and supply curves shift left wards and new equilibrium point is E2.

New equilibrium price remains same as OP and new equilibrium quantity of output is OQ2.

So equilibrium price remains unchanged and only the equilibrium quantity of output decreases from OQ1 to OQ2.

## (c) WHEN DECREASE IN DEMAND IS LESS THAN DECREASE IN SUPPLY:

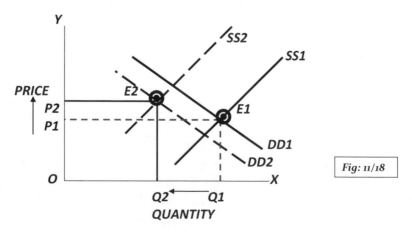

Fig: 11/18

In the above diagram E1 is the equilibrium point where equilibrium price is OP1 and equilibrium quantity of output is OQ1.

When demand decreases less than decrease in supply then both the demand and supply curves shift left wards and new equilibrium point is E2.

New equilibrium price is OP2 and new equilibrium quantity is OQ2.

So equilibrium price increases from OP1 to OP2 and the equilibrium quantity of output decreases from OQ1 to OQ2.

**Concept of Market Period, short period and long period:**

a)  Market period is that time period in which supply of a product can be increased only up to the available existing stock.
b)  Short period is that time period in which output can be increased by using more of the variable factors and keeping some factors fixed.
c)  Long period is that time period in which production of output can be increased by using all variable factors of production and no factors remain fixed.

- **SOME IMPORTANT APPLICATIONS OF DEMAND AND SUPPLY CURVES IN OUR REAL LIFE:**
  **How can you explain the Government intervention on market determined equilibrium price?**
  **(i) What happens when Government fixes maximum price lower than equilibrium price?**
                              **Or**
  **Explain Control Price or Ceiling Price and state its consequences.**

In a free market economy equilibrium price of a product is determined by the market demand and market supply forces without any interference of the Government. But sometimes this equilibrium price is too high for the consumers or too low for the producers that they require the Government intervention.

Government directly through CONTROL PRICE and SUPPORT PRICE fixes the price of the product to protect the interest of the consumers and producers respectively.

Or the Government indirectly through TAXES and SUBSIDIES control the price of the product in the economy.

## (i) CONTROL PRICE OR CEILING PRICE:

"Ceiling Price or Control Price is that maximum price which Government fixes for scarce commodities. It is fixed below equilibrium price. Producer cannot sell their product above this price. It is Government regulated or controlled price."

In our daily life there are certain essential goods like rice, wheat i.e., food grains and oil, sugar etc. if becomes scarce then their prices increase too high, as a result the poor people fail to avail these goods. Then it is the duty of the Government to control the price and to protect the interest of the consumers.

The producers cannot charge price higher than the Ceiling Price fixed by the Government.

Price Control or Ceiling price can be explained by the following diagram.

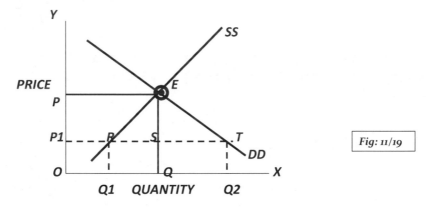

Fig: 11/19

In the above diagram the equilibrium point E is determined freely by the market demand and supply forces without the interference of the Government. Here OP is the equilibrium price and OQ is equilibrium quantity. But this equilibrium price is too high that the poor consumers cannot afford this commodity. Therefore the Govt. Interferes and fixes the maximum price that the sellers can charge is OP1, which is below equilibrium price OP. This price OP1 is called Control Price or Ceiling Price.

**CONSEQUENCES OF PRICE CONTROL:** The consequences or effects of Control Price are as follows:

(i) **SHORTAGE:** When the Control Price is lower than the equilibrium price then the producers reduce the supply of commodity because of less profit. On the other hand at low price the demand for commodity increases. Therefore demand is more than supply and the situation is called shortage and the demand of many consumers cannot be satisfied.

(ii) **RATIONING:** Since the control price is lower than the equilibrium price so there is excess demand in the market. Therefore the Government introduces rationing of product system. According to this system, the essential goods at control price will be distributed by the ration cards through the fair price shops of the Government and the quantity will depend on the number of heads in the family.

(iii) **BLACK MARKETING:** Due to control price there is excess demand in the economy and demand of many consumers remain unsatisfied for the commodity. Therefore some consumers to satisfy their demand are ready to buy the commodities at higher price illegally in the black market. This system is called black marketing where the sellers earn huge profits by charging illegally high price.

- **How can you explain the Government intervention on market determined equilibrium price?**
**(i) What happens when Government fixes minimum price which is higher than equilibrium price?**
**Or**
**Explain Minimum Support Price or Floor Price and state its consequences.**

In a free market economy equilibrium price of a product is determined by the market demand and market supply forces without any interference of the Government. But sometimes this equilibrium price is too high for the consumers or too low for the producers that they require the Government intervention.

Government directly through CONTROL PRICE and SUPPORT PRICE fixes the price of the product to protect the interest of the consumers and producers respectively.

Or the Government indirectly through TAXES and SUBSIDIES control the price of the product in the economy.

## (i) MINIMUM SUPPORT PRICE OR FLOOR PRICE:

Floor price refers to that minimum price; the producers must be paid for their product. It is fixed by the Government in order to protect the interests of the producers or the farmers.

In any economy if the production of any good increases and on the other hand the demand for the good does not increase i.e. if there is excess supply of any good in the market, the immediate effect is the price of good will decrease and the producers become losers.

In India when the supply of the agricultural product increases but its demand does not increase in the same rate then there is excess supply in the market. As a result the price decreases and the farmers become losers.

Then the Government fixes minimum support prices of different goods like wheat, rice, sugar cane etc. As a result the farmers are not compelled to sell their products at price below the floor price fixed by the Government. Floor price can be explained by the following diagram.

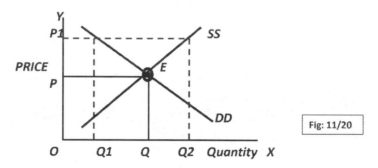

Fig: 11/20

In the above diagram the equilibrium point E is determined freely by the market demand and supply forces without the interference of the Government. Here OP is the equilibrium price and OQ is equilibrium quantity. But this equilibrium price is too low that the farmers cannot sell the commodity at this price because they become losers.

Therefore the Govt. Interferes and fixes the minimum support price or floor price below which the sellers will not sell their goods. In the above diagram OP1 is the floor price fixed by the Government. Even if the surplus product is not sold at OP1 price in the market, then the Government will buy it for its buffer stock.

## CONSEQUENCES OF MINIMUM SUPPORT PRICE OR FLOOR PRICE:

The consequences of floor price are as follows.

(i) **BUFFER STOCKS**: Under minimum support price policy at price fixed by the Government, higher than the equilibrium price, there is excess supply of goods. Then if the surplus goods are not sold in the market the Govt. will purchase it for its buffer stock and in future whenever there is need Govt. will sell it at the same price. In India it is done by the Food Corporation of India (FCI) and some State Govt. agencies.

(ii) **SUBSIDIES:** The Govt. buys the surplus food grains at floor price and keeps it in its ware houses and if necessary the Govt. sells the same product through the public distribution shops at subsidized price which is known as food subsidy.

## Distinction between Control Price and Floor Price:

| BASIS | CONTROL PRICE | FLOOR PRICE |
|---|---|---|
| 1. Objective | To protect the interest of the poor consumers. | To protect the interests of the producers. |
| 2. Price Setting | Price is set below the equilibrium price. | Price is set above the equilibrium price. |
| 3. Effects | Rationing and Black marketing. | Buffer stocks and Subsidies. |
| 4. Alternate name | Its other name is Ceiling Price. | Its other name is Minimum Support Price. |

Q. If a demand function is as DD = 19 – 3p – p2 and supply function is SS = 5p – 1 then find out the equilibrium price and equilibrium quantity of output.

Ans. At equilibrium, DD = SS

$$Or, 19 - 3p - p2 = 5p - 1$$
$$Or, p2 + 8p - 20 = 0$$
$$Or, (p + 10)(p - 2) = 0$$

Therefore, p = - 10 or 2. But price cannot be negative. So price = 2.

When p =2, then DD = 19 – 6 – 4 = 9

And SS = 5.2 – 1 = 9

So, equilibrium price = Rs.2 and equilibrium quantity of output = 9.

__*__*__*__*__*__*__*__*__*__*__*__

# IMPORTANT QUESTIONS:

1. Define equilibrium price.
2. What is meant by equilibrium quantity?
3. What happens to the equilibrium price if demand increases more than increase in supply?
4. If demand rises by 10% and supply rises by 20% then what will happen to the equilibrium price?

## 3 OR 4 MARK QUESTIONS:

1. Explain the determination of equilibrium price under perfect competition market.
2. Explain the excess demand with the help of a diagram under perfect competition market.
3. How can you explain the deficient demand by using diagram under perfect competition market?
4. What will happen to the equilibrium price when only demand increases?
5. What will happen to the equilibrium price when only supply changes?
6. Explain the effect of simultaneous changes in both demand and supply on the equilibrium price.
7. How can you explain that due to simultaneous changes in both demand and supply the equilibrium price remains unchanged?
8. What happens when market price is more than equilibrium price?
9. What happens when market price is less than equilibrium price?
10. Explain with the help of a diagram the change in the price of substitute goods on the equilibrium price of the original good.
11. How does change in technology affect the equilibrium price of a commodity?

12. How does change in income of the consumer affect the equilibrium price of a commodity?
13. What happens to the equilibrium price when demand is perfectly elastic and supply changes?
14. Explain with the help of a diagram the effect on equilibrium price when demand changes and supply is perfectly elastic.
15. Explain the ceiling price and its effects.
16. What is floor price? State its consequences.
17. Distinguish between control price and floor price.

## 6 MARK QUESTIONS:

1. How can you explain that equilibrium price may or may not change with the simultaneous shift of both demand and supply curves?
2. Explain excess demand and its effect on the equilibrium price of a commodity with the help of a diagram.
3. Explain excess supply and its effect on the equilibrium price of a commodity with the help of a diagram.
4. Explain the determination of equilibrium price of a commodity with the help of a hypothetical schedule and diagram.
5. Explain the effect of simultaneous change in both demand and supply on the equilibrium price.

—*—*—*—*—*—*—*—*—*—*—*—*—

# INTRODUCTORY MACRO ECONOMICS:

# Chapter - 1

## An Introduction To Macro Economics And Some Of Its Basic Concepts:

**Introduction to Macro Economics:**

The subject matter of economics is mainly concerned with some economic activities like production, consumption, investment, distribution, public finance and exchange.

The modern economic theory is mainly divided into two branches like micro-economics and macro-economics. Micro-economics is the analysis of the individual behaviour whereas Macro-economics is the analysis of aggregate behaviour.

In 1933, Ragner Frisch, Professor of Oslo University for the first time classified the subject matter of Economics into two branches i.e. Micro Economics and Macro Economics.

Micro Economics deals with study of individual units like individual's income, individual firm's output etc. This is already discussed in detail, in the first chapter of Micro Economics of this book.

Macro Economics deals with aggregate problems of the economy like aggregate demand, aggregate supply, national income etc.

Definition: "Macro economic theory is that part of economics which studies overall average and aggregates of the system".

**The main scope of macro economics are as follows:**

(i) Theory of national income: It includes concept and measurement of national income.
(ii) Theory of Employment: It includes determination of income, employment and output.

(iii) Theory of Money and banking
(iv) Government budget
(v) Theory of International trade: It includes Foreign exchange rate determination and balance of payments.
(vi) Theory of economic growth: It includes the problems relating to economic growth and fiscal and monetary policies of the Government.

Most of the modern economics is now macro-economics which deals with aggregate problems of the economy. Macro-economics has become more popular after the publication of J.M.Keynes' 'General theory of Employment, Interest and Money' in 1936. Besides Keynes, Malthus, Karl Marx, Fisher have great contribution for the development of macroeconomic analysis.

Gardner Ackley says, "Macro-economics deals with economic affairs in large. It concerns the overall dimensions of economic life".

## MACRO-ECONOMIC THEORY

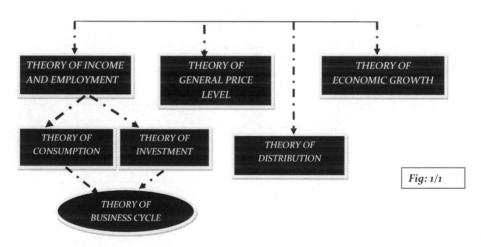

Fig: 1/1

Both micro-economics and macro-economics have place of their own and both are equally important. The two approaches are supplementary rather than substitute to each other and they are interdependent on each other.

# ▪ EVOLUTION OF MACRO ECONOMICS:

The study of macro economics is mainly dominated by two schools of thoughts. They are

**(1) Classical School of Thought and**
**(2) Keynesian School of Thought:**

## ➢ CLASSICAL SCHOOL OF THOUGHT:

It includes the economists like J. S. Mill, Malthus, A. C. Pigou and Ricardo. They advocated the following facts.

**(a) FREE ECONOMY**: There is free economy or capitalist economy without any interference of the Government.

**(b) FULL EMPLOYMENT:** Full employment equilibrium is a normal feature of the economy.

**(c) HIGHEST LEVEL OF INCOME:** Resources are fully and optimally utilised and the main aim of producers is to maximize profit. Thus the level of income is highest.

## ➢ KEYNESIAN SCHOOL OF THOUGHT:

This school of thought is dominated by Lord Keynes. He observed that in 1930's there was a worldwide depression i.e. the output in developed countries fall and unemployment increased by huge amounts. In U.S.A. from 1929 to 1933, unemployment rate increased from 3% to 25% and aggregate output decreased by 33%.

He advocated the following facts.

(a) Market economy needs to be regulated by the Government. Otherwise there might be either inflation or deflation in the economy and the economy becomes unstable.

(b) The Government should undertake large scale investment expenditure to increase the employment opportunities.

(c) There will be some unemployment i.e. full employment is not normal feature.

## ▪ Distinction between micro and macro economics:

| BASIS | MICRO ECONOMICS | MACRO ECONOMICS |
|---|---|---|
| 1. Meaning | It studies only individual economic units. | It studies aggregate problems of the economy. |
| 2. Main aim | Its main aim is price determination and allocation of resources. | Its main aim is to determine the level of national income and employment. |
| 3. Main tools | Its main tools are demand and supply of a particular product or factor. | Its main tools are aggregate demand and aggregate supply of the whole economy. |
| 4. Equilibrium. | It deals with partial equilibrium. | It deals with aggregate equilibrium. |
| 5. Examples. | Individual income, individual saving, individual firm's output etc. | National income, national savings, aggregate demand, aggregate supply etc. |

## ▪ Concept of National Income:

In any economy production generates income, income creates expenditure and expenditure calls forth production. So national income can be defined in the following three ways.

**(i) From production point view:** "National income is the sum total of money value of net flow all the final goods and services produced by normal residents of a country during a period of account."

**(ii) From income point of view: CSO** (Central Statistical Organization) has defined, "National income is the sum total of factor incomes earned by normal residents of a country in the form of rent, wages, interest and profit in an accounting year".

**(iii) From expenditure point of view:** Simon Kuznets defined national income as "National product is the net output of commodities and services flowing during the year from the country's productive system into the hands of ultimate consumers or into the net addition to the country's capital goods".

## ▪ SOME BASIC CONCEPTS OF MACRO ECONOMICS:

### (A) Consumption goods.

Consumption goods or consumer goods are those goods which directly satisfy consumers' wants. For example food, shirt, T.V. set, scooter, pen, services of a doctor or lawyer etc. are called consumer goods.

Consumer goods are classified into following categories.

1. **Durable Consumer goods**: Durable consumer goods are those goods which can be used for a long time i.e. for many years. For example car, T.V. set, refrigerator etc. are durable consumer goods.
2. **Semi-durable consumer goods:** It refers to those goods which can be used for some longer period i.e. for one or two years like furniture, clothes, electrical goods etc.
3. **Non-durable consumer goods:** It refers to those goods which can be used for once only. These are also called single use consumer goods. For example milk, fruit, petrol are non-durable goods.
4. **Services:** It refers to those non-material goods which directly satisfy human wants like services of a teacher, or of a doctor, or of a lawyer.

### (B) Capital goods:

Capital goods are those goods which are used in the process of production for many years. These goods are fixed assets of the producers. These goods include plant, machinery, stock of raw—material; semi finished and finished goods with the producer at the end of the year.

### Now let us discuss that whether all machineries are capital goods or not?

This can be answered with some examples.

(i) A sewing machine with a tailor is capital goods because here the end user is a producer. But the sewing machine with a consumer at his home cannot be called as capital goods because the end user here is a consumer not a producer. So sewing machine with consumer is called as durable consumer goods.

(ii) A refrigerator in the restaurant, for the same above reason, is capital goods whereas the same refrigerator at home with the consumer is called as durable consumer goods.

(iii) A car with a tourist service provider is capital goods whereas a car with consumer at home is durable consumer goods.

So the basis of classification is the end using of the goods.

**CLASSIFICATION OF CAPITAL GOODS:**

Capital goods are classified into two categories.

(a) **Producer goods or durable capital goods:** It refers to those goods which can be used for a long time for many years like machinery, building and other fixed assets of the business.

(b) **Non-durable capital goods:** It refers to those goods which exhaust after some time like one year for example stock of raw material, semi finished and finished goods. These are single-use producer goods.

## ▪ Distinction between consumer goods and capital goods:

| BASIS | CONSUMER GOODS | CAPITAL GOODS |
|---|---|---|
| 1. Meaning. | It refers to those goods which directly satisfy the wants of the consumers. | It refers to those goods which are used in the process of production for many years. These goods are fixed assets of the producers. |
| 2. Nature. | These goods do not promote productivity. | These goods help to promote productivity. |
| 3. Satisfaction. | These goods satisfy human wants directly. | These goods satisfy human wants indirectly. |
| 4. Example. | Food, shirt, T.V. set, scooter, pen, services of a doctor or lawyer etc. | Plant, machinery, stock of raw—material; semi finished and finished goods with the producer at the end of the year. |

## ■ What is meant by GNP deflator?

It is defined as the ratio of nominal GNP to real GNP, multiplied by 100.

$$\text{GNP deflator} = \frac{\text{NOMINAL GNP}}{\text{REAL GNP}} \times 100.$$

## ■ Distinction between intermediate goods and final goods:

| BASIS | INTERMEDIATE GOODS | FINAL GOODS |
|---|---|---|
| 1. Meaning. | It refers to those goods which are used for further production or for resale in the market. | It refers to those goods which are used for final consumption or for investment. |
| 2. Nature of demand. | These goods have derived demand. | These goods have direct demand. |
| 3. National income. | Values of these goods are not included in national income. | Value of these goods is always included in national income. |
| 4. Production boundary. | These goods remain inside the production boundary. | These goods are always outside the production boundary. |
| 5. Example. | Wheat purchased by flour mill, cotton purchased by thread making mill etc. | Television, aeroplanes, books, sweets, furniture ready for sale, service of a doctor, lawyer etc. |

## ■ Distinction between Stock and Flow variables.

| BASIS | STOCK | FLOW |
|---|---|---|
| 1. Meaning. | Stock is a variable which is measured at a particular point of time. | Flow is a variable which is measured over a period of time. |
| 2. Time dimensional | It has no time dimension. | It has time dimension like per hour, per week, per month etc. |

| 3. Interdependence. | Stock influences flow. If the stock increases then flow will increase. | Flow influences stock. If investment per month increases then stock of capital will increase. |
|---|---|---|
| 4. Example. | Wealth, capital, money supply, bank deposits, water in water tank, distance between Delhi and Kolkata etc. | Income, expenditure, capital formation, changes in money supply, interest on capital. |

## ▪ The concept of investment in Macro economics:

Investment is defined as the process of capital formation, or a process of increase in the stock of capital.

Symbolically,

$$I = \Delta K$$

Here, I is Investment, K is capital stock and $\Delta K$ is change in the capital stock during the year.

Gross investment is the gross domestic capital formation which consists of the following:

(a) Net value of machinery and equipment.
(b) Changes in the stock of finished goods and semi finished goods.
(c) Construction of road, building etc.
(d) Replacement cost or cost of depreciation.

**So investment has two components:**

(i) fixed investment and (ii) inventory investment.

(i) **Fixed investment**: It refers to increase in the stock of fixed assets of the producers during an accounting year. For example plant and machinery. Fixed investment is also called fixed capital formation.

(ii) **Inventory investment**: Change in the inventory stock of semi finished goods and finished goods and raw material during the year is called as inventory investment.

286

Investment is also classified into gross investment and net investment.

(a) **GROSS INVESTMENT:** It refers to the expenditure on the purchase of fixed assets during the accounting year. It also includes new assets, replacement of fixed assets and expenditure on the inventory stock during the accounting year.

(b) **NET INVESTMENT:** Net investment refers to net addition to the stock of capital which raises the production capacity.

Net Investment = Gross Investment – Depreciation.

## ▪ The concepts of Depreciation, Capital loss and Obsolescence:

(i) **OBSOLESCENCE:** It refers to the loss of value of fixed capital due to change in technology or due to change in demand for goods and services. For example, sometimes capital goods like machines becomes obsolete due to either change in technology or due to change in the taste and fashion resulting a fall in demand for goods and services.

This kind of Obsolescence is also called as Expected Obsolescence and it is a part of depreciation.

Whereas Unexpected Obsolescence refers to loss of value of fixed capital due to natural calamities like earthquake, flood, cyclone, fire etc. Unexpected Obsolescence is not a part of depreciation.

Now depreciation and capital loss can be explained by the following way.

➢ Distinction between capital loss and depreciation:

| BASIS | CAPITAL LOSS | DEPRECIATION |
|---|---|---|
| 1. Meaning. | It is defined as the loss in the value of fixed capital due to natural calamities and unexpected obsolescence. | It is defined as the loss in the value of fixed capital due to normal wear and tear and expected obsolescence. |
| 2. Relation with production process. | It is not the result of the production process. | It is the result of the production process. |

| 3. Provision. | Provision of capital loss is not maintained. | Provision of depreciation is maintained to replace assets. |
|---|---|---|
| 4. Nature. | It is abnormal and non-recurring in nature | It is normal and recurring in nature. |

## ▪ The concepts of Indirect taxes, Subsidies, Factor cost and Market price:

(I) **INDIRECT TAXES:** It refers to taxes which are levied by the government on production and sale of commodities. It includes excise duty, sales tax, custom duty, octroi etc.

(II) **SUBSIDIES:** It refers to cash grants given by the Government to the enterprises to encourage production of certain commodities or to sell goods at prices lower than the free market prices.

(III) **FACTOR COST:** It refers to all factor payments made by the producing units (firms) to the owners of factors of production in the form of rent, wages, interest and profit, for their factor services.

(IV) **MARKET PRICE:** It refers to the price at which a commodity is sold and purchased in the market.

Relation between Market price and Factor cost.
MARKET PRICE = FACTOR COST + INDIRECT TAXES – SUBSIDIES.
Or, MARKET PRICE = FACTOR COST + NET INDIRECT TAXES.
OR, MP = FC + NIT.
NET INDIRECT TAXES (NIT) = INDIRECT TAXES – SUBSIDIES.

## BASIC CONCEPTS OF NATIONAL INCOME ACCOUNTING:

**IMPORTANT FORMULAE:**

1. $$\frac{[\text{REAL NATIONAL INCOME}]}{\text{MONETARY NATIONAL INCOME}} = \frac{\text{BASE YEAR PRICE INDEX}}{\text{CURRENT YEAR PRICE INDEX}}$$

(Here Real national income means national income in base year and Monetary national income means national income in current year).

2. GROWTH RATE OF NATIONAL INCOME = $\frac{(M - R)}{M} \times 100$

(Here M stands for Monetary national income and R stands for Real national income).

1. Calculate national income in the current year when the real national income is Rs. 500 crores and the base year price index and current year price index are given as 100 and 120 respectively.

Solution: We know that $\frac{R.N.}{M.N.Y} = \frac{B. Y. Price index}{C. Y. Price index}$

Therefore,

$(500/M. N. Y) = (100/120)$

M. N. Y = $\frac{500 \times 120}{100}$

= 600

So, the Monetary National income = Rs. 600 crores.

2. Calculate national income at constant price when the national income in current year and price index in the current year are given as Rs. 1200 crores and 150 respectively.

Solution: We know that $\frac{R.N.Y}{M.N.Y} = \frac{B. Y. Price index}{C. Y. Price index}$

Therefore,

$(R. N.Y/1200) = (100/150)$

R. N. Y = $\frac{100 \times 1200}{150}$

= 800

So, the Real National income = Rs. 800 crores.

3. Calculate growth rate of the economy where national income at constant price is Rs. 4500 crores and national income at current year price is given as Rs. 6000 crores.

Solution: Growth Rate of the National Income = $\frac{(M - R)}{M} \times 100$

$$= \frac{(6000 - 4500)}{4500} \times 100$$
$$= (1500/4500) \times 100$$
$$= 33.3\%$$

So, the required growth rate of national income = 33.3%

4. Calculate the real per capita income for 2008-2009 with the help of following table.

| Year | N.Y at current year price (Rs. in Crores) | Population (crores) | Index No. |
|---|---|---|---|
| 2001-2002 | 30,000 | 80 | 100 |
| 2008-2009 | 170,000 | 100 | 340 |

Solution: First, let us find out the National Income at constant year price for the year 2008-2009 by the following formulae:

$\frac{R.N.Y}{M.N.Y} = \frac{B. Y. Price\ index}{C. Y. Price\ index}$

Or, (R. N.Y/170,000) = (100/340)

Or, R.N.Y = (170,000 x 100)/340

Or, R.N.Y = 50,000

So, the Real Per Capita Income = Rs. 50,000/100 = Rs. 500.

5. Calculate total value of production at base year price and current year price with the help of following table:

| Goods | 1999-2000 | | 2007-2008 | |
|---|---|---|---|---|
| | Price ($P_0$) | Quantity ($Q_0$) | Price ($P_1$) | Quantity ($Q_1$) |
| A | 20 | 150 | 40 | 150 |
| B | 30 | 200 | 50 | 200 |
| C | 40 | 250 | 80 | 250 |
| D | 25 | 400 | 50 | 400 |
| E | 50 | 450 | 90 | 450 |

Table. 1/1

Solution:

| Goods | 1999-2000 | | 2007-2008 | | $P_0Q_0$ | $P_1Q_1$ | $P_0Q_1$ | $P_1Q_0$ |
|-------|-----------|-----------|-----------|-----------|----------|----------|----------|----------|
| | Price $(P_0)$ | Quantity $(Q_0)$ | Price $(P_1)$ | Quantity $(Q_1)$ | | | | |
| A | 20 | 150 | 40 | 150 | 3000 | 6000 | 3000 | 6000 |
| B | 30 | 200 | 50 | 200 | 6000 | 10000 | 6000 | 10000 |
| C | 40 | 250 | 80 | 250 | 10000 | 20000 | 10000 | 20000 |
| D | 25 | 400 | 50 | 400 | 10000 | 20000 | 10000 | 20000 |
| E | 50 | 450 | 90 | 450 | 22500 | 40500 | 22500 | 40500 |

Therefore, The total value of production of output at current year price for 1999-2000: 22500

For 2007-2008: 40500

But the total value of output at Base year Price
For 1999-2000: 22500
And for 2007-2008: 22500

# IMPORTANT QUESTIONS:

## 1 MARK QUESTIONS:

1. What is meant by macro economics?
2. Write two examples of macro economics.
3. Who is called father of modern macro economics?
4. Define GNP deflator.
5. What is meant by factor cost?
6. Define Gross Domestic Income.
7. What is meant by Net Domestic In come?
8. When can domestic income be equal to national income?
9. Write two examples of intermediate goods used in agriculture.
10. Write two examples of intermediate goods used in industries.
11. Define nominal GNP.
12. Define real GNP.
13. What is meant by consumption of fixed capital?
14. Define subsidy.
15. Define capital loss.

## 3 OR 4 MARK QUESTIONS:

1. Distinguish between real national income and monetary national income.
2. Distinguish between GDP at MP and NDP at FC.
3. Distinguish between Domestic factor income and national income.
4. Differentiate between intermediate goods and final goods?
5. Distinguish between consumer goods and capital goods.
6. Distinguish between stock and flow variables.
7. What is meant by investment? Distinguish between net investment and gross investment.

8. Which price is better to measure national income and why?
9. Explain the classification of consumer goods.
10. Define producer goods. Explain the classification of producer goods.

# Chapter - 2

## Circular Flow Of Income:

## • CIRCULAR FLOW OF INCOME:

It refers to the continuous circular movement of money income or the flow of goods and services among different sectors of an economy. It is circular in nature because it moves in a circular way and comes back to the starting point and again continues.

National income is a flow concept because it is measured at a particular point of view. In every economy there are three activities like (a) production of goods and services, (b) generation of income in terms of rent, wages, interest and profit and (c) expenditure in the form of consumption expenditure and investment expenditure.

Production, income and expenditure are related in a circular way. Production is the result of combined efforts of factors of production like land, labour, capital and entrepreneur. The revenue generated by the net output in the production process is distributed among factors of production in the form of money income like rent, wages, interest and profit. Thus production generates income.

This income leads to increase the expenditure for both consumption and investment and expenditure in turn gives rise to further production. Therefore production generates income and income creates expenditure and expenditure helps to raise the production. So there are three phases in the circular flow of income like production, income and expenditure.

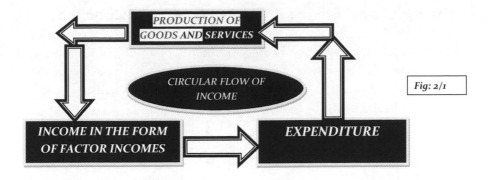

Fig: 2/1

> TWO BASIS OF CIRCULAR FLOW OF INCOME:

(1) Real flow or flow of goods and services are the reverse of money flow
(2) Flow of income among different sectors reflect relationship between the concepts of receipts and payments.

## ▪ The Real flow in a two sector economy:

Real flow refers to the flow of goods and services from firms to households and in return the flow of factor services from the households to the firms in an economy. This can be explained by the following diagram.

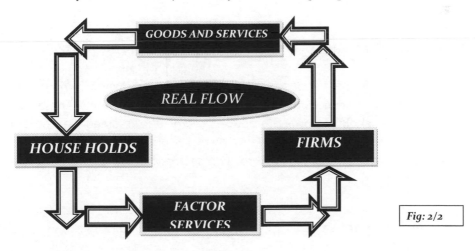

Fig: 2/2

In the above diagram the firms supply goods and services to the house hold sector and in return the house hold sector supplies factor services to the firms. This is known as real flow.

## • The concept of Money flow in a two sector economy:

Money flow refers to flow of monetary payments by the firms to household sector for their factor services and in returns the monetary payments made by the household sector to the firms for their goods and services.

This can be explained by the following diagram.

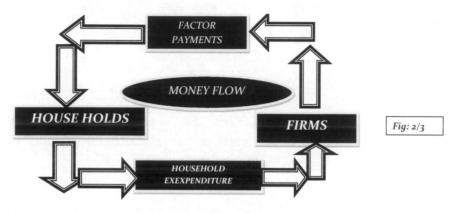

Fig: 2/3

In the above diagram it is clear that the household sector make payments to the firms for their goods and services. On the other hand the firms make the monetary payments for the factor services of the house hold sector in the form of rent, wages, interest and profit.

## • The Circular flow of income in two sector economy:

It refers to the continuous circular movement of money income or the flow of goods and services between two sectors of an economy. These two sectors are household sector and producers sector. It is assumed that there is no Government. This model has two markets like product market and factor market. The circular flow of income for two sectors can be explained by the following diagram.

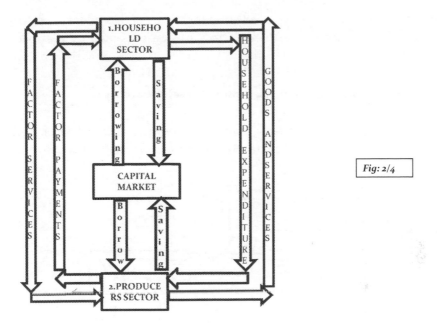

*Fig: 2/4*

In the above diagram in the absence of government in case of two sectors economy the firms supply goods and services to the households and the household make monetary payments to the firms. On the other hand the households supply factor services in the form of land, labour, capital and etc. and the firms make factor payments to the household sector in the form of rent, wages, interest and profit.

## WHEN CAPITAL MARKET IS INTRODUCED IN THE ABOVE MODEL:

When capital market is introduced in the above model then both households and firms save in the capital market and when required they can borrow from the capital market as shown in the above diagram.

## The Circular flow of income in case of three sectors economy or closed economy:

It refers to the continuous circular movement of money income or the flow of goods and services between three sectors of an economy. These three sectors are household sector, Government sector and producers sector. The circular flow of income for three sectors can be explained by the following diagram.

**We need to remember the following important points**:

1. Factor services rendered by households include land, labour, capital.
2. Factor payments made to the households include rent, wages, interest.

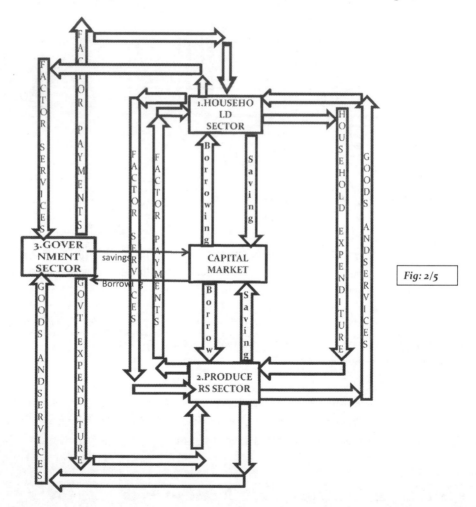

*Fig: 2/5*

In the above diagram in the presence of government in case of three sectors economy,

(i)   The firms supply goods and services to the households and the household make monetary payments to the firms. On the other hand the households supply factor services in the form of land, labour, capital and etc. and the firms make factor payments to the household sector in the form of rent, wages, interest and profit.

(ii)  WHEN CAPITAL MARKET IS INTRODUCED IN THE ABOVE MODEL:
      When capital market is introduced in the above model then both households and firms save in the capital market and when required they can borrow from the capital market as shown in the above diagram by black colour.

(iii) The firms supply goods and services to the Govt. sector and on the other hand the Govt. sector makes payments for those goods and services in the form of Govt. expenditure.

(iv)  The household sector supply factor services to the Govt. sector and the Govt. sector makes factor payments in the form of rent, wages, interest and profit.

(v)   The Govt. sector borrows from the capital market and saves into the capital market.

## • The circular flow of income in case of four sectors economy or an open economy:

It refers to the continuous circular movement of money income or the flow of goods and services between FOUR sectors of an economy. These four sectors are household sector, Government sector, producers sector and rest of the world. The circular flow of income for four sectors economy can be explained by the following diagram.

We need to remember following important points:

1.   The producers sector exports goods and services to the rest of the world and earn exports receipts from rest of the world.

2.   The producers sector also imports goods and services from the rest of the world and make import payments to the rest of the world.

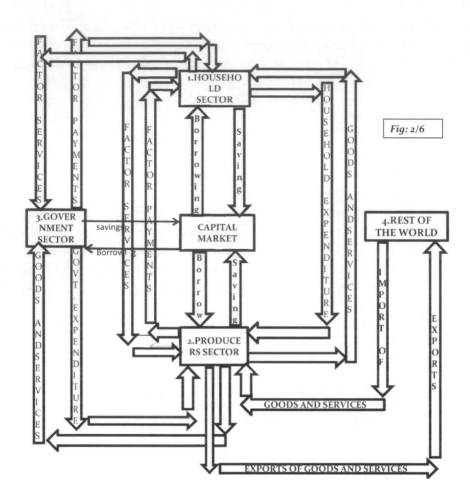

Fig: 2/6

In the above diagram in the presence of government in case of FOUR sectors economy,

(i) The firms supply goods and services to the households and the household make monetary payments to the firms. On the other hand the households supply factor services in the form of land, labour, capital and etc. and the firms make factor payments to the household sector in the form of rent, wages, interest and profit.

(ii) WHEN CAPITAL MARKET IS INTRODUCED IN THE ABOVE MODEL:
When capital market is introduced in the above model then both households and firms save in the capital market and when required they can borrow from the capital market as shown in the above diagram by black colour.

(iii) The firms supply goods and services to the Govt. sector and on the other hand the Govt. sector makes payments for those goods and services in the form of Govt. expenditure.

(iv) The household sector supply factor services to the Govt. sector and the Govt. sector makes factor payments in the form of rent, wages, interest and profit.

(v) The Govt. sector borrows from the capital market and saves into the capital market.

(vi) The rest of the world has economic relation with any country with the help of export and import. The household and producers sector get receipt from the rest of the world by exporting goods. On the other hand when the household and producers sector import goods and services from the rest of the world then they make import payments.

**For the above explanation the following diagram can also be used.**

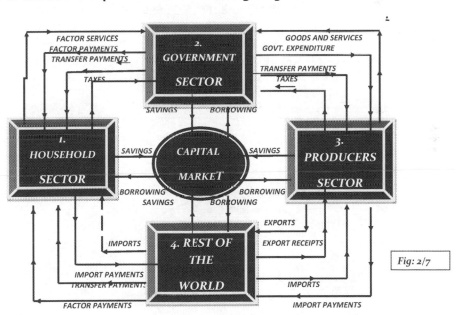

Fig: 2/7

## ▪ Distinction between the injections and leakages in the circular flow of national income:

| BASIS | INJECTIONS | LEAKAGES |
|---|---|---|
| 1. Meaning. | 'Injections' refers to those variables which help to increase the national income. | 'Leakages' refers to those variables which dampen the economic growth and reduces the national income of the country. |
| 2. Impact. | It has positive impact on an economy because it helps to increase the national income. | It has negative impact on an economy because it hampers the growth of production and thus the national income of the country. |
| 3. Contribution | It increases the size of circular flow of income. | It reduces the size of circular flow of income. |
| 4. Examples. | It includes Government expenditure, Household expenditure, Govt. investment, private investment, Foreign direct investment and Exports. | It includes savings, Imports, Taxes by the Govt., Payments of old debt of the Govt. |

'Injections' and 'Leakages' can also be clearly understood by the following diagram.

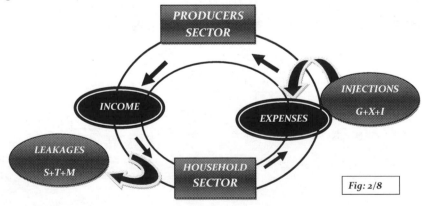

Fig: 2/8

**INJECTIONS**: It refers to those variables which introduce money income into the circular flow and thus increases the national income.

| STATE OF ECONOMY | COMPONENTS OF INJECTIONS |
|---|---|
| 1. In case of two-Sectors Economy (without Financial market) | There is no Injections |
| 2. In case of two-Sectors Economy (with Financial market) | There is injections in the form of Investment |
| 3. In case of three-Sectors Economy | Injections in the form of Investment and Government Expenditure |
| 4. In case of four-Sectors Economy | Injections in the form of Investment, Government Expenditure and Exports |

**LEAKAGES:** It refers to those variables which lead to withdraw money income from the circular flow and thus reduces the national income.

| STATE OF ECONOMY | COMPONENTS OF LEAKAGES |
|---|---|
| 1. In case of two-Sectors Economy (without Financial market) | There is no Leakages |
| 2. In case of two-Sectors Economy (with Financial market) | There is leakages in the form of Savings |
| 3. In case of three-Sectors Economy | Leakages in the form of Savings and Taxes |
| 4. In case of four-Sectors Economy | Leakages in the form of Savings, Taxes and Imports |

**EQUILIBRIUM IS ACHIEVED WHEN INJECTIONS ARE EQUAL TO LEAKAGES.**

__*__*__*__*__*__*__*__*__*__*__*__*__

# IMPORTANT QUESTIONS:

## 1 MARK QUESTIONS:

1. Define circular flow of income.
2. What is meant by household sector?
3. What is meant by producer's sector?
4. What do you mean by rest of the world?
5. Write two examples of injections of national income.
6. Give two examples of leakages of national income of our country.

## 3 OR 4 MARK QUESTIONS:

1. Explain the real flow and monetary flow with the help of example.
2. Distinguish between injections and leakages of national income.
3. How can you explain circular flow of income in case of a closed economy?
4. How can you explain circular flow of income in case of an open economy?
5. Explain the circular flow of income for three sectors and capital market.

## 6 MARK QUESTIONS:

1. Explain the circular flow of income in case of four sectors economy and capital market.
2. How can you explain injections and leakages of national income in an economy?

—*—*—*—*—*—*—*—*—*—*—*—*—

# Chapter - 3

## National Income And Its Related Aggregates:

It is better for the students to clear the concept of economy and economic activities before to study the national income and its related aggregates.

**ECONOMY**: An economy is a system which provides the people living which includes production, consumption, investment, exchange and distribution.

According to Prof. Brown, "An Economy is a system by which people get living".

We can conclude that an economy is a system which produces goods and services for the purpose of providing living to the people. It includes all agricultural activities, industrial activities and service activities which help directly or indirectly to produce goods and services for the satisfaction of human wants and their living.

**BASIC ECONOMIC ACTIVITIES:**

Basic economic activities are those functions of an economy which are required to satisfy human wants and their livelihood. It includes production, consumption and investment.

**PRODUCTION**: It is an activity which helps to produce goods and services by using the factors of production to satisfy human wants and can be measured in term of money.

It includes the following:

a) The goods are produced in order to sale in market with a view to earn profit.
b) The goods and services like school, colleges, hospitals, roads, water supply etc. provided by the Government.
c) Production for self consumption goods.
d) Construction of buildings, bridges, dams etc.

It does not include the domestic services like cooking food, cleaning floor, washing cloth etc. by a housewife, teaching by parents to their own children or nursing by parents to their own children etc. It also does not include leisure time activities.

**CONSUMPTION:** It refers to uses of goods and services to satisfy human wants. It includes the individual consumption and collective consumption.

**INVESTMENT:** Investment is defined as the process of capital formation, or a process of increase in the stock of capital.

Symbolically,

$$I = \Delta K$$

Here, I is Investment, $\Delta K$ is capital stock and change in the capital stock during the year.

## ▪ NATIONAL INCOME ACCOUNTING AND NATIONAL INCME ACCOUNTS:

Business accounting shows the performance of a business firm. Similarly national income accounting shows the performance of a country. National income accounting is a technique to measure the national income of the country in a particular year.

National income accounts are the statistical data relating to production, consumption and distribution of national income of a country in a particular year. National income accounting has the following importance:

a) It helps to measure the national income of the country.
b) It helps to compare the economic growth and national income of one country with other countries.
c) It shows the relative significance of primary, secondary and tertiary sectors of an economy.
d) It helps to formulate the policies for the growth and economic development of the country.
e) It helps to understand the structure of the economy and their contribution to national income.

## ▪ RELATION BETWEEN PRODUCTION, CONSUMPTION AND INVESTMENT:

The basic economic activities production, consumption and investment are inter-related and inter-dependent on each other. Without production consumption and investment are not possible. On the other hand without investment production is also not possible and without production consumption is also not possible. In reality,

---

**PRODUCTION = CONSUMPTION + INVESTMENT**

---

All economic activities are classified into Productive activities and Un-productive activities.

**PRODUCTIVE ACTIVITIES:** It refers to those activities which contribute to the national income of the country.

i)   These activities are bilateral in nature.
ii)  On one side there is the flow of money known as monetary flow and on other hand there is flow of goods and services known as real flow.
iii) These activities are always included in national income.

Examples: Teacher teaches in a school.
    A doctor works in a hospital.
    A shop-keeper sells goods in his shop.

**UNPRODUCTIVE ACTIVITIES:** It refers to those activities which do not contribute to the national income of the country.

i)   These activities are unilateral in nature.
ii)  There will be either flow of money i.e. monetary flow or flow of goods and services i.e. real flow.
iii) These activities are also called transfer payments.
iv)  These activities are not included in national income of the country.

Examples: A teacher teaches his own son at home.
    A nurse looks after her own child at home.
    Father gives pocket allowances to his own daughter.

**NATIONAL INCOME:** National income is the money value of all final goods and services produced by the normal residents of a country during an accounting year in addition to net factor income from abroad.

This concept of national income will be clear if the concept of domestic territory and normal residents are clear.

Now let us discuss the concept of Domestic territory and Normal residents in the context of national income of a country.

## ▪ The concept of Economic Territory of a country or Domestic territory of a country:

In ordinary language economic territory means the territory lying within the political boundary of a country. But in national income accounting the economic territory or domestic territory is used in wider sense.

According to United Nations Organization, "Economic Territory is the geographical territory administered by a Government within which persons, goods and capital circulate freely".

Domestic Territory refers to areas of operation generating domestic income. It includes the followings.

(i) Territory lying within the political boundary of a country including territorial water area.

(ii) Ships and aircrafts owned and operated by the residents between two or more countries. For instance, Indian ships moving between Pakistan, Sri Lanka regularly or passenger planes operated by Indian Airlines between USA and England and India are a part of domestic territory of India.

(iii) Fishing vessels, oil and natural gas rigs and floating platforms operated by the residents of a country in the international water areas or engaged in extraction in areas where the country has exclusive right of exploitation. For instance, fishing boats operated by Indian fishermen in Indian Ocean will be the part of domestic territory of India.

(iv) Embassies, consulates and military establishments of the country (say India) located abroad (say France) will be the part of domestic territory of India.

**Domestic territory of a country does not include the followings:**

(a) Offices of international organizations like ILO, WHO etc. located in the geographical area of the country.

(b) Embassies used and administered by the foreign governments.

## ■ The concept of 'Normal Residents' of a country:

A 'Normal Resident' refers to a person (or an institution) who ordinarily resides in a country for more than one year and whose centre of economic interest lies in the development of that country.

In this regard the following points must be clear to understand the concept of normal resident.

(i) Citizenship is not necessary to be the normal resident. A person can be citizen of one country but at the same time he can be a normal resident of another country. For instance, an NRI (Non Resident Indian) is citizen of India but at the same time he can be normal resident of that country in which he lives (say Canada or USA or any other country).

(ii) Normal residents include individuals as well as institutions or organizations.

(iii) Offices of international organizations like WHO, ILO, IMF etc. will not be the normal resident of any country but the people who are working in these offices will be normal residents of their own countries. For instance, an Indian or a Chinese or an American working in IMF, will be normal resident of India, China, and America respectively.

(iv) Domestic employees working in foreign embassies will be normal residents of their own country. For example, the Indians who are working in the embassy of USA located in India will be the normal resident of India only.

(v) Border workers who cross the border to work in other country regularly and come back at the end of work will be the normal resident of that country in which they live. For instance, the people residing in Nepal but working in India and them cross the border regularly but at the end of work they come back. So they will be normal resident of Nepal but not of India.

**SOME EXCEPTIONAL CASES:**

(a) Students studying abroad will not be considered for normal resident of that country in which they study. For example if any student goes to USA to study and he performs job also there then he will not be the normal resident of USA even if he resides more than one year in USA. This is because the main objective of the student is to study in USA not the job.

(b) Medical patients or players staying abroad will not be considered for normal resident of those countries in which they go.

## ■ National income from different point of view:

In any economy production generates income, income creates expenditure and expenditure calls forth production. So national income can be defined in the following three ways.

(i) From production point view, "National income is the sum total of money value of net flow of all the final goods and services produced by normal residents of a country during a period of account."

(ii) From income point of view Central Statistical Organization (CSO) has defined, "National income is the sum total of factor incomes earned by normal residents of a country in the form of rent, wages, interest and profit in an accounting year".

(iii) From expenditure point of view, Simon Kuznets defined national income as "National product is the net output of commodities and services flowing during the year from the country's productive system into the hands of ultimate consumers or into the net addition to the country's capital goods".

National Income can be measured by current year price and by base year price.

## • Distinction between National income at current year price and national income at base year price:

| BASIS | NATIONAL INCOME AT CURRENT YEAR PRICE. | NATIONAL INCOME AT BASE YEAR PRICE. |
|---|---|---|
| 1. Meaning. | It refers to the money value of all final goods and services produced in a country in a particular year and measured at current year market price. | It refers to the money value of all final goods and services produced in a country in a particular year and measured at base year market price. |
| 2. Other Name. | It is also called as nominal national income or monetary national income. | It is also known as real national income. |
| 3. Indicator of Growth. | It is not considered as true indicator of economic growth. | It is considered as true indicator of economic growth. |
| 4. Causes of Change. | It can be increased without any increase in production but due to increase in price level. | It cannot increase without any increase in production of output. |
| 5. Significance. | It is not significant to compare national income of different years. | It is very significant to compare the national income of different years. |

## • Which price is more suitable to measure the national income of a country and why?

National income refers to the money value of all final goods and services produced by the normal residents of a country in a particular year. National income can be measured at current year price and base year price.

National income if measured at current year price then it shows that national income of the country may increase only due to price rise and without any increase in the production of output. Therefore it does not reflect the true economic condition of the country.

Whereas if national income is measured at base year price then it shows that national income will increase only if the production increases otherwise not. Therefore the base year price is the true indicator of economic growth

311

and it is the better one to measure the national income of any country in any year. This can be explained by the following example.

| YEAR | PRODUCTION OF OUTPUT | PRICE OF OUTPUT (PER UNIT) | NATIONAL INCOME |
|------|----------------------|---------------------------|-----------------|
| 2003 | 500 units | Re. 80 per unit | 500x80 = Re. 40,000 |
| 2009 | 450 units | Re. 100 per unit | 450x100 = Re. 45,000 |
| 2009 | 450 units | Re. 80 per unit | 450x80 = Re. 36,000 |

*Table. 3/1*

From the above table it is clear that in 2009 the production of output has not increased compared to the production in 2003 but if the same production is measured at current year price (Rs. 100 per unit) then monetary national income becomes Re. 45,000 which is more than the national income in 2003 ( national income is Re.40,000). Therefore, current year price shows that the national income of the country increases only due to price rise and without any increase in output, which cannot reflect the true economic condition of the country.

On the other hand if the output of 2009 is measured at base year price (Rs. 80 per unit) then national income is Re. 36,000. i.e. national income has decreased instead of any increase.

So we can conclude that base year price is more suitable and better one to measure national income of any country for any year.

## ▪ Some important concepts of National income and its related Aggregates:

Different economists have explained national income in different forms like gross or net, domestic or national, at market price or at factor cost etc. which are known as different concepts of national income. Its main concepts are as follows.

### (i) GROSS DOMESTIC PRODUCT AT MARKET PRICE (GDP at MP):

It refers to the money value of all final goods and services produced by the residents and non-residents of the country within the domestic territory and measured at market price in a particular year.

GDP is defined as the money value of all final goods and services produced by a country's economic resources located in that country regardless of their ownership, measured in a specific time period.

**FEATURES OF GDP:**

(a) GDP includes the cost of depreciation or consumption of fixed capital.
(b) It includes only the value of final goods to avoid the problem of double accounting.
(c) GDP is monetary concept. So it is generally measured at market price.
(d) It does not include the value of second hand goods.
(e) It is domestic concept so it does not include net factor income from abroad.
(f) It is a flow concept so it is measured at a particular point of time.

GDP is generally measured at current market price but it can also be measured at base year price specially to compare the national income in different years. Then we can convert the GDP at current year price into GDP at base year price in the following way.

$$\text{GDP at Base Year Price} = \frac{\textbf{GDP at Current Year Price}}{\textbf{Current Price Index}} \times 100$$

## (ii) GROSS DOMESTIC PRODUCT AT FACTOR COST (GDP at FC):

It refers to the money value of all final goods and services produced by the residents and non-residents of the country within the domestic territory and measured at factor cost in a particular year.
Symbolically,

GDP at factor cost (GDP at FC) = GDP at MP – Net Indirect Taxes (NIT)
Net Indirect Taxes = Indirect Taxes – Subsidies.

## (iii) NET DOMESTIC PRODUCT AT MARKET PRICE (NDP at MP):

It refers to the money value of all final goods and services produced by the residents and non-residents of the country within the domestic territory less depreciation and measured at market price in a particular year.

313

Symbolically,
    NDP at MP = GDP at MP – Depreciation.

## (iv) NET DOMESTIC PRODUCT AT FACTOR COST (NDP at FC):

It refers to the money value of all final goods and services produced by the residents and non-residents of the country within the domestic territory less depreciation and measured at factor cost during a particular year.

NDP at FC can also be defined as total factor incomes earned by the factors of production accruing in the domestic territory of a country in a particular year. Its main components are compensation of employees, operating surplus and mixed income of self employed.

Therefore NDP at FC can also be defined as the sum total of factor incomes in the form of rent, wages, interest and profit.
Symbolically,
    NDP at FC = GDP at MP – Depreciation – Net Indirect Taxes.
              = NDP at MP – Net Indirect Taxes.

## (v) GROSS NATIONAL PRODUCT AT MARKET PRICE (GNP at MP):

GNP at MP is not domestic concept. It is national concept.

GNP at MP is defined as the market value of all final goods and services produced in the domestic territory of the country by the normal residents during a particular year including net factor income from abroad.

GNP at MP can also be defined as the market value of all final goods and services produced by the resources owned by the country's normal residents whether located inside the country or elsewhere.
Symbolically,
    GNP at MP = GDP at MP + Net Factor Income from Abroad.

## (vi) GROSS NATIONAL PRODUCT AT FACTOR COST (GNP at FC):

GNP at FC is not domestic concept. It is national concept.

GNP at FC is defined value of all final goods and services produced in the domestic territory of the country by the normal residents, measured at factor cost during a particular year including net factor income from abroad.

Symbolically,

GNP at FC = GNP at MP – NET INDIRECT TAXES.

= GDP at MP + (NET FACTOR INCOME FROM ABROAD).

= NATIONAL INCOME (NNP at FC) + DEPRECIATION.

## (vii) NET NATIONAL PRODUCT AT MARKET PRICE (NNP at MP):

NNP at MP is not domestic concept. It is national concept.

NNP at MP is defined as the market value of all final goods and services produced in the domestic territory of the country by the normal residents during a particular year including net factor income from abroad and less depreciation.

NNP at MP can also be defined as the market value of all final goods and services less depreciation, produced by the resources owned by the country's normal residents whether located inside the country or elsewhere.

Symbolically,

NNP at MP = GNP at MP – Depreciation.

= National Income + Net Indirect Taxes.

= NDP at MP + (Net Factor Income from Abroad).

## (viii) NET NATIONAL PRODUCT AT FACTOR COST (NNP at FC):

NNP at FC is not domestic concept. It is national concept.

NNP at FC or national income can also be defined as total factor incomes earned by the factors of production accruing in the domestic territory of a country in a particular year in addition to Net Factor Income from Abroad.

Its main components are compensation of employees, operating surplus and mixed income of self employed and Net Factor Income from abroad.

Therefore NNP at FC can also be defined as the sum total of factor incomes in the form of rent, wages, interest and profit plus net factor income from abroad.

Symbolically,

NNP at FC = NDP at FC + (Net Factor Income from Abroad).

= (Compensation of employees + Operating Surplus + Mixed income of self employed) + (Net Factor Income from Abroad).

## ▪ Net factor income from abroad and its main components:

Net factor income from abroad is defined as the difference between the income received from abroad by the normal residents of a country for rendering factor services and the similar payments made to the non-residents for rendering their factor services within the domestic territory of a country.

Net factor income from abroad (NFYA)
= Factor income from Abroad by the residents – Factor income to Abroad of non-residents in the domestic territory

Its main components are as follows.

(i)   NET COMPENSATION OF EMPLOYEES FROM ABROAD:
(ii)  NET INCOME FROM PROPERTY AND ENTREPRENEURSHIP:
(iii) NET RETAINED EARNINGS OF RESIDENTS COMPANIES FROM ABROAD:

### (i)  NET COMPENSATION OF EMPLOYEES FROM ABROAD:

It is the difference between compensation of resident employees working temporarily in foreign countries and compensation paid to non-resident foreign employees working temporarily in the domestic territory of the country.
Some important points:

- (A) Working temporarily means the time period of stay which will be less than a year. If the person stays more than one year then his income will be included in the national income of that country in which he stays.
- (B) If the person sends a part of his income to his parent country then it will be treated as remittance and current transfer and therefore it will not be included in the net factor income from abroad.

### (ii) NET INCOME FROM PROPERTY AND ENTREPRENEURSHIP:

It is the difference between factor incomes received in the form of rent, interest, dividend (income from property) and profit (income from entrepreneurship) by the resident from abroad and similar payments made to the rest of the world.

### (iii) NET RETAINED EARNINGS OF RESIDENT COMPANIES ABROAD:

Retained earnings refer to the undistributed profits of the companies which are not distributed among the share holders.

Net Retained Earnings of Resident Companies from Abroad is the difference between the retained earnings of resident companies' located abroad and retained earnings of foreign companies located within the domestic territory of a country.

Therefore, Net Factor Income from Abroad
  = (Net compensation of employees + Net income from
  Property and entrepreneurship + Net retained earnings of resident
    companies abroad).

## ▪ Domestic factor income (NDP at FC) and its main components:

Domestic factor income or domestic income refers to the income received by the factors of production for rendering factor services in the production process in the domestic territory of a country. Its main components are as follows:

### (a) Compensation of employees:

It refers to the payments made to the employees by the employer for their services, made either in cash or in kind.

According to Central Statistical Organization (CSO), "Compensation of employees is all payments by the producers of wages and salaries to their employees in cash or kind and of contribution in respect of their employees to social security scheme".

Components of COE:

### (A) Wages and salaries in cash:

  i) Wages and salaries paid to the employees in cash;
  ii) Dearness Allowances (DA), House Rent Allowances (HRA), Bonus, Overtime etc.
  (iii) Transport Allowances, commission, Honorarium etc.

**(B) Wages and salaries in kind**:

   i)   Rent free accommodation
   ii)  Free medical facilities, free education to children, free food, free uniform etc.

**(C) Employer's social security contribution**:

   i)   Contribution to provident fund by employer
   ii)  Retirement pension
   iii) Group insurance premium paid by the employer on behalf of employees.

Students must remember that Compensation of Employees does not include Travelling Allowances. It is because travelling allowances is given to the person or persons for promoting sales or for the development the business i.e. in the interest of the companies. The employees cannot spend this money for their own interest.

**(b) Operating surplus:**

It refers to the income from property in the form of rent, interest, royalty and income from entrepreneurship in the form of profit. Profit has three components like dividend, corporate taxes and undistributed profit or retained earnings.

Rent is accrued from land;

Interest is accrued from financial assets;

Profit is the income of the entrepreneur for rendering his services to produce output. It is the sum total of the following components:

Dividend: it is a part of profit distributed to the shares holders.

Corporate (profit) Tax: it is that part of profit which is paid by the firms to the Government for earning profit.

Undistributed profit: It is that part of profit which is kept by the companies (not distributed) to meet future contingencies.

**(c) Mixed income of self employed:**

It refers to the income from work as well as income from property and entrepreneurship. Generally it is the income generated by the unincorporated

318

enterprises owned by the households individually or in partnerships. For example, income of a doctor from his clinic or income of self employed lawyers. This income is from both his labour and from his property and entrepreneurship. This income is very difficult to separate into compensation of employees or in operating surplus.

Therefore,

Domestic Factor Income (NDP at Factor Cost) =

Compensation of employees
+ Operating Surplus
+ Mixed income of self-employed.

## ▪ CATEGORIES OF DOMESTIC FACTOR INCOME:\

The domestic factor income (NDP at Factor Cost) of a country is obtained by both Private sector and by the Public or Government sector.

**(A) Income from domestic product accruing to Private sector**: It refers to that part of domestic income which accrues only to the private sector.

**(B) Income from domestic product accruing to Public sector**: It refers to that part of domestic income which accrues only to the public or Government sector. It has two components which are as follows:

(i) **INCOME FROM PROPERTY AND ENTRENEURSHIP ACCRUING TO GOVERNMENT ADMINISTRATIVE DEPARTMENT**: It includes income earned by Government Departmental Enterprises (like railways, post and telegraph etc.) from property (rent, interest) and entrepreneurship (profit).

(ii) **SAVINGS OF GOVERNMENT NON-DEPARTMENTAL ENTERPRISES:** It includes retained earnings or undistributed profits of non-departmental Government enterprises (like Air India, FCI, IDBI etc.)

# ▪ Explanation of some important concepts relating to National Income:

(i) Private income, (ii) Personal income, (iii) Personal disposable Income and (iv) National disposable income:

## (i) PRIVATE INCOME:

Private income refers to that income which accrues to private sector from all sources, both within domestic territory as well as from the rest of the world and from any source i.e. earned or unearned. It does not include the income of Government sector.

According to Central Statistical Organization, "Private income is the total of factor income from all sources and current transfers from the Government and rest of the world accruing to private sector".

**Thus, main components of Private Income are as follows.**

(a) Income from domestic product accruing to Private Sector.
(b) Net factor income from abroad.
(c) Current transfers from the Government and rest of the world.
(d) Interest on national debts.

I.e. Private income = (a) + (b) + (c) + (d).

Some Important Concepts:

**Interest on National Debt**: It is defined as the interest paid by the Government of a country on borrowings from the public. It is made either for consumption or for investment or for both.

**Current Transfers**: It is defined as the payments which are made from the current income of the payer and paid for the current consumption of the payee. It can be voluntary like donations, gifts, scholarships etc. or compulsory like sales tax, excise duty etc. current transfers can be categorized into two groups:

(i) Current Transfers from the Government: it includes old age pension, donations, subsidies, unemployment allowances, scholarships etc.

(ii) Current Transfers from the rest of the world: it includes receiving gifts from abroad in cash or in kind, financial and non-financial assistance during natural calamities or during any emergency etc.

## (ii) PERSONAL INCOME:

Personal income is the sum total of current incomes actually received by households or individuals from all sources.

It includes both factor incomes and transfer incomes.

## FEATURES OF PERSONAL INCOME:

(A) It includes income actually received by the households.

(B) It includes both factor income and transfer income.

(C) It includes only current transfer income and from both Government and the rest of the world.

PERSONAL INCOME
= Private income – Undistributed profit (corporate savings)
– Corporation profit tax.

## (iii) PERSONAL DISPOSABLE INCOME:

It is that part of personal income which is actually available with the households either for spending or for saving.

According to Central Statistical Organization, "Personal disposable income is the income remaining with individuals and households after deduction of all taxes levied against their income and their property by the Government".

Personal disposable income
= Personal income – personal direct taxes – miscellaneous Government receipts like fees and fines paid by the households.

## (iv) NATIONAL DISPOSABLE INCOME:

National disposable income is the income from all sources (earned and current transfers from abroad) available to residents of a country for consumption or for saving in a particular time period.

In other words it is the net national income at market price available to a country for disposition.

It is of two types:

## (a) NET NATIONAL DISPOSABLE INCOME

= NNP at FC + Net Indirect Taxes + Net Current Transfers from the Rest of the World.

## (b) GROSS NATIONAL DISPOSABLE INCOME

= Net National Disposable Income + Depreciation.

## ▪ Distinction between change in stock and fixed capital formation:

| BASIS | CHANGE IN STOCK | FIXED CAPITAL FORMATION |
|---|---|---|
| 1. Meaning. | It is the difference between closing stock and opening stock. | It refers to the addition to stock of fixed capital assets in the domestic territory of a country. |
| 2. Depreciation. | There is no depreciation. | There is provision of depreciation. |
| 3. Change of composition. | Its composition changes with respect to time. | Its composition remains constant for a long time. |
| 4. Importance. | It is important for smooth running of the economy. | It is required for increasing economic growth. |
| 5. Relation with demand. | It depends on short run demand. | It depends on long run demand. |
| 6. Example. | It includes change in stock of raw materials, semi finished and finished goods etc. | It includes fixed capital assets like machines, plant, building, transport equipments etc. |

# • Gross Domestic Capital formation and its constituents:

It refers to the stock of capital of a country in a specific time period. It has two components like gross fixed capital formation and change in stock. These are explained in detail.

## (A) GROSS FIXED CAPITAL FORMATION:

It refers to the gross addition to the stock of fixed capital assets in a country in a specific time period. It includes (a) purchase of new assets and (b) net purchase of second hand assets from abroad.

### (a) New assets include the following.

   (i)  It includes residential buildings like flat, hostel etc. and non-residential buildings like commercial shops, office buildings etc.

  (ii)  Construction of roads, bridges, post and telegraph lines etc. made by the Government.

 (iii)  Machinery and other equipments.

 (iv)  Transport equipments.

### (b) Net purchase of second hand assets from abroad:

It refers to the difference between purchase of second hand assets from abroad and sales of second hand assets to abroad.

## (B) CHANGES IN STOCK:

It refers to the difference between stock at the beginning and stock at the end of the year. It includes the following.

   (i)  Change in stock of raw materials, semi finished goods and finished goods held by the producers.

  (ii)  Stock of strategic raw materials like steel, chemicals, and food grains and other goods like oil etc.

 (iii)  Livestock like goat, sheep etc. reared for slaughter by enterprise.

# • Distinction between Domestic income (NDP at FC) and National income (NNP at FC):

| BASIS | DOMESTIC INCOME | NATIONAL INCOME |
|---|---|---|
| 1. Meaning. | NDP at FC can be defined as total factor incomes earned by the factors of production accruing in the domestic territory of a country in a particular year. | It refers to money value of all final goods and services produced by normal residents of a country in a particular year. |
| 2. Residents and non-residents. | It includes income earned by both residents and non-residents. | It includes income earned by only the residents. |
| 3. Net factor income from abroad. | It does not include net factor income from abroad. | It includes net factor income from abroad. |
| 4. Formula. | Domestic income (NDP at FC) = National income— Net factor income from abroad. | National income = Domestic income + Net factor income from abroad. |

# • Distinction between GDP and GNP:

| BASIS | GDP | GNP |
|---|---|---|
| 1. Meaning. | GDP is defined as the money value of all final goods and services produced by a country's economic resources located in that country regardless of their ownership, measured in a specific time period. | GNP at MP can also be defined as the market value of all final goods and services produced by the resources owned by the country's normal residents whether located inside the country or elsewhere. |
| 2. Concept. | It is narrow concept. | It is wider concept. |
| 3. Nature. | It is territorial concept. | It is national concept. |
| 4. NFYA. | It does not include NFYA. | It includes NFYA. |
| 5. Formula. | GDP = GNP – NFYA. | GNP = GDP + NFYA. |

# ▪ What is GNP deflator?

It is defined as the ratio of nominal GNP to real GNP, multiplied by 100. Symbolically,

GNP deflator = $\dfrac{\text{NOMINAL GNP}}{\text{REAL GNP}}$ X 100.

# ▪ Distinction between National income and Private income:

| BASIS | NATIONAL INCOME | PRIVATE INCOME |
|---|---|---|
| 1. Meaning. | It refers to money value of all final goods and services produced by normal residents of a country in a particular year. | Private income refers to that income which accrues to private sector from all sources, both within domestic territory as well as from the rest of the world and from any source i.e. earned or unearned. |
| 2. Nature. | It includes only factor incomes but not transfer incomes. | It includes both factor incomes and transfer incomes. |
| 3. Interest on national debt. | It does not include interest on national debt. | It includes interest on national debt. |
| 4. Incomes of public and private sector. | It includes the incomes both in public and private sector. | It includes only the incomes of private sector. |

# ▪ Distinction between National income and Personal income:

| BASIS | NATIONAL INCOME | PERSONAL INCOME |
|---|---|---|
| 1. Meaning. | It refers to money value of final goods and services produced by normal residents of a country in a particular year. | Personal income is the sum total of current incomes actually received by households or individuals from all sources. |
| 2. Concept. | This concept is related to generation of income. | This concept is related to the receipts of income. |

| 3. Corporate savings and corporate taxes | It includes Corporate savings and corporate taxes. | It does not include Corporate savings and corporate taxes. |
|---|---|---|
| 4. Interest on national debt. | It does not include interest on national debt. | It includes interest on national debt. |
| 5. Nature. | It includes only factor incomes but not transfer incomes. | It includes both factor incomes and transfer incomes. |

## • Distinction between National income and National Disposable income:

| BASIS | NATIONAL INCOME | NATIONAL DISPOSABLE INCOME |
|---|---|---|
| 1. Meaning. | It refers to money value of final goods and services produced by normal residents of a country in a particular year. | National disposable income is the income from all sources (earned and current transfers from abroad) available to residents of a country for consumption or for saving in a particular time period. |
| 2. Nature. | It includes only factor incomes but not transfer incomes. | It includes both factor incomes and transfer incomes. |
| 3. Measurement. | It is measured at factor cost. | It is measured at market price. |
| 4. Formulae. | National income = National disposable income—Net indirect taxes—Net current transfers from abroad. | National Disposable income = National income + NIT + Net current Transfers from abroad. |

## • Distinction between Personal income and Personal Disposable income:

| BASIS | PERSONAL INCOME | PERSONAL DISPOSABLE INCOME |
|---|---|---|
| 1. Meaning. | Personal income is the sum total of current incomes actually received by households or individuals from all sources. | It is that part of personal income which is actually available with the households either for spending or for saving after deduction of all types of taxes relating to their income. |
| 2. Concept. | It is broader concept. | It is narrow concept. |
| 3. Personal direct taxes. | It includes personal direct taxes. | It does not include personal direct taxes. |
| 4. Formulae. | Personal income = Personal Disposable income + Personal direct taxes + Miscellaneous expenses like fees, fines etc. | Personal Disposable Income = Personal income— Personal direct taxes – Miscellaneous expenses like fees, fines tec. |

## • Distinction between National disposable income and Personal disposable income:

| BASIS | NATIONAL DISPOSABLE INCOME | PERSONAL DISPOSABLE INCOME |
|---|---|---|
| 1. Meaning. | National disposable income is the income from all sources (earned and current transfers from abroad) available to residents of a country for consumption or for saving in a particular time period. | It is that part of personal income which is actually available with the households either for spending or for saving after deduction of all types of taxes relating to their income. |
| 2. Nature. | It is national and wider concept and it considers all production units. | It is narrow concept and it considers only individual and household units. |
| 3. Net current transfers. | It considers net current transfers from abroad. | It does not consider net current transfers from abroad. |

- ## Distinction between Private income and Personal income:

| BASIS | PRIVATE INCOME | PERSONAL INCOME |
|---|---|---|
| 1. Meaning. | Private income refers to income accrues to private sector from all sources, both within domestic territory as well as from the rest of the world and from any source i.e. earned or unearned. | Personal income is the sum total of current incomes actually received by households or individuals from all sources. |
| 2. Scope. | It is wider concept. | It is narrow concept. |
| 3. Corporate savings. | It includes corporate savings or undistributed profit. | It does not include corporate savings or undistributed profit. |
| 4. Corporate taxes. | It includes corporate taxes. | It does not include corporate taxes. |

- ## Distinction between Factor income and Transfer income:

| FACTOR INCOME (Factor payments) | TRANSFER INCOME (Transfer payments) |
|---|---|
| 1. It is bilateral concept. | 1. It is unilateral concept. |
| 2. It is an earning concept. | 2. It is a receipt concept. |
| 3. It is a reward for rendering factor services. | 3. It is received without rendering any productive or factor services. |
| 4. It is included in national income of the country. | 4. It is not included in national income of the country. |
| 5. It is earned income. | 5. It is unearned income. |
| 6. Examples: rent, wages, interest and profit. | 6. Examples: pocket allowances, donation, scholarship, old age pension etc. |

__*__*__*__*__*__*__*__*__*__*__*__*__*__

# NATIONAL INCOME AND ITS RELATED AGGREGATES:

1. INTERMEDIATE CONSUMPTION EXPENDITURE OF GENERAL GOVERNMENT:

   = (1) Expenditure on non-durable goods and services
   + (2) Expenditure on durable goods for military purposes
   + (3) Expenditure on maintenance of Government building
   + (4) Gifts (required processing) from Abroad
   _ (1) Net Sales of Second hand Goods
   _ (2) Scrap and Wastage

2. FINAL CONSUMPTION EXPENDITURE OF GENERAL GOVERNMENT:

   = (1) Intermediate Consumption by the Government
   + (2) Expenditure on Compensation of Employees
   + (3) Direct Purchases of goods and services made Abroad
   + (4) Consumption of fixed capital
   _ (1) Value of sales of goods and services

3. HOUSEHOLD PRIVATE FINAL CONSUMPTION EXPENDITURE:

   = (1) Purchase of New durable and non-durable goods and services
   + (2) Direct Purchases from Abroad
   + (3) Production for Self-consumption goods
   + (4) Net value of gifts received in kind
   + (5) Imputed rent of owner occupied houses
   + (6) Benefits received in kind (like wages/salaries, rent free accommodation)
   (-) Net Sales of Second-hand Goods
   (-) Sale of scraps and wastes

4. FINAL CONSUMPTION EXPENDITURE OF NON-PROFIT INSTITUTION SERVING HOUSEHOLDS:

= (1) Expenditure on intermediate consumption
+ (2) Compensation of Employees
+ (3) Net Receipts of Gifts
_ (1) Net Sales

5. PRIVATE FINAL CONSUMPTION EXPENDITURE:

= (1) Household Final Consumption Expenditure
+ (2) Final Consumption Expenditure of Private Non-Profit institutions

1. Calculate intermediate consumption expenditure of General Government from the following information:

|  |  | (Rs. in crores) |
|---|---|---|
| i) | Expenditure on durable goods for military purposes | 400 |
| ii) | Expenditure on non-durable goods and services | 350 |
| iii) | Expenditure on maintenance of Government building | 200 |
| iv) | Compensation of employees paid by Government | 850 |
| v) | Net sales of second-hand goods | 90 |
| vi) | Gifts from abroad required further processing | 300 |

Solution: Intermediate consumption expenditure of General Government =

(1) Expenditure on non-durable goods and services (350)
+ (2) Expenditure on durable goods for military purposes (400)
+ (3) Expenditure on maintenance of Government building (200)
+ (4) Gifts (required processing) from Abroad (300)
_ (1) Net Sales of Second hand Goods (190)

= 350 + 400 + 200 + 300 – 190 = 1250 – 190 = 1060 (Rs. in crores)

2. Calculate final consumption expenditure of Government from the following information:

|  |  | (Rs. in crores) |
|---|---|---|
| i) | Intermediate consumption expenditure of Government | 5000 |
| ii) | Direct purchases from abroad | 2500 |
| iii) | Value of Sales | 2100 |
| iv) | Compensation of employees | 8000 |
| v) | Gifts from abroad required further processing | 350 |

Solution: Government Final consumption expenditure =

= (1) Intermediate Consumption (5000)
+ (2) Compensation of Employees (8000)
+ (3) Direct Purchases made Abroad (2500)
  (1) Value of sales (2100)

= 5000 + 8000 + 2500 – 2100 = 15500 – 2100 = 13400 (Rs. in crores)

3. Calculate household final consumption expenditure from the following information:

|  |  | (Rs. in cores) |
|---|---|---|
| i) | Expenditure on purchase of new goods | 1200 |
| ii) | Net sale of second-hand goods | 350 |
| iii) | Net indirect taxes | 1000 |
| iv) | Direct purchases from abroad | 550 |
| v) | Goods produced for self-consumption | 250 |
| vi) | Compensation of employees | 2200 |

Solution: House-hold final consumption expenditure =

= (1) Purchase of New goods and services (1200)
+ (2) Direct Purchases from Abroad (550)
+ (3) Production for Self-consumption goods (250)
_ (1) Net Sales of Second-hand Goods (350)

= 1200 + 550 + 250 – 350 = 2000 – 350 = 1650 (Rs. in crores)

4. Calculate final consumption expenditure of Private Non-profit institution serving households from the following information:

|  |  | (Rs. in crores) |
|---|---|---|
| i) | Net sales | 1550 |
| ii) | Compensation of employees | 5550 |
| iii) | Intermediate consumption expenditure | 4500 |
| iv) | Gifts received from abroad | 2450 |

Solution:

= (1) Expenditure on intermediate consumption (4500)
+ (2) Compensation of Employees (5550)
+ (3) Net Receipts of Gifts (2450)
_ (1) Net Sales (1550)

= 4500 + 5550 + 2450 – 1550 = 12500 – 1550 = 10950 (Rs. in crores)

5. Calculate Private final consumption expenditure from the following information:

|  |  |  |
|---|---|---|
| i) | House-hold final consumption expenditure | 45000 |
| ii) | Final consumption expenditure of Private non-profit institutions | 25000 |
| iii) | Net sales | 4500 |
| iv) | Compensation of employees | 15000 |

Private final consumption expenditure

= (1) Household Final Consumption Expenditure (45000)
+ (2) Final Consumption Expenditure of Private Non-Profit institutions (25000)
= 45000 + 25000
= 70000 (Rs. in crores)

6. Calculate gross domestic capital formation from the following information:

i)   Purchases of new assets                                                              15000
ii)  Import of new assets                                                                  10000
iii) Purchase of second-hand assets from abroad                              4500
iv)  Sales of second-hand assets to abroad                                       5000

Solution: Gross Domestic Capital Formation =

   (i) Purchase of new assets (15000)
   + (ii) Import of new assets (10000)
   + (iii) Net purchase of second-hand assets from abroad (4500 – 5000)
   = 15000 + 10000 + 4500 – 5000
   = 29500 – 5000 = 24500 (Rs. in crores)

Q. How can you explain that increase in the GDP is not the appropriate index of welfare?

Ans. Welfare refers to the feeling of well-being among the people. Generally Increase in the GDP is regarded as an important index of welfare. But there are some exceptions to this generalization. Sometimes increase in the GDP necessarily does not reflect as the appropriate index of welfare because of the following limitations.

1. Distribution of GDP: If there is an unequal distribution of income by which the rich persons become richer and the poor persons become poorer then increase in GDP does not increase the welfare of the people.
2. High Growth Rate of Population: If the growth rate of population is more than the growth rate of real GDP then it reduces instead of increase the welfare of the people.
3. Composition of GDP: GDP will not increase the social welfare of the country if the GDP increases because of increase in the production of defence goods or due to increase in the production of wine or tobacco.
4. Externalities: Externalities refer to good and bad impact of an economic activity without making any payments or penalties. For example, the air pollution caused by the emitting of smoke by the chimneys or water pollution caused by throwing of waste materials and garbage into the river, decreases the social welfare of the country.

# IMPORTANT QUESTIONS:

1. Define an economy.
2. What is meant by an economic activity?
3. Define productive activity and give two examples.
4. Define unproductive activity with two examples.
5. State three basic economic activities.
6. What is meant by production?
7. Define investment.
8. What do you mean by change in stock?
9. What is meant by fixed capital formation?
10. Define national income accounting.
11. Define national income.
12. Define the term 'Normal residents'.
13. What is GDP at MP?
14. What is NDP at FC?
15. What is meant by national disposable income?
16. Define personal disposable income.
17. What is meant by GNP deflator?
18. Define real national income.
19. Define nominal national income.
20. How do you get Real GDP from Monetary GDP?
21. When will domestic factor income be more than national income?
22. When will be national income be more than domestic factor income?
23. Under what condition GDP will be equal to GNP?
24. When will be GDP at MP will be equal to GDP at Factor Cost?

## 3 OR 4 MARK QUESTIONS:

1. Distinguish between real national income and monetary national income.
2. Distinguish between private income and personal income.
3. Differentiate between personal disposable income and personal disposable income.
4. Which price is better to measure national income of the country and why?
5. Distinguish between national income and private income.
6. Distinguish between domestic factor income and national income.
7. Distinguish between change in stock and fixed capital formation.
8. What is national income accounting? Explain its main importance.
9. Distinguish between net investment and gross investment.
10. Differentiate between factor income and transfer income.
11. Why are exports included but imports are not included in national income?
12. Distinguish between net exports and net factor income from abroad.

## 6 MARK QUESTIONS:

1. Explain the concept of domestic territory of a country in the context of national income.
2. What do you mean by normal resident of a country? Explain its main features.
3. What is meant by net factor income from abroad? Explain its main components.
4. Define GDP. State its main features.

—*—*—*—*—*—*—*—*—*—*—*—*—

# Chapter - 4

## Measurement Of National Income:

National Income or NNP at FC (Net national Product at Factor Cost) is not a domestic concept. It is national concept.

NNP at FC or national income can also be defined as total factor incomes earned by the factors of production accruing in the domestic territory of a country in a particular year in addition to Net Factor Income from Abroad.

Its main components are compensation of employees, operating surplus and mixed income of self employed and Net Factor Income from abroad.

In other words national income is can be defined as an aggregate of flow of production, income and expenditure. It is measured at different stages by different methods.

Professor Schumpeter for the first time measured national income at three levels like production level, income level and expenditure level.

In India National Income is measured by Central Statistical Organization (CSO) by the following three methods.

1. Income method.
2. Expenditure method and
3. Value added or Product method.

## ■ MEASUREMENT OF NATIONAL INCOME BY INCOME METHOD AND ITS PRECAUTIONS:

Income method measures national income from the point of payments made to factors of production in the form of rent, wages, interest and profit for rendering their factor services in an accounting year.

Under this method national income is calculated by adding all factor incomes in the domestic territory in addition to net factor income from abroad.

The important steps are as follows.

## STEP—1: IDENTIFICATION AND CLASSIFICATION OF PRODUCING ENTERPRISES:

All producing enterprises are identified and classified into three categories which are as follows.

(i)   Primary sector: It includes agriculture, mining, fishing, forestry etc. This sector produces goods and services by exploiting natural resources.
(ii)  Secondary sector: It includes all manufacturing industries. This sector transforms the inputs into output.
(iii) Tertiary sector: It is also called as service sector. It does not produce goods but it provides services. It includes transport, banking, communication and insurance etc.

## STEP—2: CLASSIFICATION OF FACTOR INCOMES:

All factor incomes are classified into three categories.

### (a) Compensation of employees:

It refers to the payments made by the employer to the employees for their services, made either in cash or in kind. It includes wages, salaries, dearness allowances, free medical services, and free education to the children, bonus, contribution to provident fund made by the employer etc.

### (b) Operating surplus:

It refers to the income from property in the form of rent, interest, royalty and income from entrepreneurship in the form of profit. Profit has three components like dividend, corporate taxes and undistributed profit or retains earnings.

## (c) Mixed income of self employed:

It refers to the income from work as well as income from property and entrepreneurship like income of a doctor from his clinic.

**STEP—3: CALCULATION OF DOMESTIC INCOME:**

By adding the above mentioned factor incomes i.e. compensation of employees, operating surplus and mixed income of self employed, we get domestic income or NDP at FC.

NDP at FC = C.O.E. + O.S. + MIXED INCOME of self employed.

**STEP—4: CALCULATION OF NATIONAL INCOME:**

When we add Net factor income from abroad with domestic income or NDP at FC, then we get National income or NNP at FC.

Symbolically, NATIONAL INCOME (NNP at FC) =
                    NDP at FC + Net Factor Income from Abroad

## ▪ PRECAUTIONS UNDER INCOME METHOD:

The important precautions are as follows.

(i) Only factor incomes are included but the transfer incomes are not included in national income because transfer payments are unproductive activities.

(ii) Sale and purchase of second hand goods in the domestic territory are not included to avoid the problem of double accounting.

(iii) Illegal activities like smuggling, gambling and black marketing are not included in national income because these are unproductive activities.

(iv) Sales of shares and bonds are not included in national income because these are not related to flow of goods and services in an economy.

(v) Production for self consumption goods are included (its imputed value is included) but the production for self consumption services are not included because it is difficult to measure.

(vi) Imputed rent of owner-occupied houses should be included in national income.

## ▪ MEASUREMENT OF NATIONAL INCOME BY EXPENDITURE METHOD AND ITS PRECAUTIONS:

Expenditure method measures the national income by aggregating all final expenditures. This method actually measures the national income from the point of disposal of GDP. Therefore this method is also called as Income Disposable method or Investment method.

The important steps are as follows.

### STEP—1: IDENTIFICATION AND CLASSIFICATION OF ECONOMIC UNITS INCURRING FINAL EXPENDITURES:

All economic units incurring final expenditure are classified into four categories.

(i) Household sector: It refers to that sector which consumes goods and services.
(ii) Producing sector: It refers to that sector which produces goods and services by using factors of production.
(iii) Government sector: Its main responsibility is to provide services to both household sector and producing sector.
(iv) Rest of the world: It is mainly related with any country by exports and imports.

### STEP—2: CLASSIFICATION OF FINAL CONSUMPTION EXPENDITURE:

Aggregate final expenditure is classified into following categories.

### (A) Government final consumption expenditure:

It refers to the current expenditure on final goods and services by the Government administrative department less sales. It is called collective consumption expenditure like roads, parks, bridges etc. It includes compensation of employees paid by the Government sector, goods and services purchased by the Government sector within the country and purchases of goods and services by the Govt. from abroad.

## (B) PRIVATE FINAL CONSUMPTION EXPENDITURE:

It is obtained when the quantity of final sales of durable goods, semi-durable goods, non-durable goods and services to the consumer households and non-profit institutions serving the households are multiplied by retail prices.

It also includes

(i) The purchases of non-resident households in abroad.
(ii) Wages, salaries, gifts which are received in kind.
(iv) Imputed rent of owner-occupied houses.
(iii) Current purchases of goods and services in the domestic market.

## (C) INVESTMENT EXPENDITURE:

Investment expenditure or Gross domestic capital formation is categorized into fixed investment and inventory investment.

(i) **Fixed investment:** It refers to the expenditure made by the producers on the purchase of fixed assets like machinery, plant. It is further classified into three following groups.

(a) Business fixed investment.
(b) Government fixed investment.
(c) Residential Construction fixed investment.

(ii) **INVENTORY INVESTMENT:** It refers to change in stock during the year. It is estimated as the difference between closing stock and opening stock of the year.

Symbolically, Change in stock = Closing stock – opening stock.

## (D) NET EXPORTS:

Net exports are defined as the difference between exports of goods and services and import of goods and services of a country in an accounting year.

Net foreign investment is the addition of net exports and net factor income from abroad.

Net export = Export – Import.

## STEP—3: CALCULATION OF GDP at MARKET PRICE:

When we add Govt. final consumption expenditure, Private final consumption expenditure, Investment expenditure (Gross domestic capital formation) and Net exports, then we get GDP at MP.

> GDP at MP = Govt. final consumption expenditure + Private final
> Consumption expenditure + Gross domestic capital
> Formation + Net exports.

## STEP—4: CALCULATION OF NDP at FC or DOMESTIC INCOME:

Domestic income is obtained when we subtract depreciation and net indirect taxes from GDP at MP.

> Domestic income (NDP at FC)
> = GDP at MP
> (—) Depreciation (consumption of fixed capital)
> (—) Net indirect taxes (Indirect taxes – subsidies)

## STEP—5: CALCULATION OF NATIONAL INCOME:

When we add Net factor income from abroad with the domestic income then we get national income.

> National Income (NNP at FC) = Domestic income (NDP at FC)
> + (Net factor income from abroad)

## ▪ PRECAUTIONS UNDER EXPENDITURE METHOD:

The important precautions involved in this method are as follows.

(i) Only the final consumption expenditure on goods and services will be included to avoid the problem of double counting.

(ii) Expenditure on intermediate goods is not included in national income to avoid the problem of double counting.

(iii) Expenditure on second hand goods is not included in national income because the value of these goods is already included.

(iv) Expenditure on shares and bonds is not included because these are not related to goods and services. These are only paper claims and these expenditures do not cause any value addition.

(v) Expenditure on transfer payments by the Government like old age pension, scholarship etc. is not included in national income because these expenditures do not cause any value addition.

(vi) Imputed value of expenditure on production for self consumption goods is included because it causes value addition.

(vii) Imputed rent of owner-occupied houses will be included in national income.

## • VALUEADDED METHOD TO MEASURE NATIONAL INCOME AND THE PRECAUTIONS INVOLVED:

This method is also known as output method or product method. This method measures national income from the point of view of the contribution made by all the producing enterprises in the domestic territory of a country in a specific time period.

The important steps are as follows.

### STEP—1: IDENTIFICATION AND CLASSIFICATION OF PRODUCING ENTERPRISES:

All producing enterprises are identified and classified into three categories which are as follows.

(i) Primary sector: It includes agriculture, mining, fishing, forestry etc. This sector produces goods and services by exploiting natural resources.

(ii) Secondary sector: It includes all manufacturing industries. This sector transforms the inputs into output.

(iii) Tertiary sector: It is also called as service sector. It does not produce goods but it provides services. It includes transport, banking, communication and insurance etc.

## STEP—2: CALCULATION OF GROSS VALUE ADDED AT MARKET PRICE:

At first the value of output is calculated by multiplying the goods and services produced by each enterprise with their market price. It can also be calculated by the addition of sales and change in stock.

I.e. Value of Output = Price x Q (G + S):
Q (G + S) means Quantity of Goods and Services.
Or Value of Output = Sales + Change in Stock.

Next, if we subtract the cost of intermediate goods like cost of raw materials, consumption of electricity, fuel etc. i.e. cost of non-factor inputs from the value of output then we get the Gross Value Added at Market Price.

i.e. GVA at MP (GDP at MP)
= Value of Output – Cost of Intermediate goods.

## STEP—3: CALCULATION OF DOMESTIC INCOME (NDP at FC):

When we subtract the value of depreciation and net indirect taxes from the value of GVA at MP then we get domestic income or NVA at FC.

i.e. Domestic Income (NVA at FC) = GVA at MP—Depreciation
– Net Indirect Taxes.
Net Indirect Taxes = Indirect taxes – subsidies.

## STEP—4: CALCULATION OF NATIONAL INCOME:

When we add Net factor income from abroad with the domestic income (NVA at FC) then we get national income.
National Income (NNP at FC) = Domestic income (NVA at FC)
+ Net factor income from abroad.
Net factor income from abroad = Factor income from abroad
- Factor income to abroad.

## ▪ PRECAUTIONS UNDER VALUE ADDED METHOD:

The important precautions involved in this method are as follows.

(i) The sale and purchase of second hand goods will not be included in national income because value of these goods is already included in some previous year.

(ii) Value of intermediate goods will not be included in national income to avoid the problem of double counting.

(iii) The imputed value of the production for self consumption goods will be included in national income because it is a part of gross domestic product.

(iv) Own account production of fixed capital by households, firms and the Government will be included in national income because it is a part of gross domestic product.

(v) Sale and purchase of shares and bonds will not be included in national income because these are only paper claims and do not cause value addition.

(vi) The value of production for self consumption services will not be included in national income because these are free of cost.

## ▪ What is problem of double counting? How can it be avoided?

The problem of double counting means the counting of the value of a commodity more than once. For example, a good before to be transformed into a final commodity it crosses many stages. If the value of that commodity is counted at each stage then there will be a problem of double counting.

For example, a farmer produces a certain quantity of cotton and sells to Mr. A at price of Re. 5000. Mr. A uses cotton and produces Yarn and he sells it to Mr. B at price of Re. 10,000. Mr. B uses yarn to produce cloth and sells cloth at price of Re. 12,000 to the consumer in the market.

Now if the value of the same commodity is counted then total value becomes Re. (5000+10,000+12,000) = Re. 27,000. This clearly reflects the problem of double counting.

**How to avoid the problem of double counting?**

The problem of double counting can be avoided by the following way.

(i) **Final output method**: According to this method the value of only final goods will be included in national income. Final goods are those goods which are ready for consumption and cannot be resold. In case of above example the value of cloth i.e. Re. 12,000 will be included in national income because cloth is the final goods.

(ii) **Value added method:** Value added means the difference between value of output and cost of intermediate goods of the firm. According to this method the value added for the above example can be calculated by the following way with the help of a table.

| PRODUCER | VALUE OF OUTPUT (in Rs.) | INTERMEDIATE CONSUMPTION (in Rs.) | VALUE ADDED (in Rs.) |
|---|---|---|---|
| Farmer | 5000 | 00 | 5000-00=5000 |
| Mr. A | 10,000 | 5000 | 10,000-5000=5000 |
| Mr. B | 12,000 | 10,000 | 12,000-10,000=2000 |
| TOTAL | 27,000 | 15,000 | 27,000-15,000=12,000 |

*Table. 4/1*

So, from the above table it becomes clear that total value added in the economy becomes Re.12.000 which will be included in national income. This value added is equal to the value of final goods in the economy.

- **How is equality of the above three methods proved?**
- **Or reconcile three methods of measuring national income. Which method is more suitable to measure national income?**

It has been clearly observed that national income of any country can be measured by any of the three methods i.e. income method, or expenditure method or value added method. Whatever the method is followed the answer will be the same because the same physical output is measured from different angles. In any country whatever quantity of goods and services will be produced, the same amount of income will be generated. And whatever income will be generated, the same amount of final expenditure will be incurred. Therefore in the economy national income measured by any of the three methods will give the same result.

Besides, the choice of out of three methods depends upon the following factors.

(1) **NATURE OF ECONOMIC ACTIVITIES:** Different method is applied for different activities.

  (i) **Agriculture, forestry, fishing, animal husbandry etc.:** In case of these activities Product method is most appropriate to measure the national income.

  (ii) **Mining, manufacturing, banking, trade, transport and communication etc.:** In case of these activities Income method is most appropriate to measure national income.

  (iii) **Professional services:** Income method is used to measure national income.

  (iv) **Construction activities:** In case of rural and urban construction the expenditure method is used.

(2) **STRUCTURE OF ECONOMY:**

In case of under developed country where agriculture is the main occupation, product method is most appropriate to measure national income.

In case of developed country where main occupation is service sector, income method is used.

In case of mixed economy like India, China, Pakistan the mix of all methods is used to measure national income.

(3) **AVAILABILITY OF DATA:** Choice of any method to measure national income also depends on the availability and reliability of data.

## ▪ COMPENSATION OF EMPLOYEES AND ITS COMPONENTS:

Compensation of employees refers to the payments made to the employees by the employer for their factor services, made either in cash or in kind.

**(1) WAGES AND SALARIES IN CASH:** It includes the followings.

   (i)   Wages and salaries paid in cash.

   (ii)  Dearness allowances (DA), House Rent Allowances (HRA), Bonus, City Compensation Allowances (CCA), Overtime etc.

   (iii) Commissions on sales, Honorarium etc.

   (iv) Transport Allowances.

   (Note: Travelling Allowances is not included.)

**(2) WAGES AND SALARIES IN KIND:** It includes the followings.

   (i)   Rent free accommodation.

   (ii)  Free medical facilities to the employees and their children.

   (iii) Free education to the employees' children.

   (iv) Free food and free uniform.

**(3) EMPLOYERS' CONTRIBUTION TO SOCIAL SECURITY:**

It includes the followings.

   (i)   Employer's contribution for life insurance, casualty insurance etc.

   (ii)  Employer's contribution to provident fund of employees.

   (iii) Retirement pension.

## ▪ CONCEPT OF OPERATING SURPLUS AND ITS COMPONENTS:

Operating surplus refers to the income from property in the form of rent, interest, royalty and income from entrepreneurship in the form of profit. Profit has three components like dividend, corporate taxes and undistributed profit or retained earnings.

The components of operating surplus can be presented in the following way.

**(1) INCOME FROM PROPERTY:** It includes the following.

   (i)   Rent, which includes actual and impudent rent.

   (ii)  Interest.

   (iii) Royalty, which includes royalty on mineral resources, patent right, copy right and trademarks etc.

**(2) INCOME FROM ENTREPRENEURSHIP:**

It includes Profit, the reward of the entrepreneurs.

Profit further classified into three categories like Dividend, corporate tax and undistributed profit or retained earnings.

## ▪ In which sector(s) there is no operating surplus and why?

Operating Surplus does not arise in the Government sector and Subsistence sector because of the following reasons:

(i) **Government Sector:** In this sector goods and services are produced for the collective consumption of the people in the society and the main objective of Government is to promote social welfare not the maximization of profit.

(ii) **Subsistence Sector:** In this sector goods and services are produced to meet the family consumption but not for the sale in the market. Therefore there is no marketing surplus and no operating surplus.

## ▪ THE CONCEPT OF MIXED INCOME OF SELF EMPLOYED:

It refers to the income from work as well as income from property and entrepreneurship.

It includes the following.

(i) Income of self-employed persons like income of a doctor from his clinic, income of a lawyer, income of a chartered accountant etc.

(ii) Profit generated in the unincorporated enterprises like small shop-keepers, small manufacturers, or of artisans etc.

In reality mixed income of self employed person consists of the income from both sources like income from his labour as well as income from his property and entrepreneurship. For example the income of a doctor from his clinic includes the income from his labour and the income from his clinic which is his property and entrepreneurship.

## BASIC CONCEPTS OF MEASUREMENT OF NATIONAL INCOME:

There are three basic concepts to learn and remember the formula of measurement of national income. These are explained in the following way.

### (1)  RELATIONSHIP BETWEEN GROSS AND NET:

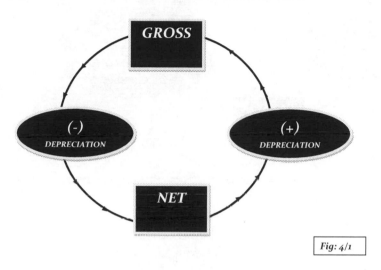

Fig: 4/1

### (2)  RELATIONSHIP BETWEEN DOMESTIC AND NATIONAL:

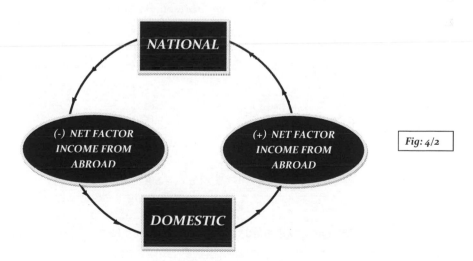

Fig: 4/2

## (3) RELATIONSHIP BETWEEN MARKET PRICE AND FACTOR COST:

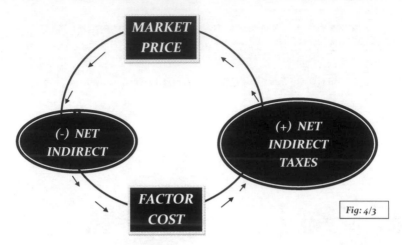

Fig: 4/3

It will be better if the students do some practices of the three basic relations (shown earlier) in the following way.

HOW WILL YOU CALCULATE (i)   NDP at FC from GDP at MP?

(ii)  GDP at MP from NDP at FC?

(iii) NNP at FC from GDP at MP?

(iv) GNP at MP from NDP at FC?

(v)  GNP at MP from NDP at FC?

If the students do practice these types of interpretations then their basic concepts will be clear and it will be easier for them to do the numerical. Let us see how to practice?

(i) NDP at FC from GDP at MP.

NDP at FC
+ Net Indirect Taxes (Because we need to go to MP from FC)
_____

= NDP at MP
+ Depreciation (Because we need to go to Gross from Net)
_____

= GDP at MP

Students are advised to practice interpretation of basic relationship explained earlier in this way as much as possible to clear concept of numerical.

## ▪ MEASUREMENT OF NATIONAL INCOME BY INCOME METHOD:

National income is measured by Income method in the following way.

COMPENSATION OF EMPLOYEES

+

OPERATING SURPLUS

+

MIXED INCOME OF SELF EMPLOYED

---

= DOMESTIC INCOME OR NDP at FC

+

NET FACTOR INCOME FROM ABROAD (NFYA)

---

= NATIONAL INCOME OR NNP at FC

Sometimes the above data are not directly given in the question then we have to find out the required data by using the components. Therefore we have to remember the following points.

(i)   Compensation of employees and its components.
      (Already discussed earlier).
(ii)  Operating Surplus and its components.
      (Already discussed earlier).
(iii) Mixed income of self employed is generally directly given.

## 2. MEASUREMENT OF NATIONAL INCOME BY EXPENDITURE METHOD:

GOVERNMENT FINAL CONSUMPTION EXPENDITURE

+

PRIVATE FINAL CONSUMPTION EXPENDITURE

+

GROSS DOMESTIC CAPITAL FORMATION

+

NET EXPORT (EXPORT-IMPORT)

---

= GROSS DOMESTIC PRODUCT at MARKET PRICE (GDP at MP)

(-) DEPRECIATION OR CONSUMPTION OF FIXED CAPITAL

---

= NET DOMESTIC PRODUCT at MARKET PRICE (NDP at MP)

(-) NET INDIRECT TAXES OR NIT

---

=DOMESTIC INCOME OR NDP at FC

+

NET FACTOR INCOME FROM ABROAD (NFYA)

---

= NATIONAL INCOME OR NNP at FC

### GROSS DOMEST CAPITAL FORMATION:

Sometimes it is directly not given in the question then any of the following formula will be used on the basis of data given in the question.

(i)   Gross Domestic Capital Formation

= Gross Fixed Capital formation + Change in Stock.

(Change in Stock = closing-opening stock).

(ii) = Net Fixed capital formation + Depreciation + Change in Stock.

(iii) = Net domestic capital formation + Depreciation

(iv) = Gross Fixed Capital Formation

+ Change in Stock + Net Acquisition of Valuables.

## 3. MEASUREMENT OF NATIONAL INCOME BY VALUE ADDED METHOD:

SALES (DOMESTIC SALES + EXPORTS)

+

CHANGE IN STOCK (closing –opening stock)

---

= VALUE OF OUTPUT

(-) INTERMEDIATE CONSUMPTION

---

= GROSS VALUE ADDED AT MARKET PRICE (GVA at MP)

(-) DEPRECIATION OR CONSUMPTION OF FIXED CAPITAL

---

= NET VALUE ADDED at MARKET PRICE (NVA at MP)

(-) NET INDIRECT TAXES OR NIT

---

=DOMESTIC INCOME OR NVA at FC

+

NET FACTOR INCOME FROM ABROAD (NFYA)

---

= NATIONAL INCOME OR NNP at FC

Students must remember that GVA at MP or GDP at MP both are used synonymously to calculate the numerical.

Sometimes the question may be given in the following format like **VALUE OF OUTPUT AND INTERMEDIATE CONSUMPTION OF Primary, Secondary and Tertiary sector are given, and then we get** the GVA at MP in the following way.

**Primary Sector:**
Value of Output – intermediate consumption = Value Added in P. S.

**Secondary Sector**:                                      +
Value of Output – intermediate consumption = Value Added in S. S.

**Tertiary Sector:**                                        +
Value of Output – intermediate consumption = Value Added in T. S.
                                          = GVA at MP

353

## ▪ How to calculate NET NATIONAL DISPOSABLE INCOME and GROSS NATIONAL DISPOSABLE INCOME?

(a) NET NATIONAL DISPOSABLE INCOME

=

NATIONAL INCOME (NNP at FC)
+ NET INDIRECT TAXES
+ NET CURRENT TRANSFERS FROM ABROAD.

(b) GROSS DISPOSABLE INCOME

= NET NATIONAL DISPOSABLE INCOME + DEPRECIATION

## ▪ How to calculate PRIVATE INCOME, PERSONAL INCOME AND PERSONAL DISPOSABLE INCOME?

Income from domestic product accruing to Private sector is the most important part of Private income. Let us see how we can get this part from NDP at FC when it is not directly given.

If we subtract NFYA from National Income then we get NDP at FC. NDP at FC has two parts: income from domestic product accruing to private sector and income from domestic product accruing to Govt. sector. Now the income from domestic product accruing to Govt. sector has two parts like income from property and entrepreneurship accruing to Govt. administrative department and savings of non-departmental enterprises.

Therefore if the income from domestic product accruing to Govt. sector is subtracted from NDP at FC then we get the main part of Private income i.e. income from domestic product accruing to Private sector, let it be denoted as x. Then we add 4 factors to the 'x' to get Private income as explained in the next page.

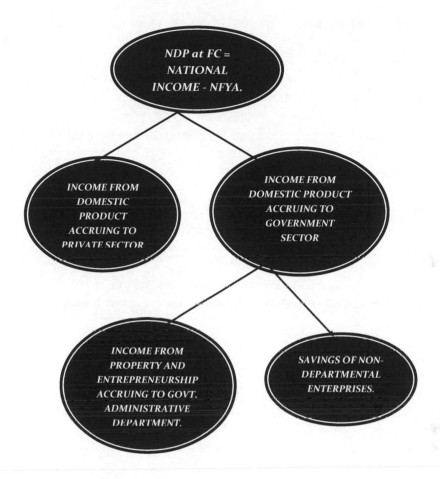

**(A) PRIVATE INCOME:** (x + 4) means as following.

Income from domestic product accruing to PRIVATE Sector

+

Net Factor Income from Abroad

+

Interest on National Debt

+

Current Transfers from Government

+

Current Transfers from Abroad

---

= PRIVATE INCOME

## (B) PERSONAL INCOME:

PERSONAL INCOME = PRIVATE INCOME
     —SAVINGS OF CORPORATE SECTOR
     —CORPORATE PROFIT TAXES.

Savings of corporate sector is also called as undistributed profit or retained earnings.

## (C) PERSONAL DISPOSABLE INCOME:

PERSONAL DISPOSABLE INCOME = PERSONAL INCOME
       —PERSONAL DIRECT TAXES
       —MISCELLANEOUS EXPENSES.

Personal direct taxes mean income tax paid by households.

Miscellaneous expenses means fees, fines etc. paid by the households to the Government.

Ultimately,

PERSONAL DISPOSABLE INCOME =
PERSONAL (HOUSEHOLD) CONSUMPTION + PERSONAL(HOUSEHOLD) SAVINGS

# ▪ NUMERICAL OF NATIONAL INCOME AND ITS RELATED AGGREGATES:

1. Calculate the net value added at factor cost from the following:

|  |  | (Rs. In Crore) |
|---|---|---|
| (i) | Consumption of fixed capital | 30 |
| (ii) | Opening stock | 15 |
| (iii) | Sales | 500 |
| (iv) | Purchase of raw material | 45 |
| (v) | Purchase of services from labourer | 20 |
| (vi) | Purchase of machinery from abroad | 40 |
| (vii) | Sales tax | 10 |
| (viii) | Excise duty | 15 |
| (ix) | Closing stock | 12 |

Ans.

Value of output = Sales + Changes in Stock (closing-opening stock)
$$= 500 + (12 - 15)$$
$$= 500 - 3$$
$$= 497$$

| | | |
|---|---|---|
| Value of Output | = | 497 |
| - Intermediate Consumption | = | -45 |
| GVA at MP | = | 452 |
| - Consumption of Fixed capital | = | -30 |
| NVA at MP | = | 422 |
| - NIT (Indirect Taxes - subsidies) | = | - (10+15-0) = - 25 |
| NVA at FC | = | 397 |

- Here indirect taxes = sales tax + excise duty.
- Purchase of services is not included in intermediate consumption because it is factor services.
- Purchase of machinery is not included in intermediate consumption because it is capital goods.

2. From the following data calculate NVA at FC and show that it is equal to income generated.

|  |  | (Rs. In Crore) |
|---|---|---|
| (i) | Domestic sales | 1200 |
| (ii) | Purchase of raw materials | 450 |
| (iii) | Export | 150 |
| (iv) | Depreciation | 65 |
| (v) | Import of raw materials | 85 |
| (vi) | Increase in stock | 100 |
| (vii) | Dividend | 120 |
| (viii) | Undistributed Profit | 80 |
| (ix) | Interest | 285 |
| (x) | Wages and salaries | 280 |
| (xi) | Rent | 50 |
| (xii) | Indirect taxes | 35 |

Ans.

Value of output = Sales + Changes in Stock
$$= (1200 + 150) + 100$$
$$= 1350 + 100$$
$$= 1450$$

| Value of Output | = | 1450 |
|---|---|---|
| (-) Intermediate Consumption | = | - (450+85) = 535 |
| GVA at MP | = | 915 |
| (-) Depreciation | = | - 65 |
| NVA at MP | = | 850 |
| -   NIT (Indirect Taxes - subsidies) | = | - 35 |
| NVA at FC | = | 815 Crore. |

| Income Generated | = | Sum of factor incomes. |
|---|---|---|
| Compensation of Employees | = | 280 |
| +   Operating Surplus | = | 50+285 + (120+80) = 535 |
| Income Generated (NDP at FC) | = | 815 Crore. |

3.  Calculate value added by firm A and firm B and GVA at FC from the following:

|     |                                        | (Rs. In Lakhs) |
| --- | -------------------------------------- | -------------- |
| (i) | Sales by Firm B to Households          | 125 |
| (ii) | Sales BY Firm A                       | 620 |
| (iii) | Purchases by Government from Firm B  | 250 |
| (iv) | Export by Firm B                     | 75 |
| (v) | Chang in stock of Firm A              | 15 |
| (vi) | Change in stock of Firm B            | 25 |
| (vii) | Imports by Firm A                   | 90 |
| (viii) | Sales by Firm C to Firm A          | 325 |
| (ix) | Purchases by Firm B from Firm A      | 150 |
| (x) | Net indirect taxes                    | 85 |

Ans.

| FIRMS | VALUE OF OUTPUT | INTERMEDIATE CONSUMPTION | VALUE ADDED |
| --- | --- | --- | --- |
| A | 620 + 15=635 | 90 + 325 = 415 | 635-415= 220 |
| B | 125+75+25+250 =475 | 150 | 475-150= 325 |
| TOTAL | 1110 | 565 | 545 |

So GVA at MP = 545

GVA at FC = GVA at MP – NIT

= 545 – 85

= 460 (Rs.in Lakh)

4.  Calculate value added of firm X and firm Y from the following data.

(Rs. In Lakh)

| | |
|---|---:|
| (i) Closing stock of firm X | 15 |
| (ii) Closing stock of firm Y | 25 |
| (iii) Opening stock of firm Y | 35 |
| (iv) Opening stock of firm X | 10 |
| (v) Sales by firm X | 400 |
| (vi) Purchase by firm X from firm Y | 90 |
| (vii) Purchase by firm Y from firm X | 120 |
| (viii) Sales by firm Y | 300 |
| (ix) Import of raw material by firm X | 60 |
| (x) Export by firm Y | 40 |

Ans.

| FIRMS | VALUE OF OUTPUT | INTERMEDIATE CONSUMPTION | VALUE ADDED |
|:---:|:---|:---|:---|
| X | 400+(15-10) = 405 | 90 + 60 = 150 | 405-150 = 255 |
| Y | 300+(25-35)+40 = 330 | 120 | 330-120=210 |
| TOTAL | 735 | 270 | 465 |

GVA at MP = 735-270

= 465 (Rs. In lakh)

5. Calculate the value of output from the following data.

|  | (Rs. In lakh) |
|---|---|
| (i) Net value added at factor cost | 200 |
| (ii) Excise duty | 30 |
| (iii) Sales tax | 15 |
| (iv) Depreciation | 60 |
| (v) Subsidy | 10 |
| (vi) Intermediate consumption | 80 |

Ans. Let value of output is X.

| | |
|---|---|
| Value of output | = X |
| (-) Intermediate consumption | = 80 |
| GVA at MP | = X-80 |
| (-) Depreciation | = 60 |
| NVA at MP | = X - 140 |
| (-) Net indirect tax | = (30+15-10) = 35 |
| NVA at FC | = X - 175 |

Therefore, X – 175 = 200

Or, value of output, X = 200 + 175 = 375 (Rs. In lakh).

6. Calculate intermediate consumption from the following data.

| | | (Rs. In lakh) |
|---|---|---|
| (i) | Net value added at factor cost | 150 |
| (ii) | Excise duty | 20 |
| (iii) | Sales tax | 15 |
| (iv) | Depreciation | 40 |
| (v) | Subsidy | 10 |
| (vi) | Value of output | 340 |

Ans. Let intermediate consumption is M.

| | | |
|---|---|---|
| | Value of output | = 340 |
| (-) | Intermediate consumption | = X |
| | GVA at MP | = 340 - X |
| (-) | Depreciation | = 40 |
| | NVA at MP | = 340 – X – 40 = 300 - X |
| (-) | Net indirect tax | = (20+15-10) = 25 |
| | NVA at FC | = 275 - X |

Therefore, 275 - X = 150

Or, intermediate consumption, M = 275 - 150 = 125 (Rs. In lakh).

7. Calculate sales from the following data.

|  |  | (Rs. In lakh) |
|---|---|---|
| (i) | Net value added at factor cost | 150 |
| (ii) | Indirect tax | 25 |
| (iii) | Depreciation | 50 |
| (iv) | Subsidy | 10 |
| (v) | Change in stock | (-) 40 |
| (vi) | Intermediate consumption | 140 |

Let sales is X.

| | |
|---|---|
| Value of output = sales + change in stock | = X + (-40) = X - 40 |
| (-)  Intermediate consumption | = 140 |
| GVA at MP | = X - 40 – 140 = X-180 |
| (-)  Depreciation | = 50 |
| NVA at MP | = X – 230 |
| (-)  Net indirect tax | = (25-10) = 15 |
| NVA at FC | = X - 245 |

Therefore, X - 245 = 150

Or, Sales, X = 245 + 150 = 395 (Rs. In lakh).

8. Calculate National Income from the following data.

|  |  | (Rs. In lakh) |
|---|---|---|
| (i) | Private final consumption expenditure | 80 |
| (ii) | Net factor income to abroad | 10 |
| (iii) | Subsidies | 5 |
| (iv) | Rent | 5 |
| (v) | Government final consumption expenditure | 40 |
| (vi) | Indirect taxes | 25 |
| (vii) | Net domestic fixed capital formation | 35 |
| (viii) | Addition to stock | (-10) |
| (ix) | Interest and profit | 20 |
| (x) | Wages and salaries | 60 |
| (xi) | Net exports | 50 |
| (xii) | Social security contribution by employer | 5 |
| (xiii) | Mixed income of self employed | 45 |
| (xiv) | Depreciation | 35 |

Ans. By using Income method

|  |  |  |
|---|---|---|
|  | Wages and salaries | 60 |
| + | Social security contribution by employer | 5 |
|  | (i) Compensation of employees | = 65 |
| + | (ii) Operating surplus | = 25 |
| + | (iii) Mixed income of self employed | = 45 |
|  | = Domestic income or NDP at FC | = 135 |
| + | Net factor income from abroad | = + (-10) |
| = | National income or NNP at FC | = 125 |

By using Expenditure method

| | | |
|---|---|---|
| | Govt. final consumption expenditure | = 40 |
| + | Private final consumption expenditure | = 80 |
| + | Gross domestic capital formation | |
| | (Net fixed capital formation + Depreciation | |
| + | Change in stock) = 35+0+(-10) = | = 25 |
| + | Net exports | = 50 |
| = | Gross Domestic Product at MP or GDP at MP | = 190 |
| - | Depreciation | = 35 |
| = | NDP at MP | = 155 |
| - | Net indirect taxes (NIT) = (25-5) = | = 20 |
| = | NDP at FC = 135 | |
| + | Net factor income from abroad | = + (-10) |
| = | National income or NNP at FC | = 125 |

So the national income by both methods is Rs. 125 lakh.

Note: Here in the question net factor income to abroad is given in place of net factor income from abroad. We took the opposite of net factor income to abroad i.e. (-10).

9. Calculate GNP at MP by income method and value added method from the following data.

| | | |
|---|---|---|
| (i) | Value of output | 700 |
| (ii) | Consumption of fixed capital | 30 |
| (iii) | Change in stock | 40 |
| (iv) | Indirect taxes | 30 |
| (v) | Purchasing of raw materials | 200 |
| (vi) | Profit | 10 |
| (vii) | Net factor income from abroad | 20 |
| (viii) | Wages and salaries | 220 |
| (ix) | Operating surplus | 20 |
| (x) | Contribution to provident fund by employer | 25 |
| (xi) | Mixed income of self employed | 85 |

By using value added method

| | | |
|---|---|---|
| | Value of output | = 610 |
| - | Intermediate consumption | = 200 |
| = | Gross Value Added at MP | = 410 |
| + | Net Factor Income from Abroad | = 20 |
| = | GNP at MP | = 430 |

By using Income method:

| | | |
|---|---|---|
| | Wages and salaries | = 220 |
| + | Contribution to Provident fund by employer | = 25 |
| = | (i) Compensation of employees | = 245 |
| + | (ii) Operating surplus | = 20 |
| + | (iii) Mixed income of self employed | = 85 |
| = | Domestic income or NDP at FC | = 350 |
| + | Net factor income from abroad | = (20) |
| = | National income or NNP at FC | = 370 |
| + | Net Indirect Taxes (Indirect tax-subsidies) | = 30 |
| = | NNP at MP | = 400 |
| + | Consumption of fixed capital | = 30 |
| = | GNP at MP | = 430 |

10. Calculate NNP at FC by expenditure method and by value added method from the following data.

| | (Rs. In Crores) |
|---|---|
| (i) Gross domestic fixed capital formation | 210 |
| (ii) Net exports | (-) 50 |
| (iii) Private Final consumption expenditure | 900 |
| (iv) Value of output of | |
| a) Primary sector | 890 |
| b) Secondary sector | 780 |
| c) Tertiary sector | 400 |
| (v) Value of intermediate consumption of | |
| a) Primary sector | 400 |
| b) Secondary sector | 300 |
| c) Tertiary sector | 200 |
| (vi) Consumption of fixed capital | 80 |
| (vii) Net indirect taxes | 90 |
| (viii) Government final consumption expenditure | 100 |
| (ix) Net factor income from abroad | (-) 20 |
| (x) Net increase in stock | 10 |

Ans. By using Expenditure method

| | |
|---|---|
| Govt. final consumption expenditure | = 100 |
| + Private final consumption expenditure | = 900 |
| + Gross domestic capital formation | |
| (Gross fixed capital formation | |
| + Change in stock) = 210 +10 = 220 | = 220 |
| + Net exports | = (-50) |
| = Gross Domestic Product at MP or GDP at MP | = 1170 |
| - Depreciation | = 80 |
| = NDP at MP | = 1090 |
| - Net indirect taxes (NIT) | = 90 |
| = NDP at FC | = 1000 |
| + Net factor income from abroad | = + (-20) |
| = National income or NNP at FC | = 980 |

By using value added method

Value of output of

| | | |
|---|---|---|
| (a) Primary sector | = 890 | |
| (b) Secondary sector | = 780 | |
| (c) Tertiary sector | = 400 | |
| (A) Gross Value of output | = 2070 | |

Intermediate consumption

| | | |
|---|---|---|
| (a) Primary sector | = 400 | |
| (b) Secondary sector | = 300 | |
| (c) Tertiary sector | = 200 | |
| (B) Gross intermediate consumption | = 900 | |

| | | |
|---|---|---|
| = | Gross Value Added at MP | = (A) – (B) |
| = | 2070 – 900 | = 1170 |
| | GVA at MP = | = 1170 |
| - | Depreciation | = 80 |
| | NVA at MP | = 1090 |
| - | NIT (Net indirect taxes) | = 90 |
| | NVA at FC | = 1000 |
| + | (Net factor income from abroad) | = + (-20) |
| = | National income or NNP at FC | = 980 |

So,

By both the methods the required national income is Rs. 980 Crore.

11. Calculate (i)Private income, (ii) Personal income, (iii) Personal disposable income, (iv) National disposable income and (v) Gross national disposable income from the following data.

|     |                                                                                          | (Rs. In Crore) |
| --- | ---------------------------------------------------------------------------------------- | -------------- |
| (a) | Net domestic product at factor cost                                                      | 650            |
| (b) | Indirect taxes                                                                           | 60             |
| (c) | Subsidies                                                                                | 10             |
| (d) | Net factor income from abroad                                                            | (-20)          |
| (e) | Income from entrepreneurship and property Accruing to Govt. administrative department    | 30             |
| (f) | Savings of Non-departmental enterprises                                                  | 10             |
| (g) | Current transfers from Govt. Department                                                  | 100            |
| (h) | Current transfers from abroad                                                            | 50             |
| (i) | Corporate profit tax                                                                      | 15             |
| (j) | Net exports                                                                              | 25             |
| (k) | Consumption of fixed capital                                                             | 50             |
| (l) | Savings of private corporate sector                                                      | 30             |
| (j) | Direct taxes paid by households                                                          | 150            |
| (k) | Miscellaneous expenses                                                                   | 60             |
| (l) | Interest on national debt.                                                               | 20             |

Ans.

|   |                                                                                          |         |
| - | ---------------------------------------------------------------------------------------- | ------- |
|   | NDP at FC                                                                                | = 650   |
| - | Income from domestic product accruing to Govt. administrative department                 | = 30    |
| - | Savings of non-departmental enterprises                                                  | = 10    |
| = | Income from domestic product accruing to Private sector                                  | = 610   |
| + | Net factor income from abroad                                                            | = (-20) |
| + | Current transfer from the Govt.                                                          | = 100   |
| + | Current transfers from abroad                                                            | = 50    |
| + | Interest on national debt.                                                               | = 20    |
| = | Private Income                                                                           | = 760   |
| - | Savings of private corporate sector                                                      | = 30    |
| - | Corporate profit tax                                                                      | = 15    |
| = | Personal Income                                                                          | = 715   |
| - | Personal direct taxes                                                                    | = 150   |
| - | Miscellaneous expenses                                                                   | = 60    |
| = | Personal Disposable Income                                                               | = 505   |

National Disposable Income

| | | |
|---|---|---|
| = | National Income (NDP at FC + NFYA) = 650 + (-20) | = 630 |
| + | NIT = (60 - 10) | = 50 |
| + | Net current transfers from abroad | = 50 |
| | So, National Disposable Income | = 730 |
| + | Depreciation | = 50 |
| = | Gross National Disposable Income | = 780 |

(i) Private income = Rs. 760 crore.
(ii) Personal income = Rs. 715 crore.
(iii) Personal disposable income = Rs. 505 crore.
(iv) National disposable income = Rs. 730 crore.
(v) Gross national disposable income = Rs. 780 crore.

12. Calculate Private income and National income and National Disposable Income from the following data.

| | | (Rs. In Crore) |
|---|---|---|
| (i) | Personal consumption | 60 |
| (ii) | Personal savings | 45 |
| (iii) | Corporate profit tax | 20 |
| (iv) | Undistributed profit | 15 |
| (v) | National debt interest | 10 |
| (vi) | Current transfer from Govt. administrative department | 20 |
| (vii) | Current transfers from abroad | 12 |
| (viii) | Net factor income from abroad | (-15) |
| (ix) | Savings of non-departmental enterprises | 25 |
| (x) | Income from domestic product accruing to Govt. administrative department | 32 |
| (xi) | Personal Direct taxes | 25 |
| (xii) | Fees and Fines paid by individual households | 15 |
| (xiii) | Net indirect taxes | 13 |

Ans.

|   |   |   |
|---|---|---|
|   | Personal consumption | = 60 |
| + | Personal savings | = 45 |
| = | Personal Disposable income | = 105 |
| + | Personal direct taxes | = 25 |
| + | Fees and fines paid by households | = 15 |
| = | Personal income | = 145 |
| + | Undistributed profit | = 15 |
| + | Corporate profit tax | = 20 |
| = | Private income | = 180 |
| - | National debt interest | = 10 |
| - | Net factor income from abroad | = (-15) |
| - | Current transfer from Govt. | = 20 |
| - | Current transfers from abroad | = 12 |
| = | Income from domestic product | |
|   | Accruing to private sector | = 153 |
|   | Income from domestic product | |
|   | Accruing to Private sector | = 153 |
| + | Savings of non-departmental enterprises | = 25 |
| + | Income from domestic product accruing to Govt. administrative department | = 32 |
| = | NDP at FC | = 210 |
| + | Net factor income from abroad | = (-15) |
| = | National Income or NNP at FC | = 195 |
| + | Current transfers from abroad | = 12 |
| + | Net indirect taxes | = 13 |
| = | National Disposable Income | = 220 |

Private income = Rs. 180 crore.
National income = Rs. 195 crore.
National Disposable Income = Rs. 220 crore.

13. Calculate National Income from the following data.

| | | (Rs. In crore) |
|---|---|---|
| (i) | Government fixed investment | 120 |
| (ii) | Inventory investment | 80 |
| (iii) | Net Factor income from abroad | (-10) |
| (iv) | Depreciation | 45 |
| (v) | Indirect taxes | 30 |
| (vi) | Subsidies | 10 |
| (vii) | Consumption expenditure | 140 |
| (viii) | Residential construction investment | 60 |
| (ix) | Business fixed investment | 30 |

Ans.

| | | |
|---|---|---|
| | Government fixed investment | = 120 |
| + | Inventory investment | = 80 |
| + | Residential construction investment | = 60 |
| + | Business fixed investment | = 30 |
| = | Investment expenditure | = 290 |
| + | Consumption expenditure | = 140 |
| = | GDP at MP | = 430 |
| | GDP at MP | = 430 |
| - | Depreciation | = 45 |
| = | NDP at MP | = 385 |
| - | NIT (30-10) | = 20 |
| = | NDP at FC | = 365 |
| + | NFYA | = (-10) |
| = | National Income | = 355 (Rs. In crore) |

14. Calculate GVA at Factor Cost from the following data.

|  |  | (Rs. In crore) |
|---|---|---|
| (i) | Sales | 300 |
| (ii) | Opening stock | 20 |
| (iii) | Closing stock | 10 |
| (iv) | Purchasing of raw materials | 160 |
| (v) | Purchase of machinery | 100 |
| (vi) | Subsidy | 40 |

| | | |
|---|---|---|
| | Value of output = Sales + change in stock = 300 + (10-20) | = 290 |
| - | Purchasing of raw materials | = 160 |
| = | GVA at MP | = 130 |
| - | NIT (Indirect tax-subsidies) = (0 - 40) = (-40) | = (-40) |
| = | GVA at FC | = 170 |

So, GVA at FC = Rs. 170 Crore.

## Measurement Of National Income:

CERTAIN IMPORTANT POINTS:

1. COMPENSATION OF EMPLOYEES/Remuneration of employees/Emoluments: It includes the following:

1. Wages and salaries
2. Free medical facilities
3. Free education to children
4. Rent free accommodation
5. Dearness allowances
6. Transport allowances
7. Employer's contribution to social security scheme (P.F)
8. Bonus
9. Commissions on sales
10. Subsidised food to employees
11. LTC (Leave Travel Concessions)
12. Retirement Pension

The following items are not included in C.O.E

1. Travelling Allowances
2. Employees' contribution to Social Security Schemes
3. Old age pension.
4. Free uniform or gifts provided to employees by employer in any occasion like Diwali/Durgapuja etc.

2.      OPERATING SURPLUS:

It includes rent, interest, profit and royalty.

Profit includes dividend, corporate tax and undistributed profit or retained earnings.

## Some Numerical Of Generation Of Income:

1. Calculate compensation of employees from the following information:

|      |                                    | (Rs. in crores) |
|------|------------------------------------|-----------------|
| i)   | Dearness allowances                | 55              |
| ii)  | Old age pension                    | 65              |
| iii) | Wages and salaries                 | 125             |
| iv)  | Subsidy on lunch to employees      | 20              |
| v)   | Free medical treatment             | 35              |
| vi)  | House rent allowances              | 70              |
| vii) | Bonus                              | 22              |
| viii)| Travelling allowances              | 28              |
| ix)  | Employer's contribution to P.F.    | 18              |

Solution: Compensation of Employees
$$= i) + iii) + iv) + v) + vi) + vii) + ix)$$
$$= 55 + 125 + 20 + 35 + 70 + 22 + 18$$
$$= 345 \ (Rs. \ in \ crores)$$

2. Calculate Gross Operating Surplus and Net Operating Surplus from the following information:

|  |  | (Rs. in crores) |
|---|---|---|
| i) | Intermediate consumption | 25000 |
| ii) | Value of output | 75000 |
| iii) | Mixed income of self-employed | 15000 |
| iv) | Remuneration to employees | 20000 |
| v) | Depreciation (consumption of fixed capital) | 8000 |
| vi) | Indirect taxes | 1500 |
| vii) | Subsidies | 100 |
| viii) | Rent, interest | 3000 |

Solution: Value of output – intermediate consumption = GVA at MP
 So, GVA at MP = 75000 – 25000 = 50000
Now, GVA at MP – Depreciation = NVA at MP
 So, NVA at MP = 50000 – 8000 = 42000
Now, NVA at MP – NIT = NVA at FC
 So, NVA at FC = 42000 – (1500-100)
= 42000 – 1400 = 40600

Now, NVA at FC
 = C.O.E. + Operating Surplus + Mixed income of self-employed
Or, 40600 = 20000 + Operating Surplus + 15000
Or, Operating Surplus = 40600 – 35000 = 5600

Net Operating Surplus = Gross Operating Surplus – rent, interest
 = 5600 – 3000 = 2600 (Rs. in crores)

# How will the Following be Treated while Calculating National Income of India?

**1. Production for self-consumption goods and services:**

Imputed value of production for self consumption goods will be included in national income because it contributes to the national income. But production for self consumption services will be not included in national income because it is difficult to measure its contribution.

**2. Sale and purchase of second hand goods:**

Sale and purchase of second hand goods inside the domestic territory will not be included in national income because its value is already included. So if it is included then there will be the problem of double counting. But sale and purchase of second hand goods from abroad will be included in national income.

**3. Sales and purchase of shares, bonds and debentures:**

These are not included in national income these do not contribute to the flow of goods and services in the economy. These are only financial transactions or paper claims.

**4. Commissions on sales:**

These are included in national income because these are part of compensation of employees.

### 5. National debt interest:

It is not included in national income because it is spent by the Govt. for social welfare and it is a part of Private income.

### 6. Bonus to employees:

It is included because it is a part of compensation of employees.

### 7. Profit earned by the State Bank of India in America:

It is included in the national income of India because it is a part of factor income from abroad.

### 8. Net indirect taxes:

It is not included in national income but it is a part of GNP at MP.

### 9. Income from smuggling, gambling or winning prize from lottery:

These are not included in national income because these are activities are not legal activities.

### 10. Tuitions by a school teacher or college teacher:

This is not included because this has no legal sanction.

### 11. Old age pension and retirement pension:

Old age pension is not included in national income because it is transfer payment. But the retirement pension is included in national income because it is a part of compensation of employees.

### 12. Ration and uniform facilities to army employees:

These are included in national income because these are a part of compensation of employees.

**13. kBlack money:**

This is not included in national income because this is an illegal activity.

**14. Tip to bearer in a hotel:**

It is included in national income because it contributes to the flow of goods and services in the economy.

**15. Tip to a beggar:**

It is not included in national income because it does not contribute to the flow of goods and services.

**16. Financial help received by the parents from their son from abroad.**

It is not included in national income because it is transfer payments.

**17. Financial help to the victims of natural calamities:**

It is not included in national income because it is transfer payments.

**18. Travelling Allowances paid by the employer:**

This is not included in national income because it is not a part of factor income.

**19. Purchase of vegetables by a restaurant:**

It is not included in national income because it is intermediate consumption.

**20. Allowances to M.P.**

It is included in national income because it is a part of his factor income.

**21. Salary paid to an American official working in India;**

It is not included in national income of India because it is a part of factor income to abroad.

## 22. Payment of installment on home loans:

It is not included in national income because it is not a part of factor income.

## 23. Admission fees paid by a student:

It is included in national income because it is a part of factor income.

## 24. Consultation fees to the lawyer:

It is included in national income because it is a part of factor income.

## 25. Defence and security services:

These services may be taken as intermediary or final. These are final services because these services provide security and peace to the country. On the other hand these services are intermediary because these services provide peaceful environment to the productive process.

## 26. Expenditure on repair and maintenance of fixed assets:

These will not be included in national income because these are intermediate consumption.

## 27. Money deposited in banks or post offices:
These will not be included in national income because these are only financial transactions and do not contribute to the flow of goods and services in the economy.

## 28. Dividend received by individual households:

These will be included in national income because these are reward for the use of capital and these add to the flow of goods and services in the economy.

## 29. Salary paid to the servant in a family:

It is included in national income because it is payment for the factor services.

**30. Bus fare paid by the passengers:**

This will be included in national income because this is reward of factor services and ads to the flow of services in the economy.

**31. Increase in the price of stocks lying with traders:**

It is not included in national income as it does not contribute to the flow of goods and services in the economy.

**32. Profit earned by a foreign bank located in India:**

It is a part of domestic income of India but not of national income of India because it is a part of factor income to abroad.

**33. Purchases by foreign tourists in India:**

Yes, it is included in national income of India as it is treated a part of our exports and thus by expenditure method it is included.

**34. Rent received by Indian residents on their house/building in America:**

Yes, it is included in national income of India as a part of factor income from abroad.

**35. Payment of fees to a lawyer engaged by a firm:**

No, it is not included in National income because it is treated as intermediate expenditure of the firm.

**36. Profits earned by Tata steel industries located in abroad:**

Yes, it is included in national income of India as a part of factor income from abroad.

**37. Salaries earned by Indian workers working in American embassy located in India:**

Yes, it is included in national income of India as a part of factor income from abroad. And it is included in the GDP of America but not of India's GDP.

**38. Expenditure made by a firm on advertisement for its product:**

No, it is not included because it is treated as intermediate expenditure of firm.

**39. Expenditure made by Government to provide free education in the country:**

Yes, it is included in the national income of India as it is a part of Government final consumption expenditure.

**40. School fees paid by a student:**

Yes, it is included as it is a part of private final consumption expenditure.

**41. Purchase of a truck for transporting goods by a firm:**

Yes, it is included in national income as it is a part of gross domestic fixed capital formation.

**42. Transport expenses incurred by a firm to carry goods:**

No, it is not included in national income as it is treated as intermediate consumption expenditure.

**43. Purchase of a machinery by a firm:**

Yes, it is included in national income as this investment is a part of gross domestic capital formation.

**44. Interest paid by an individual taken loan to build a house or to buy a car:**

Yes, it is included in national income as it is a part of private final consumption expenditure.

**45. Vegetables grown by a farmer for the consumption of his family:**

Yes, it is included in national income as imputed value of production of self consumption goods.

**46. Purchase of a tractor and fertilizers by a farmer:**

Purchase of a tractor is an investment of the farmer and therefore it is included in national income as a part of gross domestic capital formation. But the purchase of fertilizers will not be included in national income because it is treated as intermediate consumption expenditure.

**47. Expenditure made by a school for the payment of electricity bill:**

No, it is not included in national income as it is treated as intermediate consumption expenditure.

**48. Expenditure made by a household for the payment of electricity bill:**

Yes, it is included in national income as it is treated as private final consumption expenditure.

**49. Expenditure on maintenance of school building:**

It is not included in national income as it is treated as intermediate consumption expenditure.

**50. Expenditure on a machine to improve its performances:**

Yes, it is included in national income as it is treated as investment expenditure.

## ▪ How will you treat purchase of a machine in estimating national income?

(a) Machine like washing machine or vacuum cleaner purchased by a household is a final good. So it is included in national income.

(b) Machine purchased by a firm is also final good as it is used by the producer finally in the production process. So it is included in national income.

(c) But machine purchased by one firm from another in order to resale in the market is treated as intermediate goods. So it is not included in national income.

## ▪ How will you treat defence and security services in estimation of national income?

The defence and security services provided by Government may be treated as intermediate or final services.

(a) These services are final as long as they provide services for peaceful life of the households.

(b) These services are intermediary as long as they provide peaceful environment for the production process.

4Finally, as a matter of convenient these services are treated as final services and thus included in national income of India.

___*___*___*___*___*___*___*___*___*___*___*___*___*___

# IMPORTANT QUESTIONS:

## 1 MARK QUESTIONS:

1. State the methods to measure the national income of India.
2. How can the problem of double counting method be avoided?
3. Define compensation of employees.
4. What is meant by operating surplus?
5. Define value added.
6. State the components of net domestic income.
7. Name the components of net factor income from abroad.
8. State the components of final consumption expenditure.
9. Define factor income.
10. Define transfer income.
11. State the components of profit.
12. What do you mean by net domestic capital formation?

## 3 OR 4 MARK QUESTIONS:

1. What do you mean by domestic factor income? Explain its main components.
2. Define operating surplus. How is it different from mixed income of self-employed?
3. Explain the main components of compensation of employees.
4. Explain the concept of mixed income of self employed with the help of an example.
5. What is net factor income from abroad? Explain its main components.
6. Show that in any economy the net value added is always equal to sum of all factor incomes.

7. Explain the components of final consumption expenditure with the help of example.
8. Briefly explain the steps to calculate national income by value added method.
9. Briefly explain the steps to calculate national income by income method.
10. Briefly explain the steps to calculate national income by expenditure method.
11. State the precautions involved in calculation of national income by value added method.
12. State the precautions involved in calculation of national income by income method.
13. State the precautions involved in calculation of national income by expenditure method.
14. Whether the following will be included in domestic factor income of India? Answer with reasons.

    a) Salaries paid to the employees by Pakistan Embassy in India.
    b) Salary paid to a non-resident Professor teaching in an engineering college in India.
    c) Profits earned by a branch of State Bank of India located in America.
    d) Profits earned by a foreign company in India.

15. Explain the problem of double counting with the help of an example. How can it be avoided?
16. State whether the following intermediate goods or final goods?

    a) A new car purchased by a taxi driver.
    b) A new refrigerator purchased by a restaurant.
    c) A new fighter air craft F-16 purchased by Defence department of Government of India.
    d) A bread purchased by a consumer household.

## 6 MARK QUESTIONS:

1. Explain the steps involved in calculation of national income by income method along with its precautions.

2.  Explain the steps involved in calculation of national income by product or value added method along with its precautions.
3.  Explain the steps involved in calculation of national income by expenditure method along with its precautions.
    4.  Numerical:

# Chapter - 5

## Money And Money Supply:

## • EVOLUTION OF CONCEPT OF MONEY IN THE ECONOMY:

Money is defined as anything which is accepted as a medium of exchange.

The term money has been derived from the Latin word 'Moneta' the name of Goddess Juno or Moneta.

Money was not discovered in one day by any one individual. There are two theories regarding the discovery of money which are as follows.

(i) **Spontaneous Growth theory of money:** According to Professor Spalding, money was not discovered by any particular individual. Its growth was spontaneous. With the growth of human civilization the concept of money was developed in different time periods.

(ii) **Theory of evolution of money:** According to Professor Crowther, money has come into being as a result of specific human effort. He said money is most fundamental of all men's inventions.

However the evolution of money has passed through following stages.

**Stage-1: Commodity Money:** In the hunting stage people used animal skin, bows and arrows as money. Next they used goats, sheep, oxen, bulls, cows etc. as money. Then they used food grains as money. In this stage transfer of value was very difficult and there was no medium of exchange.

**Stage-2: Metallic Money:** Metallic money was introduced to meet the difficulties of commodity money. Man started to use iron, gold, brass, copper, silver etc. as money. Gradually uniform metal coin was introduced as money in 8th Century by King Midas. The limited metal coins failed to satisfy their demand in the country.

**Stage-3: Paper Money:** The transfer of metallic coins from one to another place was not convenient. So paper money was introduced for the first time in China in 807 A.D. Since then paper money has become very important part of our daily life.

**Stage-4: Credit Money:** Growth of banking system has led to create credit money. It included cheques, promissory notes, drafts, credit cards, bills of exchange, Plastic money in the form of debit card and etc.

**Stage-5: Near Money:** Near money refers to those promissory notes which are readily converted into money. It includes Treasury bills, Exchange Bills, Bonds, Government securities, Fixed deposits with banks, insurance policies etc. Near money is less liquid compared to paper money.

## ▪ BARTER ECONOMY AND ITS MAIN PROBLEMS:

In the Primitive economy wants were not so much and they used to satisfy by producing and exchanging goods and services and that economy was called as barter economy.

According to Chandler, "The direct exchange of economic goods for one another is called barter."

The barter economy is also called as C-C economy i.e. Commodity against commodity.

The main problems of barter economy are as follows:

(i) **Lack of double coincidence of wants:** Double coincidence of wants refers to the simultaneous satisfaction of wants of both the buyers and sellers. There was lack of double coincidence of wants in barter economy and the exchange of goods was really very difficult. For example, in barter economy, suppose Mr. X has rice and he wants wheat. Now Mr. X will get wheat only when any person who has wheat and wants rice. This means the exchange will be possible if there is double coincidence of wants otherwise not.

(ii) **Difficulty of common measure of value:** In barter economy there was no common measure (unit) of value. Goods were exchanged against goods but the proportion was not fixed for lack of measurement of value of commodity. Therefore it was difficult to measure the exchange value of any commodity in terms of goods.

**(iii) Difficulty of deferred payments:** Deferred payments are those payments which are made in future. In barter economy it was difficult for both the buyers and sellers to engage in any contract which involve future payments in terms of goods because of disagreement of change in the exchange value of goods and change in the quality of goods.

**(iv) Difficulty in storing wealth or value:** In barter economy it was difficult for the people to store wealth in terms of goods like rice, wheat, cattle etc. because it involved costly storage, a large space and some goods were perishable like food grains.

**(v) Indivisibility of certain goods:** In barter economy it was difficult to exchange goods because certain goods are not divisible. For example, suppose an ox owner can exchange an ox for four sheep but if he wants two sheep only then the exchange becomes difficult because he requires exchanging half of the ox for two sheep, which is not possible.

**(vi) Difficulty of transfer of value:** Transfer of value was another difficulty in barter economy. If a person thinks to move from one place to another he could carry only the movable goods like cattle, weapons, utensils but he was unable to transfer his land, house and other immovable properties.

## ▪ SOLUTIONS OF PROBLEMS OF BARTER ECONOMY:

A barter economy refers to that economy in which goods are exchanged for goods. There were many problems like double coincidence of wealth, lack of common measure of value, difficulty of storing wealth, deferred payments, transfer of value etc. All these problems are solved when money was introduced in the economy. Money helped to solve the problems of barter economy in the following way.

**(i) Money as a medium of exchange**: As a medium of exchange, money solves the problem of double coincidence of wants. People sell their goods and get money. They use money to get their necessary goods. So money has transformed the C-C economy into

C-M-C (Commodity-Money-Commodity) economy and finally into M-C-M economy. M-C-M economy means men buys machineries, raw materials and other necessary goods with help of money, then goods is produced and finally the goods are sold into the market and they get money.

(ii) **Measurement of value**: As a measure of value, money solved the problem of common measure (unit) of value of any commodity. Now with the help of money the value of any commodity can be measured which was not possible in barter economy.

(iii) **Standard of deferred payments**: As a standard of deferred payments, money solved the problem of lack of standard of deferred payments. Therefore it encourages the business which involves future payments and bank-credit system.

(iv) **Store of value**: As a store of value, money solved the problem of storing of wealth of barter economy which was difficult in barter economy as it used to take large space area.

(v) **Transfer of value**: As a transfer of value, money has solved the problem of barter economy so that at present the value of immovable property can be transferred easily to a distant place which was not possible in the barter economy.

# ■ CONCEPT OF MONEY AND ITS IMPORTANT FUNCTIONS:

Generally money has been defined on the basis of its functions. Professor Walker rightly says "Money is that which money does".

According to Geoffrey Crowther, "Money can be defined as anything that is generally accepted as a means of exchange and at the same time acts as a measure and as a store of value".

**FUNCTIONS OF MONEY:** Professor Kinsley classifies the functions of money into following three categories.

(i) Primary functions.
(ii) Secondary functions.
(iii) Tertiary functions.

❖ Primary functions include the following two functions.

1. **MEDIUM OF EXCHANGE:** Money as a medium of exchange removed the problem of inconveniences in barter economy. Money by itself has no utility but it as an intermediary helps to exchange the commodities, exchange promotes specialization, which increases productivity and efficiency and encourages trade. Thus business expands in any economy.

Money helps to consumers to purchase any commodity to satisfy their demand.

2. **MEASUREMENT OF VALUE:** Money as a measurement of value of any commodity helps to measure the exchange value of any commodity which was not possible in barter economy. This function enables the firms to develop efficient system to maintain accounting. It also helps to calculate the national income of a country. This function also helps money to act as price mechanism that guides market forces to determine the price of a commodity.

❖ **SECONDARY FUNCTION:** It includes following three functions.

3. **STANDARD OF DEFERRED PAYMENTS:** Deferred payments refer to those payments which are made in future. Payments of loans are also referred to standard of deferred payments. Money is used as standard of deferred payments because its price remains stable and it is durable and acceptable to all. This function also helps to develop the financial market and credit system.

4. **STORE OF VALUE:** It is convenient to store value in terms of money because it is generally acceptable, and its value remains stable and it does not take more space. This function enables money to act as a reserve of liquid asset to meet any need in future.

5. **TRANSFER OF VALUE:** This function of money enables the people to transfer the value of immovable properties from one place to another more conveniently. This function provides mobility to the machinery, land value and goods which accelerates the growth of trade and industry.

# ▪ LEGAL TENDER MONEY AND ITS CLASSIFICATIONS:

Legal tender money refers to that money which is recognized by the Government or monetary authority of the country as a medium of all types' payments and transactions and nobody can refuse it. In India all types of coins and currencies are called legal tender money. It is of two types like limited legal tender money and unlimited legal tender money.

(a) **Limited legal tender money**: It refers to that money which no person can be forced to accept beyond a certain maximum limit fixed by law. In India coins are limited legal tender money because coins of 5, 10, 20, and 25 paisa can be accepted up to maximum sum of Rs. 25. One can refuse payments in terms of small coins beyond a sum of Rs. 25.

(b) **Unlimited legal tender money**: It refers to that money which a person has to accept up to any limit. For example in India paper notes can be used as for any amount of payments because it is unlimited legal tender money.

## ▪ NARROW AND BROAD DEFINITIONS OF MONEY:

**Narrow Definition of money:** It is narrow definition of money when money is identified as only medium of exchange and all other functions are ignored. Accordingly it includes currency (C) and demand deposits (DD).

Thus, M = C + DD i.e. M1 concept of money supply.

**Broad Definition of money**: It is broad definition of money when money is identified as medium of exchange and store of value.

According to broad definition of money, money includes currency (C), demand deposits (DD), time deposits (TD) and saving deposits (SD) in banks and post offices.

Thus, M = C + DD + TD + SD.

## ▪ DIFFERENT TYPES OF MONEY IN THE ECONOMY:

(a) **Full-bodied money**: It refers to that money for which its commodity value (for non-monetary purposes) or face value is equal to its money value or intrinsic value. For examples, gold coins, silver coins under metallic standard system were full bodied money. If Face value = Intrinsic value then it is full bodied money.

(b) **Representative full bodied money**: It is generally made of paper money. It has no value as commodity but it represents in circulation an amount of money with a commodity value equal to the value of money. It is convenient to carry from one place to another.

(c) **Credit money**: It refers to that money whose face value is greater than its material value. For example, token coins, currency notes, cheques etc.

(d) **Fiat money**: Fiat money refers to that money which is backed by the Government order to act as money. Fiat money is generally created in a country at the time of crisis like war or emergency. This money is issued without any backing of gold, silver or other reserves and therefore it is not convertible into anything than itself. For example Mark currency issued in Germany immediately after the First World War was fiat money.

(e) **Fiduciary money**: It refers to that money which is backed up by mutual trust between the payer and the payee. For example cheques and drafts etc are fiduciary money.

(f) **High Powered money**: It refers to that money which is produced by the Central Bank and held by the Commercial banks and public. It is also called as Reserve money. It includes currency (C), cash reserves (R) with commercial banks and other deposits (OD) with R.B.I. (Reserve Bank of India which is the central bank of the country).

Thus, High Powered Money (H) = C + R + OD.

## ▪ What is money supply? Describe alternative measures of Money supply as used by Reserve Bank of India:

Money supply refers to the stock of all forms of money (paper money, coins and demand deposits of banks etc.) held by public at a point of time in an economy. Here public refers to all economic units like households, firms, local authorities and non-departmental enterprises of Government. It does not include Government and banking system because they are producers of money.

Since 1977 Reserve Bank of India measured money supply in India by the following four measures.

(i) **M1 Measurement**: It is most liquid and easiest for transactions. It includes currency (C), Demand deposits (DD) and other deposits (OD).

Thus, M1 = C + DD + OD.

(ii) **M2 Measurement**: It includes all components of M1 and Post office savings deposit.

Thus, M2 = M1 + P.O. Savings Deposits.

(iii) **M3 Measurement**: It includes all components of M1 and Net Time Deposits with commercial banks.

Thus, M3 = M1 + Net Time Deposits with commercial banks.

(iv) **M4 Measurement**: It includes all components of M3 and Post Office Savings Deposits excluding National Savings Certificate. It is broad definition of money.

Thus, M4 = M3 + P.O. Savings Deposits (excluding N.S.C.).

**Which currency system is present in India now?**

At present India is following Paper Currency Standard system or Managed Currency Standard.

## ▪ THE CONTINGENT FUNCTIONS OF MONEY:

Contingent functions are those functions of money which arise on account of economic development of a country. The main contingent functions are as follows.

(i) **Distribution of National income:** Money helps for optimum distribution of national income among the owners of different factors of production. The factors of production land, labour, capital and entrepreneur are rewarded on the basis of their marginal productivity measured in terms of money.

(ii) **Maximization of satisfaction:** Every consumer maximizes his satisfaction out of his given income by equating marginal utility of goods and price ratios of goods, measured in terms of money. On the other hand every producer maximizes his profit by equating marginal productivity of factor of production and its price, measured in terms of money.

(iii) **Basis of credit:** At present most of economic transactions are made in terms of credit system where money plays the most important role. Credit creation by the banks is also possible because of money. Banks with the help of primary deposits (savings) create credit i.e. secondary deposit (loans).

(iv) **Base of liquidity:** With the introduction of money, capital as most liquid asset i.e. money, can be kept by the individuals for different motives.

   (a)  Transaction motive: To meet daily transactions.
   (b)  Precautionary motive: To meet unforeseen contingencies.
   (c)  Speculative motive: To meet speculative profit.

(v)  **Capital formation:** Under barter system, it was not possible to save and invest in terms of goods. Introduction of money has solved this problem and encourages capital formation. As a result production increases and economic development takes place.

## ▪ STATIC FUNCTIONS OF MONEY:

Paul Einzig and Coulborn have classified the functions of money into static and dynamic functions.

**STATIC FUNCTIONS:** All the basic, traditional and technical functions of money are referred as static functions. These functions help to the economy to work smoothly. These functions include all primary and secondary functions of money i.e. these includes the following functions.

   (i)    Medium of exchange.
   (ii)   Measurement of value.
   (iii)  Standard of deferred payments.
   (iv)   Store of value.
   (v)    Transfer of value.

The explanations are same as explained earlier in this chapter to state the functions of money.

## ▪ THE DYNAMIC FUNCTIONS OF MONEY:

In modern economy money plays an important role for economic development and money is not neutral. Money has a great impact on economic development of the country. The dynamic functions are as follows.

(i) Money affects the economic system through price mechanism to determine the price of a commodity.

(ii) It helps to utilize the natural resources most efficiently and optimally.

(iii) Money helps to the Government to formulate the monetary policy particularly to control inflation and deflation.

(iv) Dynamic functions of money have helped to the International Monetary Fund (IMF) to issue of Special Drawing Rights (SDR).

__*__*__*__*__*__*__*__*__*__*__*__*__

# IMPORTANT QUESTIONS:

## 1 MARK QUESTIONS:

1. Define barter economy.
2. What is meant by money?
3. Give the narrow definition of money.
4. Give the broad definition of money.
5. Define fiduciary money.
6. What is meant by fiat money?
7. Define full-bodied money.
8. What is meant by credit money?
9. What is meant by high-powered money?
10. Define limited legal tender money.
11. Which paper currency is being used at present in India?

## 3 OR 4 MARK QUESTIONS:

1. Explain the evolution of money as brief as possible.
2. Explain the main drawbacks of barter economy.
3. How does money help to solve the problems of barter system?
4. Explain the primary functions of money.
5. Explain the secondary functions of money.
6. State the contingent functions of money.
7. Explain the static functions of money.
8. Explain the dynamic functions of money.
9. Distinguish between limited legal tender and unlimited legal tender money.
10. What do you money supply? How does Reserve Bank of India measure money supply?

397

## 6 MARK QUESTIONS:

1. What is money? Explain the main functions of money.
2. Define money supply. Explain different measures of money supply used by Reserve bank of India (RBI).
3. How does money solve the problems of barter economy?

__*__*__*__*__*__*__*__*__*__*__*__*__*__

# Chapter - 6

## Banking:
## Commercial Banks And Central Bank:

## CONCEPT OF BANK AND BANKING IN ECONOMICS:

In modern age, Banking constitutes the fundamental basis of economic growth. A bank is generally defined as an institution which accepts deposits from the public and gives loans, creates credit and performs some agency work.

According to Indian Banking Companies Act, "Banking Company is one which transacts the business of banking which means the accepting for the purpose of lending or investment of deposits of money from the public repayable on demand or otherwise and withdraw-able by cheque, draft, and order or otherwise."

In brief, a bank is an institution which accepts deposits withdraw-able by cheque and makes loans and advances with a view to earn profit.

Banking is defined as the accepting of deposits from public which are withdraw-able by cheque, draft or order or otherwise and advancing of loans to the public with a view to earn profit.

## COMMERCIAL BANK AND ITS IMPORTANT FUNCTIONS:

A commercial bank is a financial institution which performs the functions of accepting deposits from public and advancing loans for investment with an objective of earning profit.

According to Culbertson, "Commercial banks are the institutions that make short term loans to business and in the process create money".

The functions of commercial banks can be classified into three groups like (A) Primary Functions, (B) Secondary Functions and (C) Social Functions.

(A) **PRIMARY FUNCTIONS:** It includes two functions (i) Accepting Deposits and (ii) Advancing of Loans.

(i) A commercial bank accepts deposits from public in any of the following accounts.

1. **Current or Demand Deposit Account**: Such deposits are payable on demand and therefore these are called demand deposits. These can be withdrawn anytime by the depositors. The banks do not provide any interest on this account but provides cheque facilities. Generally businessmen and industrialists avail this account for daily transactions by using cheque facilities.

2. **Fixed or Time Deposit Account:** These are deposits for a fixed term i.e. for a period of some days to a few years. These are not cheque-able and can be withdrawn only after the maturity of a particular time period. This account attracts higher rate of interest. Longer the time period higher will be the interest and shorter the time period the interest will be less.

3. **Saving Deposit Account:** This account is meant for encouraging small savings. Certain restrictions are imposed by the bank on the amount to be withdrawn. Banks pay interest on this account but less than the Time deposit account.

4. **Recurring Deposit Account:** Under this account a specified amount is deposited every month for a specific period, say 12, 24, 36 or 60 months. This amount cannot be withdrawn before the maturity except certain exceptional circumstances. Banks pay higher rate of interest on this account.

(ii) A commercial bank advances loans mostly for the productive purposes and against securities in the following forms.

1. **Cash Credit:** A borrower is first sanctioned a credit limit and within that limit he is allowed to withdraw a certain amount on a given security. Interest is charged by the bank on the drawn amount of credit.

2. **Over-Draft:** An overdraft is an advance given by allowing a customer keeping current account to overdraw his current account up to

an agreed limit. It is a facility to a depositor for overdrawing the amount than the balance amount in his account. The security for the overdraft is generally financial facilities assets like shares, debentures, life insurance policies of the account holder.

3. **Demand Loans:** A loan which can be recalled on demand is called demand loan. The entire amount of loan is paid in lump sum by crediting it to the loan account of the borrower. Generally security brokers whose credit needs fluctuate take such loans on personal security and financial assets.

4. **Short-term loans:** Short-term loans are given against some security or collateral as personal loans to finance working capital or as priority sector advances. The entire amount is repaid in one installment or many installments.

5. **Bills of exchange:** It is another method to supply credit by commercial banks. Under this system banks give loans to their customers on the basis of their bills of exchange before the maturity of bills. A deduction is made out of the face value of the bill for the remaining period of maturity which is called as discounting of bills of exchange. The bills are discounted at the market rate of interest. After the maturity the amount mentioned in the bill is collected from the party concerned by the bank.

(iii) **Credit creation:** It is one of the important functions of commercial banks. Commercial banks with the help of primary deposits create the credit i.e. secondary deposits.

(B) **SECONDARY FUNCTIONS:** It includes agency functions and general utility functions which are as follows.

## AGENCY FUNCTIONS OF MONEY:

As an agent commercial banks perform the following functions.

1. Collection of funds: Commercial bank collects funds through cheques, bills, demand drafts etc. on behalf of customers.

2. Payments of various items: It makes payments on behalf of customers for payments of taxes, house rent, insurance premium, electricity bills etc.

3. Transfer of funds: It helps for easy and cheap remittance of funds on behalf of its customers, from one place to another place through demand drafts, mail transfers or internet banking etc.

4. Sale and purchase of securities: Commercial banks sale and purchase securities on behalf of customers.

5. Sale and purchase of foreign exchange: Commercial banks on behalf of Central bank sale and purchase the foreign exchange to promote international trade.

6. Collection of dividend and interest: It collects dividend on shares and interest on debentures on behalf of its customers.

7. Letter of references: It gives the information of economic conditions of its customers to traders and the similar information regarding the traders to its customers.

## GENERAL UTILITY SERVICES:

It includes the following functions.

1. Locker facilities: commercial bank provides locker facilities to its customers against a nominal rent.

2. Traveler's cheque: It provides traveler's cheques to the customers which makes easier to carry fund from one place to another without any risk.

3. Business information and statistics: Banks provide the necessary information and statistics to its customers on demand.

4. Underwriting securities issued by the Government, public or private bodies.

5. Letters of credit are issued by the banks to their customers certifying their credit worthiness.

## CREDIT CREATION BY COMMERCIAL BANK AND ITS LIMITATIONS:

Credit creation is considered as the main function of commercial banks these days. Commercial banks create credit on the basis of their primary deposits.

Credit creation by commercial banks is determined by the amount of initial fresh deposits or primary deposits and by the Cash Reserve Ratio. Cash Reserve Ratio (CRR) is the minimum ratio of deposit legally required to be kept as cash with commercial banks.

**Credit creation is based on certain assumptions.**

i.   All banks strictly maintain Cash Reserve Ratio.
ii.  All depositors will not withdraw their funds at one and at the same time.
iii. Banks do not pay any amount in cash. Amount is paid only in cheque.
iv.  Bank expands credit on the basis of excess reserve.
v.   All banks act simultaneously and they receive primary deposits also simultaneously.

## Process of Credit Creation on the basis of Credit Multiplier:

Commercial banks create credit (secondary deposits) on the basis of its collected deposits i.e. primary deposits. This can be explained by the following example:

Let a person Mr. X deposits Rs. 10,000 in a bank. This amount to the bank is known as primary deposit. Suppose CRR is 10%. So bank keeps 10% of 10,000 = Rs. 1000 in cash reserve and advances the rest of amount i.e. Rs. 9000 as loans to Mr. B in cheque (not in cash).

Let us assume that Mr. B owes Rs. 9000 to Mr. C and therefore he issues a cheque of Rs. 9000 to Mr. C. and Mr. C deposits the cheque in the same bank in his account. So the bank will debit Rs. 9000 in the account of Mr. B and credit of Rs. 9000 in the account of Mr. C. So the bank increases its deposits by Rs. 9000.

Again the bank keeps 10 % of this deposit (Rs. 9000 x 105 = Rs.900) as its reserve and gives loan of Rs.8100 (Rs. 9000 – Rs. 900) to another person Mr. D in cheque. Suppose Mr. D owes to Mr. E of Rs.8100 which he pays to Mr. E by issuing a cheque and Mr. E deposits the cheque in the same bank in his account. The bank will debit Rs. 8100 in the account of Mr. D and credit of Rs. 8100 in the account of Mr. E. So the bank increases its deposits by Rs. 8100. This process will go on for a long time and ultimately total credit creation will be Rs. 100,000.

Total Credit Creation = Initial Deposit x Credit Multiplier

= Primary Deposit x $\dfrac{1}{\text{CRR}}$

= Rs. 10,000 x $\dfrac{1}{10\%}$

= Rs. 100,000.

This can be explained by the following table.

| ROUND | PRIMARY DEPOSIT | CRR (10%) | CREDIT OR SECONDARY DEPOSIT |
|---|---|---|---|
| First | Rs. 10,000 | Rs. 1000 | Rs. 9000 |
| Second | Rs. 9000 | Rs. 900 | Rs. 8100 |
| Third | Rs. 8100 | Rs. 810 | Rs. 7290 |
| — | — | — | — |
| — | — | — | — |
| TOTAL | Rs. 100,000 | Rs. 10,000 | Rs. 90,000 |

From the above table it is clear that total credit created will be Rs.100, 000. Out of this Rs. 10,000 will be kept in bank as LRR (Legal Reserve Ratio)and the remaining Rs. 90,000 will be given as loans or be called as secondary deposit.

# ■ LIMITATIONS OF CREDIT CREATION:

Commercial bank cannot extend credit creation endlessly because it has following limitations.

(i) CRR: The credit creation depends on CRR. If CRR is less, then credit creation will be more. If CRR is high, then there will be less scope for credit creation.

(ii) Amount of primary deposit: If the amount of primary deposit is more in bank, then credit creation capacity will be more.

(iii) Credit policy of Central bank: Credit creation of commercial bank depends up on the credit policy of Central bank which decides the CRR.

(iv) Normal condition: Credit creation is possible only when there is normal condition exist in the economy. If there is depression or war like situation in the country then credit creation policy will not be successful.

# CENTRAL BANK AND ITS IMPORTANT FUNCTIONS:

Central bank is an apex financial institution which controls monetary policy as well as the banking structure of the whole country.

According to De Kock, "A central bank is a bank which constitutes the apex of the monetary and banking structure of its country." In every country Central bank plays the most important role for the economic development of the country with the help of its credit policy or monetary policy. In India the name of the central bank is Reserve Bank of India (RBI). RBI starts its operation from 1st April, 1935 and it was nationalized on 1st April, 1949.

The main functions of Central bank are as follows.

## (1) ISSUING OF NOTES:

Now a day in every country the central bank enjoys the monopoly right to issue currency notes. In India the central bank known as Reserve Bank of India has the right to issue all notes except one rupee note. The central bank issues notes generally against some reserves of gold, silver and foreign securities. Central bank has the right of note issuing because to maintain stability of domestic price level and external exchange rate.

## (2) BANKER OF THE GOVERNMENT:

In almost all countries central bank functions as a banker to the Government. The central bank accepts receipts and makes payments for the Government. It also maintains the accounts of the central and state Governments. It provides short-term loans to the Government for temporary period without charging any interest. It collects taxes and other payments on behalf of the Government. On the other hand it also gives advices to the Government on financial, fiscal and monetary matters. Central bank is very much concerned with the public finance and monetary matters.

## (3) BANKER'S BANK:

In all countries the central bank acts as banker of the commercial banks. Central bank has almost the same relationship with commercial banks as the latter have with the general public. As a custodian of cash reserves, every central bank maintains cash reserves of commercial banks. The ratio of cash reserves is determined by the central bank and it can be used by the commercial banks whenever the commercial banks require. The central bank supervises, regulates and controls the commercial banks. The licensing policy, liquidity of assets, management, merging of banks etc. are supervised by the central bank of the country.

## (4) LENDER OF THE LAST RESORT:

The central bank functions as a lender of last resort for the commercial banks of a country. This means that when the commercial banks fail to collect credit supply from any other source during emergencies then they depend upon the central bank. The central bank advances loans to the commercial banks against adequate securities, subject to certain terms and conditions. Either the commercial banks take loans from the central bank against some securities or the commercial banks may get funds by rediscounting of their eligible bills of exchange by the central bank at the time of emergency.

## (5) CUSTODIAN OF FOREIGN EXCHANGE RESERVES:

The central bank functions as a custodian of country's foreign exchange reserves and gold. It maintains the stability of exchange rate of the country fixed by the Government. It observes the external value of its currency and undertakes exchange control management. This function of central bank also helps to the country to overcome the balance of payments difficulties and to stable the foreign exchange rate.

## (6) CLEARING HOUSE FUNCTION:

The central bank also functions as a clearing house. Every commercial bank has an account with the central bank. The central bank can settle the claims of various commercial banks against each other with minimum uses of cash, by making cross payments with necessary adjustments in their accounts.

## (7) CONTROL OF CREDIT:

Credit control is an important function of central bank. Credit control means expansion or contraction of the supply of credit in the economy according to the need of the country. Excessive supply of credit causes inflation and shortage of credit causes deflation in the economy. Therefore the central bank controls credit supply by using various instruments of monetary policy like bank rate, open market operation, changes in cash reserve ratio, change in marginal requirement of loans etc.

## (8) COLLECTION OF STATISTICS:

The central bank collects a variety of statistical data concerning banking, monetary and foreign exchange activity which are published from time to time. These data can be used as important information for the economic growth and development of the country.

## (9) OTHER FUNCTIONS:

(i)   The central bank in many countries supplies agricultural credit.
(ii)  It represents as the highest financial authority of the country in international monetary organizations like IMF, IBRD etc.
(iii) It organizes the money and bill market of the country.
(iv)  It helps to replace the torn notes with new ones.

## CREDIT CONTROL BY CENTRAL BANK IN AN ECONOMY:

In modern times the main function of the central bank is to regulate and control the credit supply in the economy with a view to promote the economic growth rate and economic development in the country. The main instruments of monetary policy are classified into two categories like quantitative credit control and qualitative credit control.

Quantitative credit control includes the following instruments.

## (1) BANK RATE:

It is the rate at which the central bank lends funds to the commercial banks against securities or bills of exchange.

Whenever the central bank wants to contract the credit in the economy it follows Dear Money Policy which means it raises the bank rate that causes an increase in the market rate of interest. This discourages the borrowing from the banks.

On the other hand if the central bank wants to expand the credit in the economy it follows Chap Money Policy which means it reduces the bank rate that causes a decrease in the market rate of interest. This encourages the borrowing from the banks.

## (2) OPEN MARKET OPERATIONS:

It means sale and purchase of Government securities by the central bank to/from the public or banks.

Whenever the central bank wants to contract the credit supply in the economy it follows Dear Money Policy which means it sales the securities in the open market to the people. So the money flows from the commercial banks (by withdrawal) to the central bank. So the cash with commercial banks decreases and credit supply decreases.

Whenever the central bank wants to expand the credit supply in the economy it follows Cheap Money Policy which means it purchases the securities in the open market from the people. So the money flows from the central bank to the commercial banks. This causes increase of the cash with commercial banks and increase of credit supply in the economy.

## (3) CASH RESERVE RATIO (CRR):

Every commercial bank by law of banking is bound to keep certain
Percentage of its total deposit with central bank which is known as minimum cash reserve ratio (CRR).

Whenever the central bank wants to expand the credit, CRR is decreased which means more liquidity remains with the commercial banks so that credit supply increases.

On the other hand whenever the central bank wants to contract the credit, CRR is increased which means less liquidity remains with the commercial banks so that credit supply decreases.

## (4) STATUTORY LIQUIDITY RATIO (SLR):

It refers to a fixed percentage of cash balances that the commercial banks should keep with them as liquid assets to discharge the customers' liabilities in time.

If the central bank wants to expand credit supply, then the SLR is decreased.

On the other hand if it wants to contract credit supply, then the SLR is increased.

The CRR and SLR together are called as Legal Reserve Ratio (LRR). It refers to minimum percentage (fixed by Central bank) of commercial banks' total deposits which is legally and compulsorily kept in cash.

## (5) REPO RATE:

It is that rate at which the central bank of a country advances credit to the commercial banks for very short time period. If repo rate rises then the rate of interest of commercial banks on deposits and loans will increase.

Qualitative credit control includes the following instruments.

## (6) MARGINAL REQUIREMENT OF LOANS:

It refers to the difference between the value of the security and the amount of loan sanctioned against the security. Central bank fixes the marginal requirement ratio for different commodities. When it wants to expand the credit supply against a particular commodity, it reduces marginal requirement ratio so that customers get more credit supply.

When it wants to contract the credit supply against a particular commodity, it raises marginal requirement ratio so that customers get less credit supply.

## (7) DIRECT ACTION:

Central bank can take direct action against any commercial bank if the commercial bank does not follow the guidelines and instructions of the central bank. Direct action includes refusal to give loans to the commercial bank, imposition of monetary penalty, refusal to give re-discount facilities.

## (8) RATIONING OF CREDIT:

It refers to fixation of credit limits for different business activities with a view to control credit supply in the economy. Commercial banks cannot supply loan more than the quota limits. Thus central bank controls the credit supply in the economy. This method is more suitable in planned economies.

## (9)    MORAL SUASION:

Sometimes central bank persuades the commercial banks to adopt its credit control policy regarding the expansion and contraction of credit supply in the economy. The success of this instrument depends on the co-operation between the central bank and commercial banks and full control of money market by the central bank.

## DISTINCTION BETWEEN CENTRAL BANK AND COMMERCIAL BANK:

| BASIS | CENTRAL BANK | COMMERCIAL BANK |
|---|---|---|
| 1. Objective | To maximize social welfare. | To maximize profit. |
| 2. Public Dealing. | It has no direct dealing with public. | It directly deals with general public. |
| 3. Management | It is completely state owned institution. | It is owned by either private or public. |
| 4. Note Issue | It has monopoly right of note issue. | It cannot issue notes. |
| 5. Foreign Exchange. | It is custodian of country's foreign exchange. | It can deal with foreign exchange on the permission of central bank. |
| 6. Credit. | It controls credit. | It creates credit. |
| 7. Function. | It regulates the banking system of the country. | It functions under the supervision of central bank. |

## ▪ Explain the concept of Legal Reserve Ratio (LRR):

Legal Reserve Ratio (LRR) refers to that legal minimum percentage of total deposits (fixed by RBI) which the commercial banks under compulsion keep as cash with themselves.

410

It has two variants:

## (i) CASH RESERVE RATIO (CRR):

Every commercial bank by law of banking is bound to keep a certain percentage out of its total deposit with central bank as minimum cash reserve ratio (CRR).

Whenever the central bank wants to expand the credit, CRR is decreased which means more liquidity remains with the commercial banks so that credit supply increases.

On the other hand whenever the central bank wants to contract the credit, CRR is increased which means less liquidity remains with the commercial banks so that credit supply decreases.

## (ii) STATUTORY LIQUIDITY RATIO (SLR):

It refers to a fixed percentage of cash balances that the commercial banks should keep with them as liquid assets to discharge the customers' liabilities in time.

If the central bank wants to expand credit, the SLR is decreased.

On the other hand if it wants to contract credit, the SLR is increased.

The CRR and SLR together are called as Legal Reserve Ratio (LRR). It refers to minimum percentage (fixed by Central bank) of commercial banks' total deposits which is legally and compulsorily kept in cash.

## ❖ STERELISATION POLICY OF CENTRAL BANK OF THE COUNTRY:

It refers to the actions and policy of central bank of a country to neutralize the monetary impact of inflow of foreign currency on the domestic economy of a country caused by the surplus or deficit in Balance of Payments.

The basic objective of sterilization policy of the central bank of the country is to keep the domestic money supply unchanged despite external shocks or any changes, including the inflow or outflow of capital.

The central bank of the country uses the open market operations instrument for sterilization the monetary effect of foreign capital on domestic economy particularly during currency appreciation and inflation.

—*—*—*—*—*—*—*—*—*—*—*—*—*—

# IMPORTANT QUESTIONS:

## 1 MARK QUESTIONS:

1. What do you mean by a bank?
2. Define commercial bank.
3. Define central bank.
4. Write different types of deposit accounts of commercial bank.
5. What is meant by bank rate?
6. Define Statutory Liquidity Ratio (SLR).
7. What is meant by Cash Reserve Ratio (CRR)?
8. What is meant by Open Market Operations?
9. Define demand deposit.
   10. What is meant by marginal requirement of loans?

## 3 OR 4 MARK QUESTIONS:

1. Explain the agency functions of commercial bank.
2. How can you explain acceptance of deposit function of commercial bank?
3. Explain the lending function of commercial bank.
4. State the general utility services of commercial bank.
5. Explain briefly the functions of a central bank.
6. Explain the function of 'issue of currency' of central bank.
7. Explain the function of 'lender of last resort' of central bank.
8. Explain the function of 'banker to Government' of central bank.
9. Explain the function of 'open market operation' of central bank.
10. Explain the function of 'controller of credit' of central bank.
11. What do you mean by "Bank rate"? How does it affect the credit control function of central bank?
12. Explain the Cash Reserve Ratio (CRR) as a credit control function of Central bank?

13. Define Marginal requirement of loan function of central bank to control credit in the economy.
14. State the quantitative credit control functions of central bank.
15. State the qualitative credit control functions of central bank.
16. Write the name of instruments of monetary policy of central bank. How does central bank (RBI) stabilize money supply against exogenous shocks?

## 6 MARK QUESTIONS:

1. Explain the functions of commercial banks.
2. Explain the credit creation function of commercial bank. State the limitations of credit creation of commercial bank.
3. Distinguish between central bank and commercial bank.
4. Explain the functions of central bank.
5. How does the central bank control credit availability in the economy?

# Chapter - 7

## Aggregate Demand And Aggregate Supply:

J. M. Keynes was the first economist to put forward a systematic theory to explain the theory of income and employment.

Actually in 1930 the classical theory failed to explain that why did investment not increase even at very low rate of interest.

In USA during the period of 'Great Depression' from 1929 to 1933, unemployment rate increased from 3% to 25% and aggregate output decreased by about 33%. The classical economists could not find any reason for this increase in unemployment and decrease in output. They assumed the possibility of voluntary unemployment and frictional unemployment as the reasons for this incident.

Then, J. M. Keynes in his book 'The General Theory of Employment, Interest and Money' published in 1936 explained that there is less than full employment in the economy because of involuntary nature of unemployment and he also explained the theory of income and employment with the help of concept of effective demand which was revolutionary in macro-economic theory.

## ▪ THE CONCEPT OF EFFECTIVE DEMAND IN MACRO ECONOMICS:

It refers to that level of aggregate demand in the economy at which it is equal to aggregate supply. Therefore there is no tendency on the part of entrepreneurs to either expand or contract production.

Effective demand determines the level of income and employment in the economy and lack of effective demand results unemployment.

The total effective demand consists of demand for consumption goods or consumption demand and demand for capital goods or investment demand.

The two main determinants of effective demand are aggregate demand function and aggregate supply function. To increase the level of income and employment, increase in effective demand is essential.

Effective demand refers to that level of demand at which it is equal to aggregate supply. Effective demand determines the level of income and employment and lack of effective demand results unemployment.

The effective demand consists of (i) demand for consumption goods or consumption demand and (ii) demand for capital goods or investment demand. The main components of effective demand are as follows:

(A) AGGREGATE DEMAND FUNCTION AND
(B) AGGREGATE SUPLY FUNCTION.

## ■ CONCEPT OF AGGREGATE DEMAND AND ITS COMPONENTS:

Aggregate Demand refers to total demand for all final goods and services produced in an economy during a certain period. AD can be measured in terms of expenditure.

AD may be defined in the following forms.

Aggregate Demand refers to total demand for all final goods and services produced in an economy in a particular time period.

Aggregate Demand refers to total expenditure incurred by the people on the purchase of goods and services in an economy during a particular time period.

Therefore AD is the sum of total consumption demand and total investment demand.

The consumption demand originates from the private household (private consumption) and from the Government (public consumption).

The investment demand originates from the private entrepreneurs (demand for capital goods known as private investment) and from the Government (demand for capital goods known as public investment).

So, AD = Consumption Demand + Investment Demand.

Or, AD = C + I

## ▪ BEHAVIOUR OF AGGREGATE DEMAND:

1.  AD depends upon the level of income. Higher the level of income more will be the level of AD and vice-versa.
2.  Always there will be minimum level of AD even at zero level of income because people need to consume something at least for their survival which is known as autonomous consumption.
3.  Up to a certain level of income AD is greater than income level. Beyond that point AD is less than income level.
4.  AD curve rises at diminishing rate because as the employment and income level increases, people spend a smaller proportion of their income and starts savings.

## ▪ SLOPE OF AGGREGATE DEMAND CURVE:

The slope of the aggregate demand curve diminishes because people tend to spend a smaller proportion of their income when their income increases and they start saving for future. Therefore, the aggregate demand curve rises at a diminishing rate.

Aggregate demand has mainly two components like consumption demand and investment demand. Consumption demand consists of private consumption and public consumption. Investment demand consists of private investment and public investment.

## ▪ COMPONENTS OF AGGREGATE DEMAND:

There are four components of AD which are as follows.

### 1. PRIVATE CONSUMPTION EXPENDITURE OR HOUSEHOLD CONSUMPTION EXPENDITURE (C):

It refers to total amount of expenditure incurred by all households or private individuals to purchase goods and services to satisfy their wants. It depends up on the level of disposable income of households. There is a positive relationship between disposable income and household consumption expenditure i.e. C = f (Y). as income increases consumption also increases.

## 2. INVESTMENT EXPENDITURE (I):

It refers to planned expenditure incurred by all private entrepreneurs or firms to purchase capital assets. It includes expenditure on plant, machineries, equipments, factory building etc. and increase in the stock of raw materials, semi-finished goods and finished-goods. It depends up on Marginal Efficiency of Investment and rate of interest. There is a negative relationship between investment demand and rate of interest.

## 3. GOVERNMENT CONSUMPTION EXPENDITURE (G):

It refers to the expenditure made by the Government (Central Government, State Government, Local authorities). It includes the following: wages and salaries of civilians and armed forces, purchase of capital goods, public utility services like schools, colleges, hospitals, roads, water, electricity etc. and maintenance of law and order. It depends up on economic planning, fiscal policy and monetary policy of the Government.

## 4. NET EXPORTS (X – M):

It refers to the difference between export and import of goods and services of a country in a particular time period. It reflects the net foreign demand of our goods and services. It depends up on foreign exchange rate, terms of trade, relative prices of goods and services and trade policy of the Government.

Thus AD can be written as AD = C + I + G + (X - M).

# ▪ CONSTRUCTION OF AD CURVE FROM AD SCHEDULE:

Aggregate Demand refers to total expenditure incurred by the people on the purchase of goods and services in an economy during a particular time period.

AD curve can be drawn from AD schedule in the following way:

### AD curve from AD schedule:

| Income level (Rs. crores) | Consumption expenditure (Rs. crores) | Investment expenditure (Rs. crores) | AD = C + I (Rs. crores) |
|---|---|---|---|
| 0 | 50 | 50 | 100 |
| 50 | 75 | 50 | 125 |
| 100 | 100 | 50 | 150 |
| 150 | 125 | 50 | 175 |
| 200 | 150 | 50 | 200 |
| 250 | 175 | 50 | 225 |

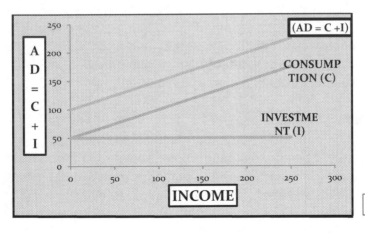

Fig: 7/1

From the above table and diagram it is clear that at zero level of income there is some consumption which is called as autonomous consumption. As the income increases consumption also increases but not at the same rate. At first, consumption is higher than income up to Rs. 100 crore income level. After Rs. 100 crore income is greater than consumption. Here aggregate investment is assumed as autonomous investment and therefore it is parallel to OX axis. AD is obtained by vertical summation of consumption and investment expenditure.

## ▪ CONCEPT OF AGGREGATE SUPPLY AND ITS MAIN COMPONENTS AND ITS SHAPE:

Aggregate Supply (AS) refers to the total value of all the final goods and services produced in the economy in a particular time period.

AS may be defined in the following three forms:

1. AS can be defined as the total value of all final goods and services produced by the producers in an economy in a particular time period. Thus AS is equal to total value added in the economy which is finally equal to cost of production.
2. Aggregate Supply is defined as minimum amount of receipts required by the producers to pay for the services of factors of production in the form of rent, interest, wages and profit.

This is equal to national income in the economy.

3. AS is also the sum total of consumption and savings of the economy

i.e. $AS = Y = C + S$.

Symbolically, $AS = f(N)$; AS is the function of number of workers employed (N).

The Aggregate Supply curve can be drawn from Aggregate Supply schedule in the following way.

| Income level (Rs. crores) (Y) | Consumption expenditure (Rs. crores) (C) | Savings (S) = Y – C | AS = C + S (Rs. crores) | |
|---|---|---|---|---|
| 0 | 50 | - 50 | 0 | |
| 50 | 75 | - 25 | 50 | |
| 100 | 100 | 0 | 100 | |
| 150 | 125 | 25 | 150 | |
| 200 | 150 | 50 | 200 | |
| 250 | 175 | 75 | 250 | Table. 7/2 |

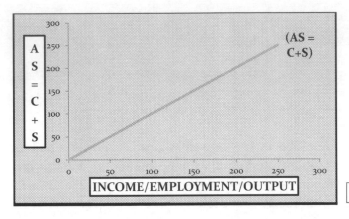

Fig: 7/2

# ▪ Behaviour of Aggregate Supply:

1. AS depends upon the utilization of available resources and technological advancement.
2. AS and level of income or employment are positively related. This means as employment increases the AS also increases.
3. Each point on the AS curve is equidistant from both X-axis and Y-axis which means total income is equal to aggregate of consumption and savings or total expenditure.
4. The slope of AS increases with the increase in the level of employment because cost of production rises at increasing rate as the employment increases.

# ▪ SHAPE OF AGGREGATE SUPPLY CURVE:

Aggregate Supply can increase till the level of full employment only. Beyond this level any increase in cost cannot generate employment. Therefore AS curve after reaching full employment it becomes vertical i.e. parallel to OY-axis.

According to Classical concept, AS curve is perfectly inelastic with respect to price but according to Keynesian concept with respect to price, AS is perfectly elastic till the level of full employment. Beyond the level of full employment (point F) AS curve becomes perfectly inelastic. This is shown by the following diagrams.

According to Keynesian concept with respect to level of employment AS becomes 45 degree line with X-axis till the level of full employment and after the full employment it becomes perfectly inelastic.

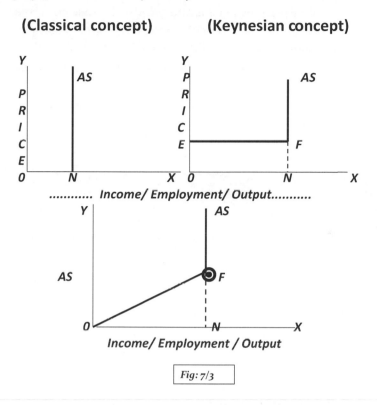

Fig: 7/3

## ▪ THE CONSUMPTION FUNCTION OR KEYNES' PSYCHOLOGICAL LAW OF CONSUMPTION:

Keynes explained the consumption behaviour of an individual with the help of Psychological Law of Consumption. According to this law, "Men are disposed, as a rule and on the average, to increase their consumption as their income increases, but not as much as the increase in their income".

In other words Keynes' Psychological law of consumption means that as the income increases the consumption also increases but at lower rate than the rate of increase in income. This is because the individuals save a part of their income.

Symbolically, C = f (Y).

**This law is based on certain assumptions**.

i.   The consumption habits of the people, the pattern of income distribution, price movement, and growth of population remain constant.
ii.  The condition of economy is absolutely normal i.e. there is absence of war, depression, hyper inflation etc.
iii. There is existence of capitalistic laissez-faire free market economy.

Keynes explained consumption function with the help of propensity to consume and save.

## ▪ GRAPHICAL PRESENTATION OF CONSUMPTION FUNCTION OR PROPENSITY TO CONSUME:

Consumption function or propensity to consume refers to the positive relationship between consumption and income.

Symbolically, $C = f(Y)$
C is consumption, Y is disposable income.

The consumption function states that as the income increases the consumption also increases.

**Behaviour of consumption function:**

1. As the income increases the consumption also increases as but by less than the increase in income.
2. Consumption is always positive even when the income is zero because people need to consume for their food and to live.
3. Consumption at zero level of income is called as autonomous consumption.
4. Consumption function is stable in short run.

Finally a consumption function can be written as

$C = f(Y)$

Or, $C = \overline{C} + bY;$

Where $\overline{C}$ is autonomous consumption and greater than zero, b is Marginal Propensity o Consume (0<MPC<1) and Y is disposable income.

Graphically a consumption curve can be drawn from the consumption schedule in the following way.

| LEVEL OF INCOME (Rs. IN CRORE) | CONSUMPTION (Rs. IN CRORE) |
|---|---|
| 0 | 50 |
| 100 | 100 |
| 200 | 150 |
| 300 | 200 |
| 400 | 250 |
| 500 | 300 |

Table. 7/3

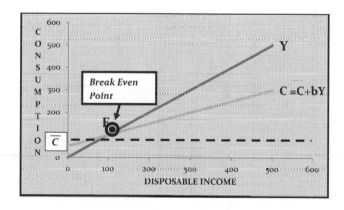

Fig: 7/4

The above table and diagram present that as the income increases the consumption also increases but less than the increase in income.

The consumption function $C = \overline{C} + by$, shows that $\overline{C}$ is the positive intercept which indicates autonomous consumption and b measures the slope of the consumption curve known as MPC, and Y is the disposable income.

In the above diagram at point E consumption expenditure is equal to income and this point is called as Breakeven Point.

Propensity to consume has two aspects Average Propensity to Consume (APC) and Marginal Propensity to Consume (MPC).

# ▪ CONCEPT OF AVERAGE PROPENSITY TO CONSUME AND MARGINAL PROPENSITY TO CONSUME:

Consumption function or propensity to consume refers to the positive relationship between consumption and income.

Symbolically, C = f (Y)

C is consumption, Y is disposable income.

The consumption function states that as the income increases the consumption also increases but less than increase in income.

Propensity to consume has two aspects which are as follows.

1. APC and 2. MPC.

### 1. Average Propensity to Consume:

It refers to the ratio of total consumption expenditure to total income.

Symbolically, APC = C/Y; where C is total consumption expenditure and Y is national income.

For example, if at particular level of national income of Rs. 500 crore the consumption expenditure is Rs. 300 crore, then Average Propensity to Consume (APC) = 300/500 = 0.6 or 60 %.

APC curve can be drawn from the following APC schedule.

| Income (Rs. In crore) | Consumption (Rs. In crore) | APC = C/Y | Shown by points In the diagram |
|---|---|---|---|
| 100 | 75 | 75/100 = 0.75 | A |
| 150 | 100 | 100/150 = 0.67 | B |

Table. 7/4

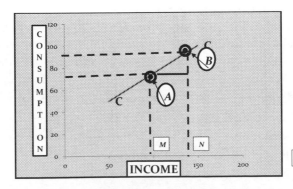

Fig: 7/5

424

The above table and diagram represents CC is the consumption curve which indicates APC at points A and B measured in the following way.

At point A, APC = C/Y = AM/OM = 75/100 = 0.75 and

At point B, APC = C/Y = BN/ON = 100/150 = 0.66.

## Properties of APC:

1. APC falls as income increases.
2. APC can never be zero because even at zero level of income survival needs some minimum consumption known as autonomous consumption.
3. APC becomes greater than one when consumption is more than income.
4. APC can be less than one when income is more than consumption.

## 2. Marginal Propensity to Consume (MPC):

It refers to the ratio of change in consumption to change in income.

Symbolically, $MPC = \frac{\Delta C}{\Delta Y}$, where $\Delta C$ is the change in consumption and $\Delta Y$ is change in disposable income.

For example, if consumption increases from Rs. 75 crore to Rs. 100 crore as a result of increase in income from Rs. 100 crore to Rs. 150 crore then $MPC = \frac{\Delta C}{\Delta Y} = 25/50 = 0.5$

The MPC curve can be drawn from the MPC schedule in the following way.

| Income (Rs. in crore) | Change in income = $\Delta Y$ | Consumption (Rs. In crore) | Change in consumption = $\Delta Y$ | MPC = $\Delta C/\Delta Y$ |
|---|---|---|---|---|
| 100 | - | 75 | - | - |
| 150 | 50 | 100 | 25 | 25/50 = 0.5 |
| 200 | 50 | 125 | 25 | 25/50 = 0.5 |

Table. 7/5

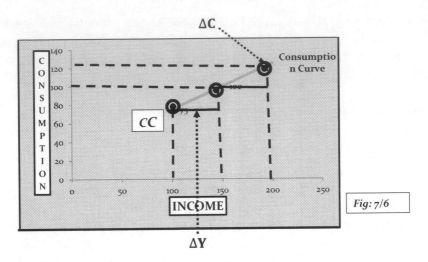

Fig: 7/6

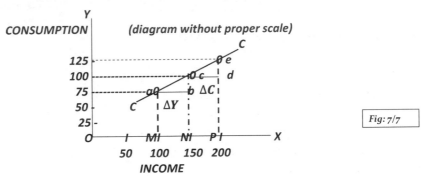

Fig: 7/7

The above table and diagram represents CC is the consumption curve which indicates MPC at different points on the curve.

At point c, MPC = cb/ba = 25/50 = 0.5 and

At point e, MPC = ed/dc = 25/50 = 0.5.

## Properties of MPC:

1. MPC remains constant in case of linear consumption curve but for non-linear consumption curve MPC decreases as income increases.
2. The value of MPC always lies between zero and one.
3. MPC of the poor class is higher than the MPC of rich class because the poor class spent most of the increment of their income to satisfy their basic needs.
4. MPC is stable in short-run because it depends on certain psychological factors which do not change in short-run.

426

## • THE RELATIONSHIP BETWEEN APC AND MPC:

APC refers to the ratio of total consumption expenditure to total income.

Symbolically, APC = C/Y; where C is total consumption expenditure and Y is disposable income.

MPC refers to the ratio of change in consumption to change in income.

Symbolically, MPC = $\frac{\Delta C}{\Delta Y}$, where $\Delta C$ is the change in consumption and $\Delta Y$ is change in income.

In case of linear consumption curve the relationship between APC and MPC can be explained by the following diagrams.

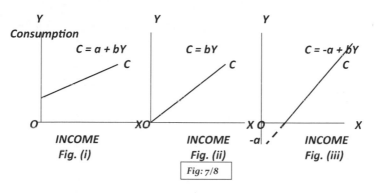

Fig. (i)    Fig. (ii)    Fig. (iii)

Fig: 7/8

Fig. (i) Shows that the linear consumption curve is C = a + bY

Here 'a' is autonomous consumption and 'b' is MPC, the slope of consumption curve.

APC = C/Y = (a + bY)/Y = a/Y + b = a/Y + MPC.

I.e. APC > MPC.

Fig. (ii) Shows that the linear consumption curve is C = bY.

Here 'a' is zero and 'b' is MPC, the slope of consumption curve.

So, APC = C/Y = bY/Y = b = MPC.

I.e. APC = MPC and constant.

Fig. (iii) Shows that the linear consumption curve C =—a + bY has negative intercept of '–a' and 'b' is MPC or slope of the consumption curve.

Here, APC = C/Y = (-a + bY)/Y =—a/Y + b

Or, APC = MPC – a/Y

I.e. APC < MPC

## • Graphical Presentation of Saving function and its different aspects Or Average Propensity to Save and Marginal Propensity to Save:

Saving is defined as that part of income which is not spent on current consumption expenditure.

Saving function refers to the functional relationship between saving and income.

Symbolically, S = f (Y); where 'S' is saving and 'Y' is income.

The above function shows that as income increases the saving also increases.

We can derive saving function from consumption function in the following way.

C = f (Y)

Or, C = a + b Y where 'a' is autonomous consumption, 'b' is MPC and Y is disposable income.

Therefore, Y = C + S

Or, S = Y − C = Y − a − bY

Or, S = − a + (1 − b) Y.

The saving curve can be drawn from the saving schedule in the following way.

| INCOME (Y) (Rs.) | CONSUMPTION (C) (Rs.) | SAVINGS (S) (Rs.) |
|---|---|---|
| 0 | 50 | − 50 |
| 50 | 75 | − 25 |
| 100 | 100 | 0 |
| 150 | 125 | 25 |
| 200 | 150 | 50 |

*Table. 7/6*

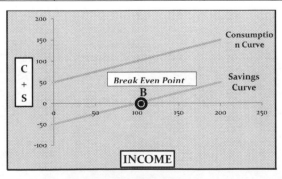

*Fig: 7/9*

428

The above table and diagram present the positive relationship between income and savings. The linear savings curve shows the constant slope or MPS. The saving line cuts the income line at point B which is known as breakeven point where Y = C or Savings = 0.

To the left of breakeven point savings is negative and to the right of breakeven point savings is positive.

Propensity to save has two aspects. They are as follows.

1.  Average propensity to save (APS) and
2.  Marginal propensity to save (MPS).

## 1.  Average propensity to save:

It is the ratio of total savings to total income. Symbolically, APS = S/Y.

For example, if income is Rs. 100 crore and saving is Rs. 25 crore, then APS = 25/100 = 0.25. This can be explained from the following table and diagram.

| Income (Rs. In crore) | Consumption (Rs. In crore) | Savings (Rs. In crore) | APS = S/Y |
|---|---|---|---|
| 100 | 75 | 25 | 25/100 = 0.25 |
| 150 | 100 | 50 | 50/150 = 0.33 |
| 200 | 125 | 75 | 75/200 = 0.38 |

*Table. 7/7*

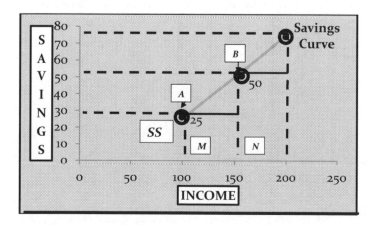

*Fig: 7/10*

The above table and diagram represents SS is the savings curve which indicates APS at points A and B measured in the following way.

At point A, APS = S/Y = AM/OM = 25/100 = 0.25 and

At point B, APS = S/Y = BN/ON = 50/150 = 0.33.

## Properties of APS:

1. Value of APS can be both positive and negative. APS is positive when consumption expenditure is less than income.

APS is negative when Consumption expenditure is more than income.

## 2. Marginal propensity to save:

It is the ratio of change in saving to change in income. It measures the slope of the savings curve.

Symbolically,

MPS $=\frac{\Delta S}{\Delta Y}$, where $\Delta s$ is the change in saving and $\Delta Y$ is change in income.

For example, if consumption increases from Rs. 75 crore to Rs. 100 crore as a result of increase in income from Rs. 100 crore to Rs. 150 crore then savings increases from Rs. 25 crore to Rs. 50 crore.

So MPS = $\frac{\Delta S}{\Delta Y}$ = 25/50 = 0.5

The MPC curve can be drawn from the MPC schedule in the following way.

| Income (Rs. In crore) | Change in income = ΔY | Consumption (Rs. In crore) | Savings | ΔS | Change in consumption = ΔC | MPS = ΔS/ΔY |
|---|---|---|---|---|---|---|
| 100 | - | 75 | 25 | - | - | - |
| 150 | 50 | 100 | 50 | 25 | 25 | 25/50 = 0.5 |
| 200 | 50 | 125 | 75 | 25 | 25 | 25/50 = 0.5 |

*Table. 7/8*

The above table and diagram represents SS is the savings curve which indicates MPS at different points on the curve.

At point c, MPS = cb/ba = 25/50 = 0.5 and

At point e, MPS = ed/dc = 25/50 = 0.5.

**Properties of MPS:**

1. The value of MPS lies always between 0 and 1.
   MPS will be zero if there is no savings i.e. if the additional income is fully consumed.
   MPS will be 1 if the additional income is fully saved.

## ▪ The relationship between the followings.

(a) APC and APS,
(b) MPC and MPS.

Relationship between APC and APS:
The sum of APC and APS is always equal to one.
Symbolically, APC + APS = 1
Proof: APC + APS = C/Y + S/Y = (C+S)/Y = Y/Y = 1 (since C + S = Y).
Therefore, APC = 1 – APS and
APS = 1 – APC.

## ▪ Relationship between MPC and MPS:

The sum of MPC and MPS is always equal to 1.
Symbolically, MPC + MPS = 1.

Proof: MPC + MPS = $\frac{\Delta C}{\Delta Y} + \frac{\Delta S}{\Delta Y}$ =(ΔC+ ΔS)/ΔY = ΔY/ΔY = 1.
Therefore, MPC = 1 – MPS and
MPS = 1 – MPC.

Note: (i) The value of MPC = 1, when MPS = 0 because whole of the disposable income is spent on consumption.
(ii) The value of MPC cannot be greater than 1 because change in consumption (ΔC) cannot be more than change in income (ΔY).

## ■ SOME BASIC CONCEPTS RELATING TO EMPLOYMENT IN MACRO ECONOMICS:

(a) Full employment.
(b) Natural rate of unemployment.
(c) Voluntary unemployment
(d) Involuntary unemployment.

### (a) FULL EMPLOYMENT:

It refers to the situation in which every able person that is willing to work at the existing rate of wage, is employed. It is a situation in which there is no involuntary unemployment.

In reality full employment never exists because it is always possible to find some people uninterested to do any productive work even when they are physically and mentally able. On the other hand there are some people who remain unemployed temporarily because either they are trying to change their jobs or due to introduction of new technology which is called as frictional unemployment.

This means full employment does not mean zero unemployment because there exists frictional, structural and voluntary unemployment.

### (b) NATURAL RATE OF UNEMPLOYMENT:

It refers to that situation in which there are some types of unemployment even at full employment. It includes frictional unemployment, structural unemployment and voluntary unemployment. It occurs due to the following factors.

1. Time required for shifting from one job to another job.
2. Time required adjusting with new technology.

### (c) VOLUNTARY UNEMPLOYMENT:

It refers to that situation in which the able bodied person do not get their jobs because they are not interested to do the jobs. They are called voluntarily unemployed.

## (d) INVOLUNTARY UNEMPLOYMENT:

It refers to that situation in which the able bodied persons who are interested to do the jobs at the existing wage rate but do not get the jobs. This is one of the main problems of every economy at present.

## ▪ THE FACTORS WHICH AFFECT PROPENSITY TO CONSUME AND SAVE:

Consumption function or propensity to consume refers to the positive relationship between consumption and income.

Symbolically, C = f (Y)

C is consumption, Y is disposable income.

The consumption function states that as the income increases the consumption also increases.

Propensity to consume has two aspects 1) APC and 2) MPC.

The factors which affect the propensity to consume are as follows.

1. **Disposable income:** Initially with the rise of disposable income the propensity to consume increases and propensity to save decreases but after a certain high level of increase in income the propensity to save increases and propensity to consume decreases.
2. **Distribution of income:** If in any economy there is more income inequality then the propensity to consume will be less and propensity to save will be more and vice-versa.
3. **Credit availability:** If credit availability is easy in any economy then there will be higher propensity to consume and lower propensity to save.
4. **Rate of interest:** With the rise in the rate of interest propensity to consume will fall and propensity to save will be more and vice-versa.
5. **Price level:** With the rise in price level the propensity to consume will fall and propensity to save will rise and vice-versa.

## ▪ Distinguish between the followings:

(a) Autonomous investment and induced investment,
(b) Ex-ante saving and ex-ante investment,
(c) Ex-post saving and ex-post investment.

(d) Ex-ante investment and Ex-post investment.

(e) Full Employment equilibrium VS under Employment equilibrium:

## (a) Autonomous investment VS Induced investment.

| BASIS | AUTONOMOUS INVESTMENT | INDUCED INVESTMENT |
|---|---|---|
| 1. Profit. | It does not depend upon level of profit. | It depends upon profit motive of the entrepreneur. |
| 2. Income Elasticity. | It is not affected by the changes in the level of national income i.e. it is income inelastic. | It increases with the increase in the national income and vice-versa. So it is income elastic. |
| 3. Sector. | Most of the investment made by the Government with an objective of social welfare (expenditure on school, college, hospitals etc.) is autonomous investment. | It is generally done by the private entrepreneurs with an objective of profit maximization like purchasing of machineries, raw materials etc. |
| 4. Determinants | It depends upon socio-economic and political conditions of the country. It is influenced by improvement in technology, discovery of new resources, growth of population etc. | It depends upon national income, innovations, taxation policy of Government, size of consumers, stability of the Government policy etc. |
| 5. Diagram. | *investment* <br><br> *autonomous* <br><br> o ——————— x <br> *Income* | *Induced Investment* <br> *investment* <br><br> O —————— x <br> *Income* |

## (b) Ex-ante (Planned) saving VS Ex-ante (Planned) investment.

(i) Ex-ante saving refers to the savings which are planned or intended to be made by all the households in an economy at the beginning of a particular time period.

Ex-ante investment refers to the investment which are planned or intended to be made by all the firms or entrepreneurs in an economy at the beginning of a particular time period.

(ii) The amount of ex-ante savings is given by saving function or propensity to save.

The amount of ex-ante investment is given by the investment demand function.

(iii) Equilibrium in the economy occurs only when ex-ante savings is equal to ex-ante investment. If they are not equal then output needs to be adjusted up or down until they are equal again.

## (c) Ex-post savings (Actual) VS Ex-post (Actual) investment:

(i) Ex-post savings refers to the actual or realized savings by the all households in an economy during a particular time period.

Ex-post investment refers to the actual or realized investment made by all the firms or entrepreneurs in an economy during a particular time period.

(ii) Ex-post savings and ex-post investment are always equal at all levels of income.

---

**ONE IMPORTANT POINT: STUDENTS MUST REMEMBER THAT AT EQUILIBRIUM LEVEL OF INCOME IN ANY ECONOMY, EX-ANTE SAVING = EX-ANTE INVESTMENT = EX-POST SAVING = EX-POST INVESTMENT.**

---

## (d) Ex-ante (Planned) Investment VS Ex-post (Actual) Investment:

(i) Ex-ante investment refers to the investment which are planned or intended to be made by all the firms or entrepreneurs in an economy at the beginning of a particular time period.

Ex-post investment refers to the actual or realized investment made by all the firms or entrepreneurs in an economy during a particular time period.

(ii) From the point of equilibrium level of national income, Ex-ante investment may or may not be equal to Ex-ante saving. But Ex-post investment is always equal to Ex-post saving.

### (e) Full Employment Equilibrium VS under Employment Equilibrium:

(i)  Full Employment refers to the situation in which every able person that is willing to work at the existing rate of wage, is employed. It is a situation in which there is no involuntary unemployment. Full employment equilibrium is reached when AD = AS.

Under-employment refers to a situation in which every able person that is willing to work at the existing rate of wage but does not get the job, or gets the job but not for the full length of hour or according to their qualification. In this situation AD = AS.

(ii)  In reality full employment never exists because it is always possible to find some people uninterested to do any productive work even when they are physically and mentally able. On the other hand there are some people who remain unemployed temporarily because either they are trying to change their jobs or due to introduction of new technology which is called as frictional unemployment. So under employment is realistic.

(iii) At full employment equilibrium real output becomes maximum whereas at under employment equilibrium real output does not reach at its maximum level.

(iv) Full employment equilibrium is a stable equilibrium but under employment equilibrium is not a stable equilibrium.

## ▪ What do you mean by Paradox of thrift?

Since the beginning of human civilization it is believed that the savings or thrift is a virtue. So the people try to save by reducing their consumption. But J. M. Keynes explained very clearly that what is good for one not good for the whole economy. He said that if every individual save then total consumption decreases in the economy. As a result demand for goods decreases and unsold stock increases.

Therefore the demand for factors of production decreases and finally unemployment increases. So income decreases and savings decreases. This paradoxical result is known as paradox of thrift.

The paradox can be explained by the following diagram.

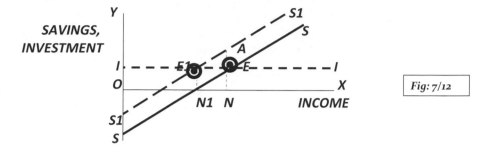

Fig: 7/12

In the above diagram SS is the saving curve and II is the investment curve and both the curve intersect each other at point E which is called equilibrium point and ON is equilibrium level of income.

Now suppose the economy becomes thrifty and increases savings by AE. As a result saving curve shifts upward to S1S1, this intersects the investment curve II at point E1, the new equilibrium point. Due to increase in savings in the economy the consumption decreases, as a result demand for goods decreases and production and employment decreases which reduces the national income from ON to ON1. This decrease in equilibrium level of income is known as paradox of thrift.

- **Explain the concept of parametric shift and parallel shift of consumption curve with the help of diagram.**

Parametric shift in a consumption curve refers to the change in the position of consumption curve due to change in its slope. The slope is called as the MPC denoted by b.

This can be explained by the following diagrams.

The consumption function can be expressed as $C = a + bY$ where 'a' is autonomous consumption does not depend upon income and b is the slope of consumption curve (MPC) depends upon the disposable income.

**Figure (a):**

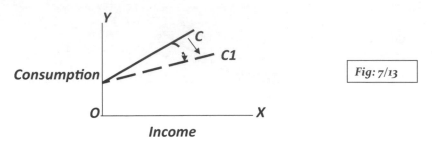

The above diagram shows that if the slope decreases i.e. value of 'b' decreases then the consumption curve swings downwards which is known as parametric shift of the consumption curve.

**Figure (b):**

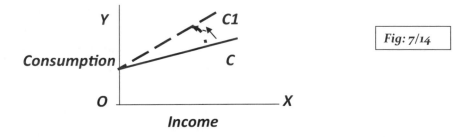

The above diagram shows that if the slope increases i.e. value of 'b' increases then the consumption curve swings upwards which is also known as parametric shift of the consumption curve.

## ▪ PARALLEL SHIFT OF CONSUMPTION CURVE:

It refers to the shift of the consumption curve depending upon the value of its intercept i.e. value of autonomous consumption 'a' which does not depend upon level of income.

If the value of intercept 'a' increases then the consumption curve shifts upward and if the value of 'a' decreases then the consumption curve shifts downwards as shown in the following diagram.

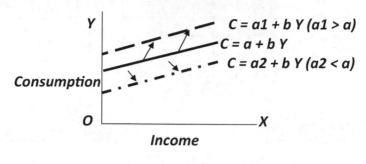

Fig: 7/15

## ▪ KEYNES' THEORY OF INCOME/EMPLOYMENT/ OUTPUT AT A GLANCE:

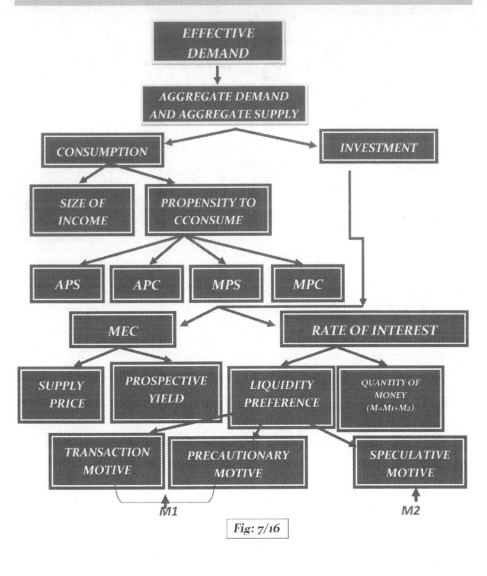

Fig: 7/16

__*__*__*__*__*__*__*__*__*__*__*__*__

# IMPORTANT QUESTIONS:

1. Who is called as father of modern macro economics?
2. Write the name of famous macro economics book by J.M.Keynes.
3. What is effective demand?
4. Define aggregate demand.
5. Define aggregate supply.
6. State the components of Aggregate demand.
7. What are the components of Aggregate supply?
8. Define consumption function.
9. Define saving function.
10. What do you mean by average propensity to consume (APC)?
11. What do you mean by average propensity to save (APS)?
12. Define marginal propensity to consume (MPC).
13. Define marginal propensity to save (MPS).
14. State the relationship between APC and APS.
15. State the relationship between MPC and MPS.
16. If APC = 0.4 then find out the value of APS.
17. If APS = 0.8 then find out the value of APC.
18. If MPC = 0.75 then find out the value of MPS.
19. If MPS = 0.45 then find out the value of MPC.
20. Define full employment.
21. Define voluntary unemployment.
22. What do you mean by involuntary unemployment?
23. Define natural rate of unemployment.
24. What is meant by autonomous investment?
25. Define induced investment.
26. Define ex-ante saving.
27. Define ex-ante investment.

28. What is meant by ex-post saving?
29. What is meant by ex-post investment?
30. When can APC = MPC?

## 3 OR 4 MARK QUESTIONS:

1. What is aggregate demand? Explain its main components.
2. Define aggregate supply and explain its main components.
3. Explain average propensity to consume with the help of a table and diagram.
4. Explain marginal propensity to consume with the help of a table and diagram.
5. Explain average propensity to save and marginal propensity to save with the help of a table.
6. Explain propensity to consume or consumption function.
7. Explain the propensity to save or saving function.
8. How can you explain the relationship between APC and APS?
9. How can you explain the relationship between MPC and MPS?
10. Explain the relationship between APC and MPC.
11. Distinguish between APC and MPC. Can the value of APC be more than MPC? Answer with reasons.
12. Distinguish between APC and MPC. The value of which of these two can be greater than one and when?
13. Explain the concept of effective demand in macro economics.
14. Distinguish between parametric shift and parallel shift of consumption curve.
15. How can you derive the consumption curve from the saving curve?
16. Explain the derivation of saving function from the function of consumption with the help of a diagram.
17. Distinguish between autonomous investment and induced investment.
18. Explain the factors which affect propensity to consume and propensity to save.
19. Explain the break-even point with the help of a diagram.
20. Explain the concept of paradox of thrift.

## 6 MARK QUESTIONS:

1.  What is Aggregate demand? Explain its components and behaviour.
2.  What is meant by aggregate supply? Distinguish between the Classical and Keynesian concept of aggregate supply curve.
3.  Distinguish between APC and MPC. How can you draw a hypothetical propensity to consume curve from hypothetical propensity to save curve?
4.  Distinguish between APS and MPS. How can you draw a hypothetical propensity to save curve from hypothetical propensity to consume curve?

# Chapter - 8

## Determination Of Equilibrium Level Of National Income And Employment And Output:

### ■ Determination of equilibrium level of income, output and employment in an economy:

In any economy the equilibrium level of income is that level of income at which aggregate demand is equal to aggregate supply or planned saving is equal to planned investment.

Equilibrium level of income or employment or output is determined

With the help of aggregate demand and aggregate supply or savings and investment curves.

There are two approaches: 1. AD and AS approach and
                          2. Saving and Investment approach.

**AD and AS approach:**

According to Keynes, equilibrium level of income and employment is determined at that point at which AD is equal to AS.

**Aggregate Demand:**

Aggregate Demand refers to total expenditure incurred by the people on the purchase of goods and services in an economy during a particular time period.

Therefore AD is the sum of total consumption demand and total investment demand.

The consumption demand originates from the private household (private consumption) and from the Government (public consumption).

The investment demand originates from the private entrepreneurs (demand for capital goods known as private investment) and from the Government (demand for capital goods known as public investment).

So, AD = Consumption Demand + Investment Demand.

Or, AD = C + I

## Aggregate Supply:

Aggregate Supply can be defined as the total value of all final goods and services produced by the producers in an economy in a particular time period. Thus AS is equal to total value added in the economy which is finally equal to cost of production.

AS is also the sum total of consumption and savings of the economy i.e. AS = Y = C + S.

Symbolically, Aggregate Supply, AS = f (N); AS is the function of number of workers employed (N).

The Aggregate Demand and Aggregate Supply curves can be drawn from the following schedule.

Table. 8/1

| Level of Income (Y)(Rs.) | Level of Consumption (C)(Rs.) | Level of Investment (I) | Level of Savings (S) | AD = C + I | AS = C + S |
|---|---|---|---|---|---|
| 0 | 50 | 50 | - 50 | 100 | 0 |
| 100 | 100 | 50 | 0 | 150 | 100 |
| **200** | **150** | **50** | **50** | **200** | **200** |
| 300 | 200 | 50 | 100 | 250 | 300 |
| 400 | 250 | 50 | 150 | 300 | 400 |
| 500 | 300 | 50 | 200 | 350 | 500 |

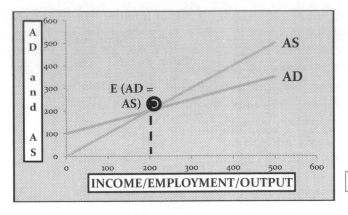

Fig: 8/1

From the above table and diagram it is clear that the equilibrium level of income and employment is determined at that point at which Aggregate Demand is equal to Aggregate Supply. Here equilibrium level of income is Rs. 200 crore determined at which

AD = AS = Rs. 200 crore. At this equilibrium point E,

**Ex-ante saving = Ex-ante investment = Ex-post saving = Ex-post Investment**

## • Saving-Investment approach:

According to this approach the equilibrium level of income is determined at that point at which planned saving (Ex-ante saving) is equal to planned investment (Ex-ante investment).

The same above table can be used to show the equilibrium level of income determination.

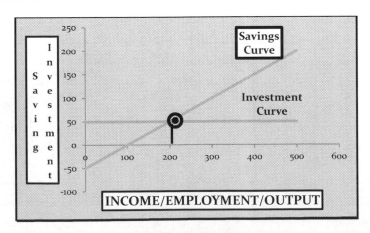

Fig: 8/2

From the above diagram it is clear that equilibrium level of income is determined at that point where S = I. Here equilibrium level of income Rs. 200 crore is determined at that point where

Saving = Investment = Rs. 50 crore.

In equilibrium, AD = AS
Or, C + I = C + S
OR, I = S.

Either to the right or to the left of the equilibrium point E, there is disequilibrium.

## ▪ Is full employment a necessary condition for equilibrium?

It is not necessary that the equilibrium level of income will be determined only at the full employment.

According to classical economists equilibrium level of income is determined only at full employment level but according to Keynes the equilibrium level of income can be determined in any of the three following situations i.e. either at full employment, or at under employment or at over employment. Whatever the situation is, the AD must be equal to AS to determine the equilibrium level of income or employment. This AD is called as effective demand.

It is clear from the above that the effective demand may or may not generate full employment. According to Keynes under employment is a normal situation of free capitalist economy and full employment is only an exception. A country can hope to achieve full employment only in periods of extreme prosperity. Full employment equilibrium is established in an economy when investment demand is able to fill the gap between the aggregate supply price corresponding to full employment and the consumption demand at full employment. In other words shortage of investment to cover the gap between income and consumption is responsible for under employment equilibrium.

### FROM UNDER EMPLOYMENT TO FULL EMPLOYMENT EQUILIBRIUM:

The economy can attain full employment equilibrium by increasing investment expenditure. This may be achieved by providing some concessions to the investors in the form of tax relief or by supplying credit at low rate of interest. The Government can also take initiative by increasing investment in public work programme like construction of roads, establishment of schools, colleges and hospitals etc.

## • Mathematical derivation of equilibrium level of income:

Aggregate Demand (AD) = C + I and Consumption function C = a+bY
Where, a is autonomous consumption, b = MPC and Y is income;
Here, I = $I_0$ (autonomous investment).
Aggregate Supply (AS) = Y = C+S
Therefore, at equilibrium, Y = C + I

$$OR, Y = a + by + I_0$$
$$OR, Y - b Y = a + I_0$$
$$Or, Y (1 - b) = a + I_0$$
$$Or, Y = \frac{a+I_0}{1-b}$$

Here, C + I are total expenditure on goods and services, is autonomous investment, 'a' is autonomous consumption, 'b' is Marginal propensity to consume which depends upon disposable income (Y).

## • Consumption plus investment (or AD and AS approach) approach to determine equilibrium level of income, output and employment in an economy. If AD is not equal to AS then how will the equilibrium is restored?

Answer of the first part is discussed already earlier. The second part can be explained in the following way.

If AD and AS are not equal then it will be either of the following two situations.

Either (1) AD > AS or (2) AD < AS

### 1. When AD > AS (Excess demand) or Ex-ante (Planned) Investment > Ex-ante (Planned) Saving:

When planned investment is greater than planned saving then the effect can be summarized in the following way.

1. Flow of goods and services will be less than their demand.
2. There will be no unsold stock with the producers.
3. Producers will be encouraged to increase their production.
4. The demand for factors of production will increase in the economy.
5. So AS would increase in the economy which raises the national income.
6. AS will increase until it becomes equal to AD and equilibrium level of income is reached in the economy.

**2. When AD < AS (Deficient demand) or Ex-ante (Planned) Investment < Ex-ante (Planned) Saving:**

When planned investment is less than planned investment then the effect can be summarized in the following way.

1. Flow of goods and services will be more than their demand.
2. Unsold stock of goods with the producers will increase in the economy.
3. Producers are discouraged to increase their production.
4. So, demand for factors of production will decrease.
5. AS will decrease in the economy which reduces the national income.
6. AS will decrease until it becomes equal to AD and equilibrium level of income is reached in the economy.

- **Explain saving—investment approach to determine equilibrium level of income, output and employment. If saving is not equal to investment then how will the equilibrium is restored.**

Answer is already discussed earlier.

- **How can you draw a propensity to save curve from a hypothetical propensity to consume curve? Or how can you derive saving function from consumption function diagrammatically?**

In any economy income is equal to sum of consumption and saving (Y = C + S) because income is either consumed or saved.

Thus if the income is given then the saving function can be directly derived from the consumption function as shown in the following diagram.

The diagram has two parts part A and part B. In part A, CC is the consumption curve and OP, the 45° line which presents income line. All the points on the income line OP are equidistant from X-axis and Y-axis. CC curve and OP curve intersect each other at point B where consumption = income. So this point B is called break-even point where saving = 0. To the right of break-even point saving is positive and to the left of point B, saving is negative.

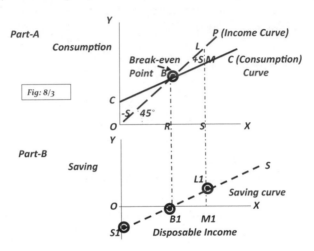

In part-B, we derive the propensity to save curve from the propensity to consume curve. In part-A the vertical distance between income line (OP) and consumption line (CC) determines the saving or dis-saving in the economy. If this vertical distance is drawn in part-B of the diagram and join the points then we get the propensity to save curve.

For example,

(i) In part-A, at zero level of income, the vertical distance between OP and CC is OC (shows dis-saving), is shown by OS1 in part-B.

(ii) In part-A, at OR level of income, the vertical distance between OP and CC is Point B (saving is zero), is shown by point B1 in part-B.

(iii) In part-A, at OS level of income, the vertical distance between OP and CC is LM (shows saving), is shown by L1M1 in part-B.

Now if we join the points S1, B1, L1 we get the propensity to save curve.

# Derivation of a consumption curve from a hypothetically drawn straight line saving curve? Explain APC at different points.

In any economy income is equal to sum of consumption and saving (Y = C + S) because income is either consumed or saved.

Thus if the income is given then the propensity to consume curve can be directly derived from the propensity to save curve as shown in the following diagram.

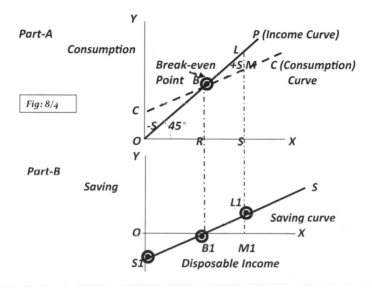

The diagram has two parts part A and part B. In part B, SS is the saving curve and OP, the 45 line which presents income line. All the points on the income line OP are equidistant from X-axis and Y-axis.

From the above diagram 1-A and 1-B we get the following points.

(i) At zero level of income, the vertical distances OS1 in part-B shows dis-saving which is equal to autonomous consumption OC in part-A.

(ii) At OR level of income saving is zero (point B1) in Part-B i.e. whole amount of income is consumed and nothing is saved. So at point R consumption = income, which is equal to BR in part-A.

(iii) At OM1 level of income, L1M1 is positive saving in Part-B. This means at this level income is greater than consumption which is shown by LM in Part-A of the diagram.

451

Now if we join the points C, B and M then we get the consumption curve or propensity to consume curve CC.

We should remember that at break-even point income = consumption, therefore at this point APC = C/Y = C/C = 1.

To the right of break-even point, income > consumption, therefore to the right of break-even point, APC > 1

To the left of break-even point the, since the income < consumption, therefore APC < 1

## ▪ The concept of full employment equilibrium with the help of a diagram:

Full employment equilibrium refers to that situation where aggregate demand is equal to aggregate supply and all the resources are fully utilised and there is no involuntary unemployment. This can be explained by the following diagram.

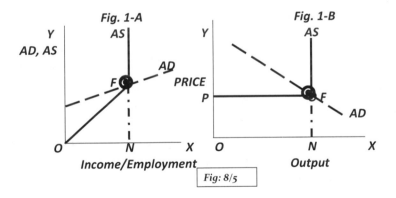

Fig: 8/5

In both the diagrams point E is the full employment equilibrium where AD = AS. In fig. 1-A, equilibrium income is ON and in Fig. 1-B, equilibrium output is ON.

Classical economists said that AS will be equal to AD only at full employment level. Classical economists' AS curve is a vertical line and parallel to OY-axis (perfectly price elastic).

# The concept of under employment equilibrium with the help of a diagram. How can under employment equilibrium be removed?

Under employment equilibrium refers to that situation at which AD is equal to AS at less than full employment and the resources are not fully utilised.

This situation occurs not by low level of AS but by deficiency of AD in the economy. This can be shown by the following diagram.

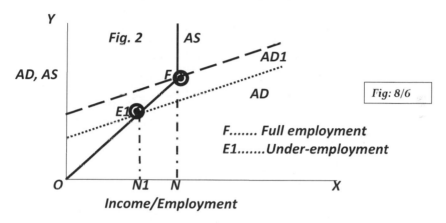

In the above diagram Point F indicates full employment equilibrium where AD = AS and the resources are fully utilised equal to ON.

Point E1 indicates under employment equilibrium where AD = AS but the resources are not fully utilised. ON1 resources are utilised out of ON resources available in the economy.

Actually, Keynes introduced the idea of under employment equilibrium.

## ADJUSTMENT MECHANISM TO CORRECT UNDER EMPLOYMENT EQUILIBRIUM:

Under employment equilibrium is corrected by the following measures.

(i) If the rate of capital formation increases in the economy by the cheap credit policy.

(ii) If the public expenditure increases.

(iii) If export of goods and services increases in the economy.

(iv) If the household expenditure increases in the economy.

# ▪ The concept of over employment equilibrium with the help of a diagram.

It refers to a situation in which AD = AS beyond full employment level. Here involuntary unemployment does not exist. It can be shown by the following diagram.

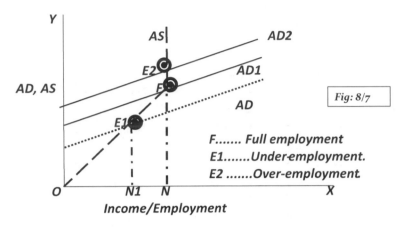

In the above diagram point F is full employment equilibrium where all resources are fully utilized. Now if the AD increases then we get new equilibrium point E2, beyond the full employment level. This point E2 is called over employment equilibrium and E2N – FN = E2F is called as excess demand.

This problem of over-employment can be solved by the following measures.

(i) If the economy adopts dear money policy.
(ii) If the public expenditure decreases.
(iii) If household expenditure decreases in the economy.

❖ **Distinguish between Classical theory and Keynesian theory of income and employment.**

| Basis | Classical Theory | Keynesian Theory |
|---|---|---|
| 1. Full employment | Equilibrium level of income is determined only at full employment level. | Full employment is not necessary but equilibrium income is determined when AD = AS |

| 2. Normal situation | Full employment is a normal situation. | Less than full employment or under-employment is a normal situation. |
|---|---|---|
| 3. Basis of law. | It is based on Say's law that supply creates its own demand. | It is based on the law that demand creates its own supply. |
| 4. Over production. | There is no possibility of over production or unemployment. | There is possibility of over production and unemployment. |
| 5. causes of equilibrium of S = I | Change in the rate of interest establishes saving-investment equilibrium. | Change in income establishes saving-investment equilibrium. |
| 6. Interference of Govt. | It follows policy of laissez faire and non-interference of Govt. | It emphasizes on the interference of Govt. to bring equilibrium of AD and AS. |
| 7. Policy to remove unemployment. | It suggests that temporary unemployment can be removed by cut in money wage policy. | It suggests increasing the effective demand to reduce unemployment but not the cut in money wage. |
| 8. Time period. | It is based on the assumption of long-run full employment equilibrium. | It is based on short-run full employment equilibrium. |

## ■ What is multiplier? Explain its working or explain the forward action and backward action of multiplier.

The concept of investment multiplier was first time introduced by R. F. Kahn to explain the effect of change in investment on change in income.

**Definition**: According to Kurihara, "The multiplier is the ratio of change in income to the change in investment".

Symbolically, $K = \frac{\Delta Y}{\Delta I}$ ; where K is multiplier, $\Delta Y$ is change in income and $\Delta I$ is change in investment.

For example if due to increase in investment of Rs. 50 crore the income increases by Rs. 200 crore then the value of multiplier is

= 200/50 = 4; So it is a co-efficient and it has no unit.

**Working of multiplier:** Working of multiplier can be explained by AD and AS approach and Saving – Investment approach diagrammatically.

**AD and AS approach:** AD is aggregate expenditure consisting of consumption expenditure and investment expenditure i.e. AD = C + I.

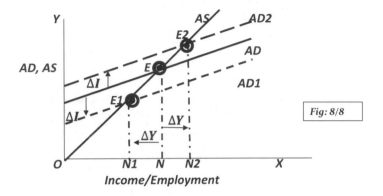

Fig: 8/8

The working of multiplier is of two types (i) Forward action of multiplier and (ii) Backward action of multiplier. Both can be explained by the above diagram.

(i) **Forward Action of Multiplier**: Equilibrium level of income is determined at point E where AD = AS and equilibrium level of income = ON.

If AD increases due to increase in investment then new equilibrium point is E2 and equilibrium level of income increases from ON to ON2. This is known as Forward Action of Multiplier.

(ii) **Backward Action of Multiplier**: Equilibrium level of income is determined at point E where AD = AS and equilibrium level of income = ON.

If AD decreases due to decrease in investment then the new equilibrium point is E1 and equilibrium level of income decreases from ON to ON1. This is known as Backward Action of Multiplier.

## ▪ Working of multiplier by Saving-Investment Approach:

The working of multiplier can be explained by using saving-investment approach in the following way.

In the following diagram SS is the saving curve and the investment curve (I) and they intersect each other at point E which is called equilibrium point. Here the equilibrium level of income is OY determined.

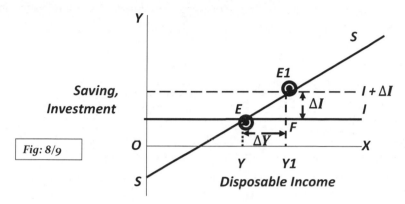

Fig: 8/9

Now if investment increases by $\Delta I$ then the new investment curve becomes (I +$\Delta I$) which intersects the saving curve SS at point E1 which is called new equilibrium point. The new equilibrium level of income is OY1.

So the income increases from OY to OY1 due to increase in investment. This ratio $\frac{\Delta Y}{\Delta I}$ is called multiplier. In the above diagram the slope of saving curve is E1F/EF = MPS = $\frac{\Delta I}{\Delta Y}$.

So the Multiplier = $\frac{\Delta Y}{\Delta I}$ = 1/MPS.

Similarly we can show the backward action of multiplier with the help of saving-investment approach where income decreases due to decrease in investment.

## ▪ Explain the working process of investment multiplier when MPC = 0.5 and investment increases by Rs. 100 crore.

Investment Multiplier is a co-efficient which measures the ratio of change in income to change in investment. It is denoted by K.

$K = \frac{\Delta Y}{\Delta I}$

Here MPC = 0.5; So Multiplier (K) = $\frac{1}{1-MPC} = \frac{1}{1-0.5} = 1/0.5 = 2$.

Here, $\Delta I$ = Rs. 100 crore.

So, K = $\frac{\Delta Y}{\Delta I} = \Delta Y/100$

Or, $2 = \Delta Y/100$

Or, $\Delta Y = 200$; so income will increase by Rs. 200 crore.

Now, this working process can be explained by the following table.

**Process of working of Multiplier:**

Table. 8/2

| Round No. | Initial Investment (Rs.) | Change in income $\Delta Y$ (Rs.) | Change in consumption $\Delta C$ (Rs.) | Saving or leakages $\Delta Y$ (Rs.) |
|---|---|---|---|---|
| 1 | 100 | 100 | 50 | 50 |
| 2 | | 50 | 25 | 25 |
| 3 | | 25 | 12.5 | 12.5 |
| 4 | | 12.5 | 6.25 | 6.25 |
| : | | : | : | : |
| T | | : | : | : |
| Total | 100 | 200 | 100 | 100 |

The table shows that as a result of initial increase in investment by Rs. 100 crore in round-1 income rises by Rs. 100 crore. MPC = 0.5 so consumption increases by Rs. 50 crore and Rs. 50 crore saved. In round-2, the consumption of Rs. 50 crore raises the income to Rs. 50 crore which is spent Rs. 25 on consumption and Rs. 25 is saved. In this way investment raises the income and income leads to increase the consumption.

Consumption of one individual becomes the income of another individual. Once again income increases and this process goes on for a long time until consumption becomes is zero. Finally income increases by Rs. 200 crore. Here we should remember that multiplier works effectively if investment increases steadily and we also should remember that there are certain limitations for the working of multiplier.

## ▪ Explain the relationship between multiplier and MPC and MPS or Derive the multiplier from the basic income expenditure identity:

At equilibrium of economy Y = C + I

Or, $\Delta Y = \Delta C + \Delta I$

Dividing both sides by $\Delta Y$,

Then we have, $1 = \frac{\Delta C}{\Delta Y} + \frac{\Delta I}{\Delta Y}$

Or, $\frac{\Delta I}{\Delta Y} = 1 - \frac{\Delta C}{\Delta Y}$

Or, $1/K = 1 - MPC$

Or, $K = 1/(1-MPC) \ldots \ldots (1)$

Or, $K = 1/MPS \ldots \ldots (2)$

## ▪ Derive the multiplier formula on the basis of functional relation between consumption and income:

The basic equilibrium condition: $Y = C + I \ldots \ldots (1)$

We also know that consumption (C) is the function of income (Y)

$$C = a + bY \ldots (2)$$

From (1) and (2) we get, $Y = a + bY + I$

Or, $Y - bY = a + I$

Or, $Y(1 - b) = a + I$

Or, $Y = \frac{a+I}{1-b} \ldots \ldots \ldots (3)$

Now, if investment increases by $\Delta I$ and change in income by $\Delta Y$, then the equilibrium condition can be rewritten as $\Delta Y = \frac{\Delta I}{1-b} \ldots (4)$

By adding (3) and (4),

We have $Y + \Delta Y = \frac{a+I}{1-b} + \frac{\Delta I}{1-b}$

Or, $\Delta Y = \left/ \frac{a+I}{1-b} + \frac{\Delta I}{1-b} \right/ - \frac{a+I}{1-b}$

Or, $\Delta Y = \frac{\Delta I}{1-b}$

Or, $K = \frac{\Delta Y}{\Delta I} = \frac{1}{1-MPC}$ ; (b = MPC)

$= 1/MPS$

## ▪ POSITIVE RELATIONSHIP BETWEEN Multiplier and MPC:

From $K = 1/(1-MPC)$, we get that there is positive relationship between multiplier (K) and MPC. This means if the value of MPC rises then the value of multiplier increases.

For example, if MPC = .5 and .8 then the value of K will be as follows.

(i)   When MPC = 0.5, $K = 1/(1-0.5) = 1/0.5 = 2$.
(ii)  When MPC = 0.8, $K = 1/(1-0.8) = 1/0.2 = 5$

So, with the increase of value of MPC the value of multiplier increases.

## ▪ INVERSE RELATIONSHIP BETWEEN MULTIPLIER AND MPS:

From $K = 1/MPS$, we get that there is inverse relationship between multiplier (K) and MPS. This means if the value of MPS rises then the value of multiplier decreases.

For example, if MPS = .5 and .8 then the value of K will be as follows.

(i)   When MPS = 0.5, $K = 1/0.5 = 2$.
(ii)  When MPS = 0.8, $K = 1/0.8 = 1.25$

So, with the increase of value of MPS, the value of multiplier decreases.

## ▪ What can be the minimum and maximum value of multiplier?

The value of multiplier depends upon the value of MPC. This can be explained if we take two extreme values of MPC i.e. 1 and 0.

(a)  When MPC = 0, then MPS = 1.
So, $K = 1/MPS = 1/1 = 1$.
This is minimum value of multiplier.

(b)  When MPC = 1, then MPS = $1 - 1 = 0$.
So, $K = 1/MPS = 1/0 = \infty$
This is maximum value of multiplier.
Therefore the value of multiplier lies between 1 and $\infty$.

## ▪ The relationship between the value of multiplier, MPC and MPS can be summarized by the following table:

| MPC | MPS=1-MPC | MULTIPLIER CO-EFFICIENT (K) |
|:---:|:---:|:---:|
| 0 | 1 | 1 |
| 1/2 | 1/2 | 2 |
| 2/3 | 1/3 | 3 |
| 3/4 | 1/4 | 4 |
| 4/5 | 1/5 | 5 |
| 5/6 | 1/6 | 6 |
| 6/7 | 1/7 | 7 |
| 7/8 | 1/8 | 8 |
| 8/9 | 1/9 | 9 |
| 9/10 | 1/10 | 10 |
| 10/10=1 | 0 | infinity |

Table. 8/3

### Numerical of multiplier:

Q. Calculate the change in income when (i) MPC = 0.5 and change in investment = Rs. 250 crore.

Ans. We know multiplier, K = 1/ (1-MPC) = 1/ (1-0.5) = 1/0.5 = 2.

$$\text{We also know that K} = \frac{\Delta Y}{\Delta I} = \Delta Y/250$$

$$\text{Or, } 2 = \Delta Y/250$$

$$\text{Or, } \Delta Y = 500$$

So, change in income = Rs. 500 crore.

Q. If the investment in any economy increases by Rs. 500 crore and income increases by Rs.1250 crore then find out the value of MPS and MPC.

Ans. We know multiplier, $K = \frac{\Delta Y}{\Delta I} = 1250/500 = 2.5$

$$\text{We also know K} = 1/\text{MPS}$$

$$\text{Or, } 2.5 = 1/\text{MPS}$$

$$\text{Or, MPS} = 1/2.5 = 0.4$$

$$\text{Therefore, MPC} = 1 - \text{MPS} = 1 - 0.4 = 0.6$$

Q. If in any economy investment increases by Rs. 500 crore and MPC = 0.8 then find out the increase in income.

$$We\ also\ know\ that\ K = \frac{\Delta Y}{\Delta I} = \Delta Y/500$$
$$Or,\ 5 = \Delta Y/500$$
$$Or,\ \Delta Y = 2500$$
So, change in income = Rs.2500 crore.

Q. In any economy saving, S = - 100 + 0.1Y and I = Rs.700 crore. Calculate (i) Equilibrium level of income.

(ii) The consumption expenditure at equilibrium level of income.
(iii) The value of MPS.
(iv) The value of multiplier.

Ans. (i) In any economy at equilibrium point,
    Saving = Investment
    So, - 100 + 0.1Y = 700
    Or, 0.1Y = 700 + 100 = 800
    Or, Y = 8000.
So the increase in income = Rs. 8000 crore.

(ii) We also know that at equilibrium point,
    Y = C + I
    Or, 8000 = C + 700
    Or, C = 8000 – 700 = 7300.
So the consumption expenditure = Rs. 7300 crore.

(iii) In the question given, S = - 100 + 0.1Y
    This means MPC = 0.1
    So, MPS = 1 – 0.1 = 0.9

(iv) The value of multiplier = 1/MPS = 1/0.9 = 10/9 = 1.11

Q. In an economy the actual level of income is Rs. 600 crores and the full employment level of income = Rs. 900 crores. If MPC = 0.5, calculate the increase in investment required to achieve full employment level of income.

Ans. Increase in income required = 900 – 600 = Rs. 300 crore.
The value of multiplier, K = 1/ (1-MPC) = 1/ (1-0.5) = 1/0.5 = 2.
So the required increase in investment can be obtained by the following way-

$$K = \frac{\Delta Y}{\Delta I} = 300/\Delta I$$
$$\text{Or, } 2 = 300/\Delta I$$
$$\text{Or, } \Delta I = 300/2 = 150$$

So, the investment required to increase by Rs. 150 crore.

Q. In an economy every time income rises, 80% of increase in income is spent on consumption. Now suppose in the same economy investment rises by Rs. 500 crore. Calculate change in income and change in saving.

Ans. Spending of 80% of increase in income means MPC = 80/100.
So, multiplier (K) = 1/ (1-MPC) = 1/ (1 – 0.8) = 1/ 0.2 = 5.
In the economy investment rises by Rs. 500 crores.

$$K = \frac{\Delta Y}{\Delta I} = \Delta Y/500$$
$$\text{Or, } 5 = \Delta Y/500$$
$$\text{Or, } \Delta Y = 2500$$

So, change in income = Rs.2500 crore.
We know that MPS = 1 - MPC = 1 – 0.8 = 0.2 = 20%
Therefore, change in saving = 20% of change in income
= 20% of Rs. 2500 = Rs. 500 crore.

## MORE NUMERICAL ON
## DETERMINATION OF EQUILIBRIUM LEVEL OF INCOME AND
## EMPLOYMENT:

1.  In an economy saving, S = - 100 + 0.1Y and I = 700
    Calculate (a) The equilibrium level of income
    And (b) The consumption expenditure at equilibrium level of income.

Solution: We know at equilibrium, S = I
                  So, - 100 + 0.1Y = 700
                        Or, 0.1Y = 800
                          Or, Y = 8000
    So, equilibrium level of income = 8000 (Rs. in crores)
              We also know that, Y = C + I
                      Or, 8000 = C + 700
                        Or, C = 7300 (Rs. in crores)

2. If the value of multiplier is 4, what will be the effect on income of an economy if investment increases by Rs. 150 crores?

Solution: Multiplier, $K = \dfrac{\Delta Y}{\Delta I}$

$$Or, 4 = \dfrac{\Delta Y}{100}$$
$$Or, \Delta Y = 400 \text{ (Rs. in crores)}$$

3. Given below is the consumption function in an economy:
          C = 100 + 0.5Y
With the help of a numerical example show that in this economy as income increases APC will decrease.
[CBSE Sample paper 2012]

Solution: C = 100 + 0.5Y
Let Income Y = 100, then C = 100 + 0.5 (100) = 150; Now APC = 150/100 = 1.5;
Again, Y = 200, then C = 100 + 0.5 (200) = 200; Now APC = 200/200 = 1;
Therefore, as income increases from 100 to 200, APC decreases from 1.5 to 1.

4. The saving function of an economy is S = -200 + 0.25Y. The economy is in equilibrium when income is equal to 2000. Calculate:

    (i) Investment expenditure at equilibrium level of income:
    (ii) Autonomous consumption.

(iii) Investment multiplier. [CBSE Sample Paper 2012]

Solution: Saving function, S = -200 + 0.25Y;
When Y = 2000,
(i) At equilibrium level of income, S = I

$$\text{Or, } -200 + 0.25Y = I$$
$$\text{Or, } I = -200 + 0.25 \times 2000 = -200 + 500 = 300$$

(ii) At zero level of income the consumption is known as autonomous consumption.

$$Y = C + S$$
$$\text{Or, } C = Y - S = 0 - [-200 + 0.25 \times 0] = 200$$

(iii) Investment multiplier, (K) = 1/(1 – MPC) = 1/MPS = 1/0.25 = 4


5. Find out the equilibrium level of national income when autonomous consumption is Rs. 200 crore, MPC = 0.75 and Investment = Rs. 500 crore.

Solution: We know C = a + by; where a = autonomous consumption, b = MPC;
We also know that, Y = C + I

$$\text{Or, } Y = a + by + I = 200 + 0.75 \times 500 = 200 + 375 = \text{Rs. 575 Cr.}$$


6. In an economy the equilibrium level of national income is Rs. 20,000 crore, The ratio of MPC to MPS is 4:1. Calculate the additional investment needed to reach new equilibrium level of income of Rs. 32,000 crore.

Solution: Present National Income, Y – Rs. 20,000 Crore
And expected final income = Rs. 32,000 Crore
Therefore, ΔY = Rs. 32000 – Rs.20, 000 = Rs. 12,000 crore

Now, MPC: MPS = 4:1
If, MPC = 4x then MPS = x;
We know, MPC + MPS =1

$$\text{Or, } 4x + x = 1; \text{ or, } x = 1/5 = 0.2$$

So, MPC = 4x = 4 x 0.2 = 0.8 and MPS = 0.2

Now, multiplier, K = 1/MPS = 1/0.2 = 5
Again, K = ΔY/ΔI

$$\text{Or, } 5 = (12,000)/ΔI$$
$$\text{Or, } ΔI = 12, 000/5 = 2400$$

Hence, the required level of additional investment = Rs. 2400 crore.

## ▪ Algebraic derivation of investment multiplier:

Aggregate Demand (AD) = C + I and Consumption function C = a+bY

Where, a is autonomous consumption, b = MPC and Y is income;

Here, I = $I_0$ (autonomous investment).

Aggregate Supply (AS) = Y = C+S

Therefore, at equilibrium, Y = C + I

OR, Y = a + by + $I_0$

OR, Y – bY = a + $I_0$

Or, Y (1 - b) = a + $I_0$

Or, $Y = \dfrac{a + I_0}{1 - b}$ . . . . . . . . . (1)

Here, C + I are total expenditure on goods and services, $I_0$ is autonomous investment, 'a' is autonomous consumption, 'b' is Marginal propensity to consume which depends upon disposable income (Y).

Now, let autonomous investment increases by ΔI and new equilibrium level of income increases by ΔY

Then, we can write, $Y + \Delta Y = \dfrac{a+I_0+\Delta I}{1-b} = \dfrac{a+I_0}{1-b} + \dfrac{\Delta I}{1-b}$ . . . . . . . (2)

Now, by subtracting (1) from (2) we have,

$$Y + \Delta Y - Y = \dfrac{a+I_0}{1-b} + \dfrac{\Delta I}{1-b} - \dfrac{a+I_0}{1-b} = \dfrac{\Delta I}{1-b}$$

$$\Delta Y = \dfrac{\Delta I}{1-b}$$

$$\text{Or, } \dfrac{\Delta Y}{\Delta I} = \dfrac{1}{1-b}$$

$$\text{Or, } K = \dfrac{1}{1-MPC} = \dfrac{1}{MPS}$$

—*—*—*—*—*—*—*—*—*—*—*—*—*—

# IMPORTANT QUESTIONS:

1. What is meant by equilibrium level of income?
2. What happens to national income when AD > AS?
3. What happens to national income when AD < AS?
4. Define investment multiplier.
5. How is investment multiplier related to MPC?
6. How is investment multiplier related to MPS?
7. If MPC = 0.4 then find out the value of multiplier.
8. If MPS = 0.75 then find out the value of multiplier.
9. If the value of multiplier is 5 then find out the value of MPC.
10. If the value of multiplier is 4 then find out the value of MPS.
11. If the value of multiplier is 5 and investment increases by Rs. 200 crore then what will be the effect on income in the economy?
12. If MPC = MPS then find out the value of multiplier.
13. If MPC: MPS = 3:1 then find out the value of multiplier.
14. What is Say's law of market?
15. Define full-employment equilibrium level of income.

3 OR 4 MARK QUESTIONS:

1. Explain AD-AS approach to determine equilibrium level of income or employment in an economy.
2. Explain Saving-investment approach to determine equilibrium level of income.
3. Define investment multiplier. Explain the relationship between multiplier and MPC with the help of a table and diagram.

4. Define investment multiplier. Explain the relationship between multiplier and MPS with the help of a table and diagram.
5. What is meant by investment multiplier? What can be its minimum value and why?
6. Explain the working of investment multiplier with the help of a diagram.
7. Explain the working of multiplier when MPC = 0.5 and investment increases by Rs. 200 crore.
8. Distinguish between ex-ante saving and ex-ante investment.
9. Explain the classical theory of income and employment.
10. Explain the Keynesian theory of income and employment.
11. Explain the concept of different types of equilibrium.
12. Complete the following table:

| Income (Rs.) | Saving (Rs.) | MPC | APC |
|:---:|:---:|:---:|:---:|
| 0 | -20 | — | — |
| 50 | -10 | — | — |
| 100 | 0 | — | — |
| 150 | 30 | — | — |
| 200 | 60 | — | — |

13. In an economy income increases by Rs. 10,000 as a result of rise in investment expenditure by Rs. 1000. Calculate

a) Investment multiplier.
b) The value of MPC.

14. Calculate the amount of new investment when the value of multiplier is 4.5 and income increases by Rs. 500.
15. Measure the level of ex-ante aggregate demand when autonomous investment and consumption expenditure (A) is Rs. 50 crore and MPS = 0.5 and the level of income is Rs. 10,000 crores. State whether the economy is in equilibrium or not?
(Hints: AD = A + bY = 50 + 0.5 x 10,000 = 5050 but AS or Y = 10,000. Here A is the sum of autonomous investment and autonomous consumption expenditure. So AD < AS and economy is not in equilibrium).

## 6 MARK QUESTIONS:

1.  Explain the equilibrium level of income and employment with the help of AD-AS approach. Do you think that the equilibrium will be always at full employment?
2.  Explain the equilibrium level of income and employment with the help of saving-investment approach. Is equality between saving and investment necessary for full employment?
3.  Explain the saving-investment approach to determine the equilibrium level of income. If savings exceeds planned investment, then what changes will bring about for the equality between them?
4.  In an economy if planned saving and planned investment is not equal then how will they be equal to bring the equilibrium level of income?
5.  In an economy the consumption function is given as
    $C = 100 + 0.5Y$
    With the help of a numerical example show that in this economy as income increases the value of APC will decrease.
6.  In an economy the saving function is given as
    $S = -200 + 0.25Y.$
    The economy is in equilibrium when income is equal to Rs. 2000. Calculate

    a)  Investment expenditure at equilibrium level of income.
    b)  Autonomous consumption.
    c)  Investment multiplier.

7.  Calculate the investment when National income = Rs. 800 Crore, autonomous consumption = Rs. 250 Crore and MPC = 0.5
8.  Calculate the consumption expenditure when autonomous consumption = Rs. 250 Crore, MPC = 0.25 and national income = Rs. 2500 Crore.
9.  Calculate the national income when autonomous consumption = Rs. 500 Crore, MPC = 0.6 and investment = Rs. 1000 Crore.
10. In an economy the consumption function is $C = 500 + 0.75Y$; where C is autonomous consumption expenditure and Y is national income. Calculate the equilibrium level of income and consumption expenditure when investment expenditure is Rs. 5000 crore.

469

# Chapter - 9

## Problem Of Excess Demand And Deficient Demand:

- ### EXCESS DEMAND OR INFLATIONARY GAP AND ITS CAUSES AND EFFECTS (IMPACTS) IN AN ECONOMY:

Excess demand refers to a situation when aggregate demand is more than aggregate supply corresponding to full employment.

The gap between aggregate demand and aggregate supply at full employment level for which the price rises (inflation) is called as inflationary gap.

The excess demand or inflationary gap can be explained by the following diagram.

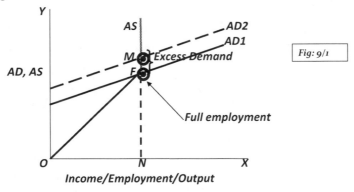

Fig: 9/1

From the above diagram we get the following.

(i)   Full employment level of income = ON.

(ii)  Aggregate Demand at full employment = FN.

(iii) Actual Aggregate Demand = MN.

So, excess demand or inflationary gap = MN – FN = MF.

**Causes of Excess Demand:** The main factors which are responsible for the excess demand are as follows.

1. **Propensity to consume:** If the household consumption expenditure increases due to increase in the propensity to consume then it causes excess demand.
2. **Deficit financing:** If deficit financing rises by borrowing and printing of currencies then money supply in the economy increases which causes excess demand in the economy.
3. **Government expenditure:** If Government expenditure increases due to more social welfare programmes like establishment of schools, colleges or expenditure for construction of roads or establishment of hospitals etc. then it causes excess demand in the economy.
4. **Surplus in Balance of payments:** If there is surplus in balance of payments due to increase in exports over imports then it causes excess demand in the economy.
5. **Private investment:** If private investment increases then also it causes excess demand.

## ▪ IMPACT OR EFFECT OF EXCESS DEMAND:

1. **Impact on Output:** Excess demand has not any effect on output because the economy has already reached at full employment level and all factors of production are fully utilised. Now the production can increase by improving technology but Keynes has assumed that state of technology remains unchanged in short-run.
2. **Impact on Employment:** Excess demand has no impact on employment because the economy has already reached full employment level and there is no involuntary unemployment.
3. **Impact on Price:** Excess demand leads to increase the price which is called as inflation.

## ▪ DEFICIENT DEMAND OR DEFLATIONARY GAP AND ITS CAUSES AND IMPACTS (EFFECTS) IN AN ECONOMY:

Deficient demand refers to a situation when aggregate demand is less than aggregate supply corresponding to full employment.

The gap between aggregate demand and aggregate supply at full employment level for which the price decreases (deflation) is called as deflationary gap.

The deficient demand or deflationary gap can be explained by the following diagram.

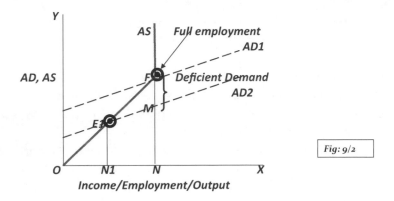

Fig: 9/2

From the above diagram we get the following.

(i)   Full employment level of income = ON.
(ii)  Aggregate Demand at full employment = FN.
(iii) Actual Aggregate Demand = MN.

So, deficient demand or deflationary gap = FN – MN = FM.

**CAUSES OF DEFICIENT DEMAND:** The main causes of deficient demand are as follows:

1.  **Propensity to consume:** If the household consumption expenditure decreases due to decrease in the propensity to consume then it causes deficient demand.
2.  **Deficit financing:** If deficit financing decreases by reduction in printing of new currencies then money supply in the economy decreases which causes deficient demand in the economy.
3.  **Government expenditure:** If Government expenditure decreases due to less social welfare programmes like establishment of schools, colleges or reduction in the Govt. expenditure for construction of roads or establishment of hospitals etc. then it causes deficient demand in the economy.

472

4. **Deficit in Balance of payments:** If there is deficit in balance of payments due to increase in imports over exports then it causes deficient demand in the economy.

5. **Private investment:** If private investment decreases then also it causes deficient demand.

## ▪ IMPACT OR EFFECT OF DEFICIENT DEMAND:

1. **Impact on Output:** Output will decrease in lesser proportion in competitive economy compared to oligopolistic economies. If labour unions are strong then they will not allow reducing wages so output will reduce considerably.

2. **Impact on Employment:** In competitive economies unemployment will be less compared to oligopolistic economies. Unemployment will be much less if trade unions have not strong bargaining power.

3. **Impact on Price:** Price will decrease more in competitive economies compared to oligopolistic economies. If trade unions have strong bargaining power then they will not allow reducing wages so price will fall much less.

## ▪ FISCAL POLICY AND ITS USES TO CORRECT EXCESS DEMAND AND DEFICIENT DEMAND IN THE ECONOMY:

Fiscal policy refers to the revenue and expenditure policy of the Government in order to correct excess demand and deficient demand in the economy.

The main instruments of fiscal policy are as follows.

1. **Taxes:** Taxes are the compulsory legal transfer payments made to the Government by the households and producers sector.

   (a) In order to correct excess demand the tax rate will increase. Therefore the burden on consumers and producers increases and their purchasing power decreases and aggregate demand decreases.

   (b) In order to correct deficient demand in the economy the tax rate decreases. Therefore the burden on the consumers and producers decreases and their purchasing power increases and aggregate demand increases.

2. **Government expenditure:** It refers to expenditure made by the Government for social welfare programmes like for example, expenditure for public construction and establishment of schools, colleges, hospitals, or for defence expenditure, subsidies etc.

   (a) In order to correct excess demand in the economy the Government reduces public expenditure to its minimum.
   (b) In order to correct deficient demand the Government increases the public expenditure so as to increase the aggregate demand in the economy.

3. **Public Borrowing:** It refers to borrowing by the Government from the public which is called as public debt.

   (a) In order to correct excess demand in the economy the Government increases the public borrowing which reduces the money supply and liquidity with the people. Thus aggregate demand decreases.
   (b) In order to correct deficient demand in the economy the Government reduces the public borrowing which increases the money supply and liquidity with the people. Thus aggregate demand increases.

4. **Deficit Financing:** It refers to the borrowing by the Government from the Central bank (RBI), foreign Governments and other institutions for financing the budgetary deficit.

   (a) In order to correct excess demand in the economy deficit financing should be very much restricted, new currency notes should not be printed. This will reduce the purchasing power of the people and aggregate demand will decrease.
   (b) In order to correct deficient demand in the economy deficit financing should be encouraged and new currency notes should be printed. This will inject more money supply in the economy and aggregate demand will increase.

## ▪ MONETARY POLICY AND ITS USES TO CORRECT EXCESS DEMAND AND DEFICIENT DEMAND IN THE ECONOMY:

Monetary policy refers to the policy of the central bank of a country to regulate and control money supply and supply of credit in the economy.

The main instruments of monetary policy can be categorized into Quantitative measures and Qualitative measures.

# ▪ QUANTITATIVE MEASURES OR QUANTITATIVE CREDIT CONTROL:

It includes the following instruments.

1.  **Bank Rate:** It refers to that rate of interest at which a Central Bank lends to the commercial banks.

Commercial banks lend to the public at higher rate than the bank rate.

   (a) In order to correct excess demand in the economy the bank rate is increased so that credit becomes dearer. This discourages the people to borrow money from the banks. The purchasing power of the people decreases which reduces aggregate demand in the economy.
   (b) In order to correct deficient demand the central bank reduces the bank rate so that credit becomes cheaper. This encourages the people to borrow money from the banks. The purchasing power of the people increases which raises the aggregate demand in the economy.

2.  **Open Market Operations:** It refers to the sale and purchase of Government securities in the open market by the central bank. This helps the central bank to control the cash reserves with commercial banks and the cost of availability of credit in the economy.

   (a) In order to correct excess demand the central bank purchases the Government securities which reduce the purchasing power of the people and thus it reduces aggregate demand in the economy.
   (b) In order to correct deficient demand the central bank sales the Government securities which increases the purchasing power of the people and thus it raises the aggregate demand.

3.  **Change in Cash Reserve Ratio (CRR):** It refers to the minimum percentage of the time deposits and demand deposits of commercial banks that they are required to keep in cash with the central bank.

(a) In order to correct excess demand the central bank raises the CRR which reduces the cash reserves with the commercial banks. So the commercial banks are forced to contract credit supply.

(b) In order to correct deficient demand in the economy the central bank reduces the CRR which raises the cash reserves with the commercial banks. So the banks are encouraged to supply credit.

4. **Change in Statutory Liquidity Ratio (SLR):** It refers to that percentage of total deposits which the commercial banks are required to keep with them in the form of liquid assets.

(a) In order to correct excess demand in the economy the central bank raises the SLR which reduces the cash reserves with the commercial banks and this discourages the supply of credit in the economy.

(b) In order to correct deficient demand in the economy the central bank reduces the SLR which raises the cash reserves with the commercial banks and encourages the supply of credit in the economy.

(5) **REPO RATE:** It is that rate at which the central bank of a country advances credit to the commercial banks for very short time period. If repo rate rises then the rate of interest of commercial banks on deposits and loans will increase. In order to correct excess demand repo rate will increase and in order to correct deficient demand the repo rate will decrease.

## ▪ QUALITATIVE MEASURES OR QUALITATIVE CREDIT CONTROL OR SELECTIVE CREDIT CONTROL:

It includes the following instruments.

1. **Marginal Requirement of Loans:** It refers to the difference between the value of security and the value of loans borrowed against the security.

(a) In order to correct the excess demand in the economy the margin is increased which restricted the credit supply and thus reduces the purchasing power of people and reduces aggregate demand in the economy.

476

(b) In order to correct deficient demand the margin is decreased which increases the credit supply in the economy and thus the purchasing power of the people increases and aggregate demand increases.

2. **Moral Suasion:** It refers to moral pressure on the commercial banks by the central bank to be liberal to provide more loans during deficient demand and to be selective and restrict the credit during excess demand in the economy.

3. **Rationing of Credit:** In order to restrict the supply of credit in the economy sometimes the central bank introduce credit quotas and fix ceiling on the loans lent by the commercial banks.

4. **Direct Action:** Sometimes central bank takes direct action against those commercial banks which disobey its directives from time to time. Direct action implies refusal to give loans to banks, refusal to give rediscount facility, imposition of monetary penalty on them etc.

## ▪ DISTINCTION BETWEEN INFLATIONARY GAP (EXCESS DEMAND) AND DEFLATIONARY GAP (DEFICIENT DEMAND) IN AN ECONOMY:

| BASIS | EXCESS DEMAND | DEFICIENT DEMAND |
|---|---|---|
| 1. Meaning. | It is a situation where AD is more than AS corresponding to full employment level. | It is a situation where AD is less than AS corresponding to full employment level. |
| 2. Level of employment. | It indicates over full employment equilibrium. | It indicates under employment equilibrium. |
| 3. Effect on price. | It causes inflation in the economy. | It causes deflation in the economy. |
| 4. Causes. | Its main causes are rise in household expenditure and Govt. expenditure, growth of black money, deficit financing etc. | Its causes are fall in household and Govt. expenditure, fall in black money, less deficit financing etc. |
| 5. Effects. | Rise in price, leads to prosperity or boom situation in the business cycle etc. | Fall in price, leads to recession, depression situation in the business cycle etc. |

## • CYCLICAL FLUCTUATION IN BUSINESS CYCLE AND ITS DIFFERENT PHASES WITH THE HELP OF DIAGRAMATIC PRESENTATION:

The term business cycle or trade cycle is used to denote the fluctuations in economic activity.

According to Keynes, "Business cycles are periodic fluctuations of employment, income and output".

The four phases of business cycle are Prosperity, Recession, Depression and Recovery. These phases can be explained by the following diagram.

1.  **Cyclical Boom:** It refers to that stage of economic activity where demand rises, price, income, employment and output are at highest level. It is also called as prosperity phase of economic activity. In the following diagram Boom is shown as the highest stage like points A, C.

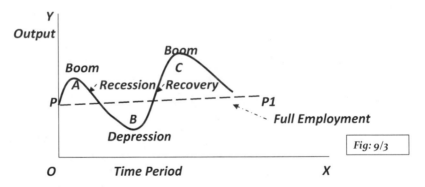

2.  **Recession:** It is that phase of business cycle where production of output tends to decrease, income and employment and price also decreases and demand also decreases. The AB stage in the above diagram is called as recession.

3.  **Depression:** It is the lowest stage of economic activity where income, output, employment and price become minimum. In the above diagram Point B indicates Stage of Depression.

4.  **Recovery:** It refers to that phase of business cycle where production of output, income, employment, investment and price tend to increase. In the above diagram BC phase of business cycle shows the Recovery stage.

## ▪ Out of fiscal policy and monetary policy which one is better to combat inflation and deflation in an economy?

Both monetary policy and fiscal policy can be used to correct inflation and deflation in an economy but their nature is different.

It has been realized that fiscal policy is more successful in controlling deficient demand whereas monetary policy is more successful to reduce excess demand in an economy.

Neither the fiscal policy nor the monetary policy alone can be useful for the stability of the economy. They act as complementary and they are not substitute to each other.

The effects of fiscal policy are more direct because it includes taxation, public expenditure, deficit financing. On the other hand the effects of monetary policy are indirect and it depends on availability of credit and cost of credit.

Therefore there is a need for co-ordination between fiscal policy and monetary policy to combat the excess demand and deficient demand in an economy. The fiscal policy will be more effective if it is free from the clutches of political pressure and monetary policy will be more effective if the central bank is given freedom to act independently.

# IMPORTANT QUESTIONS:

## 1 MARK QUESTIONS:

1. Define excess demand.
2. What is meant by deflationary gap?
3. Define deficient demand.
4. What is meant by inflationary gap?
5. What is meant by cyclical boom?
6. What is meant by cyclical depression in an economy?
7. What is the effect on output of excess demand in an economy?
8. What is the effect on output of deficient demand?
9. What is fiscal policy?
10. Define monetary policy.
11. What is bank rate?
12. What is meant by open market operations?

## 3 OR 4 MARKS QUESTIONS:

1. Explain with the help of a diagram the inflationary gap.
2. How can you explain excess demand in an economy?
3. Explain the deflationary gap with the help of a diagram.
4. How can you explain deficient demand by using diagram?
5. Distinguish between excess demand and deficient demand.
6. What is meant by fiscal policy? How is it useful to correct excess demand in an economy?
7. What is meant by fiscal policy? How is it useful to correct deficient demand in an economy?
8. What is meant by monetary policy? How is it useful to correct excess demand in an economy?

9. What is meant by monetary policy? How is it useful to correct deficient demand in an economy?
10. Would you advocate cheap money policy or dear money policy in a situation of excess demand in an economy?
11. Explain the role of bank rate and cash reserve ratio to correct excess demand in an economy.
12. Explain the role of taxation and Government expenditure policy to correct deficient demand in an economy.
13. If there is an excess demand or a deficient demand in an economy then advocate whether fiscal policy or monetary policy will be more effective to correct it?
14. Define excess demand. State its impact on output, employment and price in an economy.
15. Define deficient demand. State its impact on output, employment and price in an economy.

## 6 MARK QUESTIONS:

1. What is meant by monetary policy? How is it useful to correct excess demand and deficient demand in an economy?
2. What is meant by fiscal policy? How is it useful to correct excess demand and deficient demand in an economy?
3. Explain the role of following instruments to correct excess demand and deficient demand in an economy.

   a) Bank rate.
   b) Taxation.
   c) Statutory Liquidity Ratio (SLR).
   d) Public expenditure.

4. Distinguish between inflationary gap and deflationary gap.

# Chapter - 10

## Government Budget And Economy:

## ▪ CONCEPT OF THE GOVERNMENT BUDGET:

According to Findley Shirras, "A budget includes a statement of receipts and expenditure of previous year and estimates of the receipts and expenditure of the ensuring financial year and the proposals as to the ways and means for meeting deficit or distributing surplus, if any".

According to Indian Constitution, "Budget means the financial statement containing an estimate of all anticipated revenue and expenditure of the Government for the coming financial year".

Therefore a Government budget is an annual financial statement of the estimated receipts and estimated expenditure over a particular year.

## ▪ OBJECTIVES OF THE GOVERNMENT BUDGET:

**OBJECTIVES OF GOVERNMENT BUDGET:** The main objectives are as follows.

1. **Optimum allocation of Resources**: Government with the help of budget's taxation and public expenditure policy can highly influence the allocation of resources so that a balance is maintained between profit maximization and social welfare maximization policy of the Government.

2. **Reduction of Income inequalities**: Government reduces progressive taxation policy i.e. high rate of taxation on rich people and low rate of tax on low income group people. Even Govt. provides necessary goods at subsidized rate to the lower income group people. In this way Govt. tries to reduce income inequality.

3. **Price Stability**: Government tries to control unnecessary inflation during boom or deflation during depression by using taxation policy, expenditure and borrowing policy which are reflected in the budget.
4. **Economic Growth and Social Welfare:** The budget aims to promote rapid and balanced economic growth in agriculture and industry simultaneously in the country and to maximize the social welfare of the country.
5. **Managing Public Enterprises**: The budget also aims to manage and improve the performance of the public enterprises like railways.

## ▪ STRUCTURE OR COMPONENTS OF GOVERNMENT BUDGET:

The structure or components of budget are classified into two parts like Budget Receipts and Budget Expenditure.

Budget Receipts is divided into Revenue Receipt and Capital Receipts.

The Budget Expenditure is similarly divided into Revenue Expenditure and Capital Expenditure.

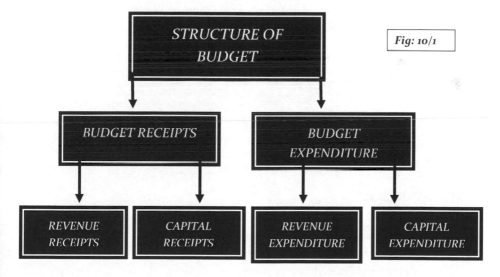

Fig: 10/1

## ▪ Budget Receipts are divided into two parts.

1. **REVENUE RECEIPTS:** Revenue Receipts are those receipts which neither create any liability nor cause any reduction in the assets of the Government. For example, income tax, corporation tax etc.
2. **CAPITAL RECEIPTS:** Capital Receipts are those receipts which either create a liability for Government or cause any reduction in the assets of the Government. For example, borrowing, disinvestment of Public companies etc.

## ▪ Budget expenditure is also divided into two parts.

1. **REVENUE EXPENDITURE:** It refers to that expenditure which neither creates assets nor reduces liability for the Government. For example, salaries to Govt. employees, pension, subsidies etc.
2. **CAPITAL EXPENDITURE:** It refers to that expenditure which either creates an asset or reduces liability of the Government. For example, repayment of loans, expenditure of Govt. to purchase land, building and machineries etc.

## ▪ TAX and its main features:

Generally a tax is defined as the compulsory payment which is paid by the people to the Government of the country for its expenditure for the common benefit of the people.

**FEATURES OF TAX:**

1. It is compulsory payment of the people to the Government.
2. It is duty of the tax-payer to pay tax.
3. Tax is a legal obligation.
4. Tax can be imposed on income of the people, or on the goods or on the services.

## ▪ DISTINCTION BETWEEN DIRECT TAX AND INDIRECT TAX:

| BASIS | DIRECT TAX | INDIRECT TAX |
|---|---|---|
| 1. Meaning. | It is really paid by the person on whom it is legally imposed. | It is imposed on one person but really paid by other person. |
| 2. Incidence of Tax. | Impact and incidence of direct taxes are on the same person. | Impact and incidence of indirect taxes are on different persons. |
| 3. Shift of Tax Burden. | Burden of this tax cannot be shifted. | Burden of this tax can be shifted. |
| 4. Base of tax. | It is imposed on the basis of income and wealth. | It is imposed on sales, production and expenditure. |

## ▪ DISTINCTION BETWEEN TAX REVENUE AND NON-TAX REVENUE:

| REFERENCE | TAX REVENUE | NON-TAX REVENUE |
|---|---|---|
| 1. Basis. | It accrues from tax for which no benefit in return is expected. | It accrues from that amount for which a special benefit is expected. |
| 2. Share of Government. | It contributes a major share of Govt. revenue. | It contributes a very small share of Govt. revenue. |
| 3. Examples. | It includes income tax, corporate tax, sales tax, excise duty etc. | It includes fees, fines, penalties, grants and gifts etc. |

## ▪ DISTINCTION BETWEN REVENUE RECEIPTS AND CAPITAL RECEIPTS:

| BASIS | REVENUE RECEIPTS | CAPITAL RECEIPTS |
|---|---|---|
| 1. Meaning. | Revenue receipts are those receipts which do not create liabilities nor reduce assets of the Govt. | Capital receipts are those receipts which either create liabilities or reduce assets of Govt. |
| 2. Effect. | These do not create liabilities nor reduce assets. | These create liabilities or reduce assets of Govt. |

| 3. Obligation to Return. | These are never returned and these create no obligation on Govt. | These are generally returned and these are obligations on the Govt. |
| 4. Examples. | It includes direct taxes, indirect taxes, fees, fines, penalties etc. | It includes borrowings, recovery of loans, disinvestment etc. |

# ▪ DISTINCTION BETWEEN REVENUE EXPENDITURE AND CAPITAL EXPENDITURE:

| BASIS | REVENUE EXPENDITURE | CAPITAL EXPENDITURE |
|---|---|---|
| 1. Meaning. | It means that expenditure which does not create assets nor reduces liability of Govt. | It means that expenditure which either creates assets or reduces liability of Govt. |
| 2. Purpose. | Main purpose is normal functioning of Govt. | Main purpose is to build capital assets or to reduce liabilities. |
| 3. Period. | It is generally for the short period. | It is generally for the long period. |
| 4. Nature. | It is of recurring nature. | It is of non-recurring nature. |
| 5. Example. | It includes payment of salaries, interest payments, subsidies, expenditure on defence, education, health etc. | It includes repayment of loans, expenditure of Govt. to purchase land, building and machineries etc. |

# ▪ DISTINCTION BETWEEN DEVELOPMENTAL EXPENDITURE AND NON-DEVELOPMENTAL EXPENDITURE:

| BASIS | DEVELOPMENTAL EXPENDITURE | NON-DEVELOPMENTAL EXPENDITURE |
|---|---|---|
| 1. Meaning. | It means the expenditure on economic growth and social development of the country. | It means the expenditure on those activities which help the Govt. to function smoothly. |
| 2. Productive. | This expenditure is productive. | This expenditure is not concerned with productivity of working class. |

| 3. Period. | It is meant for long period. | It is meant for short period. |
|---|---|---|
| 4. Nature. | It is of non-recurring nature. | It is of recurring nature. |
| 5. Example. | It includes construction of roads and railways, development of irrigation facilities, education, electricity, water etc. | It includes expenditure on maintaining law and order, for administration, defence, interest on loans etc. |

## ▪ DISTINCTION BETWEEN PLAN EXPENDITURE AND NON-PLAN EXPENDITURE:

| BASIS | PLAN EXPENDITURE | NON-PLAN EXPENDITURE |
|---|---|---|
| 1. Meaning. | It refers to expenditure provided in the budget on different programmes and projects under current five year plan. | It refers to the expenditure provided in the budget for regular functioning of the Government. |
| 2. Relation with five year plan. | It is related with the current five year plan. | It has no relation with current five year plan. |
| 3. Examples. | It includes the expenditure on central plans and projects, loans to state and U.T. Governments etc. | It includes the expenditure on payment of salaries, interest, subsidies, health, education, defence etc. |

## ▪ BUDGETARY DEFICIT AND ITS CLASSIFICATION:

Budgetary deficit refers to the difference between budgetary expenditure and budgetary receipts.

Budgetary Deficit = Budgetary Expenditure – Budgetary Receipts.

It is classified into three categories like

1. Revenue Deficit,
2. Fiscal Deficit,
3. Primary Deficit.

# REVENUE DEFICIT AND ITS IMPLICATIONS IN AN ECONOMY:

Revenue Deficit is defined as the excess of revenue expenditure over the revenue receipts.

Revenue Deficit = Revenue Expenditure – Revenue Receipts.

# SIGNIFICANCE OR IMPLICATIONS OF REVENUE DEFICIT:

1. It indicates the borrowing of the Govt. in current account to meet current expenditure.
2. It also indicates dis-savings on Govt. current account because Govt. has to obtain the funds by selling its assets.
3. The borrowings of Govt. lead to inflationary situation in the economy.
4. Larger the borrowing more will be the liability and interest payments. So the burden for the Govt. and future generation will increase.

# FISCAL DEFICIT AND ITS IMPLICATIONS IN AN ECONOMY:

Fiscal deficit is defined as the excess of anticipated Government expenditure over the anticipated Government receipts in both revenue account and capital account excluding the borrowing.

So, Fiscal Deficit = Total Expenditure – Revenue Receipts – Capital Receipts
(Excluding Borrowing).

# SIGNIFICANCE OR IMPLICATIONS OF FISCAL DEFICIT:

1. Fiscal deficit indicates the extent of dependence of Govt. on borrowings to meet the budgetary expenditure.
2. Larger the borrowing more will be the liability and interest payments. So the burden for the Govt. and future generation will increase.
3. Govt. mainly borrows from RBI which means more printing of currency notes. So money supply increases in the economy which causes inflationary pressure in the economy.

4. If the Govt. borrows from the foreign countries then Govt. loses its sovereignty and the foreign countries interfere into our domestic economic policy.

5. If the borrowing is very large then the Country might be caught in debt trap because it has to borrow to pay huge rate of interest on the loans.

## ▪ PRIMARY DEFICIT AND ITS IMPLICATIONS IN AN ECONOMY:

Primary deficit is defined as the difference between fiscal deficit and interest payments.

So, Primary Deficit = Fiscal Deficit – Interest Payments.

Actually it is Gross Primary Deficit.

Net Primary Deficit = Gross Primary Deficit – Interest receipts.

## ▪ SIGNIFICANCE OR IMPLICATIONS OF PRIMARY DEFICIT:

1. It indicates borrowing requirements of the Govt. to meet deficit net of interest payments.

2. If there is zero primary deficits then it indicates that the Govt. has to resort to borrowings only to make interest payments.

3. Larger the borrowing more will be the liability and interest payments. So the burden for the Govt. and future generation will increase.

## ▪ DISTINCTION BETWEEN REVENUE DEFICIT, FISCAL DEFICIT AND PRIMARY DEFICIT IN AN ECONOMY:

| BASIS | REVENUE DEFICIT | FISCAL DEFICIT | PRIMARY DEFICIT |
|---|---|---|---|
| 1. Meaning. | It means excess of total revenue expenditure over revenue receipts. | It means excess of budgetary expenditure over budgetary receipts excluding borrowings. | It means fiscal deficit minus interest payments. |

| 2. Formulae. | R.D. = R.E. – R.R. | F.D. = B.E.—B.R. (Excluding borrowing) | P.D. = F.D. – INTEREST PAYMENTS. |
|---|---|---|---|
| 3. Effects. | It leads to inflationary situation. | It is a liability for the interest payments on loan. | It increases the burden of debt. |
| 4. Indicator. | It indicates the indebtedness in current account. | It indicates borrowing requirements of the Govt. for repayment of loan with interest. | It indicates borrowing requirements of Govt. to meet fiscal deficit excluding interest payments. |

## ▪ BALANCED BUDGET AND ITS CHARACTERISTICS:

Balanced budget means a budget in which total Govt. expenditure is equal to total Govt. receipts.

## ▪ FEATURES OF BALANCED BUDGET:

1. **CONDITION**: This budget is recommended in normal economic conditions.
2. **EFFECTS**: This budget helps to maintain the economic conditions.
3. **PRACTICABILITY:** This is not a practical concept of today's economics.

## ▪ What is unbalanced budget?

Unbalanced budget is that budget in which total Govt. expenditure is not equal to total Govt. receipts.

It is of two types: Surplus budget and Deficit budget.

## ▪ What is surplus budget? State its main features.

Surplus budget is that budget in which total Govt. receipts are more than the total Govt. expenditure.

## ▪ FEATURES OF SURPLUS BUDGET:

1. **CONDITION:** This budget is recommended in the situations of inflationary trends.
2. **EFFECTS:** This budget helps to reduce inflation.
3. **PRACTICABILITY:** This is not a practical concept.

## ▪ DEFICIT BUDGET AND ITS MAIN CHARACTERISTICS:

Deficit budget is that budget in which total Govt. expenditure is more than total Govt. receipts.

## ▪ FEATURES OF DEFICIT BUDGET:

1. **CONDITION:** This budget is recommended in the situations of depression.
2. **EFFECTS:** This budget leads to increase the inflation.
3. **PRACTICABILITY:** This budget is a practical concept of today's economics.

## ▪ Can there be any fiscal deficit without Revenue deficit?

Yes, it is possible under the following situations.

(i) When Revenue budget is balanced but Capital budget shows a deficit.
(ii) When there is surplus in Revenue budget but deficit in Capital budget and this deficit is more than the surplus of Revenue budget.

## ▪ Numerical of Budget:

Q.1. The following figures are based on budget estimates of Government for the year 2008-09. On the basis of it calculate

(i) Revenue deficit, (ii) Fiscal deficit and (iii) Primary deficit

| COMPONENTS | Rs. In Crore | Rs. In Crore |
|---|---|---|
| 1. Revenue Receipts (2 + 3) | | 602,935 |
| 2. Tax revenue | 507,150 | |
| 3. Non-tax revenue | 95,785 | |
| 4. Capital Receipts (5 + 6 + 7) | | 147,949 |
| 5. Recoveries of loans | 4497 | |
| 6. Other receipts | 10,165 | |
| 7. Borrowing & Other liabilities | 133,287 | |
| 8. Total Receipts (1 +4) | | 750,884 |
| 9. Non-Plan Expenditure (10 + 12) | | 507,498 |
| 10. On the revenue account | 448,352 | |
| 11. (Of which interest payments) | 190,807 | |
| 12. On capital account | 59,146 | |
| 13. Plan expenditure (14 + 15) | | 243,386 |
| 14. On revenue account | 209,767 | |
| 15. On capital account | 33,619 | |
| 16. Total expenditure (9 + 13) | | 750,884 |
| 17. Revenue expenditure (10 + 14) | 658,119 | |
| 18. Capital Expenditure (12 + 15) | 92,765 | |

*Table. 10/1*

(i) Revenue Deficit = 17 − 1 = 658,119 − 602,935 = 55,184 Crores.

(ii) Fiscal Deficit = 16 − (1 +5 +6)

$$= 750,884 - (602,935 + 4497 + 10,165)$$

$$= 133,287 \text{ Crores.}$$

(iii) Primary Deficit = Fiscal Deficit − Interest Payments

$$= 133,287 - 190,807 = - 507,520 \text{ Crores.}$$

## GOVERNMENT BUDGET:
## SOME IMPORTANT POINTS RELATING TO GOVERNMENT BUDGET AND NUMERICAL:

1.  RECEIPTS = REVENUE RECEIPTS (A) + CAPITAL RECEIPTS (B):

2.  EXPENDITURE = REVENUE EXPENDITURE (C) + CAPITAL EXPENDITURE (D):

3.  REVENUE DEFICIT = REVENUE EXPENDITURE – REVENUE RECEIPTS
4.  FISCAL DEFICIT = TOTAL EXPENDITURE (REVENUE EXPENDITURE + CAPITAL EXPENDITURE) – REVENUE RECEIPTS – CAPITAL RECEIPTS (EXCLUDING BORROWING)

    OR

    FISCAL DEFICIT = TOTAL EXPENDITURE – NON-DEBT CAPITAL RECEIPTS (RECOVERIES OF LOANS AND DISINVESTMENT OF PSUs).

    FISCAL DEFICIT = BORROWINGS AND OTHER LIABILITIES

5.  PRIMARY DEFICIT = FISCAL DEFICIT – INTERESTPAYMENTS

6.  REVENUE RECEIPTS INCLUDES = TAX REVENUE (A1)
                                 + NON-TAX REVENUE (A2)

7.  **TAX REVENUE (A1) INCLUDES**:

    (a)  Income tax, (b) Corporation tax, (c) Customs,
    (d)  Union excise duties, (e) Service tax.

8.  **NON-TAX REVENUE (A2) INCLUDES**:

    (a)  Interest receipts, (b) Dividends and Profits,
    (c)  External grants.

9. CAPITAL RECEIPTS (B) INCLUDES:

   (a) Recoveries of loans,
   (b) Market Borrowings and other loans,
   (c) External assistance,
   (d) Disinvestment of PSUs.

10. REVENUE EXPENDITURE (C) INCLUDES: Expenditure by Government on

   (a) Subsidies,
   (b) Interest on Government loans,
   (c) Public administration,
   (d) Defence.

11. CAPITAL EXPENDITURE (D) INCLUDES:

   (a) Defence capital,
   (b) Non-plan capital expenditure,
   (c) Loans to Public enterprises,
   (d) Loans to States,
   (e) Loans to Foreign Governments.

1. Calculate (i) revenue deficit, (ii) fiscal deficit and (iii) Primary deficit from the following data of a Government budget.

|  |  | (Rs. in crores) |
|---|---|---|
| (i) | Tax revenue | 47 |
| (ii) | Capital receipts | 34 |
| (iii) | Non-tax revenue | 10 |
| (iv) | Borrowings | 32 |
| (v) | Revenue expenditure | 80 |
| (vi) | Interest payments | 10 |
| (vii) | Interest received | 5 |

Solution:

   (i) Revenue deficit = Revenue expenditure − revenue receipts
   = 80 − (47 + 10)
   = 80 − 57 = 23 (Rs. in crores)

(ii) Fiscal deficit
= Revenue expenditure + capital expenditure – Revenue receipts
– capital receipts (excluding borrowing)

| |
|---|
| **HERE 32 IS SUBTRACTED FROM CAPITAL RECEIPTS OF 34, AS CAPITAL RECEIPTS DOES NOT INCLUDE BORROWINGS** |

$$= 80 - 47 - 10 - (34 - 32)$$
$$= 80 - 57 - 2$$
$$= 21 \text{ (Rs. in crores)}$$

(iii) Primary deficit = Fiscal deficit – interest payments
$$= 21 - 10 = 11 \text{ (Rs. in crores)}$$

(iv) Net Primary Deficit = Primary Deficit – Interest Received
$$= 11 - 5 = 6 \text{ (Rs. in crore)}$$

—*—*—*—*—*—*—*—*—*—*—*—*—*—

# IMPORTANT QUESTIONS:

## 1 MARK QUESTIONS:

1. Define Government budget.
2. What is revenue budget?
3. Define capital budget.
4. What is meant by tax?
5. Define tax revenue.
6. Define capital receipts.
7. What is meant by revenue expenditure?
8. What is meant by capital expenditure?
9. Define developmental expenditure.
10. Define non-developmental expenditure.
11. What is meant by balanced budget?
12. Define surplus budget.
13. Define deficit budget.
14. What is meant by fiscal deficit?
15. What is meant by revenue deficit?
16. Define primary deficit.
17. What does zero primary deficit indicate?
18. How is primary deficit calculated?
19. State any one objective of Government budget.
20. Define direct tax.

## 3 OR 4 MARK QUESTIONS:

1. Define Government budget. State its main objectives.
2. Distinguish between revenue receipts and capital receipts.
3. Distinguish between revenue expenditure and capital expenditure.
4. Explain the structure of Government budget.

5. Distinguish between direct tax and indirect tax.
6. How can you differentiate between tax revenue and non-tax revenue?
7. Explain the basis of classification of Government expenditure into revenue expenditure and capital expenditure.
8. Distinguish between balanced budget and un-balanced budget.
9. Explain the basis of classification of expenditure into planned expenditure and non-planned expenditure.
10. Define revenue deficit. State its main implications.
11. What is meant by fiscal deficit? State its main implications.
12. Define primary deficit. What are the implications of primary deficit?
13. Distinguish between fiscal deficit and primary deficit.
14. How can the deficit in Government budget be reduced?
15. State with reasons whether the following examples are revenue receipts or capital receipts?

    a) Recovery of loans
    b) Interest received on loans
    c) Dividend received from public enterprises
    d) Grants from foreign Government.

## 6 MARK QUESTIONS:

1. What is Government budget? Explain various components of budget receipts?
2. Define budgetary deficit? How can it be financed?
3. Describe the various measures to correct different deficits.

# Chapter - 11

## Foreign Exchange Rate:

Foreign exchange rate refers to that rate at which one unit of a currency of one country is exchanged for the number units of currencies of another country. It is also called as external value of the currency.

■ **TYPES OF FOREIGN EXCHANGE RATE:**

There are mainly three types of foreign exchange rate which are as follows.

1. Fixed exchange rate system.
2. Flexible exchange rate.
3. Managed Floating System.

■ **FIXED EXCHANGE RATE AND ITS VARIANTS:**

Fixed rate of exchange refers to that rate of exchange which is fixed by the Government or by any monetary authority of the country.

This rate has two variants like Gold Standard system of exchange and Bretton Woods system of exchange rate.

(a) **Gold Exchange Rate System**:

According to this system gold was considered as the common unit of parity and the value of currency of each country was defined in term of gold.

This system was continued from 1870 to 1914. This system was also known as mint parity system.

### (b) Bretton Woods System:

This system replaced the gold standard and established parity for each currency in terms of both the US dollar and gold. It introduced a new exchange rate system, viz. The adjustable peg system. This meant that exchange rates were fixed by the Govt. but it is adjustable from time to time. This system thus created an adjustable system which was the best for the world. It could maintain the stability of the gold standard, which would encourage trade and capital flows in the country.

From 1945 to 1970, the world was on a dollar standard which was the key currency under Bretton Woods's system. But this system broke down in 1970 because of USA's trade deficit and budgetary deficit due to overvalued currency and huge accumulation of dollar with Germany and Japan.

Since 1971, world has been operating under hybrid system of clean floating, dirty floating, crawling peg, currency block etc.

## ■ FIXED EXCHANGE RATE AND ITS MERITS AND DEMERITS:

Fixed rate of exchange refers to that rate of exchange which is fixed by the Government or by any monetary authority of the country.

### ❖ MERITS OF FIXED EXCHANGE RATE:

1. **Stability in Exchange rate**: Fixed exchange rate system ensures stability in exchange rate which encourages the exporters and importers to trade freely. Thus it promotes world trade.

2. **Capital Inflow**: Fixed exchange rate system encourages foreign investment in the country which promotes economic growth.

3. **Capital Outflow**: Fixed exchange rate system prevents capital outflow from the country.

4.  **Speculation:** This system prevents speculation in the foreign exchange market.

5.  **Inflation:** This system helps to Government to check inflation in the country by eliminating unwanted fluctuations in prices.

❖ **DEMERITS OF FIXED EXCHANGE RATE:**

1.  **No Free market**: It contradicts the objective of free market economy.

2.  **Price Fluctuation**: This system is responsible for the internal price fluctuation because expansion and contraction of money supply is required to maintain fixed exchange rate.

3.  **Gold Reserves**: Under this system each country requires to keep a large quantity of gold reserves because currencies of different countries are convertible into gold.

4.  **Venture Capital**: This system does not encourage venture capital in the international money market. Venture capital means the capital invested in the business where the owner accepts risk for the company's profit or losses.

5.  **Difficult to determine equilibrium rate**: Under this system it is very difficult to determine equilibrium rate of exchange because it does not consider demand and supply of foreign exchange to determine the equilibrium in the international market. Therefore there is every possibility of either deficit or surplus balance of payments.

## ▪ FLEXIBLE EXCHANGE RATE AND ITS MERITS AND DEMERITS:

Flexible rate of exchange is that rate which is freely determined by the market demand and supply of foreign exchanges.

The rate at which demand for foreign exchange is equal to supply of foreign exchange that rate is called equilibrium rate of exchange.

## ➢ MERITS OF FLEXIBLE RATE OF EXCHANGE:

1.  **Free Movement of Capital**: Since in this system there is no restriction so there is free movement of capital which promotes international trade.

2.  **Gold Reserve is not necessary**: In this system there is no need for the country to keep huge gold reserves. Thus the problem of international liquidity is solved.

3.  **Free from BOP problem**: This system solves the problem of balance of payments by removing the problem of disequilibrium by devaluation or revaluation of currencies.

4.  **Venture Capital**: This system encourages the venture capital in the international money market.

## ➢ DEMERITS OF FLEXIBLE RATE OF EXCHANGE:

1.  **Instability in the Economy**: This system creates uncertainty and instability in the economy which highly affects foreign trade and capital movements in the country.

2.  **Bad impact on Exporters**: This system leads to uncertainty in the international trade. Exporters will not be able to plan their export revenue or import expenditure because of fluctuation of foreign exchange rate.

3.  **Problem of Speculation**: This system leads to problem of speculation. A country with continuous deficit has a tendency to devalue its currency. Speculators will demand foreign currencies by selling their domestic currencies. This will create excess demand for foreign currencies which may lead to black-marketing and manipulation of prices of foreign currencies.

4.  **Danger of Global Depreciation**: Under this system all the countries want to increase their exports and decrease their imports in order to create favourable balance of payments position. This creates the danger of competitive depreciation which leads to global depreciation.

## ▪ Explain the determination of flexible exchange rate.
### Or
### How is equilibrium rate of foreign exchange determined?

The equilibrium rate of foreign exchange rate is determined at that point at which the demand for foreign exchanges is equal to supply of foreign exchanges.

The determination of foreign exchange depends on the demand and supply of foreign exchanges.

**DEMAND FOR FOREIGN EXCHANGE:**

The demand for foreign exchange arises because of the following factors.

(i) When individuals, business firms or Government import goods and services from abroad they demand for foreign currencies.

(ii) When the individuals, firms or Government repay the loans to abroad they require repaying in term of foreign exchanges.

(iii) When the domestic residents want to invest in abroad they need foreign currencies.

(iv) When the domestic residents want to go to abroad for either travelling, or for medical treatment or for study then they require foreign currencies for their expenditure.

There is an inverse relationship between demand for foreign exchange and the rate of foreign exchange. This means other factors remaining same, if the rate of exchange increases then the demand for foreign exchange decreases and vice-versa.

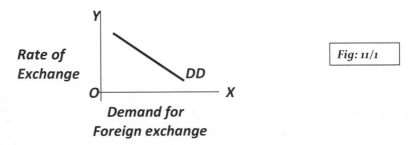

Fig: 11/1

The demand for foreign exchange curve is negatively sloped downwards from left to right. This means more foreign currencies are demanded at low rate of foreign exchange and vice-versa.

**SUPPLY OF FOREIGN EXCHANGE:**

The sources of supply of foreign exchange are as follows.

1. When the domestic exporters like individuals, or business firms or Government export goods and services to abroad then they collect foreign exchanges.
2. When the domestic residents of a country take loan from abroad then they collect foreign exchanges.
3. When the foreign investors invest in the county then the supply of foreign currencies increases in the country.
4. When the foreigners come to our country for travelling or for medical treatment or for study then also the supply of foreign currencies increases in the country.

There is a positive relationship between supply of foreign exchange and the rate of foreign exchange. This means other factors remaining same, if the rate of exchange increases then the supply for foreign exchange increases and if the rate of foreign exchange decreases then its supply decreases.

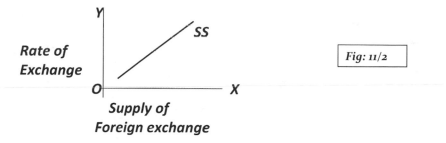

Fig: 11/2

The supply of foreign exchange curve is positively sloped upwards from left to right. This means more foreign currencies are supplied at higher rate of foreign exchange and vice-versa.

## ▪ DETERMINATION OF EQUILIBRIUM FOREIGN EXCHANGE RATE:

The equilibrium rate of foreign exchange is determined at that point where the demand for foreign exchange is equal to the supply of foreign exchange. This is explained with the help of following table and diagram.

| Rate of exchange | 10 | 20 | 30 | 40 | 50 |
|---|---|---|---|---|---|
| Demand for foreign exchange | 50 | 40 | 30 | 20 | 10 |
| Supply of foreign exchange | 10 | 20 | 30 | 40 | 50 |

Table. 11/1

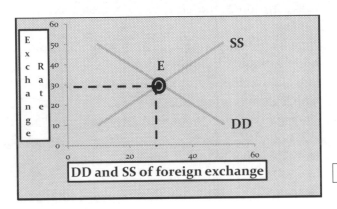

DD and SS of foreign exchange

Fig: 11/3

In the above diagram point E is the equilibrium point where the demand for foreign exchange is equal to the supply of foreign exchange and OR is the equilibrium rate of foreign exchange determined.

## ▪ DIFFERENT SOURCES OF DEMAND FOR FOREIGN EXCHANGE RATE:

The demand for foreign exchange arises because of the following factors.

(i) When individuals, business firms or Government import goods and services from abroad they demand for foreign currencies.

(ii) When the individuals, firms or Government repay the loans to abroad they require repaying in term of foreign exchanges.

(iii) When the domestic residents want to invest in abroad they need foreign currencies.

(iv) When the domestic residents want to go to abroad for either travelling, or for medical treatment or for study then they require foreign currencies for their expenditure.

There is an inverse relationship between demand for foreign exchange and the rate of foreign exchange. This means other factors remaining same, if the rate of exchange increases then the demand for foreign exchange decreases and vice-versa.

**Rate of Exchange**

*Demand for Foreign exchange*

Fig: 11/3

The demand for foreign exchange curve is negatively sloped downwards from left to right. This means more foreign currencies are demanded at low rate of foreign exchange and vice-versa.

## ▪ DIFFERENT SOURCES OF SUPPLY OF FOREIGN EXCHANGE RATE:

The sources of supply of foreign exchange are as follows.

1. When the domestic exporters like individuals, or business firms or Government export goods and services to abroad then they collect foreign exchanges.
2. When the domestic residents of a country take loan from abroad then they collect foreign exchanges.
3. When the foreign investors invest in the county then the supply of foreign currencies increases in the country.
4. When the foreigners come to our country for travelling or for medical treatment or for study then also the supply of foreign currencies increases in the country.

There is a positive relationship between supply of foreign exchange and the rate of foreign exchange. This means other factors remaining same, if the rate of exchange increases then the supply for foreign exchange increases and if the rate of foreign exchange decreases then its supply decreases.

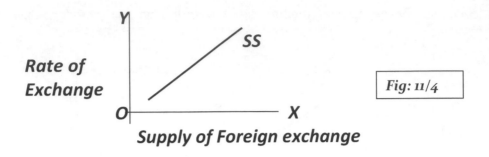

Rate of Exchange

Supply of Foreign exchange

Fig: 11/4

The supply of foreign exchange curve is positively sloped upwards from left to right. This means more foreign currencies are supplied at higher rate of foreign exchange and vice-versa.

# FOREIGN EXCHANGE MARKET AND ITS MAIN FUNCTIONS:

Foreign Exchange Market is defined as the market situation in which foreign currencies are sold and bought by the central bank, commercial banks, brokers, exporters, importers and investors.

According to Kindleberger, "The foreign exchange market is the market for a national currency anywhere in the world."

Foreign exchange market does not necessary means to any particular place.

**Main Functions of Foreign Exchange Market:**

1. **Exchange Function**: It helps to exchange the currency of one country for the currencies of other countries.
2. **Credit Function**: It helps to a country by supplying credit and thus it facilitates the international trade.
3. **Hedging Function**: It protects to a country against the risk related fluctuations in foreign exchange rate.

# Write short notes on the following.

(i) Appreciation of domestic currency.
(ii) Depreciation of domestic currency.

(i) **Appreciation of domestic currency**: It refers to rise in the value of domestic currency compared to the value of foreign currency.

For example, if the value of Indian currency i.e. Rupee increases (say at first One Dollar = Rs. 48 and now One Dollar = Rs.45) compared to the value of U.S. dollar then we can say that there is appreciation of Indian currency or conversely depreciation of U.S. dollar.

**Main Cause**: If the supply of foreign exchange (say U.S. dollar) increases and other factors remaining same.

**Diagram:**
This appreciation of domestic currency can be explained by the following diagram.

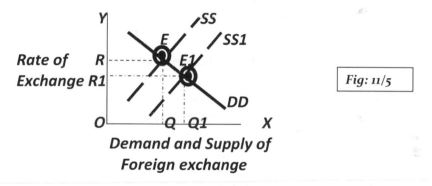

Fig: 11/5

**Demand and Supply of Foreign exchange**

In the above diagram as the supply of foreign exchange increases (shown by the shifting of supply curve to the right from SS to SS1) in the country then the value of rate of exchange decreases from OR to OR1 and the value of domestic currency increases i.e. appreciation of domestic currency takes place.

(ii) **Depreciation of domestic currency**: It refers to fall in the value of domestic currency compared to the value of foreign currency. For example, if the value of Indian currency i.e. rupee decreases compared to the value of U.S. dollar (say at first One dollar = Rs. 45 and now it is One Dollar = Rs. 50) then we can say that there is depreciation of Indian currency or conversely appreciation of U.S. dollar.

**Main Cause**: If the demand for foreign exchange (say U.S. dollar) increases and other factors remaining same.

**Diagram:**
This Depreciation of domestic currency can be explained by the following diagram.

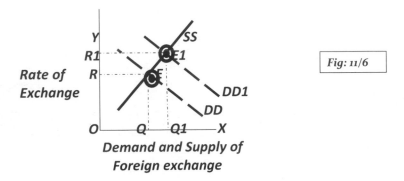

Fig: 11/6

Demand and Supply of
Foreign exchange

In the above diagram as the demand for foreign exchange increases (shown by the shifting of demand curve to the right from DD to DD1) in the country then the value of rate of exchange increases from OR to OR1 and the value of domestic currency decreases i.e. depreciation of domestic currency takes place.

## ▪ Write short notes on the following:

    (a)  Revaluation of domestic currency.
    (b)  Devaluation of domestic currency.

(a) **Revaluation of Domestic currency**: Revaluation refers to rise in the value of domestic currency compared to the value of foreign currency. It is similar to appreciation of domestic currency.

**The difference** is that the appreciation is related to flexible rate of exchange whereas the revaluation is related to the fixed rate of exchange system.

**Objective**: Main objective is to discourage the exports and to encourage the imports of raw materials, machineries and other inputs and finished goods.

(b) **Devaluation of domestic currency**: It refers to the decrease in the value of domestic currency compared to the value of foreign currency.

**The difference** is that the depreciation is related to flexible rate of exchange whereas the devaluation is related to the fixed rate of exchange system.

**Objective**: The main objective is to encourage exports. Due to devaluation, the price of Indian products in abroad decreases which leads to increase the demand for Indian product. As a result exports increases in abroad.

## ▪ What is meant by managed floating?

Managed floating is a system which allows official adjustments in exchange rate fixed by the Govt. according to the rules and regulations announced by the Foreign exchange market.
This system is a hybrid system between fixed and flexible rate of exchange.

## ▪ What is meant by dirty floating?

It is a system when managed floating is used by a country to adjust its exchange rate without caring rules and regulations of foreign exchange market.

## ▪ What is crawling Peg?

Crawling Peg is a scheme by which a country specifies a parity value for its currency and permits a small change around that parity (+/-1% from parity).
However, the parity rate is adjusted regularly by small amount as expected by the position of international reserves held by a country, or changes in money supply, or prices or changes in the exchange rate.

## ▪ Write a short note on Effective Exchange Rate (EER).

EER is a measure of strength of one currency compared to currencies of other countries in the international money market.
EER is of two types which are as follows.

(a) **Nominal Effective Exchange Rate (NEER)**: It is the measure of average relative strength of a given currency of one country compared to the currencies of other countries without considering change in price level.

(b) **Real Effective Exchange Rate (REER):** It is the real exchange rate. It is calculated on the basis of currency ratios on constant prices.

## ▪ Distinction between currency appreciation and currency depreciation:

| Basis | Currency Appreciation | Currency Depreciation |
|---|---|---|
| 1. Meaning | It refers to the increase in the value of domestic currency with respect to foreign currency. | It refers to the decrease in the value of domestic currency with respect to foreign currency. |
| 2. Effect on Export or on Import | It makes foreign goods cheaper i.e. imports become cheaper. So it leads to increase imports. | It makes domestic goods cheaper i.e. exports become cheaper. So it leads to increase exports. |
| 3. Example | A change from $1 = Rs. 50 to $1 = Rs. 45 shows Indian rupee is appreciating. | A change from $1 = Rs. 50 to $1 = Rs. 65 shows Indian rupee is depreciating. |

—*—*—*—*—*—*—*—*—*—*—*—*—

# IMPORTANT QUESTIONS:

## 1 MARK QUESTIONS:

1. What is meant by foreign exchange rate?
2. Define foreign exchange market.
3. What is meant by fixed foreign exchange rate?
4. Define flexible rate of exchange.
5. Write two sources of demand for foreign exchange.
6. Write two sources of supply of foreign exchange.
7. Define devaluation of rupee.
8. What is meant by currency appreciation?
9. What is meant by currency depreciation?
10. What is meant by equilibrium rate of foreign exchange?
11. The price of 1 US Dollar has decreased from Rs. 48 to Rs. 45. Has the Indian currency appreciated or depreciated?
12. Write two merits of fixed exchange rate.
13. What is crawling peg?
14. What is hedging?
15. What is meant by managed floating?

## 3 OR 4 MARK QUESTIONS:

1. Define foreign exchange rate. Distinguish between fixed exchange rate and flexible rate of exchange.
2. Explain the merits of fixed exchange rate.
3. Explain the demerits of fixed exchange rate.
4. Explain the merits of flexible exchange rate.
5. Explain the demerits of flexible exchange rate.
6. Write the main sources of demand for foreign exchange.
7. State the main sources of supply of foreign exchange.

8. Why does demand for foreign exchange increase?
9. Why does supply of foreign exchange rise?
10. Distinguish between nominal effective rate of exchange and real effective rate of exchange.
11. Distinguish between managed floating and dirty floating.
12. Distinguish between devaluation of domestic currency and revaluation of domestic currency.
13. Explain the appreciation of domestic currency with the help of a diagram.
14. Explain the depreciation of domestic currency with the help of a diagram.
15. What is foreign exchange rate? State its main functions.
16. Explain Bretton Woods's system.
17. How is equilibrium rate of foreign exchange rate determined?
18. Explain the effect of appreciation of domestic currency on imports.
19. Explain the effect of depreciation of domestic currency on exports.
20. What is meant by gold exchange rate system? State its limitations.

## ▪ 6 MARK QUESTIONS:

1. Explain the determination of flexible rate of exchange with the help of a diagram.
2. What is foreign exchange market? State its main functions.
3. Define foreign exchange rate. Distinguish between fixed rate of exchange and flexible rate of exchange.
4. Distinguish between devaluation and depreciation of the domestic currency.

—*—*—*—*—*—*—*—*—*—*—*—*—

# Chapter - 12

## Balance Of Payments:

### ■ BALANCE OF PAYMENTS AND ITS IMPORTANT FEATURES:

Balance of Payments is a systematic record of all economic transactions between the residents of a country and the residents of the rest of world in a particular time period.

According to Kindleberger, "The Balance of Payments of a country is a systematic record of all economic transactions between its residents and residents of foreign countries."

### FEATURES OF BOP:

1. Record: BOP is a systematic record of all economic transactions.
2. Time Period: It is related to a particular time period, usually one year.
3. System: BOP is based on double entry book keeping system in which total credit must be equal to total debit.
4. Balanced: BOP is always balanced because of double entry book keeping system.

### ■ BALANCE OF TRADE AND ITS DIFFRENT TYPES:

According to Prof. Benham, "Balance of trade of a country is the relationship between the prices of exports and imports during a certain period."

Balance of Trade (BOT) is defined as the difference between the money value of exports and imports of only visible goods of a country in a particular year.

**TYPES OF BALANCE OF TRADE:** BOT is of three types which are as follows.

(i) **Favourable Balance of Trade**: It is also called as surplus in BOT. A country has favourable BOT when the value of country's total exported goods is more than the value of its imported goods.

(ii) **Unfavourable Balance of Trade:** It is also called as deficit in BOT. A country has unfavourable BOT when the value of country's total exported goods is less than the value of its imported goods.

(iii) **Equilibrium in BOT**: A country has equilibrium balance of trade when the value of country's total exported goods is equal to the value of its total imported goods.

## ▪ DISTINCTION BETWEEN BALANCE OF PAYMENTS AND BALANCE OF TRADE:

| BASIS | BALANCE OF PAYMENTS | BALANCE OF TRADE |
|---|---|---|
| 1. Meaning. | It is a systematic record of all economic transactions of a country with the rest of the world. | It is defined as the difference between exports and imports of a country. |
| 2. Items included. | It includes both the visible and invisible items. | It includes only the visible items. |
| 3. Capital transactions. | It records capital transactions also. | It does not include capital transactions. |
| 4. Nature. | It is wider concept and includes balance of trade. | It is a narrow concept and it is a part of balance of payments. |
| 5. Balance. | BOP is always balanced. | BOT is not necessary to be balanced. It may be favourable or unfavourable. |
| 6. Significance. | It is a true indicator of economic growth. | It is not a true indicator of economic growth. |
| 7. Adjustment. | Disequilibrium in BOP cannot be met through BOT. | Any disequilibrium in BOT can be met by making adjustment of other components of BOP. |

# CURRENT ACCOUNT OF BALANCE OF PAYMENTS AND ITS MAIN COMPONENTS:

Balance of Payments account is divided into two accounts i.e. Current Account and Capital Account.

### Features of Current Account:

(i) It is that account which relates to all real and short term transactions.
(ii) It records imports and exports of goods and services and unilateral transfer payments.
(iii) It shows the flow aspect of a country's international transactions.

The main components of Current Account are as follows.

1. **MERCHANDISE OR VISIBLE GOODS**: It refers to export and import of only visible goods. Exports of goods are included as credit items and imports of goods are included as debit items. Actually it reflects the true picture of balance of trade.

2. **INVISIBLE GOODS OR SERVICES**: It includes the export and import of different types of services like travel, transport, banking, communication, insurance etc. It also includes the expenditure made by the Government on embassies, offices of high commissioners.

3. **UNILATERAL TRANSFER PAYMENTS**: It includes all types of donations, gifts etc. in cash or in kind. It also includes the contribution and donation from UNO, WHO etc.

4. **INVESTMENT INCOME**: It is a part of invisible trade. It includes dividend, interest of the companies. The outflow of dividend and interest from the country to the rest of the world is termed as payment concept whereas the inflow of dividend and interest to the country from abroad is termed as receipt concept.

5. **MISCELLANEOUS**: It includes all residual transactions like commissions, advertisement, royalties, patent fees, rent etc., are provided to abroad and received from abroad. The difference between receipts and payments of such items are included.

# ▪ CAPITAL ACCOUNT OF BALANCE OF PAYMENTS AND ITS MAIN COMPONENTS:

**Features of Capital Account**:

(i) Capital Account refers to that account which includes the transactions of short-term financial assets, long-term lending and borrowing and Government investments.

(ii) Capital Account shows the flow of international loans and investments.

(iii) It shows the country's financial assets and liabilities.

The main components of capital account are as follows.

1. **GOLD MOVEMENT**: It includes the transactions of gold between one country and the rest of the world. When country purchases gold from abroad then it makes payments to abroad so it is reflected under 'debit' item. On the other and when a country sells gold to abroad then it is reflected under 'credit' item.

2. **BANKING CAPITAL**: Inflow of banking capital besides the central bank from abroad is reflected under 'credit' item and the outflow of banking capital besides the central bank to abroad is reflected under 'debit' item.

3. **PRIVATE CAPITAL**: It includes the foreign loans both short-term and long-term. The loans received by private sector are reflected under 'credit' item and foreign loans repaid by private sector are reflected under 'debit' item.

4. **OFFICIAL CAPITAL**: It includes the followings.

    **(a) Loan** – It includes the loans received by the public sector from abroad including SDR from IMF which is reflected under 'credit' item and the loans given to other countries is reflected under 'debit' item.

    **(b) Amortization** – It includes repayment of official loans by other countries to home country and repayment of official loans by home country to other countries. In the above sentence the first one is reflected under 'credit' item and the second one is reflected under 'debit' item.

# • DISTINCTION BETWEEN CURRENT ACCOUNT AND CAPITAL ACCOUNT OF BALANCE OF PAYMENTS:

| BASIS | CURRENT ACCOUNT | CAPITAL ACCOUNT |
|---|---|---|
| 1. Meaning. | It relates to all real and short-term transactions. | It relates to transactions of short-term financial assets, long-term lending and borrowings and Govt. Investments. |
| 2. Significance. | It shows the flow of actual international transactions of the country. | It shows the flow of international loans and investments and the country's financial assets and liabilities. |
| 3. Components | It includes mainly visible goods, invisibles, transfer payments etc. | It includes mainly private capital, official capital, banking capital, gold movement etc. |

# • Do you think that BOP is always balanced? Why?

Balance of Payments is a systematic record of all economic transactions between the residents of a country and the residents of the rest of world in a particular time period.

BOP according to accounting sense is always balanced because this account is based on double entry book keeping system in which total credit must be equal to total debit or total receipts must be equal to total payments.

But according to operational sense, BOP may or may not be balanced. BOP will be surplus if total receipt is more than total payments. BOP will be deficit if total receipt is less than total payments.

BOP will be balanced if there is any deficit (or surplus) in current account and similar amount is surplus (or deficit) in capital account.

# ▪ DISTINCTION BETWEEN AUTONOMOUS AND ACCOMMODATING ITEMS OF BALANC OF PAYMENTS:

| BASIS | AUTONOMOUS ITEMS | ACCOMMODATING ITEMS |
|---|---|---|
| 1. Meaning. | These refer to economic transactions which take place due to some economic motives like profit maximization. | These refer to economic transactions which occur because of other activity in BOP like Government financing. |
| 2. Alternate name. | These are also called as 'above the lines'. | These are also called as 'below the lines'. |
| 3. Importance. | The BOP is deficit if autonomous receipts are less then autonomous payments. | Overall deficit or surplus in BOP results in the accommodating capital transactions which remove the surplus or deficit and BOP is balanced. |

# ▪ DISEQUILIBRIUM IN BALANCE OF PAYMENTS AND FACTORS RESPONSIBLE FOR THE DISEQUILIBRIUM:

Balance of Payments is said to be in equilibrium when total receipts is equal to total payments or net balance of all receipts and payments is zero.

BOP is said to be in disequilibrium when net balance of all receipts and payments is not zero i.e. either it is positive or it is negative.

If net balance of all receipts and payments is positive (if total receipts > total payments) then it is called Surplus BOP.

On the other hand if net balance of all receipts and payments is negative (if total receipts < total payments) then it is called Deficit BOP.

The main causes of disequilibrium in BOP can be categorized into following factors. Here we concern mainly with deficit in BOP.

1. **ECONOMIC FACTORS**: It includes the following factors.

   **(i) Development Expenditure**: If the Government makes huge development expenditure by importing goods and services from abroad then it causes 'deficit in BOP of the country.

**(ii) Inflation**: If there is high rate of inflation in the domestic market of the country then it compels to increase the imports which can cause 'deficit' in BOP.

**(iii) Business cycle**: Business cycle in the form of recession, depression, recovery and boom situations can highly affect the BOP.

During depression the income decreases so there is fall in demand in foreign countries which leads to reduce the exports of the country and it causes disequilibrium (deficit) in BOP.

On the other hand during boom situation in foreign countries exports increase which causes surplus in BOP of the domestic country.

**(iv) Import of services**: Underdeveloped countries mainly import capital, technology and other services from developed countries. As a result the value of imports increases which causes 'deficit' in BOP.

2. **POLITICAL FACTORS**: It includes the following factors.

**(i) Political Instability**: Experience shows that if there is any political instability in the country like instability of Government or any disturbances in the country then it affects the foreign direct investment in that country and it causes huge outflow of capital from that country. Finally the BOP is adversely affected and it becomes 'deficit'.

**(ii) Integration or Disintegration of countries**: If a country is disintegrated into different countries then it adversely affects BOP of the country. On the other hand if two countries are integrated into one country then it has favourable impact on BOP of the country.

3. **SOCIAL FACTORS**: It includes the following factors.

**(i) Change in Tastes and Preferences**: Change in tastes and preferences of the people causes disequilibrium in BOP by affecting the imports and exports of the country. For example if the domestic demand for imported goods increase due to favourable change for them then import increases and it causes 'deficit' in BOP.

**(ii) Population Growth:** Due to high growth rate of population in the country the need and demand for goods increases. To satisfy the needs of the people the country increases the imports which cause disequilibrium in BOP.

## How is disequilibrium in BOP corrected?

BOP is said to be in disequilibrium when net balance of all receipts and payments is not zero i.e. either it is positive or it is negative.

If net balance of all receipts and payments is positive then it is called Surplus BOP. On the other hand if net balance of all receipts and payments is negative then it is called Deficit BOP.

The measures to correct disequilibrium in BOP are as follows.

1. **EXPORT PROMOTION**: If the country's exports are encouraged by providing financial and technical assistance by the Government and monetary authorities to the exporters and manufacturers then disequilibrium (deficit) in BOP can be corrected.
2. **IMPORT SUBSTITUTION**: If the country encourages producing the import substitution goods inside the country then country's import can be reduced and disequilibrium in BOP can be corrected.
3. **DEVALUATION**: Devaluation means fall in the value of domestic currency compared to the value of foreign currency. Devaluation is done by the Govt. of the country in order to increase the exports because the value of domestic goods in abroad decreases which increases the demand and thus encourages the exports.
4. **REDUCTION OF INFLATION**: Inflation discourages exports and encourages imports. So the Government should check inflation in the country.

## THE RELATIONSHIP BETWEEN BALANCE OF PAYMENTS AND NATIONAL INCOME ACCOUNTS:

All economic activities generally reflect two types of transactions which lead to international payments and international receipts.

In any open economy, from the point of view of nation's production of goods and services or income generation, the national income is the sum total of consumption expenditure (C), Investment expenditure (I), Government expenditure (G) and exports X. This can be written as –

$$Y = C + I + G + X$$

From The disposition point of view, national income is the sum total of Consumption of goods and services (C), Savings (S), Payments of Taxes (T) and purchases of goods and services from abroad (i.e. imports or M). This can be written as—

Y = C + S + T + M

Now, from national income accounting point of view, income generated must be equal to income disposed of,

Therefore,

C + I + G + X = C + S + T + M

OR, I + G + X = S + T + M

(I + G + X) shows the planned injections and (S + T + M) shows planned leakages in the economy.

This means at the equilibrium of BOP, Planned injections must be equal to planned leakages.

# IMPORTANT QUESTIONS:

1. Define Balance of Payments (BOP).
2. What is meant by Balance of Trade (BOT)?
3. Write two items included in Balance of Trade account.
4. Define surplus Balance of Trade.
5. What is meant by deficit Balance of Trade?
6. What is meant by Balance of Payments invisibles?
7. Write two visible items of Balance of Trade.
8. State two items of current account of Balance of Payments.
9. What are accommodating items?
10. Define autonomous items.
11. What does deficit in BOT account indicate?
12. Calculate the value of imports when Balance of Trade is Rs. (-) 550 crores and value of exports is Rs. 350 crores.
13. The value of Balance of Trade of a country is Rs. 125 crores. If value of imports is Rs. 85 crores then find out the value of country's exports.
14. Balance of Trade of a country shows a deficit of Rs. 10,000 crores. Value of exports is Rs. 5000 crores then find out the value of imports.
15. State two items that are excluded in BOT but are included in BOP.

## 3 OR 4 MARK QUESTIONS:

1. What is meant by Balance of Payments? State its important features.
2. Distinguish between Balance of Payments and Balance of Trade.
3. Distinguish between current account and capital account of BOP.
4. Distinguish between autonomous items and accommodating items.
5. Explain the components of current account of BOP.
6. Explain the components of capital account of BOP.

7. Do you think that BOP is always balanced? Justify your statement.
8. Explain with the examples the visible and invisible items in the BOP account?
9. Distinguish between Balance of Trade account and balance on current account.
10. Explain the meaning of deficit in a BOP account.

## 6 MARK QUESTIONS:

1. Define disequilibrium in BOP. Explain its main causes. What measures do you suggest to correct disequilibrium in BOP?
2. State the items which are included in current account and capital account of BOP.
3. What is meant by BOP account? State the basis of recording transactions in BOP account.
4. Explain the relationship between Balance of Payments and National Income Accounts.
5. Distinguish between Balance of Trade and Balance of Payments on current account.

—*—*—*—*—*—*—*—*—*—*—*—*—

# Value Based Questions For Class – XII:

## 2012-13 Onwards:

Q.1. Can a monopoly promote social welfare in a country? How?

Ans. Yes, a monopoly firm can promote the social welfare in a country by using efficient utilization of its available resources and technology. This can be clear by the following examples:

1. In case of Indian railway, the poor people get the advantages to move from one place to another by paying less whereas the rich people pay more for the same journey.
2. In case of paying electricity bill the consumers who consume less electricity they pay less (unit price is less) whereas the consumers who consume more they pay more (unit price is also high).
3. When two or more inefficient firms merge together then the marginal cost becomes less. As a result they produce more output at lesser price and serve the society in better way.
4. The profits in monopoly market encourage inventions and innovations which is helpful for the society.

Q.2. How can you explain that farmers are badly affected by a bad monsoon?

Ans. In India at present only about 40% of cultivable land gets artificial irrigation and rest of land depends on monsoon for agricultural production. Therefore if monsoon is irregular or bad, if there is drought, then agricultural production is highly affected and its supply also decreases.

Given the market demand with decrease in supply, the equilibrium price will increase. (Students can present it with the Figure of 11/5 of Micro Economics of this Book). This will increase the total receipts of the farmers as a whole.

Since the demand for agricultural product is inelastic, sometimes some farmers in order to increase their profit, they use the practice of under cultivation of land.

Q.3. why there is power crisis in India? How can you solve this problem?

Ans—In India, the supply of electricity is not sufficient to satisfy the demand for electricity. Therefore it leads to power crisis. The main causes of this power crisis are as follows:

i)   The demand for electricity is greater than supply of electricity in India.
ii)  The supply is affected because of its low production which is due to low level of technology and low quality of coal.

This power-crisis problem can be solved by the following measures:

a)  If we import better quality of coal from other countries for the production of electricity.
b)  If we use advance technology then production can be increased and wastages will be minimum.
c)  If we use alternative sources of energy like solar energy, nuclear energy, wind energy then the demand for electricity can be satisfied.
d)  By using the energy or electricity saving devices which can reduce the consumption of electricity.

Q.4. Is perfect competition market a realistic or a myth?

Ans. Perfect competition is a market situation in which there are large number of sellers and buyers and the product is homogeneous. Practically, perfect competition is not a realistic one because of its following features.

a)  In perfect competition market the product is homogeneous but in the real world, products are not homogeneous.
b)  In this market the price is uniform but in real world, price of the product is also not uniform.
c)  In every market each seller wants to maximize its sales and profit. So it spends a large amount on advertisement which is included in the cost. As a result price differs. But in perfect competition market price of the product is uniform.

Q.5. Explain the effects on the market equilibrium by imposing ban on the sale of wine in Ahmadabad? Do you support this policy of Government?

Ans. Due to the ban on the sale of wine in Ahmadabad, the supply of wine will be reduced in this city and the firms which were producing wine earlier now they will use their factors of production for other related goods in place of wine. On the other hand the demand for wine in this city will certainly fall.

Now the question is whether the price of wine will be affected or not? It depends up on rate of fall in demand for wine and the rate of fall in the supply of wine and the policy of the Government and also on the transport cost of wine in the city.

Since wine is a harmful product for the society, so I strongly support this ban. Although the production of wine increases the GDP of the country but it is not regarded as an index of social welfare.

Therefore if the Government increases tax on wine then its price will rise, this causes a reduction in the demand for it. This will reduce the sale of this product and the profit of producer will decrease which reduces the production and the supply.

Q.6. How do you explain that the degree of monopolistic competition highly depends up on the degree of product differentiation in the market?

Ans. Under monopolistic competition market each firm produces differentiated product i.e. product of each firm is different from others due to its colour, size, outlook, packing etc. In this market the product may have close substitute but not perfectly substitutes.

Product differentiation means the product of one firm is different from another due to its size, colour, design; packing etc. but they are sold at different prices in the market.

A firm under monopolistic competition is neither a price taker nor a price maker. However, it is able to exercise its partial control over price by differentiating their products. If the degree of product differentiation is large and it does not depend on other products then the cross elasticity of demand will be low. As a result the firm cannot increase its sale by reducing its product's price.

On the other hand if the degree of product differentiation is less then it will lead to a high cross elasticity of demand. As a result the firm can influence the sale by reducing its product's price.

Therefore a firm under this monopolistic competition market can influence the price by effective advertisement and its goodwill. So we can conclude that a monopolistic competitive firm depends upon the product differentiation.

Q.7. If the production of polythene industry increases in any country then what will be the effect of it on social welfare of the country?

Ans. If the production of polythene product in any country increases then the country's Gross Domestic Product will increase which will lead to increase in the national income of the country.

But this product has a lot of harmful effects on the environment. It pollutes the air and environment which finally reduces in the social welfare of the country. Therefore the production of polythene product is not regarded as a favourable indicator of social welfare of the country.

Q.8. Which market is better Perfect competition or monopolistic competition? Explain with reasons.

Ans. In the perfect competition market the consumers enjoy maximum consumer surplus compared to any other market form because of its low price and P = MC condition. In this market the industry also enjoys large scale of economies which maximizes social welfare and minimizes wastage.

On the other hand, in monopolistic competition market, P > MC and total level of production is low. So the consumer gets very less amount of consumer surplus. On the other hand the firms are smaller in size so they do not enjoy economies of scale. So the cost of production is high. Therefore social welfare is minimum and wastages are more.

Therefore we can conclude that perfect competition market is better than monopolistic competition market.

Q.9. The supply of land is limited but the population is continuously increasing in the world. What will be the impact of it? How do you solve this problem?

Ans. It is a fact that population is increasing and the supply of land for the production of food grain is limited. So its immediate effect will be on the supply of food grains and this may lead to food crisis. This is a serious issue all over the world.

This problem can be solved by the following:

a) By using intensive cultivation: According to this the agricultural production can be increased on a given piece of land by using more of other factors of production.
b) By using modern farming: According to this agricultural production can be increased by using HYV seeds, chemical fertilizers, pesticides, better irrigation and scientific cultivation.
c) By using mixed farming: According to this two or more crops can be grown on the same piece of land simultaneously.

Q.10. How can we use the exhaustible natural resources in the production of output.

Ans. Since these natural resources are exhaustible therefore we need to use them more judiciously in the production of output especially for sustainable development. The other steps are as follows

a) We need to increase the uses of renewable resources in production of output.
b) We need to discover the substitutes of these exhaustible resources.
c) Wastage of resources should be minimum.
d) Social awareness campaign for optimum utilization of resources should be maximized so that people can realize the concept of sustainable development.

Q.11. Is supernormal profit a consequence of the price discrimination? Explain.

Ans. Price discrimination occurs when a seller charges different prices for different units of the same product from the consumers. A monopolist may charge different prices for the same product from different sets of consumers at the same time. For example, a doctor can charge less fees from poor people and can get more from the rich people for the same treatment. So he has the power to set his price without losing his entire share of the market.

By practicing price discrimination, the monopolist can influence the entire market and can earn supernormal profit (i.e. Price > AC). Total Output under discriminating monopoly will be larger compared to pure monopoly.

A single-price monopoly firm maximizes profits by selling less output at a high price and it has no tendency to increase its level of output. But a price discriminating monopolist firm has intension to increase its product because it sells a part of its total output at high price in one market and remaining output at less price (P MC) in another market, so that total profit is maximized or it can earn supernormal profit.

Q. 12. Is the law of diminishing marginal utility applicable with regard to education or knowledge of human being?

Ans—The law of diminishing marginal utility states that as the consumer continuously consumes more units of a commodity the utility derived from each unit of the commodity decreases.

But this is not applicable in term of gaining education or knowledge. In this case the marginal utility instead of decrease it increases with the gaining of knowledge and experience.

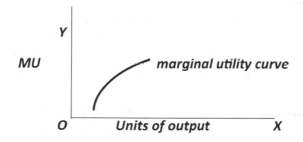

Q.13. The law of demand states as price of good rises its demand falls but in the case of petrol its demand increases even when its price rises? Explain with reasons. Can we solve this problem?

Ans—The law of demand states other factors remaining constant if the price of good rises its demand falls, if the price falls the demand for good rises.

But this is not applicable because of the following reasons.

a) The supply of petrol is very limited in the country.
b) Petrol is exhaustible resource therefore the producers' countries are not increasing its production according to its demand because of sustainable development.
c) Petrol in all countries has become a necessary good because the transport system in the country highly depends on petrol.

Therefore, even if the price of petrol rises its demand does not fall.

This problem of high demand for petrol can be solved by the following:

i)   If we use more public transport system then demand for petrol can be reduced.
ii)  By using alternative and renewable resources of petrol such as solar energy.

Q.14. A farmer is getting more profit in producing tobacco than in production of rice. In the situation of famine which crop should he produce more and why?

Ans. The main objective for any individual farmer is to maximize profit. Therefore he will always try to produce that output which yields him maximum profit.

But in famine if it is possible to produce more of rice that will be better not only for him but also for the society as a whole. This is because in the time of famine the demand for rice will be more compared to tobacco.

He will produce rice more because in the situation of famine, food grain like rice is essential commodity than tobacco. From the point of view of a society, production of tobacco is not an essential commodity and it does not increase the social welfare of any country. Whereas the production of rice is not only an essential food grain but also it increases social welfare of the country.

## MACRO ECONOMICS

Q.15. Why does India still rely on deficit budget?

Ans. In India the Government follows deficit budget because India is a developing country and Government has to arrange necessary fund for financing many development programs for the poor people and for social welfare maximization.

The Per capita income of India is comparatively low so the tax receipts of the Government are not sufficient. On the other hand an important objective of government of India is to maximize social welfare. In this country about 25% of total population lies below poverty line. So Government has to incur heavy public expenditure for the development of economy and for the upliftment of the people who are below poverty line and who are economically poor particularly for their food, health, education and their housing. So Government is compelled to follow deficit budget.

Q.16. Money supply is a necessary instrument for economic development of the country but at the same time it creates inflationary situation. How can this problem be solved?

Ans. Money supply is very necessary instrument for the economic development and for the rapid economic growth of a country but at the same time excess of money supply causes inflationary pressure in the economy. Government of the country by using its revenue and expenditure policy (Fiscal policy) can correct this inflationary situation by the following way:

a.  **Increase in Tax rates**: If the tax rate increases then it will lead to increase in price of output. This will reduce the purchasing power of people, which will reduce the demand for the output and therefore excess demand in the economy decreases.
b.  **Reduce Deficit Financing**: If deficit financing is reduced then also the excess demand can be reduced and inflationary situation will be corrected.

Q.17. Can we judge development of a country with only GDP?

Ans. No; we cannot judge development of a country with only GDP. GDP refers to the gross value of final goods and services produced in the domestic territory of a country measured in an accounting year. But GDP always does not indicate the country's welfare. For example if the production of tobacco or liquor or plastic or polythene products increase then country's GDP definitely increases but these products have harmful effect on the environment and society of the country. This will reduce the social welfare of the country. So we cannot call the country is better off.

On the other hand if the distribution of income in the country is not even or if the country ignores the sustainable development then that country cannot be called better off. In this regard we need to know the criteria used by UNDP for measuring the development of a country.

Q.18. Suppose in any country all the customers of a commercial bank prefers to withdraw their deposits simultaneously at the same time then what will happen?

Ans. If in any country all the customers of a commercial bank prefer to withdraw their bank deposits simultaneously at the same time then it will be difficult for the commercial bank to return the deposit for lack of sufficient fund available with them.

Then Central bank as the lender of the last resort helps the commercial bank with the help of required money in addition to the deposits of commercial banks.

The central bank also provides the advances if they require at this juncture.

Q.19. Is 'Saving' a virtue or a vice in an economy? Explain with reasons.

Ans. Saving is that part of income which is not spent but kept for future and used for safety purpose along with some extra return.

From the point of view of an individual, saving is good for him because it helps him for capital formation in future. But from the point of view of an economy as a whole saving is not good because it reduces the aggregate consumption in the economy and national income decreases.

If the rate of saving increases in an economy then it causes leakages in the flow of income which leads to decrease in the national income of the country. This increase in savings affects the multiplier process which creates the situation of deficient demand in economy;

On the other hand increase in savings means decrease in consumption. Since the consumption decreases in the economy, this will reduce the effective demand and unsold stock with producers will increase; this will increase the unemployment in the economy. Consequently national income will decrease.

Q.20. Will the following be included in the calculation of the GDP of the country? Answer with reasons.

a) Environmental pollution
b) Global warming

Ans. a) Yes, it should be included in the form of social cost of the country.

b) Yes, it should be included in the GDP in the form of country's social cost.

But there is one limitation: The estimation of these social costs is very difficult.

**Q.21. Define budget. How does it help to reduce poverty in a developing country like India?**

Ans. Budget is a financial statement relating to estimated receipts and expenditure of the Government of a country. India is a developing country and Indian economy is basically an agricultural economy because about 60% of total working population depends on agriculture for their livelihood. In India one of the main causes for poverty is the presence of strong income inequality. This will be clear by the following example.

In India about 20% farmers own 64% cultivated land and 80% farmers own only 36% land. So there is strong income inequality in the country. Therefore, in order to remove poverty we need to remove the inequality of 'income and wealth'.

Therefore we use the Government budget. In the budget of India if we follow the progressive tax system, then it can be a good measure to reduce the income inequality because the rich people have to pay more taxes. And the collected receipts from taxes collected from the rich people by the Government can be used to provide the poor people many social facilities like education, health & food grain at subsidized rate. Thus the poverty can be removed by reducing income inequality and by the implementation of progressive taxation policy.

**Q.22. Very recently in the month of August-September, 2013 the foreign exchange rate becomes 1$= Rs 60 to 1$= Rs 70; who becomes the gainer – exporters or importers? Answer with reasons. How will this problem be solved?**

Ans. This decrease in the exchange rate is called as the depreciation of Indian currency with respect to foreign currency (dollar). This is caused by the market forces of demand and supply of foreign currency.

Since the value of dollar has increased, the exports become cheaper and the imports become dearer. The exporters' output's price in the foreign countries will fall. So their demand will increase in abroad and exporters will be gainers.

On the other hand the importers have to pay more to import their products. So they will be losers. Particularly in importing crude oil the importers will face more financial burden, this will lead to increase the price of petrol, diesel in the country, this finally will increase the transport cost and the inflation will increase in the economy.

At this juncture Central Bank of the country (RBI in India) needs to interfere by its monetary policy in order to safeguard the interest of the importers and to control inflation in the economy.

Q.23. Define the concept of autonomous consumption. Can it be zero?

Ans. Autonomous consumption is defined as the minimum level of consumption to fulfill the basic needs of the people and this consumption does not depend up on the level of income. In other words even if the level of income is zero the autonomous consumption is positive. For example all the students have positive consumption without even any income. Or for a grand old man his consumption is positive but his income is zero. In this case the old man meets his consumption by dis-savings.

Symbolically, autonomous consumption (a) in the consumption function (C) can be written as $C = a + b\,Y$; $(a>0$, and $0<b<1)$ where 'a' and 'b' are two parameters and 'C' denotes consumption and 'Y' stands for income.

Q.24. High growth rate of 6% of GDP is not enough for a developing country like India to provide two times meal a day. Justify the statement with reasons.

Ans. 6% of GDP growth rate is no doubt a good one but for India it is not sufficient. India is a developing country and poverty and unemployment are two serious problems. At the time of independence about 48% of total population were below poverty line and at present about 25% are below poverty line. The main reasons for this are as follows:

1.  Unequal distribution of GDP: Due to unequal distribution of GDP the rich people become richer and the poor people become poorer. The poor people could not avail the opportunity of education and jobs; they remain unemployed so they are below the poverty line.

2.  Rise in price level: Due to rise in price level it becomes difficult for the poor people to sustain their life and to fulfill their basic needs of life. So they remain poor.
3.  Increase in GDP if does not create more employment opportunities in the country then it is called as jobless growth which is also another reason for increasing unemployment particularly after the policy of privatization.

Q.25. Mr. Hemant was surprised in the market at the high price of vegetables like onion at Rs.100 per Kg and brinjal at Rs. 80 per Kg. What measures can you suggest to solve his problem?

Ans. The high price of onions, brinjals and other vegetables have made very difficult for the common people to survive. They are forced to compromise to their demand by consuming very less. On the other hand the people who are not able to consume they are forced to compromise with their hunger. In this regard the role of Government is very important. Some important measures are as follows:

a)  If the Government directly provides the subsidies to the farmers who are producing vegetables to purchase the fertilizers, seeds, pesticides etc then the cost of production can be reduced. Therefore the market price of the vegetables can be reduced.
b)  If the Government increases the investment in the production of vegetables and other horticulture products by providing credit facilities at reasonable rate of interest then the farmers will be able to produce their products at right time and can sell them at reasonable price to the consumers. In this regard we need to remember the high rate of investment in fruits and vegetables during 1991 and 2003 during golden revolution that made India 2nd largest country in the production of fruits and vegetables in the world.
c)  If the consumers are provided these products at subsidized price by public distribution shops then the consumers will be benefited.
d)  If the Government by making proper law is able to remove the middle-men or illegal agents who exploit the farmers by purchasing their products at very low price and sell these products at very high price after illegal hoarding.

# C.B.S.E. Question Paper—2013

## CLASS—XII
## ALL INDIA

Time: 3 Hour                                        Max. Marks: 100

**General instructions:**

(i)   All questions in both the sections are compulsory.

(ii)  Marks for questions are indicated against each.

(iii) Questions No. 1-5 and 17-21 are very short-answer questions carrying 1 mark each. They are required to be answered in one sentence each.

(iv)  Questions No. 6-10 and 22-26 are short-answer questions carrying 3 marks each. Answers to them should normally not exceed 60 words each.

(v)   Questions No. 11-13 and 27-29 are also short-answer questions carrying 4 marks each. Answers to them should normally not exceed 70 words each.

(vi)  Questions No. 14-16 and 30-32 are also long-answer questions carrying 6 marks each. Answers to them should normally not exceed 100 words each.

(vii) Answers should be brief and to the point and the above word limits should be adhered to as far as possible.

## SECTION A

1. What does a rightward shift of demand curve indicate?                    1
2. Under which market form is a firm a price taker?                         1
3. When is demand for a good said to be perfectly inelastic?                1
4. Define marginal revenue.                                                 1
5. Give the meaning of market supply.                                       1

6. From the following table, find out the level of output at which    3
   producer will be in equilibrium. Give reasons for your answer.

| Output (units) | Marginal Revenue (Rs.) | Marginal cost (Rs.) |
|---|---|---|
| 1 | 8 | 10 |
| 2 | 8 | 8 |
| 3 | 8 | 7 |
| 4 | 8 | 8 |
| 5 | 8 | 9 |

7. A 15 percent rise in the price of a commodity raises its demand    3
   from 300 units to 345 units. Calculate its price elasticity of demand.
8. Explain the conditions of consumer's equilibrium under utility    3
   analysis.
9. Why can a firm not earn abnormal profits under perfect    3
   competition in the long run? Explain.

Or

Why the demand curve of a firm under monopolistic competition is is more elastic than under monopoly? Explain.

10. How is the demand for a good affected by a rise in the prices of    3
    other goods? Explain.
11. Equilibrium price of an essential medicine is too high. Explain    4
    what possible steps can be taken to bring down the equilibrium
    price but only through the market forces. Also explain the series
    of changes that will occur in the market.
12. Explain the meaning of opportunity cost with the help of    4
    production possibility schedule.

Or

With the help of suitable example explain the problem of 'for whom to produce'.

13. Price elasticity of demand for a good is (-0.75). Calculate the    4
    percentage fall in its price that will result in 15 percent rise in its
    demand.

14. Giving reasons, state whether the following statements are true or false:    6
    (i) Average product will increase when marginal product increases.
    (ii) With increase in level of output, average fixed cost goes on falling till it reaches zero.
    (iii) Under diminishing returns to a factor, total product continues to increase till marginal product reaches zero.

15. Explain three properties of indifference curves.    6

Or

Explain the conditions of consumer's equilibrium under indifference curve approach.

16. If equilibrium price of a good is greater than its market price, explain all the changes that will take place in the market. Use diagram.    6

## SECTION B

17. How can Reserve Bank of India help in bringing down the foreign exchange rate which is very high?    1
18. Give two examples of intermediate goods.    1
19. What one step can be taken through market to reduce the consumption of a product harmful for health?    1
20. What is revenue deficit?    1
21. State the components of supply of money.    1
22. How can budgetary policy be used to reduce inequalities of income.    3
23. State three sources each of revenue receipts and capital receipts in government budget.    3
24. Explain the 'medium of exchange' function of money.    3

Or

Explain the 'lender of last resort' function of central bank.

25. How is exchange rate determined in the foreign exchange market? Explain.     3

26. Explain the effect of depreciation of domestic currency on exports.     3

27. Distinguish between "real" gross domestic product and "nominal" gross domestic product. Which of these is a better index of welfare of the people and why?     4

Or

Distinguish between stocks and flows. Give two examples of each.

28. Calculate "Sales" from the following data:     4

| Particulars | Rs. in Crore |
|---|---|
| (i) Subsidies | 200 |
| (ii) Opening stock | 100 |
| (iii) Closing stock | 600 |
| (iv) Intermediate consumption | 3,000 |
| (v) Consumption of fixed capital | 700 |
| (vi) Profit | 750 |
| (vii) Net value added at factor cost | 2,000 |

29. Explain any two methods of credit control used by central bank.     4

30. From the following data about an economy, calculate (a) equilibrium level of national income and (b) total consumption expenditure at equilibrium level of national income.     6

    (i) $C = 200 + 0.5Y$ is the consumption function where C is consumption expenditure and Y is national income.

    (ii) Investment expenditure is 1500

31. Calculate "Gross National Product at Market Price" from the    6
    following data:

| Particulars | Rs. in Crore |
| --- | --- |
| (i)    Compensation of employees | 2,000 |
| (ii)   Interest | 500 |
| (iii)  Rent | 700 |
| (iv)   Profits | 800 |
| (v)    Employer's contribution to social security schemes | 200 |
| (vi)   Dividends | 300 |
| (vii)  Consumption of fixed capital | 100 |
| (viii) Net Indirect Taxes | 250 |
| (ix)   Net Exports | 70 |
| (x)    Net factor income to abroad | 150 |
| (xi)   Mixed income of self-employed | 1,500 |

Or

Calculate "Gross National Disposable Income" from the following data:

| Particulars | Rs. in Crore |
| --- | --- |
| (i)    Net domestic product at factor cost | 3,000 |
| (ii)   Indirect taxes | 300 |
| (iii)  Net current transfers from rest of world | 250 |
| (iv)   Current transfers from te Government | 100 |
| (v)    Net factor income to abroad | 150 |
| (vi)   Consumption of fixed capital | 200 |
| (vii)  Subsidies | 100 |

32. Explain all the changes that will take place in an economy when    6
    aggregate demand is not equal to aggregate supply.

# C.B.S.E. Question Paper—2012

## CLASS—XII
## ALL INDIA (Set-1)

Time: 3 Hour                                                    Max. Marks: 100

**General instructions:**

(i)   All questions in both the sections are compulsory.
(ii)  Marks for questions are indicated against each.
(iii) Questions No. 1-5 and 17-21 are very short-answer questions carrying 1 mark each. They are required to be answered in one sentence each.
(iv)  Questions No. 6-10 and 22-26 are short-answer questions carrying 3 marks each. Answers to them should normally not exceed 60 words each.
(v)   Questions No. 11-13 and 27-29 are also short-answer questions carrying 4 marks each. Answers to them should normally not exceed 70 words each.
(vi)  Questions No. 14-16 and 30-32 are also long-answer questions carrying 6 marks each. Answers to them should normally not exceed 100 words each.
(vii) Answers should be brief and to the point and the above word limits should be adhered to as far as possible.

### SECTION A

1.  Define microeconomics.                                           1
2.  Give one reason for a shift in demand curve.                     1
3.  What is the behaviour of Total variable Cost, as output increases?    1

4. What is the behaviour of Marginal Revenue in a market in which a firm can sell any quantity of the output it produces at a given price?   1

5. What is a price-maker firm?   1

6. Define production possibilities curve. Explain why it is downward sloping from left to right.   3

7. A consumer consumes only two goods X and Y and is in equilibrium. Price of X falls. Explain the reaction of the consumer through the utility analysis.   3

8. Draw Total Variable Cost, Total Cost, and Total Fixed Cost curves in a single diagram.   3

9. A producer starts a business by investing his own savings and hiring the labour. Identify implicit and explicit costs from this information. Explain.   3

10. Explain the implications of large number of sellers in a perfectly competitive market.

Or

Explain why there are only a few firms in an oligopoly market?   3

11. Define an indifference map. Why does indifference curve to the right show more utility? Explain.   4

12. A consumer buys 10 units of a commodity at a price of Rs. 10 per unit. He incurs an expenditure of Rs. 200 on buying 20 units. Calculate price elasticity of demand by the percentage method. Comment upon the shape of demand curve based on this information.   4

13. What does the Law of Variable proportions show? State the behaviour of marginal product according to this law.   4

Or

Explain how changes in prices of inputs influence the supply of a product.

14. Explain the difference between (i) inferior goods and normal goods and (ii) cardinal utility and ordinal utility. Give example in each case.   6

15. Explain the distinction between "change in quantity supplied" and "change in supply". Use diagram.   6

16. Market for a good is in equilibrium. There is simultaneous "decrease" both in demand and supply but there is no change in market price. Explain with the help of schedule how it is possible.

Or

Market for a good is in equilibrium. Explain the chain of reactions in the market if the price is (i) higher than equilibrium price and (ii) lower than equilibrium price.      6

## SECTION B

17. Define flow variable.      1
18. Define consumption goods.      1
19. What are time deposits?      1
20. Define a 'direct tax'.      1
21. What is a fixed exchange rate?      1
22. Find Net Value Added at Market Price.      3

| Particulars | Rs. in Crore |
|---|---|
| (i) Depreciation | 700 |
| (ii) Output sold (units) | 900 |
| (iii) Price per unit of output | 40 |
| (iv) Closing stock | 1,000 |
| (v) Opening stock | 800 |
| (vi) Sales tax | 3,000 |
| (vii) Intermediate cost | 20,000 |

23. Explain 'standard of deferred payments' function of money.      3
24. Outline the steps taken in deriving Consumption Curve from the Saving Curve. Use diagram.      3
25. Find consumption expenditure from the following:      3

| Particulars | Rs. in Crore |
|---|---|
| (i) National Income | 5,000 |
| (ii) Autonomous Consumption | 1,000 |
| (iii) Marginal Propensity to Consume | 0.80 |

26. Distinguish between revenue receipts and capital receipts in a government budget. Give example in each case.    3

Or

Explain the role of government budget in bringing economic stability.

27. Should the following be treated as final expenditure or intermediate expenditure? Give reasons for your answer.    4

    (i)  Purchase of furniture by a firm.
    (ii) Expenditure on maintenance by a firm.

28. Explain the 'lender of last resort' function of the Central bank.

Or

Explain "government banker' function of the Central bank.    4

29. Explain the concept of 'fiscal deficit' in a government budget. What does it indicate?    4

30. Find out (a) Gross National Product at Market Price and (b) Net Current Transfers to Abroad:    6

| Particulars | | Rs. in Crore |
|---|---|---|
| (i) | Private final consumption expenditure | 1,000 |
| (ii) | Depreciation | 100 |
| (iii) | Net National Disposable Income | 1,500 |
| (iv) | Closing Stock | 20 |
| (v) | Government final consumption expenditure | 300 |
| (vi) | Net Indirect tax | 50 |
| (vii) | Opening stock | 20 |
| (viii) | Net domestic fixed capital formation | 110 |
| (ix) | Net exports | 15 |
| (x) | Net factor income to abroad | (-10) |

31. Explain the concept of 'inflationary gap'. Also explain the role of 'legal reserves' in reducing it.                 6

Or

Explain the concept of 'deflationary gap'. Also explain the role of 'margin requirement' in reducing it.

32. Give the meaning of 'foreign exchange' and 'foreign exchange         6
    rate'. Give reason, explain the relation between foreign
    exchange rate and demand for exchange rate.

### (SET-2)
### Uncommon Questions to Set-1 are given only:

1. Give the meaning of an economy.                                        1
2. What is market demand?                                                 1
3. What is the behaviour of average fixed cost as output                  1
   increases?
4. What is the behaviour of average revenue in a market in which          1
   a firm can sell more only by lowering the price?
5. What is a price taker firm?                                            1
6. What is opportunity cost? Explain with the help of numerical           3
   example.
7. Given price of a good, how does a consumer decide as to how            3
   much of that good to buy?
8. Draw Average Variable Cost, Average Total Cost and Marginal            3
   Cost Curves in a single diagram.
9. An individual is both owner and the manager of a shop taken            3
   on rent. Identify implicit cost from this information. Explain.
10. Explain the implication of large number of buyers in a perfectly
    competitive market.

Or

Explain why firms are mutually interdependent in an oligopoly             3
   market.

11. Define an indifference curve. Explain why an indifference curve    4
is downward sloping from left to right.

12. When the price of a good is Rs. 7 per unit a consumer buys    4
12 units. When price falls to Rs. 6 per unit he spends Rs. 72
on the good. Calculate price elasticity of demand by using
percentage method. Comment on the likely shape of demand
curve based on this measure of elasticity.

13. What does the Law of variable Proportions show? State the    4
behaviour of Total Product according to this law.

Or

Explain the changes in prices of other products influence the supply of a
given product.

14. Explain how do the following influence demand for a good:    6

(i)   Rise in income of the consumer.
(ii)  Fall in prices of related goods.

15. Explain the conditions of a producer's equilibrium in terms of    6
marginal cost and marginal revenue. Use diagram.

16. Market for a good is in equilibrium. There is simultaneous    6
"increase" both in demand and supply of the good. Explain its
effect on market price.

Or

Market for a good is in equilibrium. There is simultaneous    6
"decrease" both in demand and supply of the good. Explain its
effect on market price.

## (SET-2)
## Uncommon Questions to Set-1 are given only:

22. Find Gross Value Added at factor cost:                                3

| Particulars | Rs. in Crore |
| --- | --- |
| (i) Units of output sold | 2,000 |
| (ii) Price per unit of output | 20 |
| (iii) Depreciation | 2,000 |
| (iv) Change in stock | (-500) |
| (v) Intermediate costs | 15,000 |
| (vi) Subsidy | 3,000 |

25. Find National Income from the following:                               3

| Particulars | Rs. in Crore |
| --- | --- |
| (i) Autonomous consumption | 100 |
| (ii) Marginal propensity to consume | 0.60 |
| (iii) Investment | 200 |

27. Give reason, explain how should the following be treated while       4
    estimating national income:

    (i)  Expenditure on free services provided by government.
    (ii) Payment of interest by a government firm.

30. Find out (a) National income and (b) Net national Disposable    6
    Income:

| Particulars | Rs. in Crore |
|---|---|
| (i)     Net imports | (-10) |
| (ii)    Net domestic fixed capital formation | 100 |
| (iii)   Private final consumption expenditure | 600 |
| (iv)    Consumption of fixed capital | 60 |
| (v)     Change in stocks | (-50) |
| (vi)    Government final consumption expenditure | 200 |
| (vii)   Net factor income to abroad | 20 |
| (viii)  Net current transfers to abroad | 30 |
| (ix)    Net indirect tax | 70 |
| (x)     Factor income from abroad | 10 |

## (SET-3)

1. Define macro economics.                                          1
2. What does an indifference curve show?                            1
3. Define marginal cost.                                            1
4. What is the behaviour of average revenue in a market in which    1
   a firm can sell any quantity of a good at a given price?
5. Define oligopoly.                                                1
6. Explain, giving reason, why production possibilities curve is    3
   concave.
7. A consumer consumes only two goods X and Y and is in            3
   equilibrium. Price of X rises. Explain the reaction of the
   consumer through the utility analysis.
8. Draw supply curves showing price elasticity of supply equal to
   (i)   Zero,
   (ii)  One and
   (iii) Infinity throughout.                                      3
9. A producer borrows money to start a business and looks after     3
   the business himself. Identify the implicit and explicit costs
   from this information. Explain.
10. Explain the implications of 'homogeneous products' in a         3
    perfectly competitive market.

Or

Explain the implications of 'differentiated products' in monopolistic competition.

11. Explain why an indifference curve is downward sloping from     4
    left to right. State the conditions of consumer's equilibrium in
    indifference curve analysis.
12. A consumer buys 13 units of a good at a price of Rs. 11 per unit.     4
    When price rises to Rs. 13 per unit he buys 11 units. Use expenditure
    approach to find price elasticity of demand. Also comment on the
    shape of the demand curve based on this information.
13. How does the change in tax on a product influence the supply of     4
    that product? Explain.

Or

What is revenue? Explain the relation between marginal revenue and the average revenue.

14. Explain the distinction between:     6

    (i) 'Change in demand' and 'change in quantity demanded'.
    (ii) Budget set and budget line.

15. State the phases of changes in Total Product in the Law of     6
    variable Proportions. Also explain the reason behind each
    phase. Use diagram.

16. Market for a good is in equilibrium. Explain the chain of reactions in the
market when there is

    (i) 'Decrease' in supply.
    (ii) 'Decrease' in demand.     6

Or

Market for a good is in equilibrium. There is simultaneous "increase" both in demand and supply but there is no change in price. Explain how it is possible. Use a schedule.

**Uncommon Questions to Set-1 are given only:**

22. Find out Net Value Added at Factor Cost     3

| Particulars | Rs. in Crores |
| --- | --- |
| (i)   Price per unit of output | 25 |
| (ii)  Output sold (units) | 1,000 |
| (iii) Excise duty | 5,000 |
| (iv) Depreciation | 1,000 |
| (v)  Change in stocks | (-500) |
| (vi) Intermediate cost | 7,000 |

25. Find investment from the following:     3

| Particulars | Rs. in Crores |
| --- | --- |
| (i)  National Income | 600 |
| (ii) Autonomous consumption | 150 |
| (iii) Marginal propensity to consume | 0.70 |

27. How should the following be treated while estimating national Income? Give reasons.     4

   (i)   Expenditure on education of children by a family.
   (ii)  Payment of electricity bill by a school.

30. Find out (a) Net National Product at Market Price and Gross    6
    National Disposable Income:

| Particulars | | Rs. in Crores |
|---|---|---|
| (i) | Undistributed profits | 20 |
| (ii) | Compensation of employees | 800 |
| (iii) | Rent | 300 |
| (iv) | Dividend | 100 |
| (v) | Royalty | 40 |
| (vi) | Net current transfers to abroad | (-30) |
| (vii) | Corporation tax | 50 |
| (viii) | Interest | 400 |
| (ix) | Depreciation | 70 |
| (x) | Net factor income from abroad | (-10) |
| (xi) | Net indirect tax | 60 |

# C.B.S.E. Question Paper—2011

## Class—XII

Time: 3 Hour

Max. Marks: 100

**General instructions:**

(i) All questions in both the sections are compulsory.

(ii) Marks for questions are indicated against each.

(iii) Questions No. 1-5 and 17-21 are very short-answer questions carrying 1 mark each. They are required to be answered in one sentence each.

(iv) Questions No. 6-10 and 22-26 are short-answer questions carrying 3 marks each. Answers to them should normally not exceed 60 words each.

(v) Questions No. 11-13 and 27-29 are also short-answer questions carrying 4 marks each. Answers to them should normally not exceed 70 words each.

(vi) Questions No. 14-16 and 30-32 are also long-answer questions carrying 6 marks each. Answers to them should normally not exceed 100 words each.

(vii) Answers should be brief and to the point and the above word limits should be adhered to as far as possible.

### SECTION A

| | | |
|---|---|---|
| 1. | Define an economy. | 1 |
| 2. | Define production function. | 1 |
| 3. | What is 'decrease' in supply? | 1 |
| 4. | Define a budget line. | 1 |
| 5. | When is a firm called price maker? | 1 |
| 6. | Explain the implications of the feature 'large number of buyers' in a perfectly competitive market. | 3 |

OR

Explain the implications of the feature 'homogeneous products' in a perfectly competitive market.

7. When price of a good is Rs. 12 per unit, the consumer buys 24 units of that good. When price rises to Rs. 14 per unit, the consumer buys 20 units. Calculate price elasticity of demand.    3

8. Draw in a single diagram the average revenue and marginal revenue curves of a firm which can sell any quantity of the good at a given price. Explain.    3

9. Distinguish between explicit cost and implicit cost and give examples.    3

10. How is production possibility curve affected by unemployment in the economy?    3

11. A consumer consumes only two goods X and Y. At a certain consumption level of these goods, he finds that the ratio of marginal utility to price in case of X is lower than in case of Y. Explain the reaction of the consumer.    4

12. Define marginal cost. Explain its relation with average cost.    4

OR

Define variable cost. Explain the behaviour of total variable cost as output increases.

13. Explain how rise in income of a consumer affects the demand of a good. Give examples.    4

14. Market for a good is in equilibrium. There is 'increase' in supply of the good. Explain the chain of effects of this change. Use diagram.    6

15. Explain any three properties of indifference curves.    6

16. What is producer's equilibrium? Explain the conditions of producer's equilibrium through the 'marginal cost and marginal revenue' approach. Use diagram.    6

**SECTION B**

17. Define 'Statutory Liquidity Ratio'.    1
18. What are stock variables?    1
19. Define 'depreciation'.    1

20. What is foreign exchange rate?    1
21. Define money.    1
22. List the transactions of current account of balance of    3
    Payments Account.
23. When price of a foreign currency falls, the demand for that    3
    foreign currency rises. Explain, why?

OR

When price of a foreign currency falls, the supply of that foreign
currency also falls. Explain, why?
24. In an economy the marginal propensity to save is 0.4.    3
    National income increases by Rs. 200 crores as a result of
    change in investment. Calculate the change in investment.
25. Explain how 'non-monetary exchanges' are a limitation in    3
    taking Gross Domestic Product as an index of welfare.
26. Explain the distinction between voluntary and involuntary    3
    unemployment.
27. From the following data about a Government Budget find (a)    4
    Revenue deficit, (b) Fiscal deficit and (c) Primary deficit:

|  |  | (Rs. in arab) |
| --- | --- | --- |
| (i) | Tax revenue | 47 |
| (ii) | Capital receipts | 34 |
| (iii) | Non-tax revenue | 10 |
| (iv) | Borrowings | 32 |
| (v) | Revenue expenditure | 80 |
| (vi) | Interest payments | 20 |

28. Explain the 'redistribution of income' objective of a    4
    Government budget.

OR

Explain the 'economic stability' objective of a Government budget.

29. Giving reasons, explain the treatment assigned to the
    following while estimating national income:                          4

    (i)  Social security contribution by employees.
    (ii) Pension paid after retirement.

30. Explain the following functions of the central bank:                 6

    (i)  Bank of issue.
    (ii) Banker's bank.

31. Explain the role of the following in correcting the                  6
    inflationary gap in an economy:

    (i)  Legal reserves.
    (ii) Bank rate.

                                OR

Explain the role of following in correcting the deflationary gap in an economy:

    (i)  Open market operations
    (ii) Margin requirements.

32. Calculate (a) 'Net National Product at market price' and (b)         6
    'Private Income' from the following:

|          |                                         | (Rs. in crore) |
|----------|-----------------------------------------|:--------------:|
| (i)      | Net current transfers to abroad         | 30             |
| (ii)     | Mixed income                            | 600            |
| (iii)    | Subsidies                               | 20             |
| (iv)     | Operating surplus                       | 200            |
| (v)      | National debt interest                  | 70             |
| (vi)     | Net factor income to abroad             | 10             |
| (vii)    | Compensation of employees               | 1400           |
| (viii)   | Indirect tax                            | 100            |
| (ix)     | Domestic product accruing to Government | 350            |
| (x)      | Current transfers by Government         | 50             |

—*—*—*—*—*—*—*—*—*—*—*—*—

# C.B.S.E. Question Paper—2010

## CLASS—XII

Time: 3 Hour                                      Max. Marks: 100

**General instructions:**

(i) All questions in both the sections are compulsory.

(ii) Marks for questions are indicated against each.

(iii) Questions No. 1-5 and 17-21 are very short-answer questions carrying 1 mark each. They are required to be answered in one sentence each.

(iv) Questions No. 6-10 and 22-26 are short-answer questions carrying 3 marks each. Answers to them should normally not exceed 60 words each.

(v) Questions No. 11-13 and 27-29 are also short-answer questions carrying 4 marks each. Answers to them should normally not exceed 70 words each.

(vi) Questions No. 14-16 and 30-32 are also long-answer questions carrying 6 marks each. Answers to them should normally not exceed 100 words each.

(vii) Answers should be brief and to the point and the above word limits should be adhered to as far as possible.

### SECTION A

1. Define a budget line.                                                      1
2. What is meant by inferior good in economics?                               1
3. In which market form can a firm not influence the price of the product?    1
4. Define monopoly.                                                           1
5. What can you say about the number of buyers and sellers under monopolistic competition?  1

6. Explain the effect of the following on the price elasticity of demand of a commodity:    3

   (i)  Number of substitutes
   (ii) Nature of the commodity.

7. Explain any two causes of 'increase' in demand of a commodity.    3

OR

Explain the inverse relationship between price and quantity demanded of a commodity.

8. A firm's average fixed cost, when it produces 2 units, is Rs. 30.    3
   Its average total cost schedule is given below. Calculate its marginal cost and average variable cost at each level of output.

| Output (units) | 1 | 2 | 3 |
|---|---|---|---|
| Average Total Cost | 80 | 48 | 40 |

9. Total revenue is Rs. 400 when the price of the commodity is    3
   Rs.2 per unit. When price rises to Rs. 3 per unit, the quantity supplied is 300 units. Calculate the price elasticity of supply.

10. Why is the number of firms small in an oligopoly market?    3
    Explain.

11. Explain the problem of 'how to produce'.    4

OR

Distinguish between microeconomics and macroeconomics. Give examples.

12. When price of a commodity falls by Re. 1 per unit, its quantity    4
    demanded rises by 3 units. Its price elasticity of demand is
    (-2). Calculate its quantity demanded if the price before the
    change was Rs. 10 per unit.

13. How does the equilibrium price of a 'normal' commodity    4
    change when income of its buyers falls? Explain the chain of
    effects.

14. State whether the following statements are true or false. Give      6
    reasons for your answer:

    (i) When marginal revenue is constant and not equal to zero, then total revenue will also be constant.
    (ii) As soon as marginal cost starts rising, average variable cost also starts rising.
    (iii) Total product always increases whether there is increasing returns or diminishing returns to a factor.

15. What are the conditions of consumer's equilibrium under the      6
    indifference curve approach? What changes will take place if
    the conditions are not fulfilled to reach equilibrium?

16. From the following schedule find out the level of output at      6
    which the producer is in equilibrium, using marginal cost and
    marginal revenue approach. Give reasons for your answer.

| Price per unit (Rs.) | Output (units) | Total Cost |
|:---:|:---:|:---:|
| 8 | 1 | 6 |
| 7 | 2 | 11 |
| 6 | 3 | 15 |
| 5 | 4 | 18 |
| 4 | 5 | 23 |

OR

Explain the law of returns to a factor with the help of total product and marginal product schedule.

## SECTION B

17. Give the meaning of money.      1
18. What is meant by revenue deficit?      1
19. What is ex-ante aggregate demand?      1
20. Give the meaning of inflationary gap.      1
21. State two sources of demand for foreign exchange.      1
22. Distinguish between real and nominal gross domestic product.      3

OR

Giving reasons, classify the following into intermediate and final goods:

(i) Machines purchased by a dealer of machines.
(ii) A car purchased by a household.

23. Explain the 'banker to the government' function of the central bank.     3

24. Explain the allocation function of a Government budget.     3

25. Distinguish between autonomous and accommodating transactions of balance of payments account.     3

26. Giving two examples, explain why there is a rise in demand for a foreign currency when its price falls.     3

27. How does a commercial bank create money?     4

OR

Explain how do 'open market operations' by the central bank affect money creation by commercial banks.

28. Giving reasons, state whether the following statements are true or false:     4

(i) When marginal propensity to consume is zero, the value of investment multiplier will also be zero.
(ii) Value of average propensity to save can never be less than zero.

29. Distinguish between:     4

(i) Capital expenditure and Revenue expenditure.
(ii) Fiscal deficit and Primary deficit.

30. How will you treat the following while estimating national income of India? Give reasons for your answer.     6

(i) Dividend received by a foreigner from investment in shares of an Indian company.
(ii) Profits earned by a branch of an Indian bank in Canada.

(iii) Scholarship given to Indian students studying in India by a foreign company.

31. In an economy the equilibrium level of income is Rs. 12,000    6
    crore. The ratio of marginal propensity to consume and
    marginal propensity to save is 3:1. Calculate the additional
    investment needed to reach a new equilibrium level of income
    of Rs. 20,000 crore.

32. Calculate (a) Gross Domestic Product at market price, and (b)
    Factor income from abroad from the following data:

|  |  | (Rs. in crores) |
|---|---|---|
| (i) | Profits | 500 |
| (ii) | Exports | 40 |
| (iii) | Compensation of employees | 1,500 |
| (iv) | Gross national product at factor cost | 2,800 |
| (v) | Net current transfers from rest of the world | 90 |
| (vi) | Rent | 300 |
| (vii) | Interest | 400 |
| (viii) | Factor income to abroad | 120 |
| (ix) | Net indirect taxes | 250 |
| (x) | Net domestic capital formation | 650 |
| (xi) | Gross fixed capital formation | 700 |
| (xii) | Change in stock | 50 |

__*__*__*__*__*__*__*__*__*__*__*__*__

# C.B.S.E. Question Paper—2009

## Class—XII

Time: 3 Hour                                                   Max. Marks: 100

**General instructions:**

(i) All questions in both the sections are compulsory.

(ii) Marks for questions are indicated against each.

(iii) Questions No. 1-5 and 17-21 are very short-answer questions carrying 1 mark each. They are required to be answered in one sentence each.

(iv) Questions No. 6-10 and 22-26 are short-answer questions carrying 3 marks each. Answers to them should normally not exceed 60 words each.

(v) Questions No. 11-13 and 27-29 are also short-answer questions carrying 4 marks each. Answers to them should normally not exceed 70 words each.

(vi) Questions No. 14-16 and 30-32 are also long-answer questions carrying 6 marks each. Answers to them should normally not exceed 100 words each.

(vii) Answers should be brief and to the point and the above word limits should be adhered to as far as possible.

### SECTION A

1. Give the meaning of opportunity cost.                                    1
2. What is meant by inferior good in economics?                             1
3. Define marginal cost.                                                    1
4. Give one reason for a rightward shift in supply curve.                   1
5. Why is average total cost greater than average variable cost?            1
6. State the law of demand and show it with the help of a schedule.         3

561

7. Explain the geometric method of measuring price elasticity of demand.    3

8. Why do problems related to allocation of resources in an economy arise? Explain.    3

OR

Explain the problem of 'for whom to produce'.

9. Complete the following table:    3

| Output (units) | Total revenue (Rs.) | Marginal revenue (Rs.) | Average revenue (Rs.) |
|---|---|---|---|
| 1 | — | — | 8 |
| 2 | — | 4 | — |
| 3 | 12 | — | 4 |
| 4 | 8 | — | 2 |

10. Explain the effect of fall in prices of other goods on the supply of a given good.    3

11. Explain two points of distinction between monopoly and monopolistic competition.    4

OR

Explain any two main features of perfect competition.

12. The price elasticity of supply of a commodity Y is half the price elasticity of supply of commodity X. 16 percent rise in the price X results in a 40 percent rise in supply. If the price of Y falls by 8 percent, calculate the percentage fall in its supply.    4

13. Given below is a cost and revenue schedule of a producer. At what level of output is the producer in equilibrium? Give reasons for your answer.    4

| Output (units) | Price (Rs.) | Total Cost |
|:---:|:---:|:---:|
| 1 | 10 | 13 |
| 2 | 10 | 22 |
| 3 | 10 | 30 |
| 4 | 10 | 38 |
| 5 | 10 | 47 |
| 6 | 10 | 57 |
| 7 | 10 | 71 |

14. With the help of a demand and supply schedule, explain the meaning of excess demand and its effect on price of a commodity.   6

OR

Define equilibrium price of a commodity. How is it determined? Explain with the help of a schedule.

15. Giving reasons, state whether the following statements are true or false:   6

(i) Average cost falls only when marginal cost falls.

(ii) The difference between average total cost and average variable cost is constant.

(iii) When total revenue is maximum, marginal revenue is also maximum.

16. Explain the effect of the following on the market demand of a commodity:   6

(i) Change in price of related goods

(ii) Change in the number of its buyers.

## SECTION B

17. Give meaning of aggregate supply.   1
18. Why are taxes received by the Government not capital receipts?   1
19. Give the meaning of excess demand in an economy.   1
20. What is meant by cash reserve ratio?   1
21. Define involuntary unemployment.   1
22. Complete the following table:   3

| Income | MPC | Saving | APS |
|--------|-----|--------|-----|
| 0 | | ( - 90) | |
| 100 | 0.6 | — | — |
| 200 | 0.6 | — | — |
| 300 | 0.6 | — | — |

23. Give the meaning of factor income to abroad and factor income from abroad. Also give an example of each.    3

OR

Distinguish between domestic product and national product. When can domestic product be more than national product?

24. Distinguish between balance of trade account and balance of current account.    3

25. State three main functions of a commercial bank. Explain any one of them.    3

26. Give the meaning of revenue deficit, fiscal deficit and primary deficit.

27. Describe the evolution of money.    4

OR

Explain any two functions of money.

28. Explain any two objectives of a Government budget.    4

29. Explain two merits each of flexible foreign exchange rate and fixed foreign exchange rate.    4

30. While estimating national income, how will you treat the following?    6

(i)   Imputed rent of self occupied houses.

(ii)  Interest received on debentures.

(iii) Financial help received by flood victims.

31. In an economy $S = -50 + 0.5 Y$ is the saving function (where $S$ = saving and $Y$ = income) and investment expenditure is 7000. Calculate:

(i)   Equilibrium level of national income.

(ii) Consumption expenditure at equilibrium level of national income. 6

OR

From the following information about an economy, calculate (i) its equilibrium level of national income, and (ii) savings at equilibrium level of national income.

Consumption function: C = 200 + 0.9 Y

(Where C = consumption expenditure and Y = national income) and Investment expenditure: I = 3000.

32. From the following data, calculate "national income" by (a) Income method and (b) expenditure method: 6

|  |  | (Rs. in crores) |
|---|---|---|
| (i) | Interest | 150 |
| (ii) | Rent | 250 |
| (iii) | Government final consumption expenditure | 600 |
| (iv) | Private final consumption expenditure | 1200 |
| (v) | Profits | 640 |
| (vi) | Compensation of employees | 1000 |
| (vii) | Net factor income to abroad | 30 |
| (viii) | Net indirect taxes | 60 |
| (ix) | Net exports | (-) 40 |
| (x) | Consumption of fixed capital | 50 |
| (xi) | Net domestic capital formation | 340 |

—*—*—*—*—*—*—*—*—*—*—*—*—

# General Instructions for C.P.T. Examination:

SUBJECT: ECONOMICS                                            M.M. 50

(I) ALL QUESTIONS ARE COMPULSORY.
(2) EACH QUESTION CARRIES (+1) MARK FOR CORRECT ANSWER AND (- 0.25) MARK FOR WRONG ANSWER.
(3) QUESTION PAPER CONTAINS 50 QUESTIONS.

### SOME IMPORTANT QUESTIONS FOR C.P.T.EXAMINATION WITH SOLUTIONS:

1.  Which branch of economics deals with the problem of allocation of resources?
    (a) Micro economics      (b) Macro economics      (c) Econometrics
    (d) Development economics.

2.  Scarcity definition of economics is given by
    (a) Adam Smith      (b) Joan Robinson
    (c) Samuelson      (d) Lord Robbins.

3   "Economics is the study of mankind in the ordinary business of life" is given by
    (a) A. Smith      (b) A. Marshall      (c) Baumol      (d) Samuelson.

4.  Capitalist economy uses _____ as the principal means of resources allocation.
    (a) Demand      (b) Supply      (c) Means of production      (d) Price.

5.  Under a free economy, prices are
    (a) Regulated                          (b) Partly regulated
    (c) Determined by demand and supply      (d) None of these.

6. A study of how increase in the price will affect natural unemployment in the economy is an example of
   (a) Micro economics          (b) Macro economics
   (c) Descriptive economics     (d) Normative economics.

7. If a point falls inside the production possibility curve, what does it indicate?
   (a) Under utilisation of resources     (b) Over utilisation of resources
   (c) Fuller utilisation of resources    (d) None of these.

8. Which of the following falls under micro economics?
   (a) National income          (b) General Price level
   (c) Factor pricing           (d) National saving and investment.

9. According to Robbins, 'means' are
   (a) Scarce     (b) Unlimited     (c) Not defined     (d) None of these.

10. If the opportunity cost is constant, then production possibility curve would be
    (a) Convex     (b) straight line     (c) Concave     (d) Backward bending

11. Economics is the study of
    (a) How society manages its unlimited resources
    (b) How to reduce our wants until we are satisfied
    (c) How society manages its scarce resources
    (d) How to fully satisfy our unlimited wants.

12. In a free economy when consumers increase their purchase of a good and the level of _____ exceed _____ then prices rise.
    (a)Demand, Supply          (b) Supply, Demand
    (c) Price, Demand          (d) Profits, Supply

13. Production possibility curve is concave because of
    (a) Increasing marginal opportunity cost
    (b) Decreasing marginal opportunity cost
    (c) Increasing MRS
    (d) Decreasing MRS.

14. Capital intensive technology is used in
    (a) Developed economies
    (b) Capital surplus economies
    (c) Underdeveloped economies
    (d) Feudal economies.

15. Movement from a point on production possibility frontier to a point inside the PPF indicates
    (a) Increasing employment      (b) Increasing unemployment
    (c) Economic growth            (d) Fuller utilisation of resources

16. In case of an inferior good, the income elasticity of demand is
    (a) Positive      (b) Zero      (c) Negative      (d) Infinite.

17. In case of Giffen goods, a fall in its price tends to
    (a) Make the demand remains constant
    (b) Reduce the demand
    (c) Increase the demand
    (d) Change the demand in abnormal way.

18. For what type of good does the demand fall with a rise in income level of households?
    (a) Inferior goods      (b) Substitutes
    (c) Luxuries            (d) Necessaries.

19. The price of Pizza increases by 15% and quantity demanded falls by 18%, this indicates that demand for Pizza is
    (a) Elastic            (b) Inelastic
    (c) Unitary elastic    (d) Perfectly inelastic

20. The price increases by 10% but the quantity demanded does not change, this indicates the demand is
    (a) One      (b) Infinite      (c) Zero      (d) None of these.

21. Which factor generally keeps the price elasticity of demand for a good low?
    (a) Variety of uses for that good
    (b) Its low price
    (c) Its Close substitutes
    (d) Middle sized income of consumer.

22. At the midpoint of straight line demand curve, elasticity of demand is
    (a) Zero     (b) 1     (c) 1.5     (d) -2.

23. For a good with unitary elastic demand, if its price rises then the total expenditure would
    (a) Increase     (b) Decrease     (c) Constant     (d) None of these.

24. If the price of any complementary good rises then demand curve would shift to
    (a) Left     (b) Right     (c) Constant     (d) None of these

25. Who said "If money is not the heart of the economic system, it can certainly be considered its blood".
    (a) R. B. Trescot     (b) Marshall     (c) A. Smith     (d) Robbins.

26. If income change by 15% and demand change by 30% then income elasticity of demand is
    (a) 0.5     (b) 2     (c) 0.3     (d) 3

27. The indifference curve is always
    (a) Concave to the origin          (b) Convex to the origin
    (c) U-shaped                       (d) L-shaped.

28. The diminishing marginal utility curve of a consumer is also his
    (a) Indifference curve             (b) Production possibility curve
    (c) Supply curve                   (d) Demand curve.

29. Which curve shows combination of two goods that yield equal level of satisfaction to the consumer?
    (a) Iso-cost curve                 (b) Indifference curve
    (c) Marginal utility curve         (d) Iso-quant curve

30. At equilibrium, the slope of the indifference curve is
    (a) Equal to the slope of budget line
    (b) Greater than slope of budget line
    (c) Smaller than slope of budget line
    (d) None of above.

31. The law of equi-marginal utility considers price of money as
    (a) Zero
    (b) Les than one
    (c) More than one
    (d) Equal to one

32. Marginal utility approach was given by
    (a) J.R. Hicks
    (b) A. Marshall
    (c) Robbins
    (d) A.C. Pigou.

33. In case of a right-angled indifference curve goods are
    (a) Perfectly complementary
    (b) Perfectly substitutes
    (c) Inferior goods
    (d) Giffen goods.

34. In case of a straight line indifference curve goods are
    (a) Perfectly complementary
    (b) Perfectly substitutes
    (c) Inferior goods
    (d) Giffen goods.

35. Two indifference curves never intersect each other because
    (a) Different level of satisfaction
    (b) Same level of satisfaction
    (c) Convexity
    (d) Concavity

36. A budget line is a result of
    (a) Price of good X
    (b) Price of good Y
    (c) Income of consumer
    (d) All of above.

37. Supply of goods means
    (a) Actual production of goods
    (b) Total stock of goods
    (c) Stock available for sale
    (d) Amount of goods offered for sale at a particular price per unit of time.

38. When supply price increase in the short-run, the profit of the producer
    (a) Increases
    (b) Decreases
    (c) Constant
    (d) None of the above

39. When supply is perfectly inelastic, elasticity of supply is equal to
    (a) +1      (b) 0      (c) – 1      (d) Infinity

40. If there is an improvement in technology then
    (a) Supply curve shifts to the left
    (b) Supply curve shifts to the left
    (c) Quantity supplied increase
    (d) Quantity supplied decrease.

41. Indifference curve slopes downwards because
    (a) Increasing marginal opportunity cost    (b) Increasing MRS
    (c) Decreasing MRS                          (d) None of these.

42. Concept of indifference curve is given by
    (a) A. Marshall    (b) Hicks    (c) Samuelson    (d) Robbins.

43. Demand for a firm's product will be highly elastic in a market where
    (a) No substitutes are available
    (b) A few substitutes are available
    (c) More substitutes are available
    (d) Infinitely large number of substitutes are available.

44. Average Fixed Cost curve is
    (a) Downward sloping curve          (b) Rectangular hyperbola
    (c) Vertical straight line           (d) Horizontal straight line.

45. Periods of less than full employment correspond to
    (a) Points outside the PPC          (b) Points inside the PPC
    (c) Points on the PPC               (d) None of these

46. In a free market economy the allocation of resources is determined by
    (a) Consumers' vote                 (b) Central planning authority
    (c) Preference of consumer          (d) Profit of the entrepreneur.

47. The structure of cold drink industry in India is best described as
    (a) Perfectly competitive           (b) Monopolistic competition
    (c) Monopoly                        (d) Oligopoly market.

48. When a firm faces a downward sloping demand curve, its Marginal revenue curve will always be
    (a) A horizontal straight line      (b) A vertical straight line
    (c) Sloping downwards               (d) Sloping upwards.

49. 'Point of satiety' is referred to a situation in which
    (a) TU is rising              (b) TU is decreasing
    (c) MU = 0                    (d) MU is negative.

50. If production of output is subject to constant marginal returns, Total Variable Cost curve will be
    (a) A horizontal straight line starting from origin
    (b) A vertical straight line starting from the origin
    (c) An upward sloping straight line starting from origin
    (d) A U-shaped curve.

## SOLUTION

1.a,   2.d,   3.b,   4.d,   5.c,   6.b,   7.a,   8.c,   9.a,   10.b,
11.c,  12.a,  13.a,  14.b,  15.b,  16.c,  17.b,  18.a,  19.a,  20.c,
21.b,  22.b,  23.c,  24.a,  25.a,  26.b,  27.b,  28.d,  29.b,  30.a,
31.d,  32.b,  33.a,  34.b,  35.a,  36.d,  37.d,  38.a,  39.b,  40.b,
41.c,  42.b,  43.d,  44.b,  45.b,  46.c,  47.d,  48.c,  49.c,  50.c.

51. As production of output increases Long-run Average Cost falls because of
    (a) Law of diminishing returns     (b) Economies of scale
    (c) Diseconomies of scale          (d) Law of variable proportion.

52. As production of output increases U-shaped Short-run Average Cost falls because of
    (a) Law of diminishing returns     (b) Economies of scale
    (c) Law of variable proportion     (d) Diseconomies of scale.

53. Iso-quants are equal to
    (a) Product lines        (b) Utility lines
    (c) Revenue lines        (d) Cost lines.

54. If MP > AP then AP is
    (a) Increasing           (b) Decreasing
    (c) Constant         (d) None of these

55. At equilibrium point an iso-quant is _____ to an iso-cost line.
    (a) Convex      (b) Perpendicular      (c) Tangent      (d) Concave

56. At the point of inflection, the Marginal Product is
    (a) Increasing     (b) Decreasing     (c) Maximum     (d) Negative

57. If Marginal Product of Labour is less than Average Product of Labour, then it is true
    (a) MP of labour is negative          (b) Marginal Product of labour = 0
    (c) AP of Labour is falling           (d) AP of Labour is negative.

58. Law of Variable proportion is valid when
    (a) Only one factor is fixed          (b) All factors are Variable
    (c) All factors are fixed             (d) None of these.

59. During second stage of Law of Diminishing returns:
    (a) MP and TP are maximum             (b) MP and AP are diminishing
    (c) AP is negative                    (d) TP is negative.

60. Innovative Entrepreneurship concept is given by
    (a) Robbins                           (b) Joan Robinson
    (c) Schumpeter                        (d) A. Marshall.

61. When Average Cost increases, Marginal Cost must be
    (a) Constant                          (b) Decreasing
    (c) Increasing                        (d) None of these

62. Economic Cost includes
    (a) Explicit + Implicit cost
    (b) Accounting Cost + Implicit cost
    (c) Accounting cost + Explicit cost
    (d) Accounting cost + Opportunity cost.

63. External economies accrue due to
    (a) Increasing return to scale        (b) Law of variable proportion
    (c) Increasing cost                   (d) None of these.

64. Which of the following is called as Planning or Envelope Curve?
    (a) Total Cost                        (b) Marginal Cost
    (c) Long-run Average Cost             (d) TVC.

65. A firm's Average Fixed Cost is Rs. 50 at 6 units of output, what will it be at 4 unit of output?
    (a) Rs. 200    (b) 12.5    (c) 75    (d) None of these

66. Write the formula of Arc elasticity of demand

    (a) $\dfrac{(Q2-Q1)}{(Q1+Q2)} \times \dfrac{(P1+P2)}{(P1-P2)}$    (b) $\dfrac{(Q1+Q2)}{(Q1-Q2)} \times \dfrac{(P1-P2)}{(P1+P2)}$

    (c) $\dfrac{(Q2-Q1)}{(Q2+Q1)} \times \dfrac{(P1-P2)}{(P1+P2)}$    (d) None of these.

67. In which market form, firm has no control over the price of its product
    (a) Monopolistic competition    (b) Monopoly
    (c) Oligopoly    (d) Perfect competition.

68. If MR = P (1 – 1/e) and e is greater than one, then
    (a) MR > 0    (b) MR < 0    (c) MR = 0    (d) None of these.

69. Profits of the firm will be more at the point where
    (a) MR = MC
    (b) Additional revenue from extra unit is equal to its additional cost
    (c) Both (a), (b)
    (d) None of these.

70. If MR > MC then what should a firm do?
    (a) Expand output    (b) Price should be lowered
    (c) Output should be decreased    (d) None of these.

71. Price discrimination monopoly is possible when
    (a) Elasticity of demand is different    (b) Costs are same
    (c) Profits are same    (d) Elasticity of demand is same.

72. A competitive firm in the short-run incur losses and still the firm continues its production if
    (a) Price = Minimum AVC    (b) Price > Minimum AVC
    (c) Both (a) and (b)    (d) None of the above.

73. The cross elasticity of demand under monopolistic competition for the product of a single firm would be
    (a) More elastic    (b) Less elastic    (c) Infinite    (d) Zero.

74. The conditions for the long-run equilibrium of competitive firm is
    (a) SMC = SAC = LMC
    (b) LMC = LAC = Price
    (c) P = MR
    (d) None.

75. Kinked demand curve concept is given by
    (a) A. Marshall
    (b) A.C. Pigou
    (c) P. Sweezy
    (d) J.R. Hicks.

76. A firm will shut down in the short-run if
    (a) Fixed Cost > Revenue
    (b) TC > TR
    (c) Variable Cost > Revenue
    (d) If the firm suffers losses.

77. Dumping is an example of which of the following market?
    (a) Oligopoly
    (b) Perfect competition
    (c) Monopolistic competition
    (d) Monopoly market.

78. If AC = MC, then which one of the following correct?
    (a) MC is minimum
    (b) AC is minimum
    (c) AC is maximum
    (d) MC is maximum.

79. The demand curve in monopoly market is _____.
    (a) Infinite    (b) Ed > 1    (c) Ed < 1    (d) Ed = 0.

80. The optimum output is the one which is produced
    (a) By the optimum firm
    (b) At zero level of output
    (c) At minimum average cost
    (d) At maximum average cost.

81. All money costs can be regarded as
    (a) Social cost
    (b) Opportunity cost
    (c) Explicit cost
    (d) Implicit cost.

82. India has nearly _____% of world's population.
    (a) 10    (b) 17    (c) 50    (d) 19.5

83. In India what %age of population are dependent on agriculture?
    (a) 72%    (b) 60%    (c) 22%    (d) None of these

84. In which year MODVAT was introduced in India?
    (a) 1988-89    (b) 1986-87    (c) 1985-86    (d) 1987-88

85. A gini index of zero represents perfect _____.
    (a) Equality      (b) Profit      (c) Loss      (d) Inequality

86. NABARD was set up in
    (a) 1982      (b) 1983      (c) 1991      (d) 2000

87. In India _____% population is below poverty line.
    (a) 40      (b) 30      (c) 10      (d) About 20

88. Which of the following instruments is used to measure income inequality?
    (a) GDP      (b) Gini index      (c) Per capita income      (d) HDI

89. In which year Reserve Bank of India was nationalised?
    (a) 1935      (b) 1947      (c) 1949      (d) 1950

90. From which sector the largest contribution to GDP comes in India?
    (a) Manufacturing      (b) Agriculture
    (c) Construction      (d) Service

91. The 10th Five Year Plan aimed to achieve growth rate of ___% in industrial sector.
    (a) 5      (b) 8      (c) 10      (d) 6

92. Share of tertiary sector in GDP in 2005-06 was_____%
    (a) 51.4      (b) 42.3      (c) 45.1      (d) 54.1

93. What type of industries was emphasized in Second Five Year Plan of Mahalanobis model?
    (a) Export oriented      (b) Agro-based
    (c) Consumer goods      (d) Capital and Basic goods.

94. AGMARK is related to
    (a) Service sector      (b) Industrial production
    (c) Agricultural products      (d) Electrical goods.

95. Which sector in India has the highest employment elasticity?
    (a) Primary      (b) Tertiary
    (c) Secondary      (d) None of these

96. The Zero Based Budgeting (ZBB) concept has been adopted from
    (a) Apr, 1987                     (b) Mar, 1969
    (c) Feb, 1999                     (d) Jan, 1985

97. In which year and in how many districts National Food For Work Programme (NFFWP) launched in India?
    (a) Nov-2004, 150                 (b) Nov-1950, 200
    (c) Jan-1991, 1500                (d) None

98. In which year for the first time India enjoyed Surplus in B.O.P?
    (a) 8th Plan        (b) 6th Plan        (c) 1st Plan        (d) 4th Plan

99. According to 2011 census, what is the total population of India?
    (a) 1.21 billion                  (b) 111.1 billion
    (c) 108.9 billion                 (d) 1.31 billion

100.    What is the literacy rate of India according to 2011 census?
    (a) 65.45%          (b) 70.45%          (c) 45.65%          (d) 74.04%

## SOLUTION

| | | | | | | | | | |
|---|---|---|---|---|---|---|---|---|---|
| 51.b, | 52.c, | 53.a, | 54.a, | 55.c, | 56.c, | 57.c, | 58.a, | 59.b, | 60.c, |
| 61.c, | 62.b, | 63.a, | 64.c, | 65.c, | 66.a, | 67.d, | 68.a, | 69.c, | 70.a, |
| 71.a, | 72.c, | 73.d, | 74.c, | 75.c, | 76.c, | 77.d, | 78.b, | 79.c, | 80.c, |
| 81.c, | 82.b, | 83.b, | 84.b, | 85.a, | 86.a, | 87.d, | 88.b, | 89.c, | 90.d, |
| 91.c, | 92.d, | 93.d, | 94.c, | 95.a, | 96.a, | 97.a, | 98.d, | 99.a, | 100.d. |

101. Which of the following is an indirect tax?
    (a) VAT        (b) Gift tax        (c) Income tax        (d) Wealth tax

102. Wealth tax on annual basis was first time introduced in the year
    (a) 1977        (b) 1957        (c) 1947        (d) 1987

103. In which year VAT was implemented in India?
    (a) April, 2000        (b) April 2003
    (c) April 2005         (d) April 2010

104. In India from which of the following highest tax revenue is earned?
    (a) Excise duty        (b) Income tax        (c) VAT        (d) None of these

105. In which year service tax was introduced in India?
   (a) 1991-92        (b) 2001-02
   (c) 1995-96        (d) 1950-51

106. Approximately life expectancy of Indian people in 2001 was
   (a) 54        (b) 45        (c) 63.8        (d) 56.8

107. India is passing through_____ stage of demographic transition
   (a) 1st        (b) 4th        (c) 3rd        (d) 2nd

108. According to 2011 census India's population accounts ___% of world's population
   (a) 14.5        (b) 17.5        (c) 18.5        (d) None of these

109. Which is the most populous state of India according to 2011 census?
   (a) West Bengal        (b) Maharashtra
   (c) Bihar              (d) U.P.

110. EAS stands for
   (a) Electric Assurance Scheme        (b) Employment Assurance Scheme
   (c) Education Assurance Scheme       (d) None of these

111. The scheme of EAS and JRY are mingled into
   (a) NFFWP        (b) SGRY        (c) SGSY        (d) IAY

112. In which of the following the National Rural Employment Guarantee Bill is not applicable?
   (a) J & K        (b) Mizoram        (c) Delhi        (d) U.P.

113. In India most of unemployment is
   (a) Frictional        (b) Structural        (c) Voluntary        (d) Technological

114. What % of Indian villages is electrified?
   (a) 66        (b) 82        (c) 76        (d) 92

115. Which energy in India contributes maximum energy?
   (a) Solar        (b) Hydel        (c) Thermal        (d) Nuclear

116. According to 2011 census what is the sex ratio in India?
     (a) 933              (b) 940          (c) 950          (d) 953

117. In which country BRIC summit, 2011 took place?
     (a) Brazil           (b) China        (c) Russia       (d) India

118. Which year is known as the 'Great year of divide'?
     (a) 1921             (b) 1931         (c) 1947         (d) 1991

119. National Literacy Mission (NLM) covers the age group of
     (a) 15-39 years          (b) 25-35 years
     (c)15-35 years           (d) 0-25 years

120. What is the major source of energy in India?
     (a) Coal     (b) Bio-gas     (c) Nuclear power        (d) Petroleum

121. What is the position of India's Postal Network?
     (a) First     (b) 10th         (c) 7th              (d) None of these

122. Indian Postal System was introduced in
     (a) 1818     (b) 1837         (c) 1827             (d) 1618

123. Which is the apex bank for agricultural credit in India?
     (a) NABARD          (b) ICICI        (c) SBI          (d) IFC

124. When too much money chases too few gods, the resulting inflation is called
     (a) Deflation            (b) Demand-pull inflation
     (c) Cost-push inflation  (d) Stagflation

125. Inflation with recession is called
     (a) Stagflation          (b) Reflation
     (c) Inflation            (d) Deflation

126. What was the maximum inflation that recorded in 1966-67?
     (a) 9.5      (b) 13.9         (c) 10.9             (d) 10

127. Revenue deficit in India is
     (a) Zero     (b) Negative     (c) Positive         (d) Balanced

128. The sum total of borrowings and other liabilities is called
    (a) Fiscal deficit       (b) Revenue deficit
    (c) Primary deficit       (d) None of these

129. When a country has a deficit in its current account, then this deficit can be financed by _____
    (a) Raising the income tax rate       (b) Reduction of its expenditure
    (c) International borrowing       (d) Increasing rate of tariff

130. Fiscal policy is a policy of which of the following
    (a) Monetary authority       (b) Government finance
    (c) Money lenders       (d) Commercial banks

131. As per IMF, B.O.P manual, import, export of goods should be presented on
    (a) FOB basis       (b) FOR basis
    (c) CIF basis       (d) None of these

132. India has witnessed a surplus for the third successive year in which account of Balance of Payments?
    (a) Trade account of BOP       (b) Current account of BOP
    (c) Both       (d) None of these

133. What % of FDI is allowed in Private Banking in India?
    (a) 100       (b) 50       (c) 49       (d) 74

134. External deficit refers to which one of the following?
    (a) Revenue deficit       (b) Current account deficit in BOP
    (c) Fiscal deficit       (d) Trade deficit

135. What was position of India among the 10 debtor countries of the world in 2005?
    (a) $1^{st}$       (b) $2^{nd}$       (c) $8^{th}$       (d) $15^{th}$

136. When external debt is more than interest obligation, then it is called as
    (a) Debt trap       (b) External trap
    (c) Liquidity trap       (d) None of these

137. Quantitative restrictions on _____ items were removed in the EX-IM policy of 2000-01
    (a) 417 (b) 100 (c) 714 (d) 471

138. From 2005 FDI limit in certain services of telecom sector was increased from 49% to _____
    (a) 100% (b) 50% (c) 74% (d) None of these

139. India's rank in paying taxes in world is ____
    (a) 164th (b) 114th (c) 130th (d) 105th

140. What was SLR during 1990-99 when it was at peak?
    (a) 48.5% (b) 38.5% (c) 28.5% (d) 49%

141. What does EPCG stand for?
    (a) Export Promotion Capital Goods
    (b) Export Promotion Consumer Goods
    (c) Export Programme for Capital Growth
    (d) None of these

142. When was EX-IM policy announced in India?
    (a) 1997 (b) 1992 (c) 1998 (d) 1990

143. In which of the following 100% Privatisation in India has taken place?
    (a) VSNL (b) CMC Limited
    (c) Centaur Hotel (d) Maruti Udyog Limited

144. Cross Holding is a method of which one of the following?
    (a) Globalisation (b) Privatisation
    (c) Disinvestment (d) None of these

145. World Trade Organisation was formed on 1st January in the year of
    (a) 1945 (b) 1995
    (c) 1999 (d) 1986

146. IMF starts its operation in
    (a) April, 1947 (b) March, 1947
    (c) Aug, 1947 (d) Oct, 1946

147. GST stands for
    (a) Goods and Services Tax          (b) Government Service Tax
    (c) Gross Sale Tax                   (d) Government Sale Tax

148. The budget of 2011 estimated a target to reduce the fiscal deficit by
    _____% for 2011-12
    (a) 4.6%            (b) 5.5%            (c) 7%            (d) 7.6%

149. According to budget 2011, for the tax concession the age limit of senior
    citizens reduced to
    (a) 60 years        (b) 58 years        (c) 65 years      (d) None of these

150. Privatization can be achieved by
    (a) Franchising        (b) Leasing        (c) Contracting  (d) All of these

## SOLUTION

101.a,  102.b,  103.c,  104.a,  105.c,  106.c,  107.d,  108.b,  109.d,  110.b,
111.b,  112.a,  113.b,  114.c,  115.c,  116.b,  117.b,  118.a,  119.c,  120.a,
121.a,  122.b,  123.a,  124.b,  125.a,  126.b,  127b,   128.a,  129.c,  130.b,
131.a,  132.b,  133.d,  134.b,  135.c,  136.a,  137.c,  138.c,  139.a,  140.b,
141.a,  142.b,  143.c,  144.c,  145.b,  146.b,  147.a,  148.a,  149.a,  150.d.

151. Which one of the following is true for perfect complementarities
    between goods x and y
    (a) MRS y x = 0                     (b) MRS x y = 0
    (c) MRS x y = MRS y x = 0           (d) None of these

152. The 'interest rate' policy is a component of which one of the following
    policy?
    (a) Monetary policy        (b) Fiscal policy
    (c) Direct control         (d) Trade policy

153. Broad money and narrow money refer to which one of the following?
    (a) M3, M1             (b) M1, M3
    (c) M2, M1             (d) M4, M2

154. 'Bills of Exchange' sometimes are also known as _____
  (a) Narrow money                 (b) Business obligations
  (c) Transferable assets          (d) Broad money

155. Which one of the following is not a part of narrow money?
  (a) Demand deposit               (b) Currencies held by public
  (c) Time deposit                 (d) None of these

156. How many banks were nationalized in India in 1969?
  (a) 17        (b) 8        (c) 14        (d) 16

157. A commercial bank normally does not pay any interest on ____
  (a) Time deposit                 (b) Long-term deposit
  (c) Demand deposit               (d) Short-term deposit

158. The rate at which central bank discounts the bills of commercial banks is called as
  (a) CRR      (b) Bank rate     (c) Reverse repo rate      (d) SLR

159. What is the number of banks present in India in 1947?
  (a) 840       (b) 640        (c) 740        (d) 500

160. How many banks were nationalized in India in 1980?
  (a) 6         (b) 14         (c) 10         (d) 8

161. A country's ability to meet interest and repayment of loans is reflected by its
  (a) Import ratio to GDP          (b) Export ratio to GDP
  (c) Debt-service ratio           (d) None of these

162. Within how many days the Central and State Governments have to repay the advances made by the Reserve Bank of India?
  (a) 15 days                      (b) 45 days
  (c) 90 days                      (d) 180 days

163. RBI issues all currency notes except
  (a) Rs. 1000 note                (b) Rs. 500 note
  (c) Re. 1 note                   (d) Rs. 100 note

164. Open market operation is an important instrument of
  (a) Monetary policy      (b) Fiscal policy
  (c) Trade policy         (d) None of these

165. Which one of the following is the monetary authority of a country?
  (a) The banking system of the country
  (b) Central Government of the country
  (c) The Central bank of the country
  (d) All of these

166. The RBI follows dear money policy to check _____ in the economy
  (a) Deflation            (b) Inflation
  (c) Both (a) and (b)     (d) None of these

167. What % of working population is engaged in service sector?
  (a) 40%    (b) 45%      (c) 55%       (d) 65%

168. NAFED is connected with which one of the following?
  (a) Agricultural implements      (b) Animal husbandry
  (c) Conservation of forest       (d) Agricultural marketing

169. The main impact of green revolution was noticed on which one of the following crop?
  (a) Cereals   (b) Pulses     (c) Fruits      (d) All of these

170. Rangarajan committee was set up on which one of the following?
  (a) Devaluation of rupee         (b) PSU investment
  (c) Deficit financing            (d) Revaluation of rupee

171. Who said that in India Black money is generated at the rate of 20% of country's GDP?
  (a) Raja Chellia                 (b) Amartya Sen
  (c) Lord Keynese                 (d) Manmohan Singh

172. What is the share of India's exports in world trade?
  (a) 0.5 %    (b) 10 %       (c) 0.8 %       (d) 20%

173. Which one of the following tax is collected by Panchayets?
  (a) Land revenue    (b) Sales tax     (c) VAT        (d) Tax on local fairs

174. In which year for the first time disinvestment committee was set up?
   (a) 1991      (b) 1999         (c) 1996          (d) 1980

175. 'Food for work' programme is renamed as
   (a) IRDP      (b) NREP         (c) TRYSEM       (d) MNP

176. Who collects the revenue of custom duty?
   (a) Partly by centre and partly by state       (b) Only by centre
   (c) Only by state                              (d) None of these

177. Who is the introducer of 'Market law'?
   (a) J.M. Keynese                (b) J.B. Say
   (c) Lord Robbins                (d) Schumpeter

178. Which one of the following is the apex organisation of industrial finance in India?
   (a) IDBI              (b) ICICI          (c) IFCI          (d) NABARD

179. What is the name of new common currency introduced among European Countries?
   (a) Euro Pound        (b) Euro Dollar  (c) Euro          (d) None of these

180. What is the position of India in the world from the point of 'Scientific and technical manpower'?
   (a) 1$^{st}$              (b) 4$^{th}$             (c) 3$^{rd}$             (d) 2$^{nd}$

181. What is the average agricultural growth that estimated in 2009-10 in India?
   (a) (-) 0.2%          (b) 5%             (c) 2%             (d) 8.6%

182. What is the target to create 'Skilled workforce' by India by the end of 2024?
   (a) 15 crore          (b) 25 crore       (c) 10 crore       (d) 13 crore

183. What is the average annual growth rate of national income and per capita income of India since independence?
   (a) 4.4% and 2.2%             (b) 5.5% and 2.5%
   (c) 6.6% and 3.3%             (d) None of these

184. Y = C + I is
    (a) An equation
    (b) An identity
    (c) A formula
    (d) A function

185. Which one of the following is not an assumption about indifference curve?
    (a) Slope downward to the right
    (b) Cardinal utility
    (c) Convex to the origin
    (d) None of these

186. Money is
    (a) Helpful for production
    (b) harmful for production\
    (c) Neutral for production
    (d) None of these

187. The economic rent earned by any factor will be highest if its elasticity of supply is
    (a) Equal to one
    (b) Infinite
    (c) Zero
    (d) Between zero and one

188. Annual growth rate of National income was recorded lowest during
    (a) Sixth plan
    (b) Third plan
    (c) Second plan
    (d) Fifth plan

189. Inflation associated with recession is called
    (a) Stagflation
    (b) Reflation
    (c) Devaluation
    (d) Hyper inflation

190. 'Intellectual Property' does not include one of the following
    (a) Copyrights
    (b) Patents
    (c) Trade marks
    (d) Agricultural subsidies

191. Self-reliance as an objective of planning was emphasised first in
    (a) Second five year plan
    (b) Third five year plan
    (c) Fifth five year plan
    (d) Fourth five year plan

192. First five year plan was introduced in
    (a) 1951      (b) 1950      (c) 1947      (d) 1948

193. Core sector included
   (a) Agricultural inputs
   (b) Iron & steel
   (c) Petroleum
   (d) All the above

194. National Stock Exchange of India was set up in
   (a) 1990    (b) 1992    (c) 1994    (d) 1996

195. SEBI was set up in India in
   (a) 1980    (b) 1984    (c) 1988    (d) 1992

196. Special Drawing Rights was created by
   (a) IMF    (b) IBRD    (c) UNDP    (d) ADB

197. MODVAT tax is related to which one of the following?
   (a) Excise tax    (b) Sales tax    (c) Estate duty    (d) Corporate tax

198. Agricultural Income is taxed by
   (a) Centre
   (b) State
   (c) Local authority
   (d) None of these

199. Which committee recommended the introduction of an agricultural tax?
   (a) Jha
   (b) Raj
   (c) Chellia
   (d) None of these

200. 'Yellow Revolution' is related to production of
   (a) Rice    (b) Wheat    (c) Oilseeds    (d) Coffee

## SOLUTION

151.C,  152.A,  153.a,  154.a,  155.c,  156.c,  157.c,  158.b,  159.b,  160.a
161.c,  162.c,  163.c,  164.a,  165.c,  166.b,  167.b,  168.d,  169.a,  170.b,
171.a,  172.c,  173.d,  174.c,  175.b,  176.b,  177.b,  178.a,  179.c,  180.d,
181.a,  182.a,  183.a,  184.b,  185.b,  186.c,  187.c,  188.b,  189.a,  190.d
191.c,  192.a,  193.d,  194.b,  195.c,  196.a,  197.a,  198.b,  199.b,  200.c

—*—*—*—*—*—*—*—*—*—*—*—

# Test Paper – 1

Time: 3 Hours        CLASS: XII        M.M.100

General Instructions: As per CBSE Question Paper

## SECTION – A (Introductory Micro Economics)

1. State two features of Production possibility curve. (1)
2. If demand curve is rectangular hyperbola then find out its price elasticity of demand. (1)
3. What happens to equilibrium price of a commodity when its demand increases but its supply decreases? (1)
4. State one feature of monopoly market. (1)
5. If two supply curves intersect each other, which one does have higher price elasticity? (1)
6. Explain any three determinants which affect market demand for a commodity. (3)
7. Explain the problem of "for whom to produce".

Or

Explain the central problem of "choice of technique" (3)

8. What will be the price elasticity of supply at a point on a positively sloped straight line supply curve? (3)
9. Explain the law of diminishing marginal utility with the help of hypothetical schedule. (3)
10. Why do households buy more of a commodity at lower price? Explain. (3)
11. Distinguish between changes in quantity supplied and changes in supply (decrease) of a commodity. (4)
12. On the basis of following information determine the level of output at which the producer will be in equilibrium under perfect competition market when the price per unit is given Rs. 7 (4)

| Output (unit) | 1 | 2 | 3 | 4 | 5 | 6 | 7 |
|---|---|---|---|---|---|---|---|
| Total cost | 7 | 15 | 22 | 28 | 33 | 40 | 48 |

13. with the rise in price by Rs. 5, the quantity demanded of a commodity changes from 100 units to 95 units. If the price elasticity of demand is (– 1.2) then find out the price before change.

Or

A firm earns revenue of Rs. 50 when the market price of a good       (4) is Rs. 10. When the market price increases to Rs. 15 then the firm earns revenue of Rs. 150. Calculate the price elasticity of supply of the firm's output.

14. Explain the likely behaviour of Total Product and Marginal       (6) Product when for increasing production when only one input is increased while all other factors kept constant.

15. There is a simultaneous "increase in demand and supply of a commodity. When will it result the following:
   i)   No change in equilibrium price.
   ii)  A fall in equilibrium price. Explain both by using diagrams.       (6)

Or

What happens when the Government fixes the following?

   i)   Ceiling price is lower than the market equilibrium price of a commodity.
   ii)  Support price is higher than the market equilibrium price of a commodity.

16. Distinguish between perfect competition market and oligopoly       (6) market.

## SECTION – B (Introductory Macro Economics)

17. What is meant by statutory Liquidity Ratio? (1)
18. State two components of money supply. (1)
19. Define involuntary unemployment. (1)
20. Give two examples of non-tax revenue receipts. (1)
21. What is a GNP deflator? (1)
22. Distinguish between consumption goods and capital goods. (3)
23. Explain the three merits of flexible exchange rate. (3)

Or

Explain three merits of fixed exchange rate.

24. Distinguish between current account and capital account of Balance of Payments. (3)
25. Differentiate between devaluation and depreciation of domestic currency. (3)
26. State three precautions to calculate Net Domestic Product of a country. (3)
27. From the following data find out whether the economy is in equilibrium or not?
    Y = Rs. 2500 crores, I (autonomous investment) = Rs. 100 crores, (4)
    MPC = 0.8 and C (autonomous consumption)= Rs. 400 crores.
28. Define excess demand. How is it corrected by quantitative credit control measures? (4)

Or

What is meant by inflationary gap? How is it corrected by qualitative credit control measures?

29. How does a commercial bank can create credit in an economy? Explain with the help of an example. (4)
30. a)  How is "revenue expenditure" different from "capital expenditure"?
    b)  State the implications of fiscal deficit. (3+3)
31. Explain determination of equilibrium level of income through the saving – investment approach. What changes are required if the economy is not in equilibrium? Explain. (6)

Or

Explain the determination of equilibrium level of national income on the basis of aggregate demand and aggregate supply approach. What changes will take place if the economy is not in equilibrium? Explain.

32. Calculate the following from the given data: (6)
   (a) Private income
   (b) Personal income and
   (c) Net National Disposable Income

|  |  | (Rs. in crores) |
|---|---|---|
| i) | National income | 3000 |
| ii) | Savings of private corporate sector | 30 |
| iii) | Corporate profit tax | 80 |
| iv) | Current transfers from Government Administrative department | 60 |
| v) | Income from property and entrepreneurship accruing to Govt. Administrative department | 150 |
| vi) | Current transfers from the rest of the world | 50 |
| vii) | Savings of non-departmental Govt. enterprises | 40 |
| viii) | Net indirect taxes | 250 |
| ix) | Direct taxes paid by households | 100 |
| x) | Net factor income from abroad | (– 10) |
| xi) | Consumption of fixed capital | 150 |

—*—*—*—*—*—*—*—*—*—*—*—*—*—

# Test Paper – 2

Time: 3 Hours                    CLASS: XII                    M.M. 100

General Instructions: As per CBSE Question Paper

## SECTION – A (Introductory Micro Economics)

1. Define marginal opportunity cost.                                    (1)
2. What happens to equilibrium price of a commodity when its        (1)
   demand decreases and its supply increases?
3. If a linear supply curve slopes upwards and starts from          (1)
   horizontal axis then what will be its price elasticity of supply?
4. If two demand curves intersect each other then which one         (1)
   does have higher price elasticity?
5. What happens to Average Cost when Average cost is less than       (1)
   Marginal Cost?
6. Explain any one central problem with the help of production      (3)
   possibility curve.
7. Explain any three factors which affect market supply of a        (3)
   commodity?
8. Why does demand curve slope downwards?                           (3)
9. How do we measure price elasticity of demand for a              (3)
   commodity at different points on a straight line demand
   curve?
10. When does a budget line shift to right wards?                   (3)

Or

Explain a budget line to show attainable and unattainable Points.
11. Explain the producer's equilibrium level of output with the help   (4)
    of MR and MC approach under perfect competition market.
12. Explain the factors which affect price elasticity of demand for a   (4)
    commodity?

592

13. When the price of a commodity changes by 10% then its    (4)
    demand falls from 250 units to 200 units. Calculate its price
    elasticity of demand?

Or

Consider the demand for a good at price Rs.40 is 250 units. If the
price of the good increases by Rs.10 per unit then its demand falls
to 220 units, calculate its price elasticity of demand.

14. Explain excess demand and deficient demand for a commodity    (6)
    under perfect competition market.
15. How can you explain the law of diminishing return to a factor    (6)
    when only one factor is variable? State its causes also.
16. Distinguish between monopoly market and oligopoly market.

Or

Explain the shape of demand curves and their causes under    (6)
perfect competition market, monopoly and monopolistic
competition market.

## SECTION – B (Introductory Macro Economics)

17. Define high powered money.    (1)
18. What is the value of multiplier when MPC = 0.75?    (1)
19. How do you calculate GNP deflator?    (1)
20. Give two examples of tax revenue receipts.    (1)
21. What is net primary deficit?    (1)
22. Explain the problem of double counting.
    How can it be avoided?    (3)
23. Distinguish between current account and capital account of    (3)
    Balance of Payments.
24. Explain the demerits of fixed exchange rate.    (3)

Or

Explain the demerits of flexible exchange rate.
25. Explain the components of net domestic factor income.    (3)
26. State the causes of deficit in Balance of Payments of India.    (3)

27. Define excess demand and state its impact on output, (4)
    employment and price in an economy.

Or

Define deficient demand and state its impact on output,
employment and price in an economy.

28. In an economy, the actual level of income is Rs. 800 crores, (4)
    whereas the full employment level of income is Rs. 1500
    crores. If the MPC is given as 0.75 then calculate the required
    increase in investment to achieve full employment income.

29. Explain the agency functions of commercial bank. (4)

30. Explain the derivation of propensity to save curve from the (6)
    propensity to consume curve and state its relevance.

Or

Explain the derivation of propensity to consume curve from the
propensity to save curve and state its relevance.

31. Explain the steps required to calculate national income by (6)
    using expenditure method.

32. Calculate NDP at Factor Cost and Personal Disposable Income (6)
    from the following data:

|  |  | (Rs. in crores) |
|---|---|---|
| i) | Private final consumption expenditure | 700 |
| ii) | Savings of non-departmental enterprises | 20 |
| iii) | Net domestic fixed capital formation | 100 |
| iv) | Undistributed profit | 15 |
| v) | Change in stock | 10 |
| vi) | Corporate tax | 35 |
| vii) | Net exports | 40 |
| viii) | Income from property and entrepreneurship accruing to the Govt. administrative department | 30 |
| ix) | National debt interest | 40 |
| x) | Govt. Final consumption expenditure | 150 |
| xi) | Current transfers from Government | 25 |

| | | |
|---|---|---|
| xii) | Net factor income from abroad | (-10) |
| xiii) | Net current transfers from the rest of world | 10 |
| xiv) | Net indirect taxes | 60 |
| xv) | Personal direct taxes | 30 |

—*—*—*—*—*—*—*—*—*—*—*—*—*—

# Test Paper – 3

Time: 3 Hours     CLASS: XII     M.M. 100

  General Instructions: As per CBSE Question Paper

## SECTION – A (Introductory Micro Economics)

1.  What does leftward shift in production possibility curve indicate? (1)
2.  Define inferior goods. (1)
3.  What happens to Average Variable Cost when it is less than Marginal Cost? (1)
4.  Define marginal opportunity cost. (1)
5.  What is meant by collusive oligopoly market? (1)
6.  Under what conditions at the given price the demand for a commodity will increase? (3)

Or

Why does demand for a commodity decrease at the given price?

7.  Explain the central problem of "for whom to produce". (3)
8.  How does price of related goods and objective of a firm affect the supply for a commodity? (3)
9.  A seller collects revenue of Rs. 500 when he sells 20 units of a commodity. If price falls by Rs.5 per unit how much will he supply if the price elasticity of supply is unity? (3)
10. State any three properties of indifference curve. (3)
11. Explain the relationship between marginal revenue and average revenue under imperfect competition market. (4)

Or

Explain the relationship between TPP and MPP when only one factor is variable.

12. Distinguish between changes in quantity demanded and (4)
changes in demand (decrease).

13. How do we measure the elasticity of supply for a commodity (4)
when the supply curve slopes positively upward?

14. Explain different degrees of price elasticity of supply of a (6)
commodity.

Or

Explain the main determinants of price elasticity of demand for a commodity.

15. Can a firm under perfect competition market earn super (6)
normal profit in long run? Explain.

16. Explain the change in the equilibrium price of a commodity (6)
when the demand and the supply change in opposite
direction.

## SECTION – B (Introductory Macro Economics)

17. Define propensity to save. (1)
18. If the value of multiplier is 2 then find out the value of MPC. (1)
19. What is meant by net operating surplus? (1)
20. Define flow variable. (1)
21. If there is deficit of Rs. 25,000 crores in balance of trade and (1)
the value of imports is Rs. 34,000 crores then find out the
value of exports?
22. State three precautions while calculating net domestic income (3)
of a country.
23. Distinguish between Balance of payments of goods and (3)
Balance of payments.
24. Distinguish between direct tax and indirect tax. (3)
25. Explain three demerits of fixed exchange rate

Or

Explain three demerits of flexible rate of exchange. (3)
26. Do you think purchasing of machines is always a final good? (3)
State the reasons for your answer.
27. Differentiate between revenue deficit and fiscal deficit. Why (4)
India has large fiscal deficit?

28. Define multiplier. How does it work in an economy? (4)
29. What is deficient demand? How is it corrected by fiscal (4)
policy?

Or

Define inflationary gap. How is it corrected by the Government revenue and expenditure policy?

30. Why must aggregate demand become equal to aggregate (6)
supply at the equilibrium level of income and output? Explain
with the help of a diagram.

Or

Calculate the following from the table given below where investment is given as Rs. 100 crores.

a) Find out the break-even point
b) State the equilibrium level of income and output in the economy
c) Calculate APC at income level of Rs. 150 crores
d) Calculate APS at income level of Rs. 250 crores
e) Calculate MPC at income level of Rs. 200 to Rs. 350
f) Calculate the value of multiplier on the basis of Q. No. (e) above.

| INCOME | CONSUMPTION |
|--------|-------------|
| 50 | 75 |
| 100 | 100 |
| 150 | 125 |
| 200 | 150 |
| 250 | 175 |
| 300 | 200 |
| 350 | 225 |

31. Explain quantitative credit control and quantitative credit (6)
control measures for the stability of equilibrium level of
national income in an economy.

32. Calculate GNP at MP by income method and NNP at FC by  (6)
    expenditure method from the following data.

|  |  | (Rs. in crores) |
|---|---|---|
| i) | Personal consumption expenditure | 700 |
| ii) | Wages and salaries | 700 |
| iii) | Employers' contribution to provident fund | 100 |
| iv) | Gross Business fixed investment | 70 |
| v) | Gross residential construction investment | 50 |
| vi) | Gross public investment | 32 |
| vii) | Inventory investment | 28 |
| viii) | Profits | 80 |
| ix) | Govt. purchases of goods and services | 200 |
| x) | Rent | 50 |
| xi) | Exports | 50 |
| xii) | Imports | 30 |
| xiii) | Interest | 60 |
| xiv) | Mixed income | 80 |
| xv) | Net factor income to abroad | 10 |
| xvi) | Depreciation | 20 |
| xvii) | Net Indirect taxes | 10 |

**ALL THE BEST**